Hitoshi Okuda was famous in Japanese amateur manga (*doujinshi*) under a pen name long before he made his professional debut. He studied under Nobuteru Yuki and Yutaka Izubuchi, two of Japan's top animators. His older works include **Radical Guardian**, published in Japan by Fujimi Shobo. His recent works include **The All-New Tenchi Muyô!**, **Ranto Mashoroku**, and **Little Dragon Restaurant**, all published in Japan by Kadokawa Shoten.

The All-New Tenchi Muyô!

Volume 5: Point and Shoot
Action Edition

STORY AND ART BY HITOSHI OKUDA

English Adaptation/Fred Burke
Translation/Lillian Olsen
Touch-up Art & Lettering/Curtis Yee
Design/Hidemi Sahara
Editor/Shaenon K. Garrity

Managing Editor/Annette Roman
Director of Production/Noboru Watanabe
Editorial Director/Alvin Lu
Sr. Director of Licensing & Acquisitions/Rika Inouye
Vice President of Sales & Marketing/Liza Coppola
Executive Vice President/Hyoe Narita
Publisher/Seiji Horibuchi

Published by VIZ, LLC
P.O. Box 77010
San Francisco, CA 94107

Action Edition
10 9 8 7 6 5 4 3 2 1
First printing, October 2004

For advertising rates or media kit, e-mail advertising@viz.com

www.animerica-mag.com

www.viz.com

store.viz.com

VIZ GRAPHIC NOVEL

THE ALL-NEW TENCHI MUYŌ!

Point and Shoot

STORY AND ART BY
HITOSHI OKUDA

CONTENTS

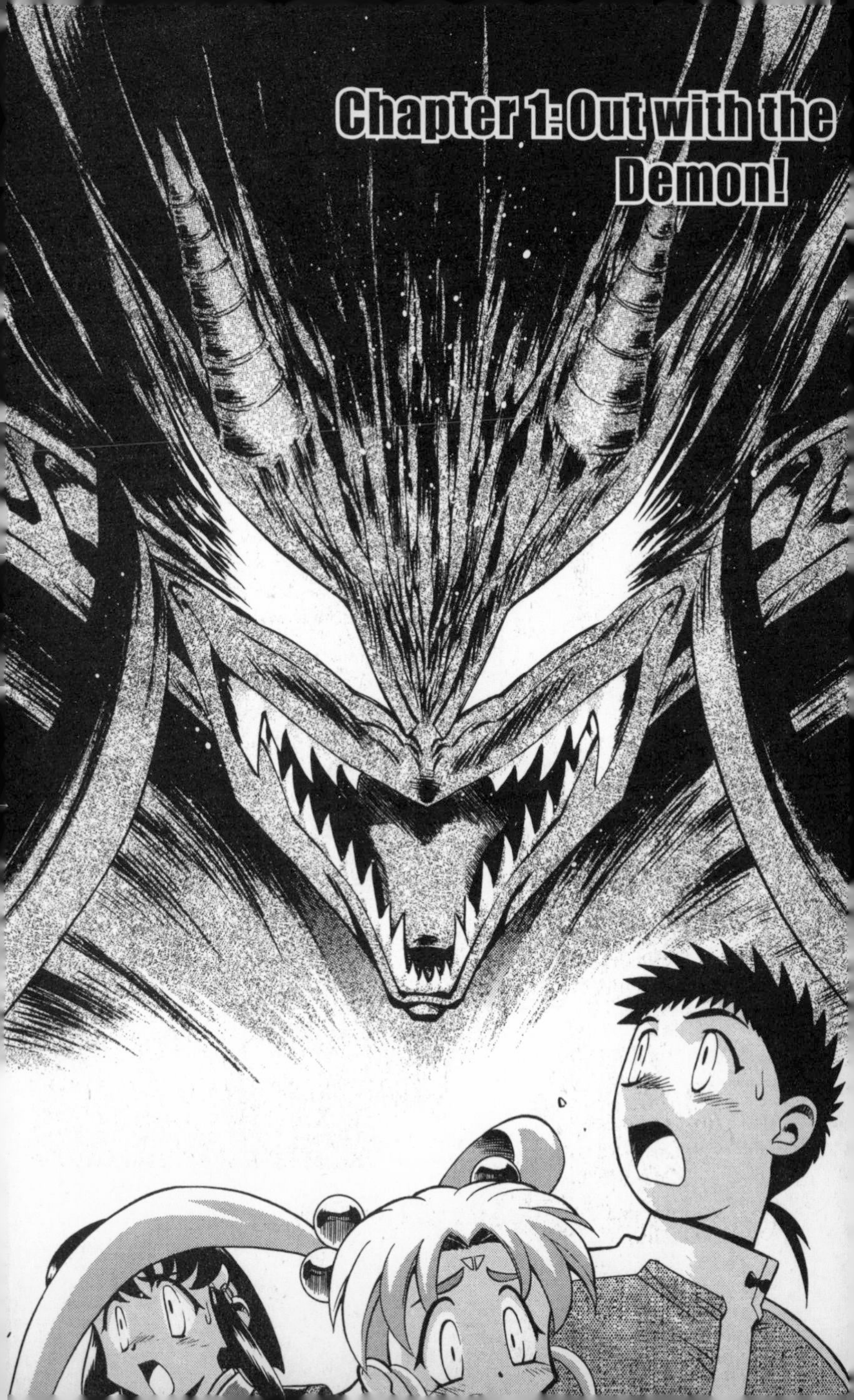
Chapter 1: Out with the Demon!

SZZZ TUP TUP TPSH

TUP TUP SZZZ

SST FSH

MREOW?

OH, THIS? I'M FRYING SOYBEANS FOR MAME-MAKI!

WE **HAVE** TO THROW THEM! TODAY IS SETSUBUN!*

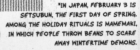

2/3 SETSUBUN

*IN JAPAN, FEBRUARY 3 IS SETSUBUN, THE FIRST DAY OF SPRING. AMONG THE HOLIDAY RITUALS IS MAMEMAKI, IN WHICH PEOPLE THROW BEANS TO SCARE AWAY WINTERTIME DEMONS.

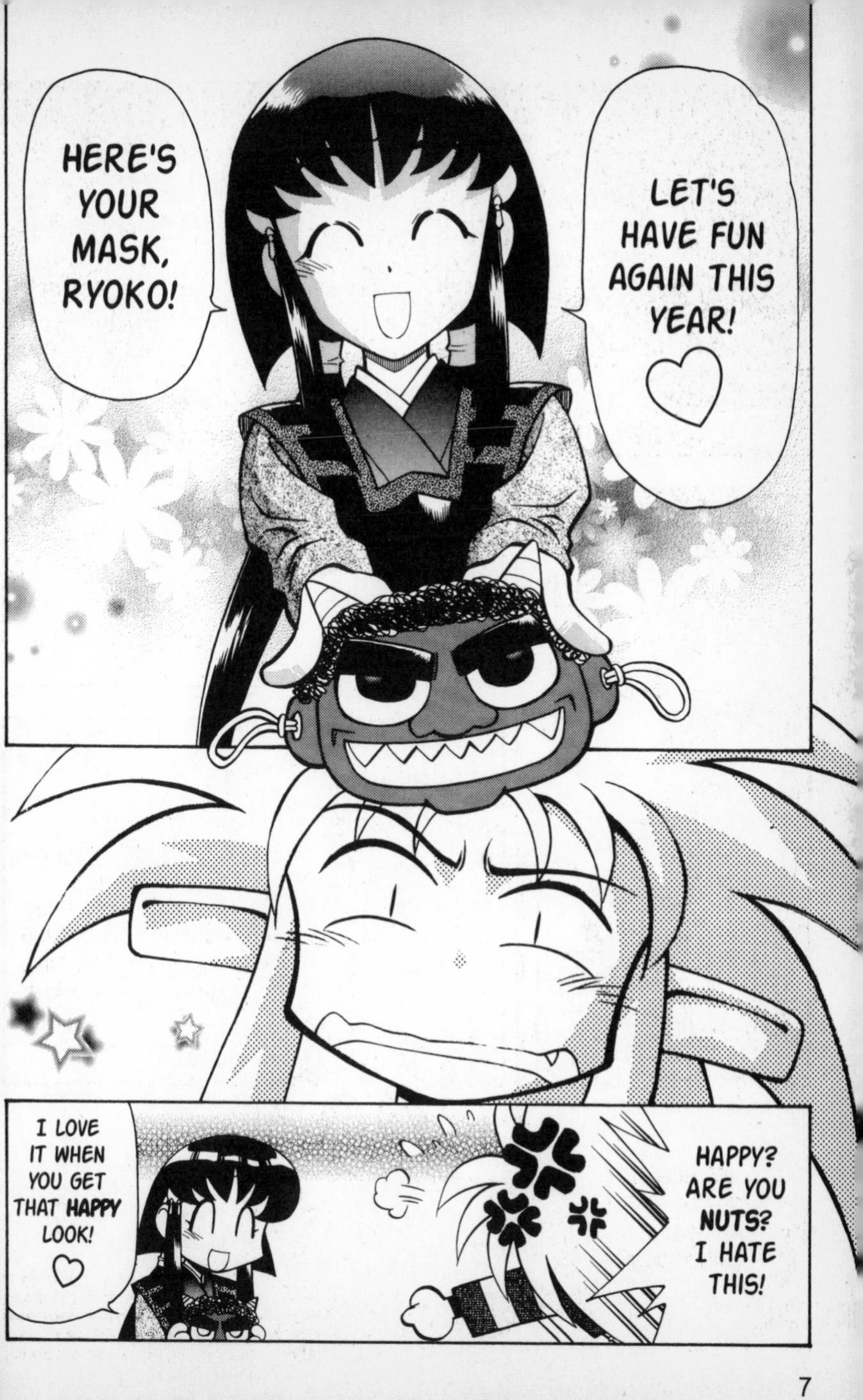
HERE'S YOUR MASK, RYOKO!
LET'S HAVE FUN AGAIN THIS YEAR! ♡
I LOVE IT WHEN YOU GET THAT **HAPPY** LOOK! ♡
HAPPY? ARE YOU **NUTS?** I HATE THIS!

BUT YOU'RE OUR VERY OWN **DEMON**, RYOKO. YOU'RE A **LEGEND**!

THAT STORY'S JUST A LIE YOSHO MADE UP... TO **RUIN** MY LIFE!

WHO'D CALL A SWEET, PRETTY THING LIKE **ME** A DEMON?

NO ONE IN HER RIGHT MIND!

BUT SHE IS.

SHE HAS TO BE.

FOR REAL, IS SHE?

STOP THAT!

NOW, NOW! RYOKO HAS A POINT HERE! YOU KNOW THAT!

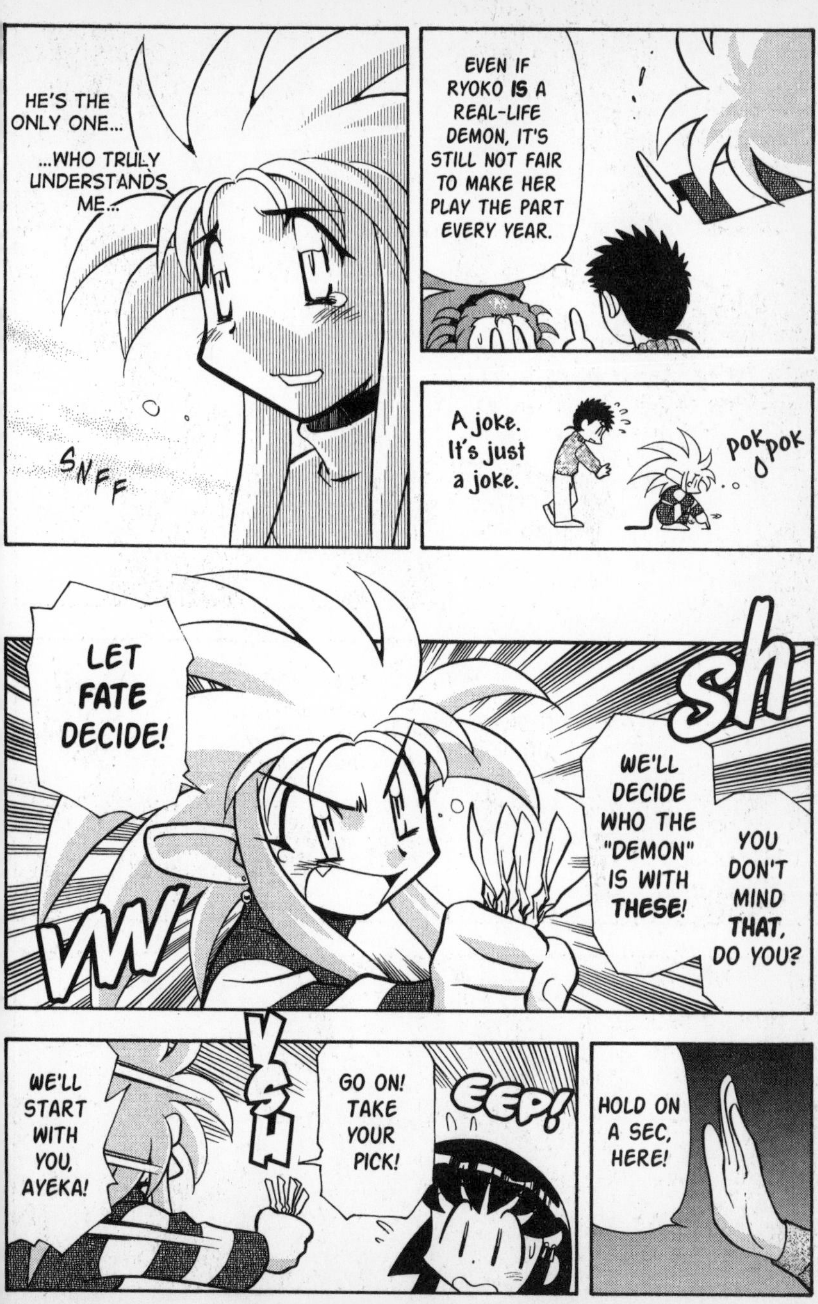

HE'S THE ONLY ONE...
...WHO TRULY UNDERSTANDS ME...
SNFF
EVEN IF RYOKO IS A REAL-LIFE DEMON, IT'S STILL NOT FAIR TO MAKE HER PLAY THE PART EVERY YEAR.
!
A joke. It's just a joke.
POK POK
LET FATE DECIDE!
sh
VW
WE'LL DECIDE WHO THE "DEMON" IS WITH THESE!
YOU DON'T MIND THAT, DO YOU?
WE'LL START WITH YOU, AYEKA!
VSH
GO ON! TAKE YOUR PICK!
EEP!
HOLD ON A SEC, HERE!

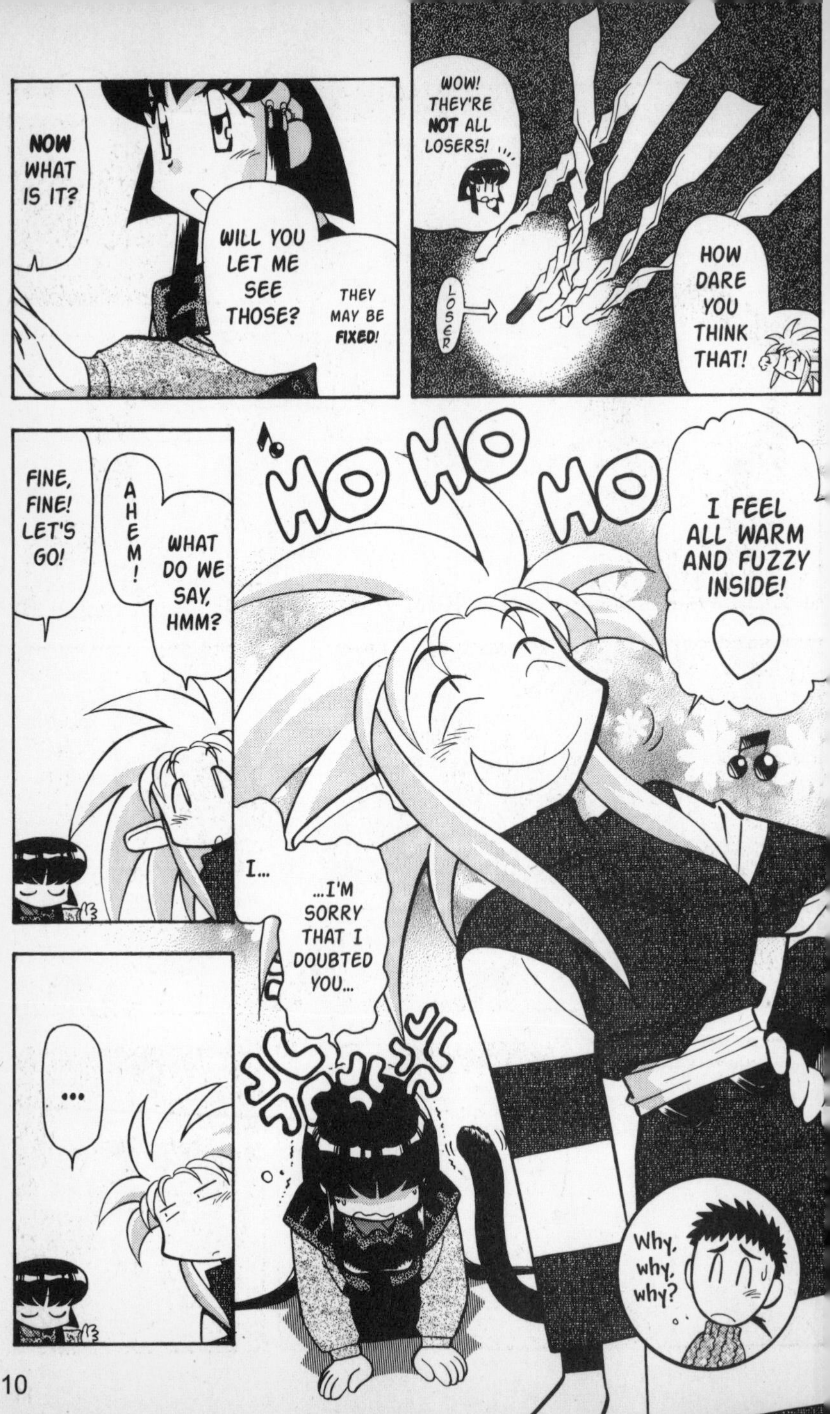
NOW WHAT IS IT?
WILL YOU LET ME SEE THOSE?
THEY MAY BE FIXED!
WOW! THEY'RE NOT ALL LOSERS!
LOSER
HOW DARE YOU THINK THAT!
FINE, FINE! LET'S GO!
AHEM!
WHAT DO WE SAY, HMM?
...
HO HO HO
I FEEL ALL WARM AND FUZZY INSIDE!
I...
...I'M SORRY THAT I DOUBTED YOU...
Why, why, why?

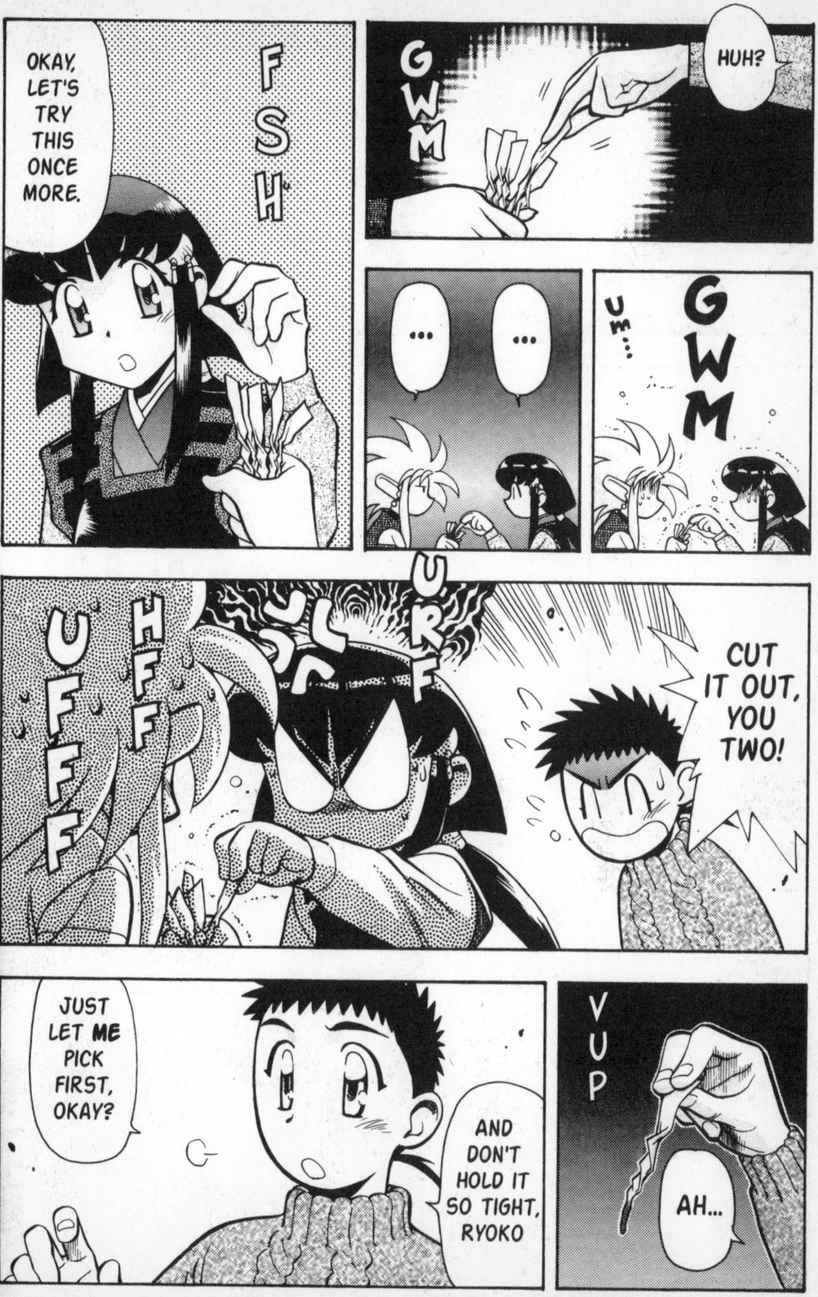
OKAY, LET'S TRY THIS ONCE MORE.
FSH
GWM
HUH?
...
...
Um...
GWM
UFFF
HFF
URF
CUT IT OUT, YOU TWO!
JUST LET ME PICK FIRST, OKAY?
AND DON'T HOLD IT SO TIGHT, RYOKO
VUP
AH...

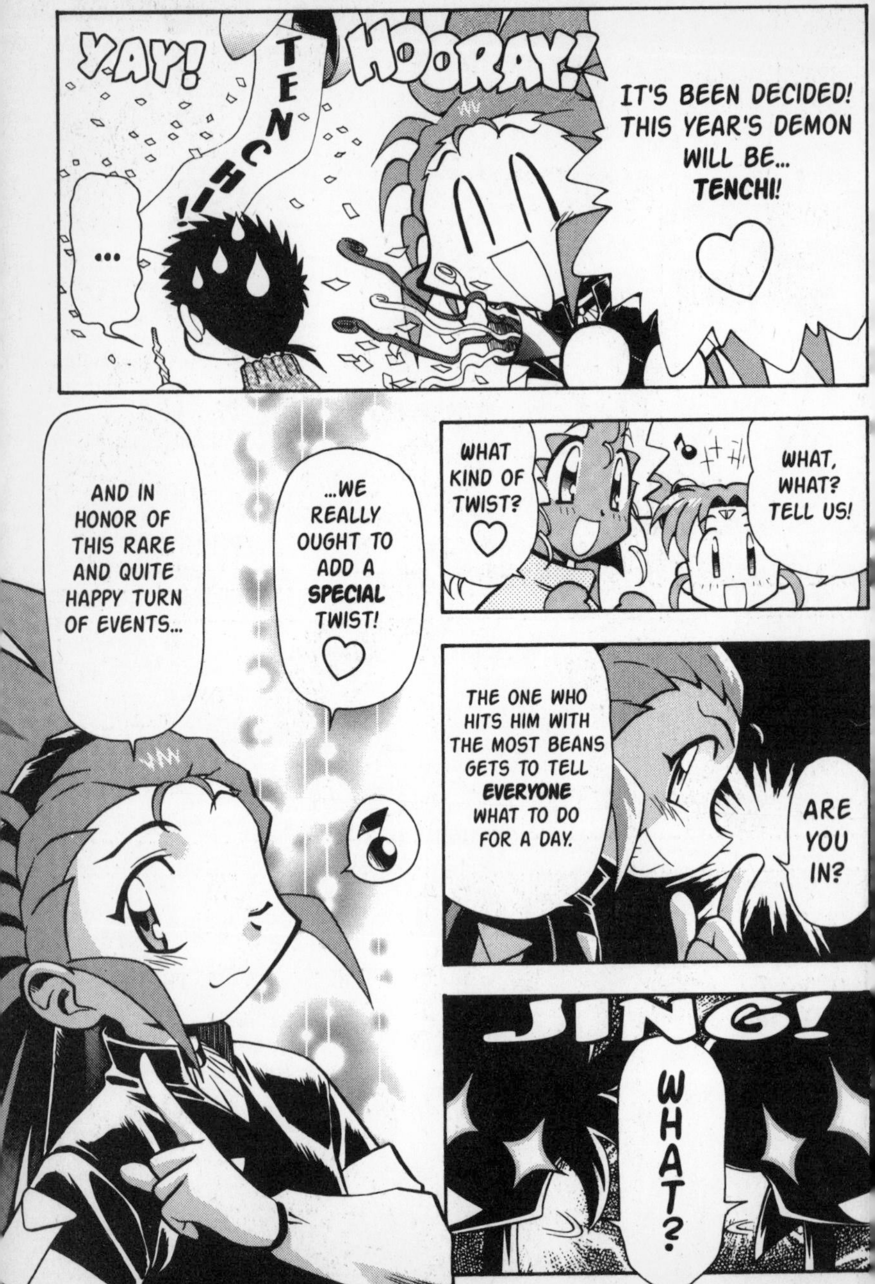
YAY!
TENCHI!
HOORAY!
IT'S BEEN DECIDED! THIS YEAR'S DEMON WILL BE... **TENCHI!**
...
AND IN HONOR OF THIS RARE AND QUITE HAPPY TURN OF EVENTS...
...WE REALLY OUGHT TO ADD A **SPECIAL** TWIST!
WHAT KIND OF TWIST?
WHAT, WHAT? TELL US!
THE ONE WHO HITS HIM WITH THE MOST BEANS GETS TO TELL **EVERYONE** WHAT TO DO FOR A DAY.
ARE YOU IN?
JING!
WHAT?

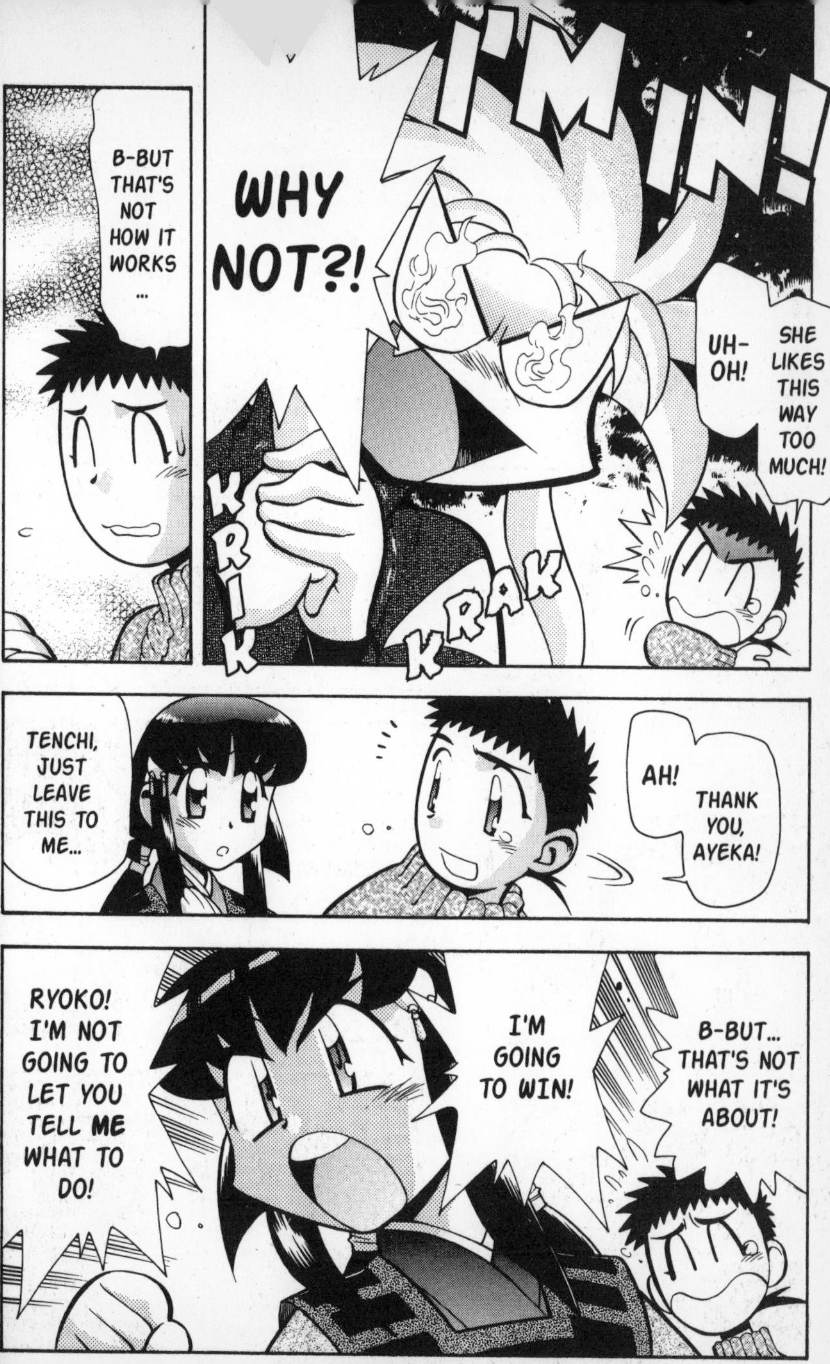
B-BUT THAT'S NOT HOW IT WORKS ...
WHY NOT?!
I'M IN!
UH-OH!
SHE LIKES THIS WAY TOO MUCH!
KRIK
KRAK
TENCHI, JUST LEAVE THIS TO ME...
AH!
THANK YOU, AYEKA!
RYOKO! I'M NOT GOING TO LET YOU TELL ME WHAT TO DO!
I'M GOING TO WIN!
B-BUT... THAT'S NOT WHAT IT'S ABOUT!

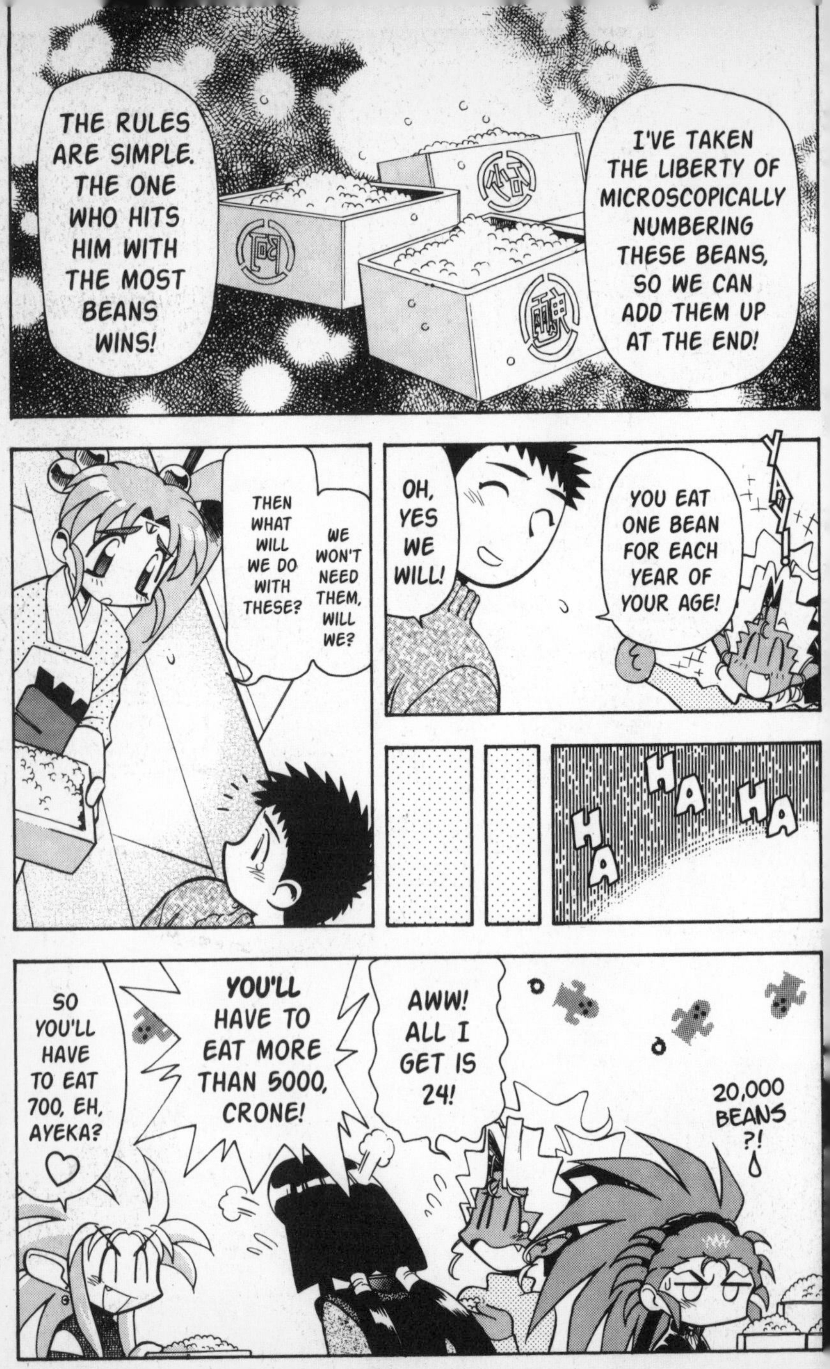
THE RULES ARE SIMPLE. THE ONE WHO HITS HIM WITH THE MOST BEANS WINS!
I'VE TAKEN THE LIBERTY OF MICROSCOPICALLY NUMBERING THESE BEANS, SO WE CAN ADD THEM UP AT THE END!
THEN WHAT WILL WE DO WITH THESE?
WE WON'T NEED THEM, WILL WE?
OH, YES WE WILL!
YOU EAT ONE BEAN FOR EACH YEAR OF YOUR AGE!
HA HA HA HA
SO YOU'LL HAVE TO EAT 700, EH, AYEKA?
YOU'LL HAVE TO EAT MORE THAN 5000, CRONE!
AWW! ALL I GET IS 24!
20,000 BEANS?!

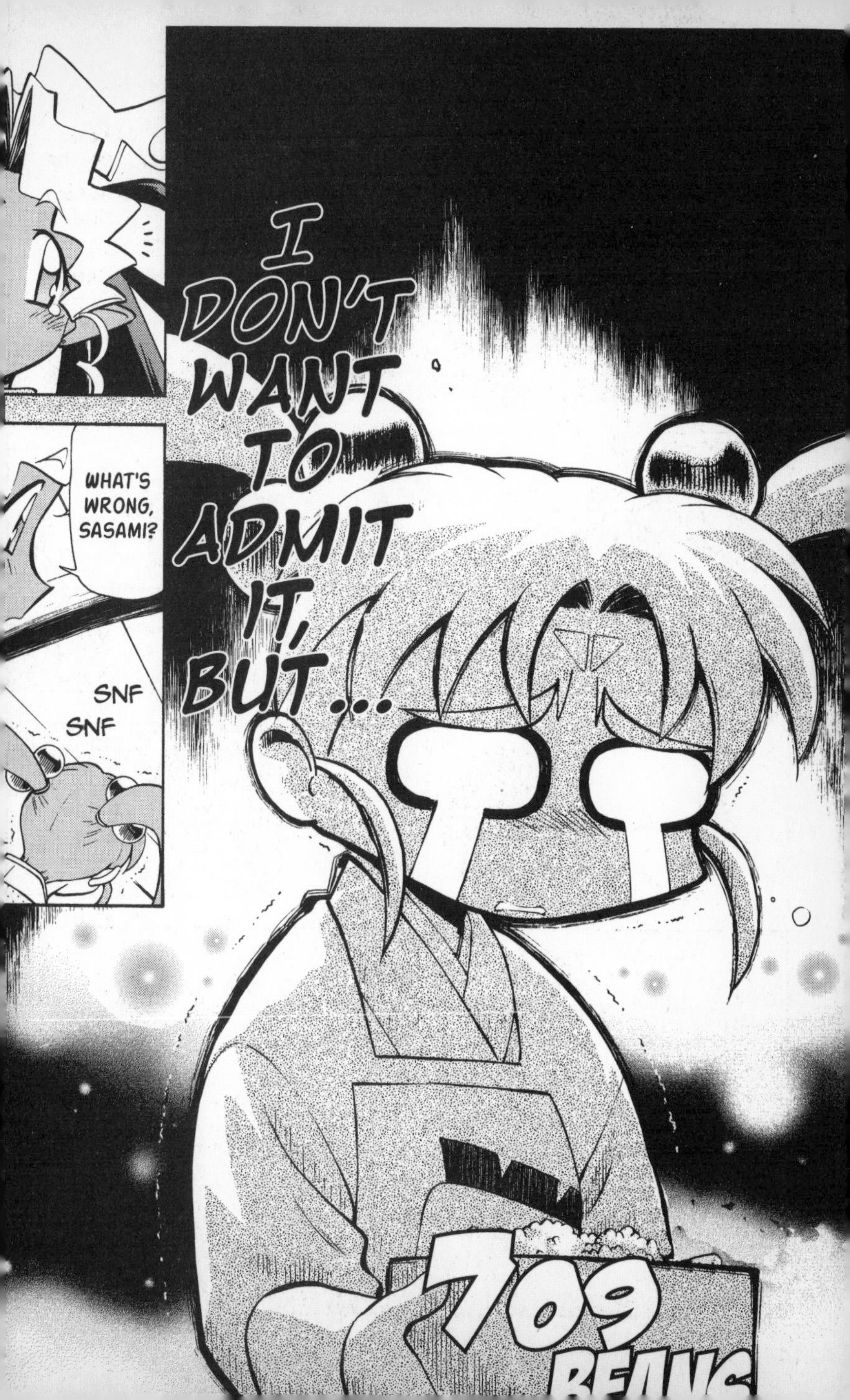
WHAT'S WRONG, SASAMI?
SNF
SNF
I DON'T WANT TO ADMIT IT, BUT...
709 BEANS

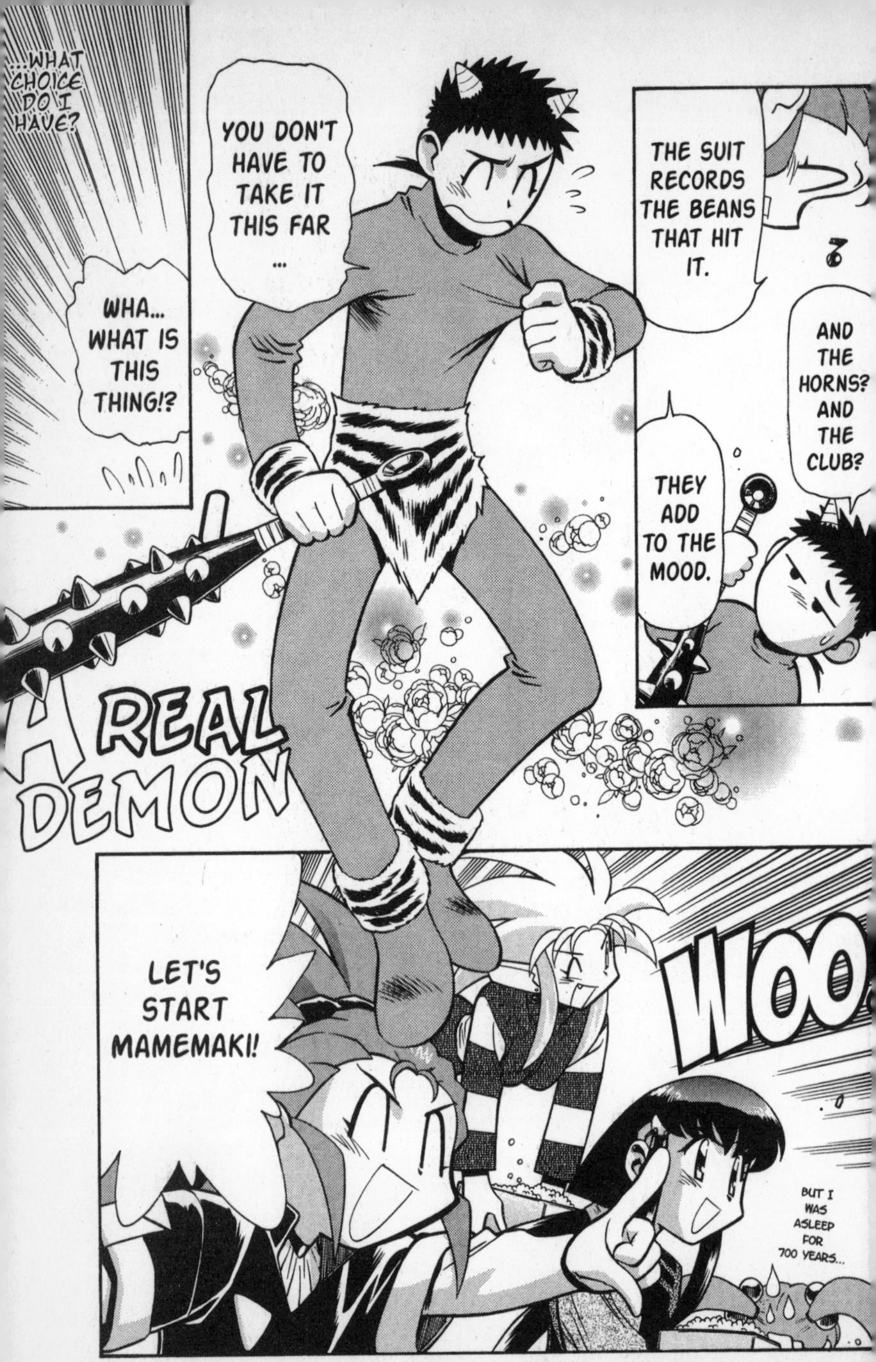

...WHAT CHOICE DO I HAVE?
WHA... WHAT IS THIS THING!?
YOU DON'T HAVE TO TAKE IT THIS FAR ...
THE SUIT RECORDS THE BEANS THAT HIT IT.
AND THE HORNS? AND THE CLUB?
THEY ADD TO THE MOOD.
A REAL DEMON
LET'S START MAMEMAKI!
WOO
BUT I WAS ASLEEP FOR 700 YEARS...

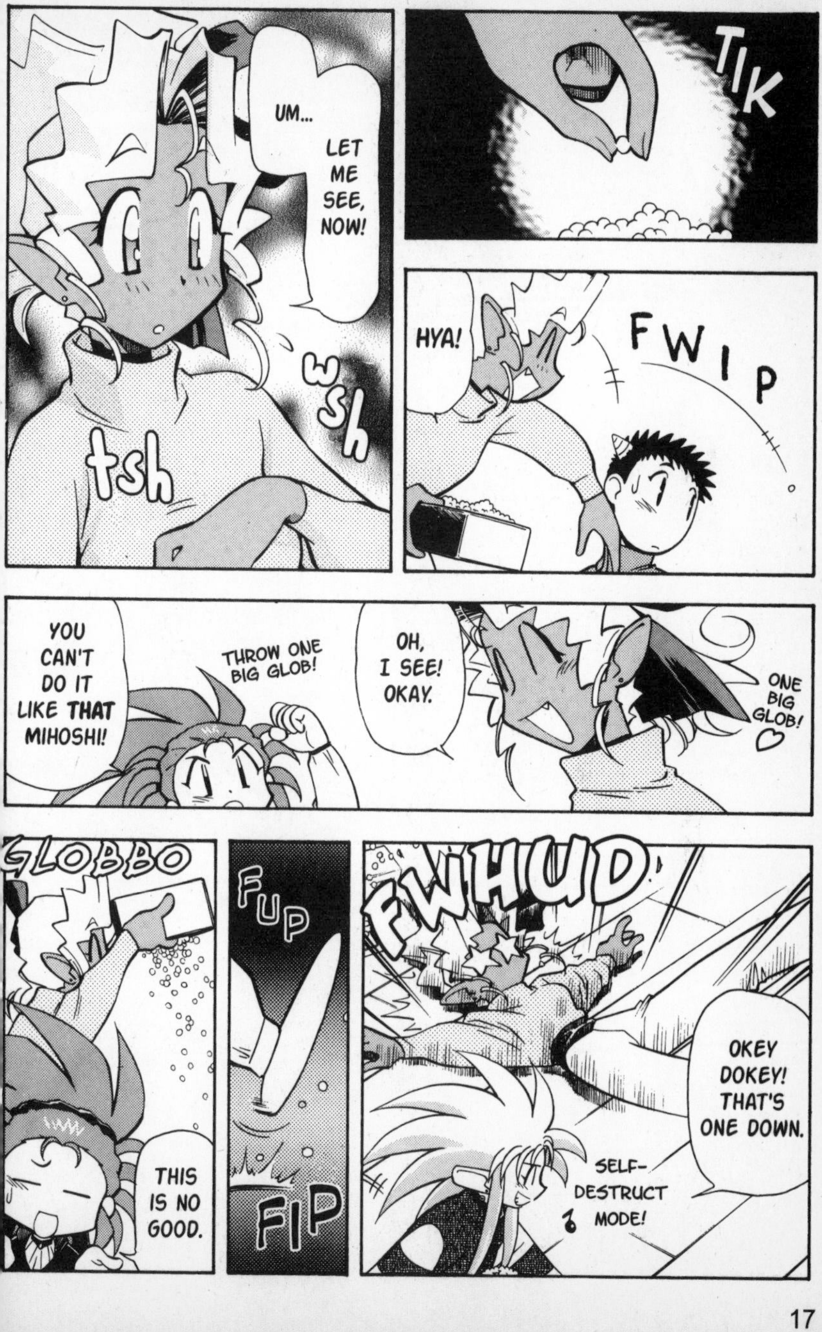
tsh
UM... LET ME SEE, NOW!
wsh
TIK
HYA!
FWIP
YOU CAN'T DO IT LIKE THAT MIHOSHI!
THROW ONE BIG GLOB!
OH, I SEE! OKAY.
ONE BIG GLOB!
GLOBBO
THIS IS NO GOOD.
FUP
FIP
FWHUD
OKEY DOKEY! THAT'S ONE DOWN.
SELF-DESTRUCT MODE!

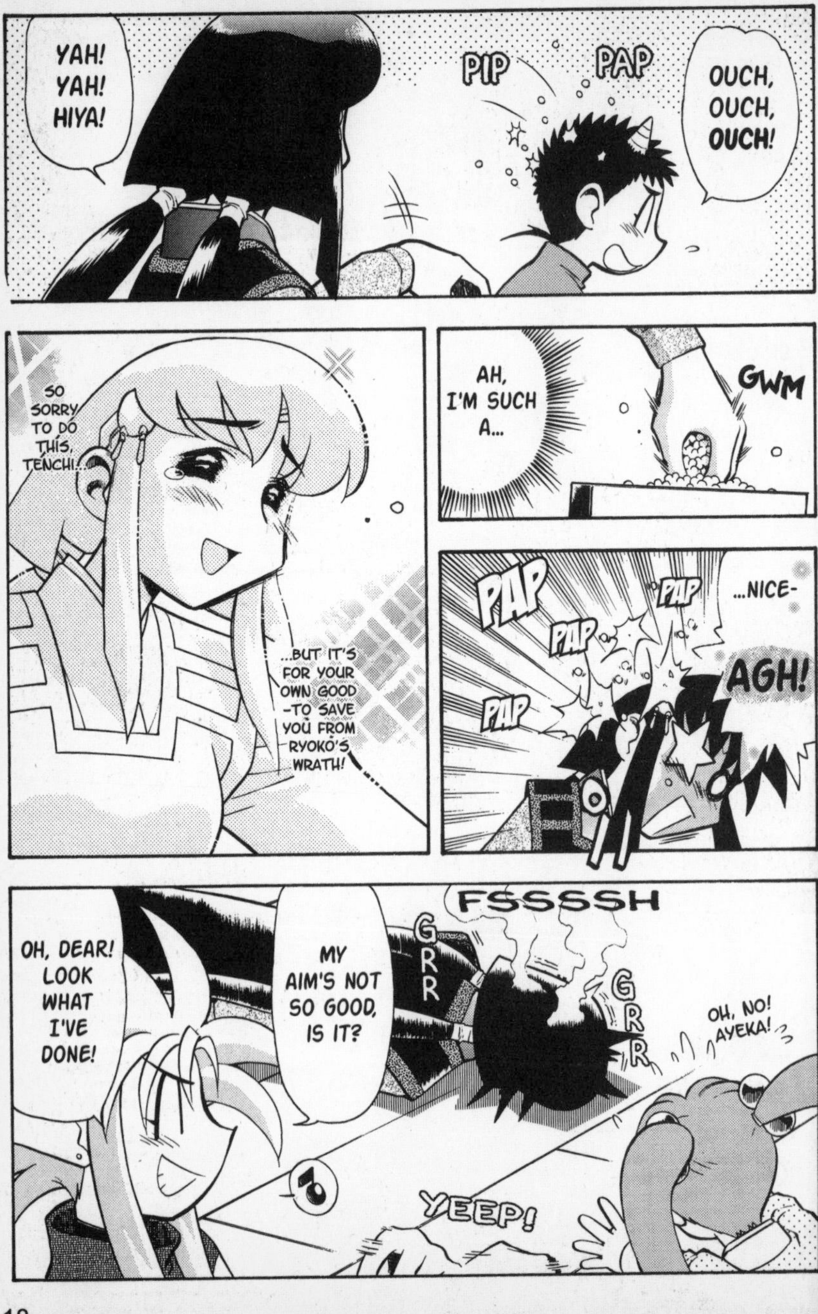
YAH! YAH! HIYA!
PIP
PAP
OUCH, OUCH, OUCH!
SO SORRY TO DO THIS, TENCHI...
...BUT IT'S FOR YOUR OWN GOOD -TO SAVE YOU FROM RYOKO'S WRATH!
AH, I'M SUCH A...
GWM
PAP
PAP
PAP
PAP
...NICE-
AGH!
OH, DEAR! LOOK WHAT I'VE DONE!
MY AIM'S NOT SO GOOD, IS IT?
FSSSSH
GRR
GRR
OH, NO! AYEKA!
YEEP!

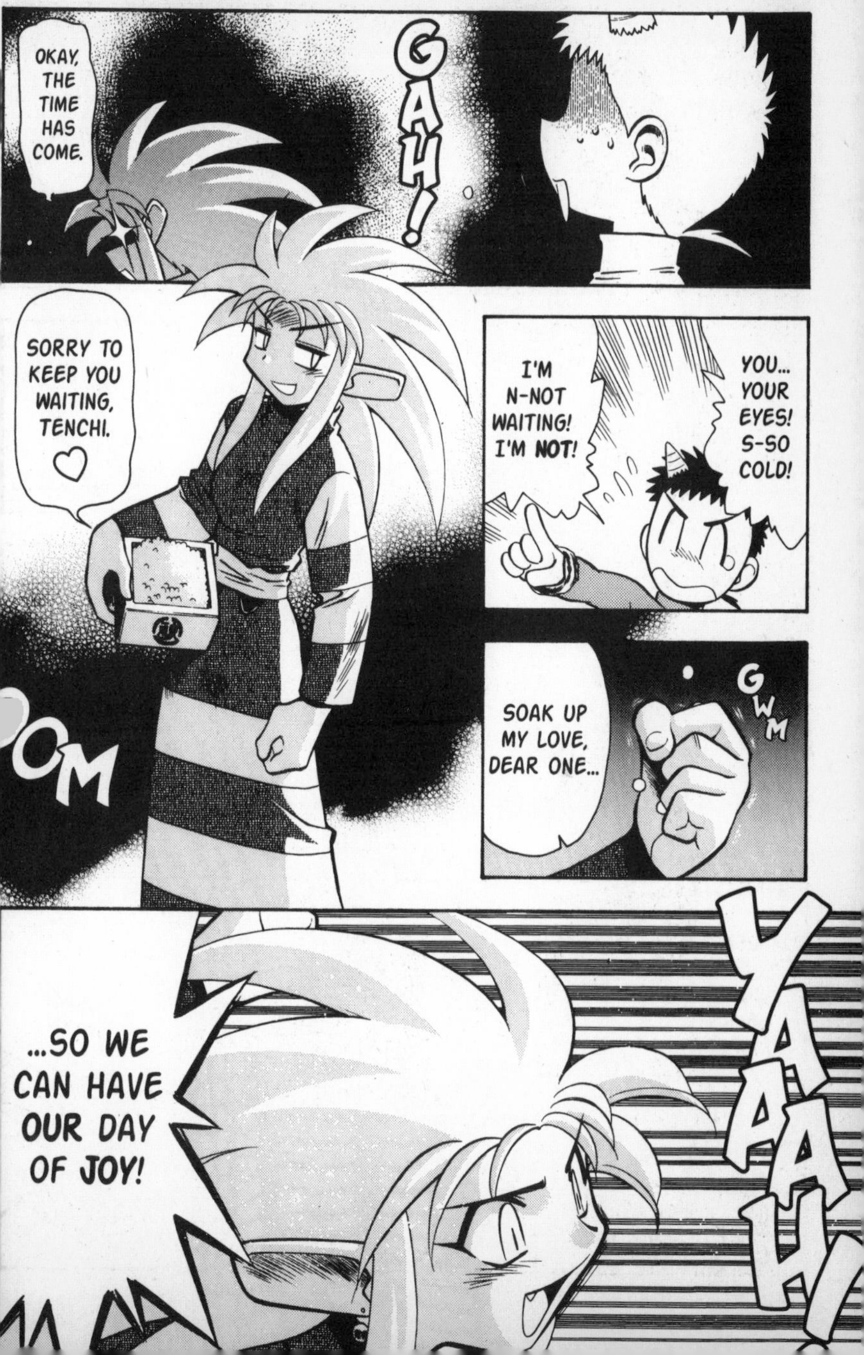

OKAY, THE TIME HAS COME.
GAAH!
SORRY TO KEEP YOU WAITING, TENCHI. ♡
OM
I'M N-NOT WAITING! I'M **NOT**!
YOU... YOUR EYES! S-SO COLD!
SOAK UP MY LOVE, DEAR ONE...
GWM
...SO WE CAN HAVE **OUR** DAY OF **JOY**!
YAAAH!

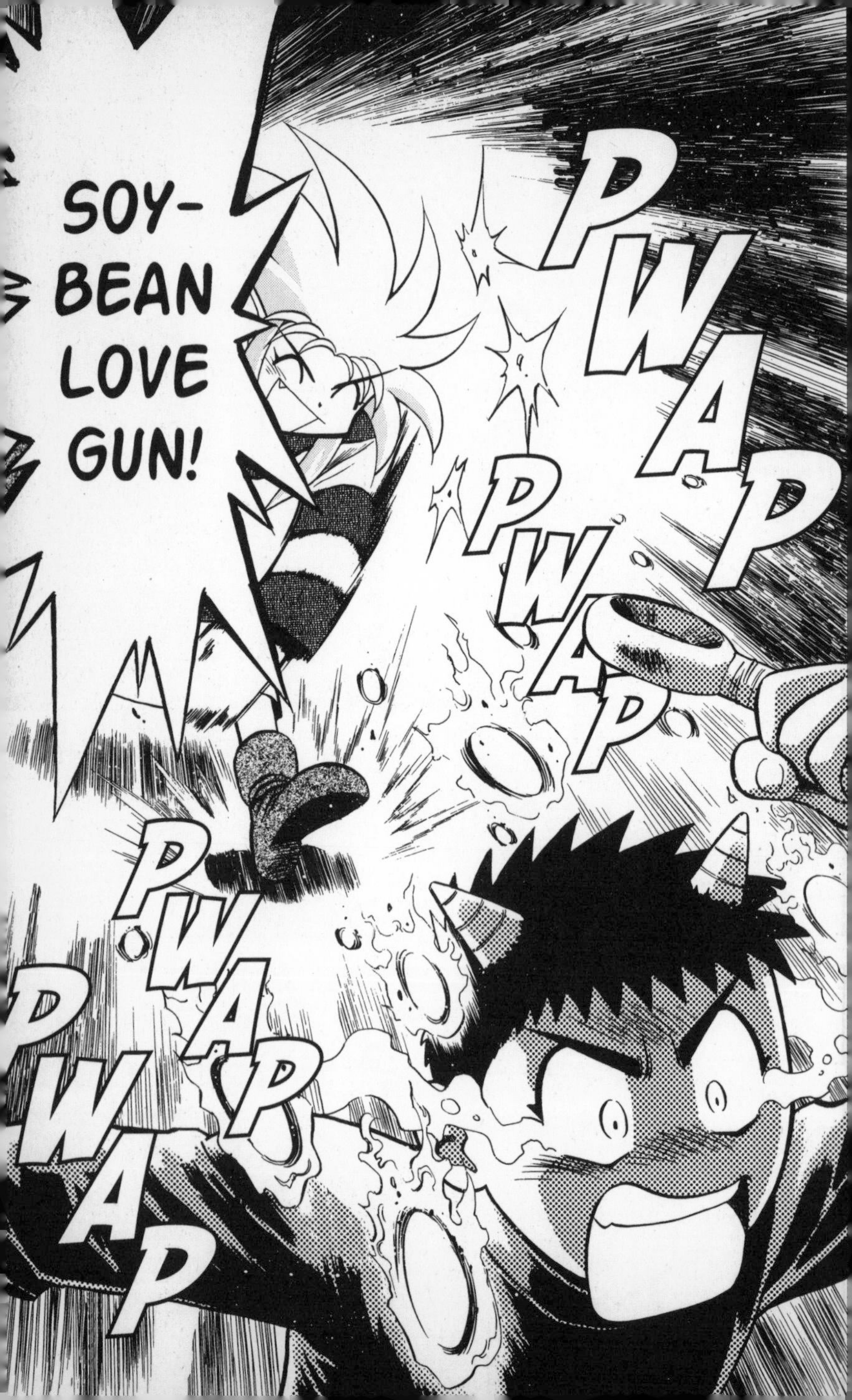
SOY-BEAN LOVE GUN!
PWAP
PWAP
PWAP
PWAP

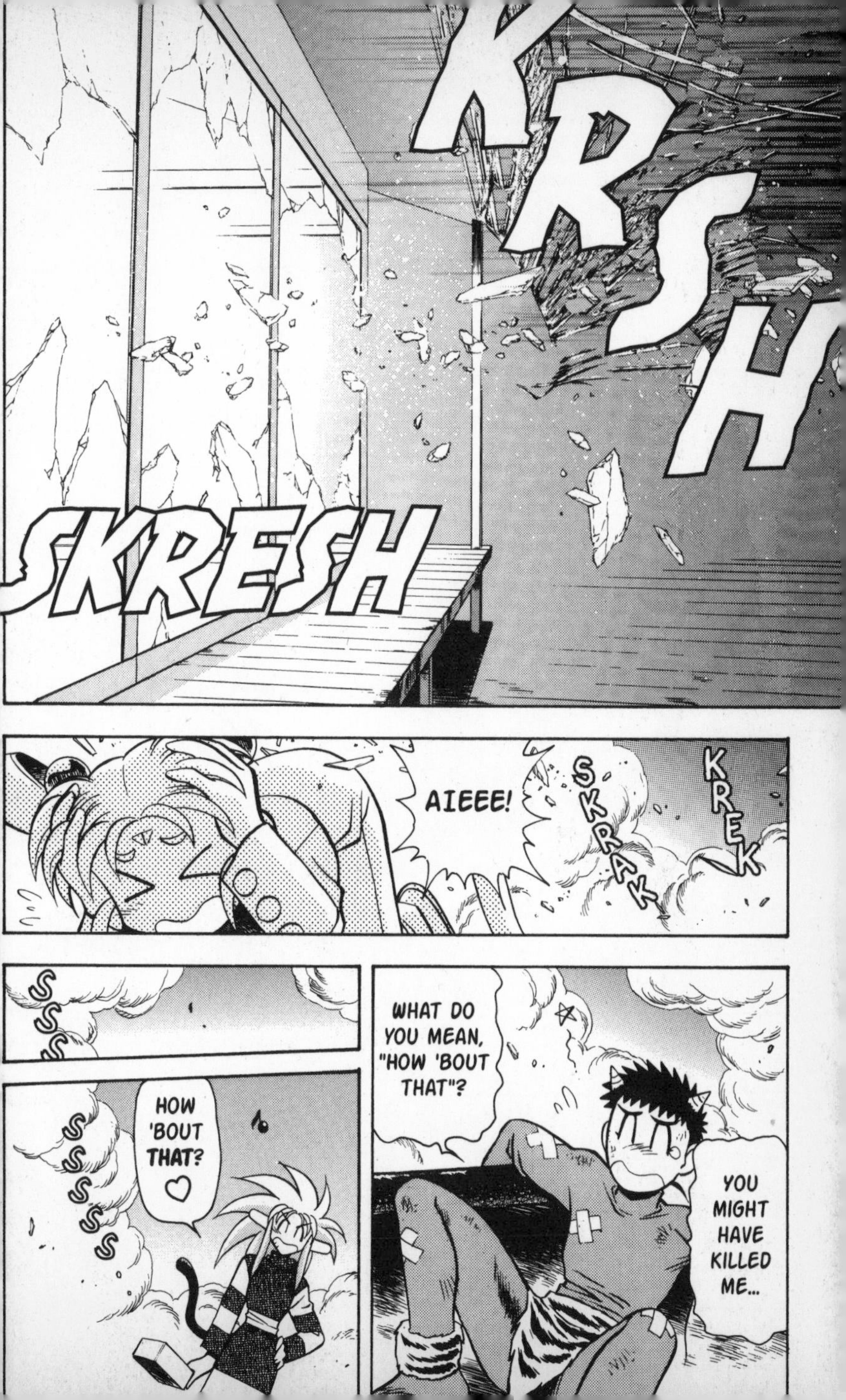
KRSH
SKRESH
AIEEE!
SKRAK
KREK
SSS
WHAT DO YOU MEAN, "HOW 'BOUT THAT"?
SSSSSS
HOW 'BOUT THAT? ♡
YOU MIGHT HAVE KILLED ME...

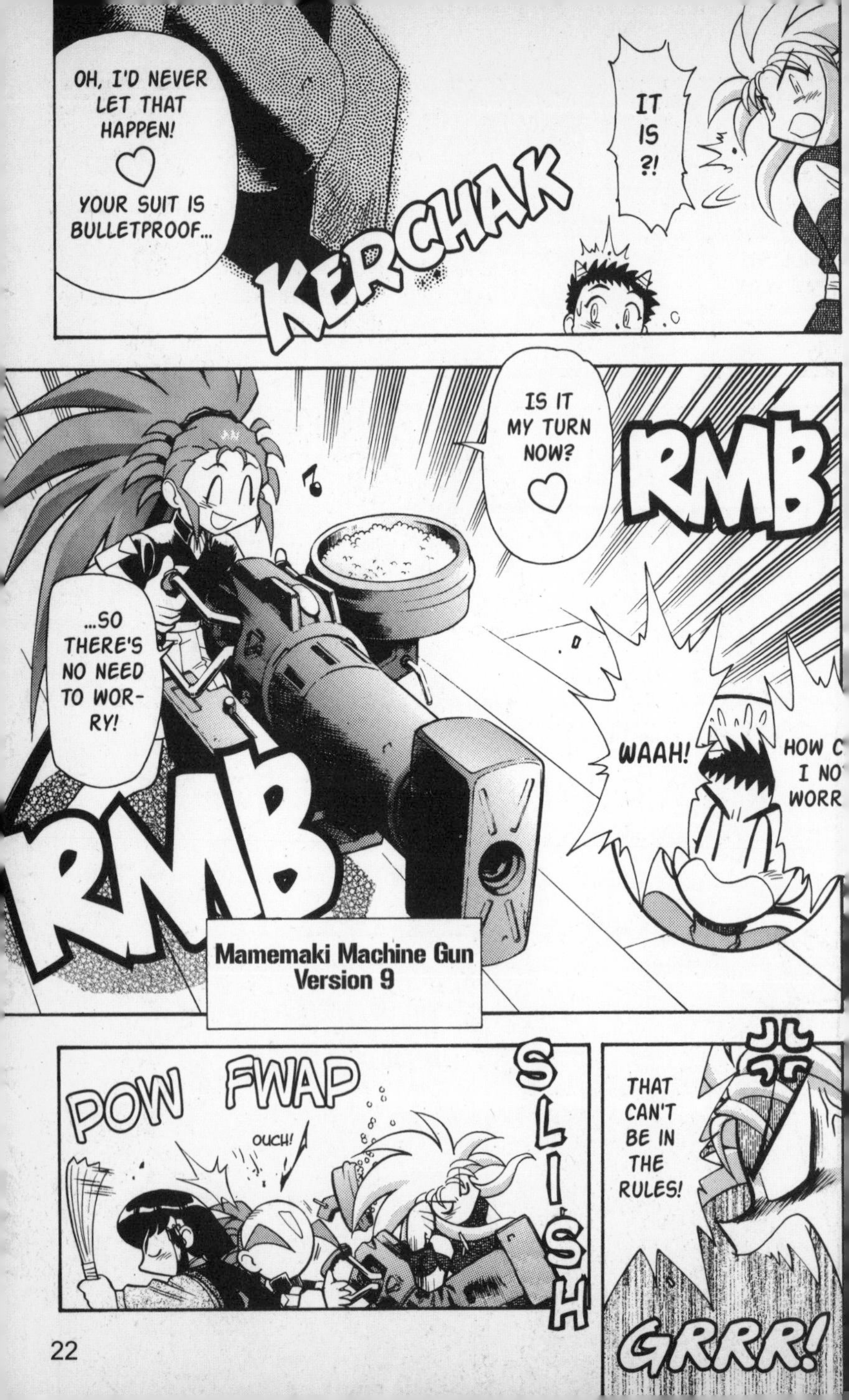

OH, I'D NEVER LET THAT HAPPEN! ♥ YOUR SUIT IS BULLETPROOF...
KERCHAK
IT IS ?!
IS IT MY TURN NOW? ♥
RMB
...SO THERE'S NO NEED TO WOR-RY!
RMB
WAAH!
HOW C I NO WORR
Mamemaki Machine Gun Version 9
POW
FWAP
OUCH!
SLISH
THAT CAN'T BE IN THE RULES!
GRRR!

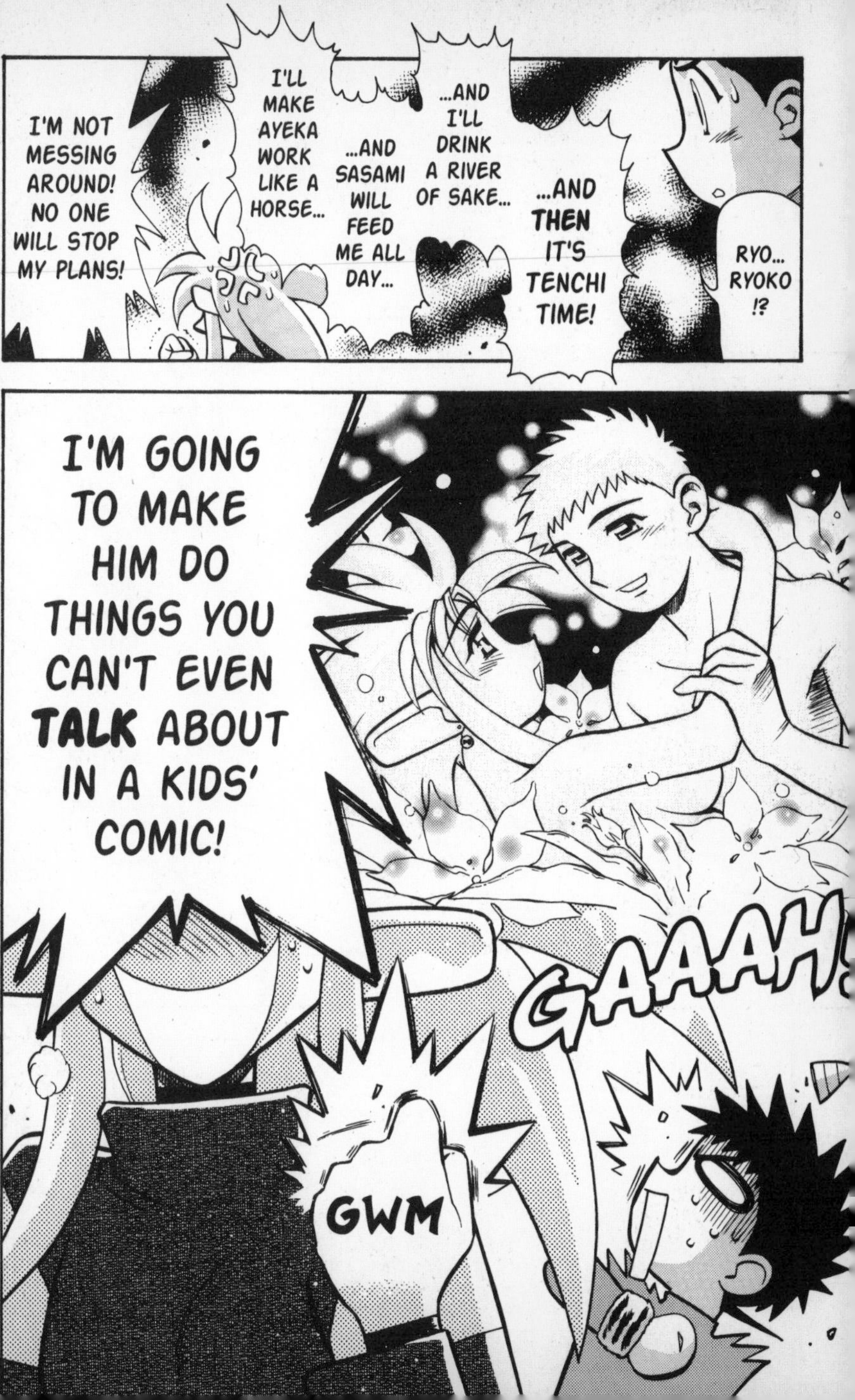

I'M NOT MESSING AROUND! NO ONE WILL STOP MY PLANS!
I'LL MAKE AYEKA WORK LIKE A HORSE...
...AND SASAMI WILL FEED ME ALL DAY...
...AND I'LL DRINK A RIVER OF SAKE...
...AND **THEN** IT'S TENCHI TIME!
RYO... RYOKO!?
I'M GOING TO MAKE HIM DO THINGS YOU CAN'T EVEN **TALK** ABOUT IN A KIDS' COMIC!
GAAAH!
GWM

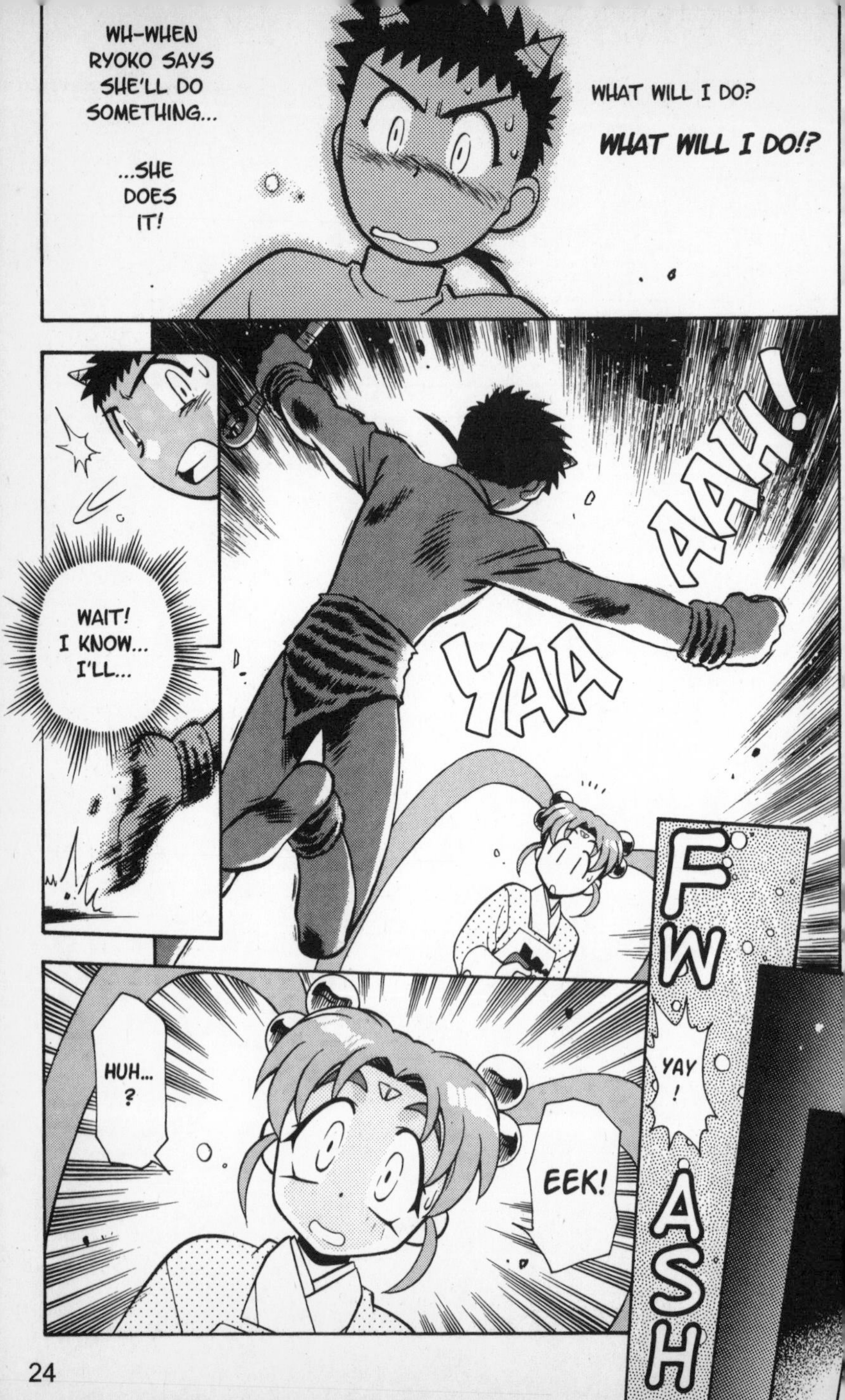
WH-WHEN RYOKO SAYS SHE'LL DO SOMETHING...
...SHE DOES IT!
WHAT WILL I DO?
WHAT WILL I DO!?
WAIT! I KNOW... I'LL...
YAA
AAH!
FWASH
HUH...?
EEK!
YAY!

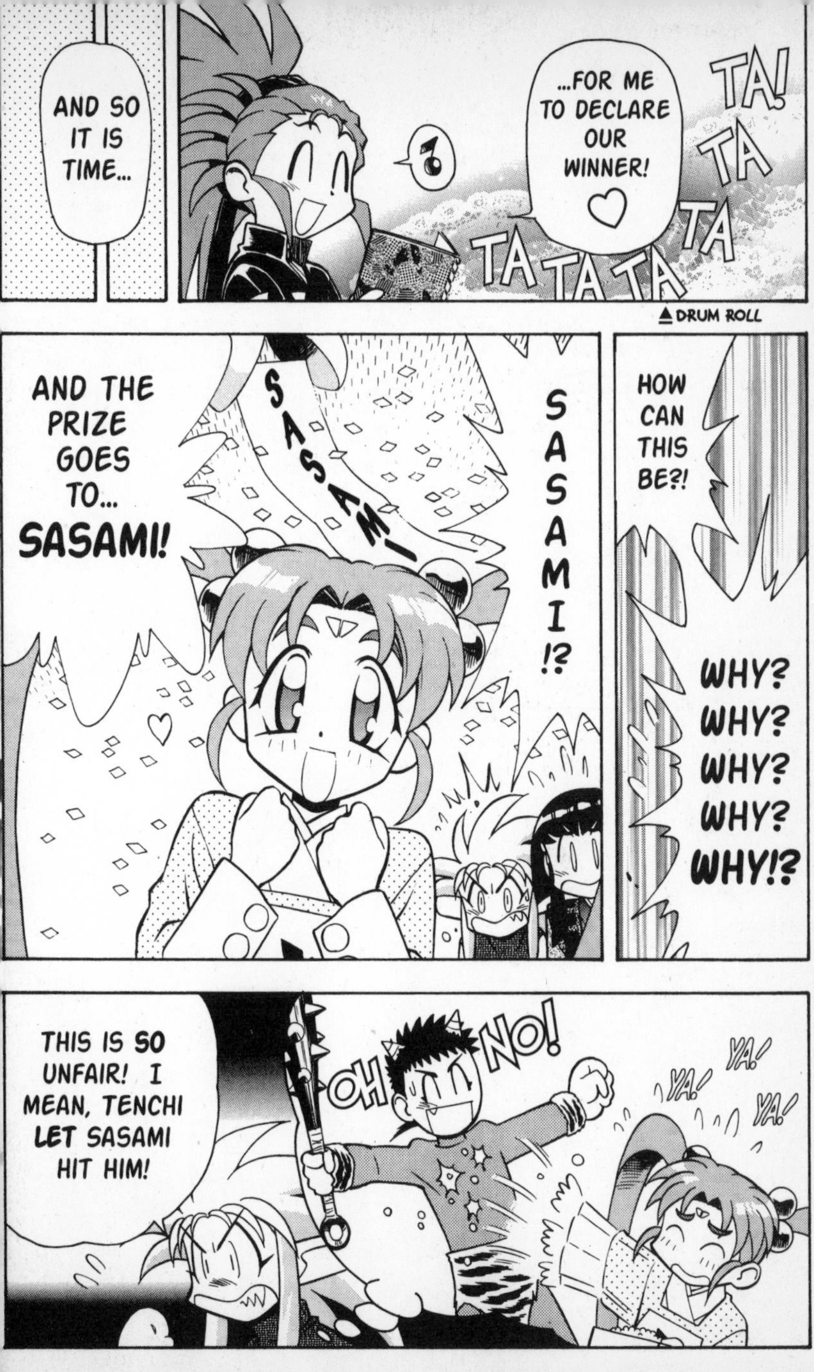
AND SO IT IS TIME...
...FOR ME TO DECLARE OUR WINNER! ♡
TA! TA TA TA TA TA TA TA
▲DRUM ROLL
AND THE PRIZE GOES TO... SASAMI!
SASAMI!
SASAMI!?
HOW CAN THIS BE?!
WHY? WHY? WHY? WHY? WHY!?
THIS IS SO UNFAIR! I MEAN, TENCHI LET SASAMI HIT HIM!
OH NO!
YA! YA! YA!

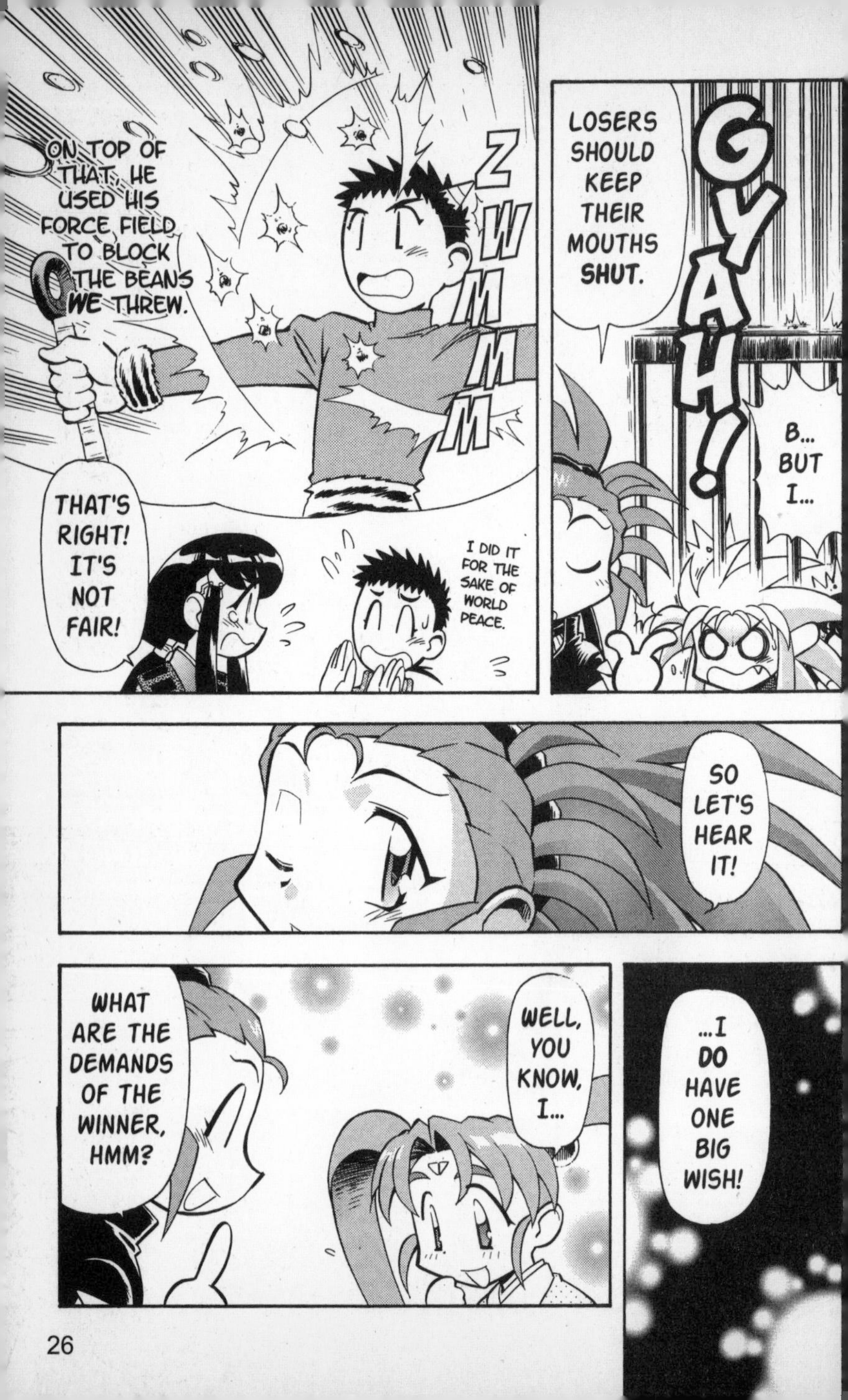
ON TOP OF THAT, HE USED HIS FORCE FIELD TO BLOCK THE BEANS WE THREW.
ZWMMMM
THAT'S RIGHT! IT'S NOT FAIR!
I DID IT FOR THE SAKE OF WORLD PEACE.
LOSERS SHOULD KEEP THEIR MOUTHS SHUT.
GYAH!
B... BUT I...
SO LET'S HEAR IT!
WHAT ARE THE DEMANDS OF THE WINNER, HMM?
WELL, YOU KNOW, I...
...I DO HAVE ONE BIG WISH!

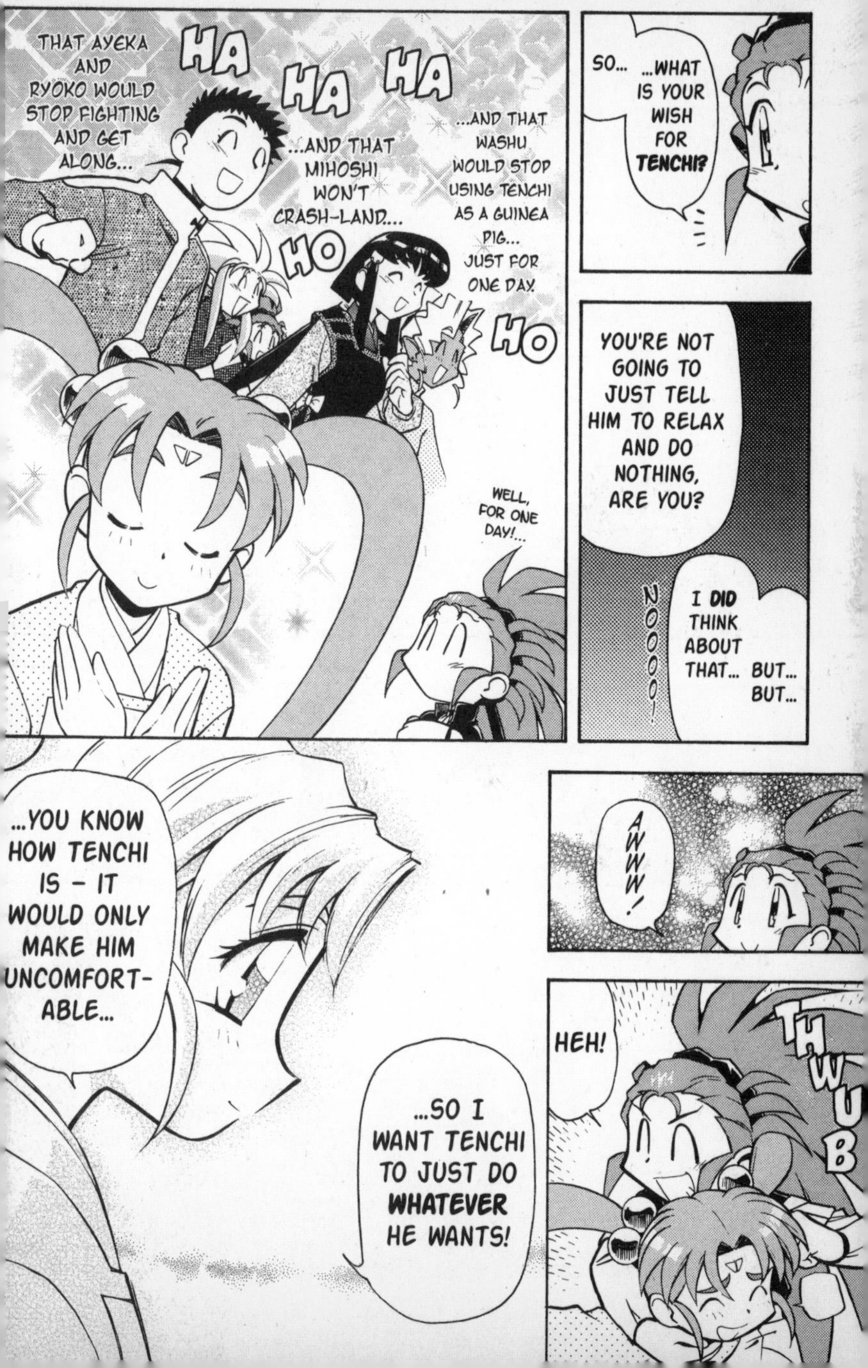
THAT AYEKA AND RYOKO WOULD STOP FIGHTING AND GET ALONG...
HA HA HA
...AND THAT MIHOSHI WON'T CRASH-LAND...
...AND THAT WASHU WOULD STOP USING TENCHI AS A GUINEA PIG... JUST FOR ONE DAY.
HO HO
WELL, FOR ONE DAY!...
SO... ...WHAT IS YOUR WISH FOR TENCHI?
YOU'RE NOT GOING TO JUST TELL HIM TO RELAX AND DO NOTHING, ARE YOU?
NOOOOO!
I DID THINK ABOUT THAT... BUT... BUT...
...YOU KNOW HOW TENCHI IS – IT WOULD ONLY MAKE HIM UNCOMFORT-ABLE...
...SO I WANT TENCHI TO JUST DO WHATEVER HE WANTS!
AWWW!
HEH!
THWUB

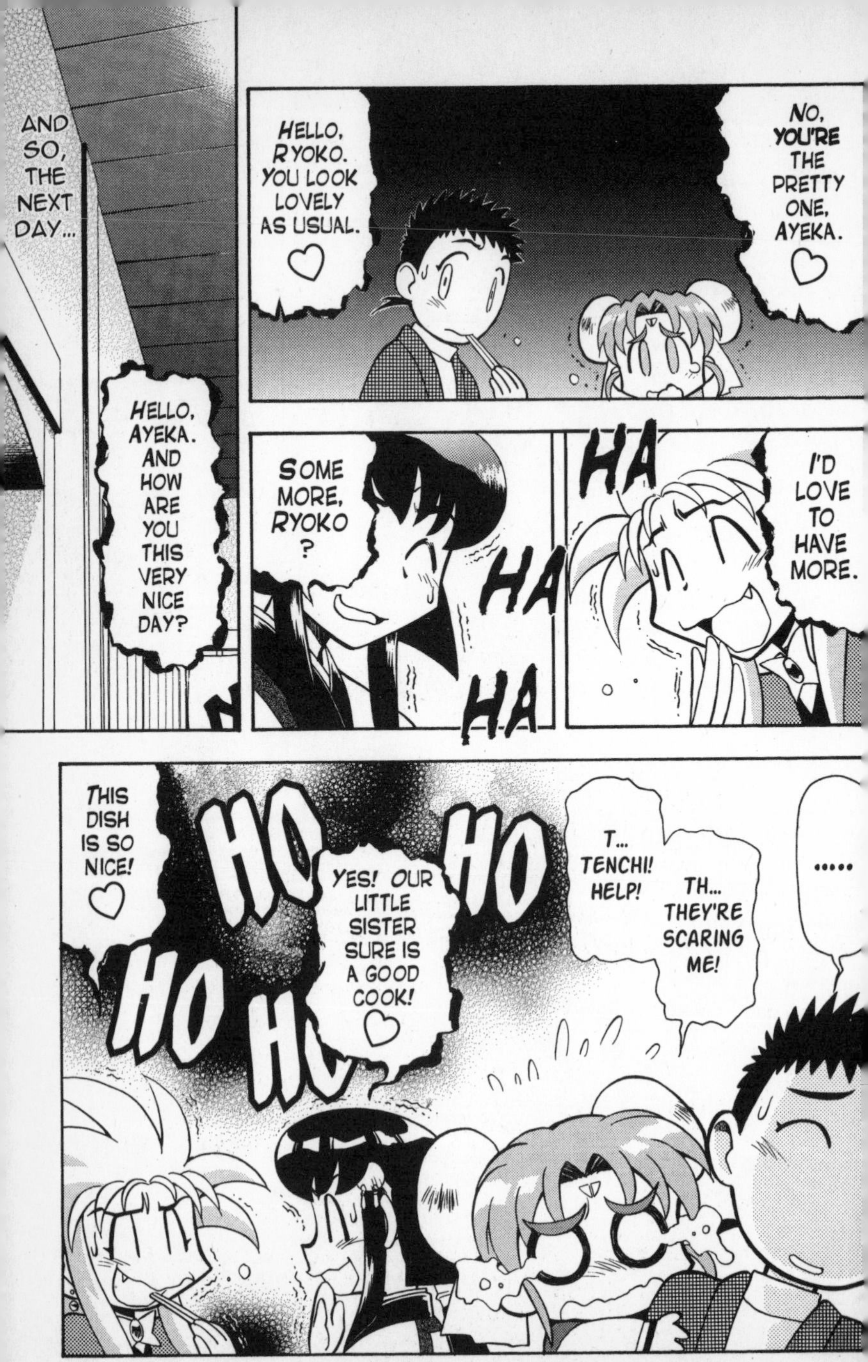
AND SO, THE NEXT DAY...
HELLO, AYEKA. AND HOW ARE YOU THIS VERY NICE DAY?
HELLO, RYOKO. YOU LOOK LOVELY AS USUAL. ♡
NO, YOU'RE THE PRETTY ONE, AYEKA. ♡
SOME MORE, RYOKO?
HA HA HA HA
I'D LOVE TO HAVE MORE.
THIS DISH IS SO NICE! ♡
HO HO
YES! OUR LITTLE SISTER SURE IS A GOOD COOK! ♡
HO
HO HO
T... TENCHI! HELP!
TH... THEY'RE SCARING ME!
.....

Chapter 2 : School Daze

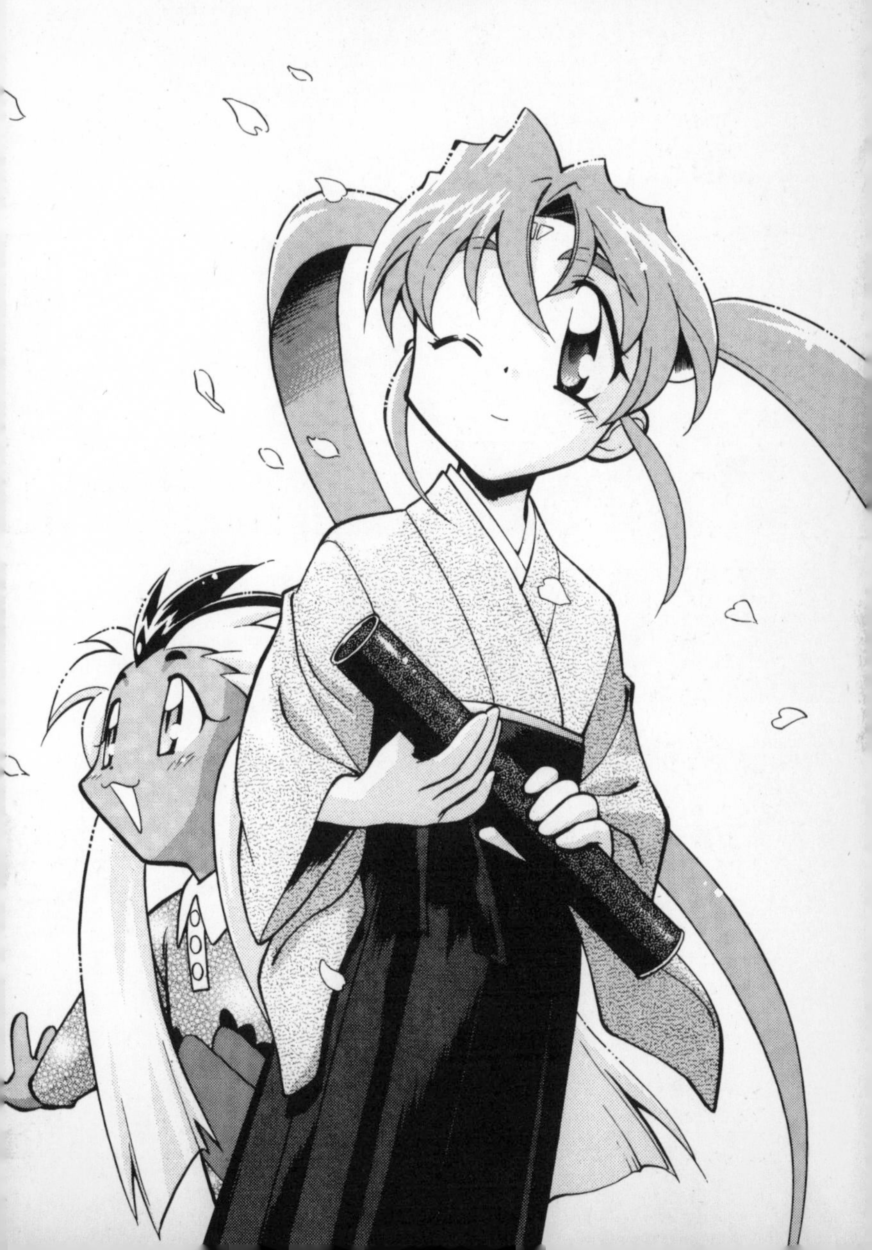

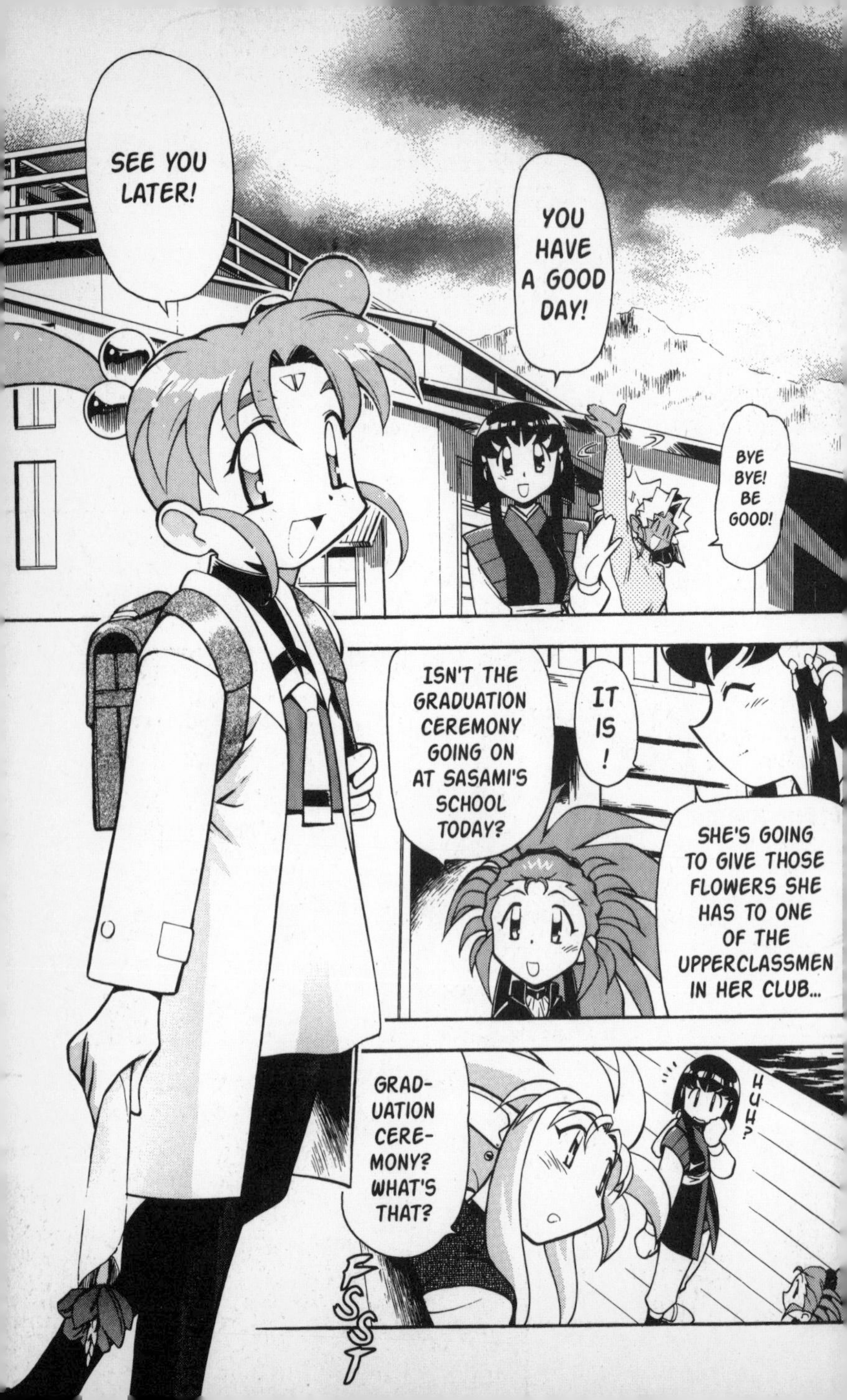
SEE YOU LATER!
YOU HAVE A GOOD DAY!
BYE BYE! BE GOOD!
ISN'T THE GRADUATION CEREMONY GOING ON AT SASAMI'S SCHOOL TODAY?
IT IS!
SHE'S GOING TO GIVE THOSE FLOWERS SHE HAS TO ONE OF THE UPPERCLASSMEN IN HER CLUB...
GRAD-UATION CERE-MONY? WHAT'S THAT?
HUH?
FSST

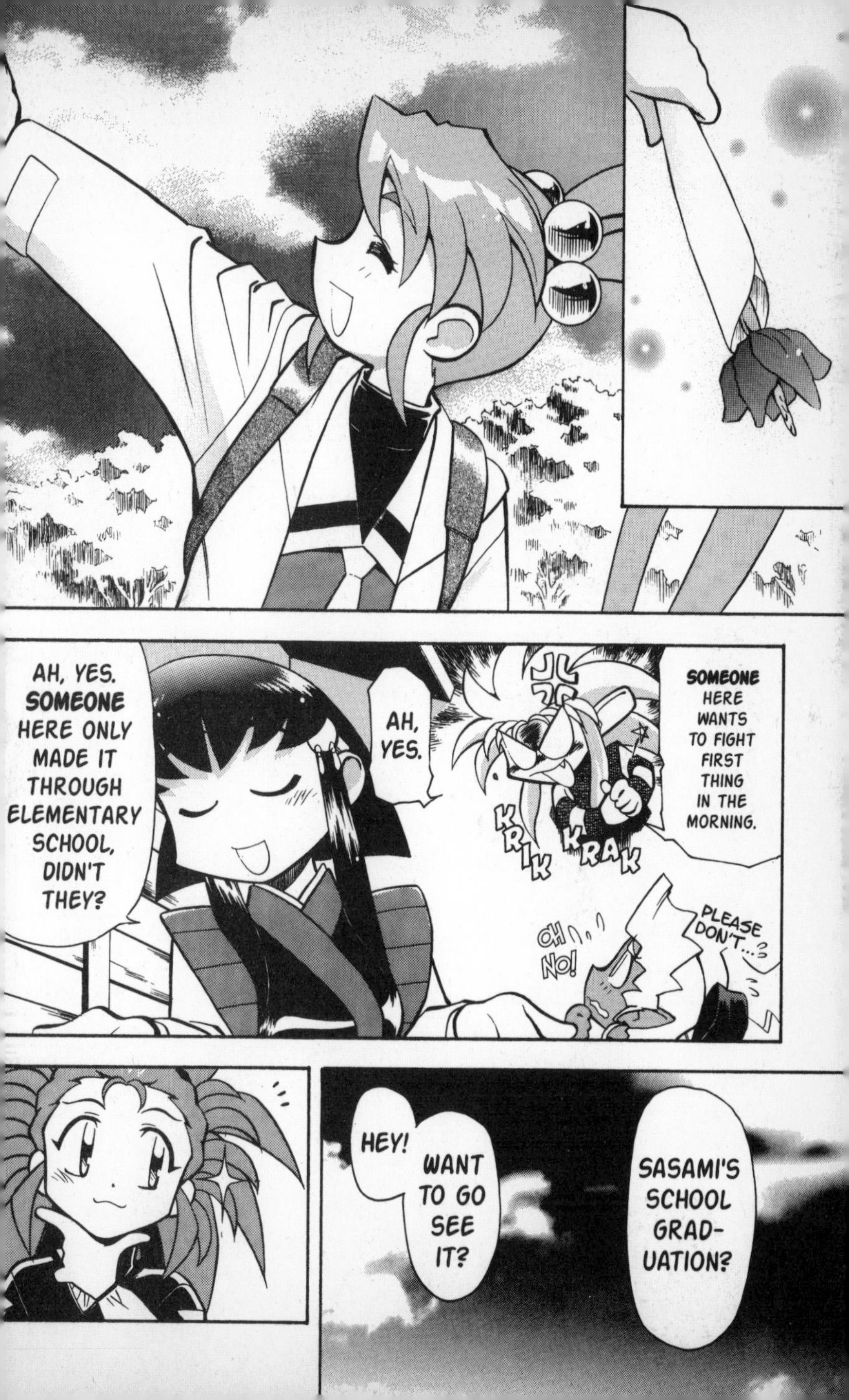
AH, YES. SOMEONE HERE ONLY MADE IT THROUGH ELEMENTARY SCHOOL, DIDN'T THEY?
AH, YES.
KRIK KRAK
SOMEONE HERE WANTS TO FIGHT FIRST THING IN THE MORNING.
OH NO!
PLEASE DON'T...
HEY!
WANT TO GO SEE IT?
SASAMI'S SCHOOL GRAD-UATION?

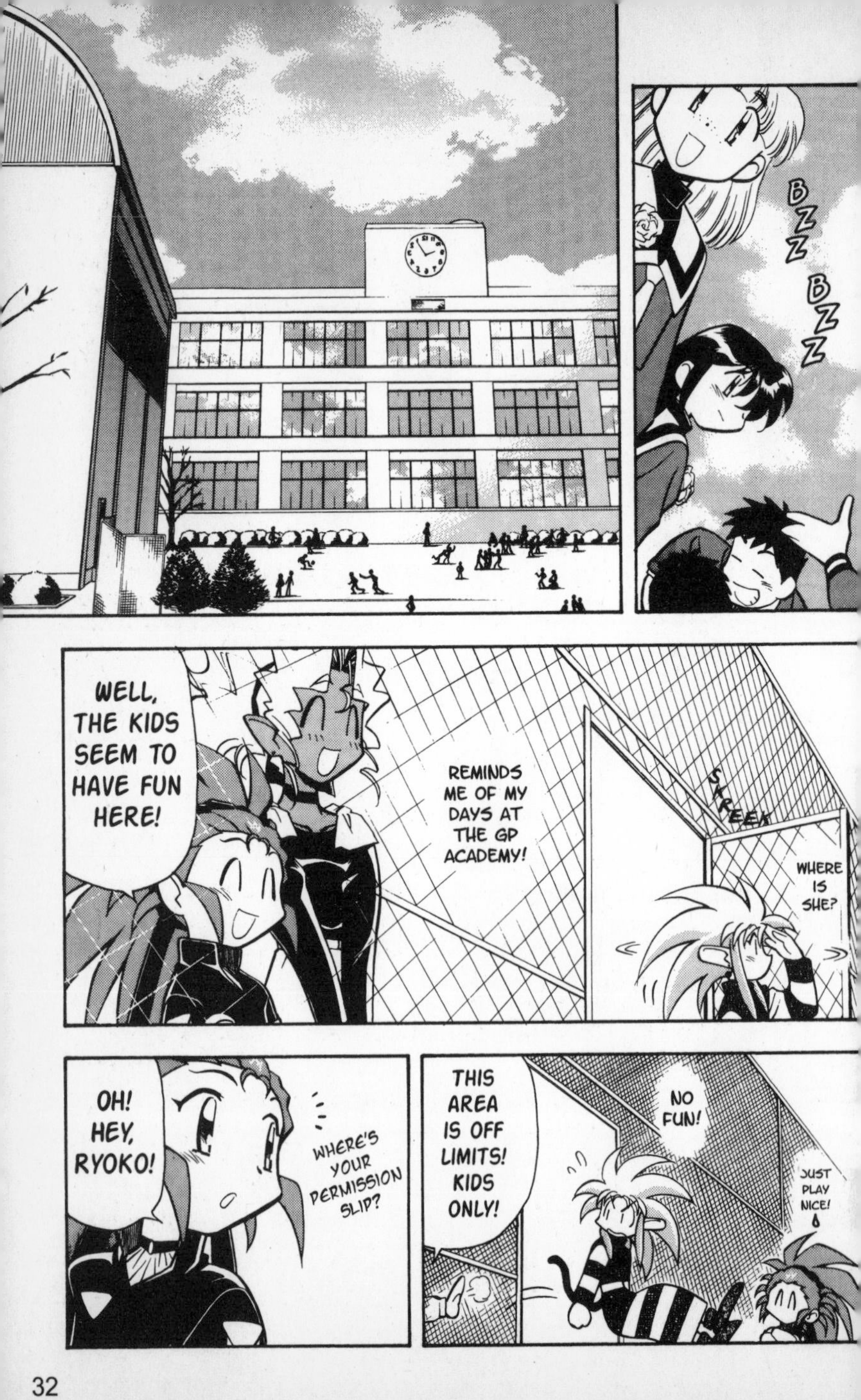
BZZ
BZZZ
WELL, THE KIDS SEEM TO HAVE FUN HERE!
REMINDS ME OF MY DAYS AT THE GP ACADEMY!
SKREEEK
WHERE IS SHE?
OH! HEY, RYOKO!
WHERE'S YOUR PERMISSION SLIP?
THIS AREA IS OFF LIMITS! KIDS ONLY!
NO FUN!
JUST PLAY NICE!

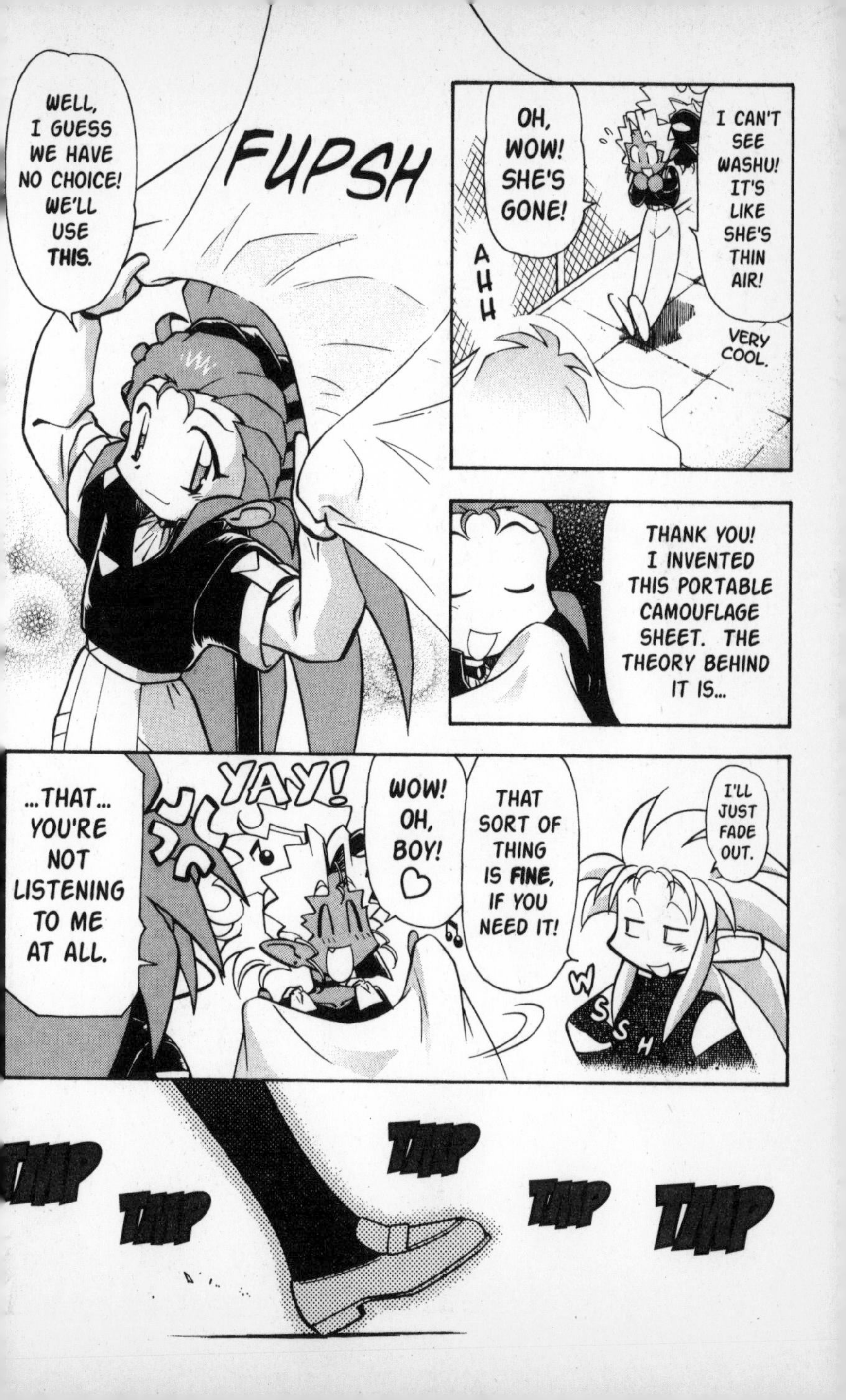
WELL, I GUESS WE HAVE NO CHOICE! WE'LL USE THIS.
FUPSH
OH, WOW! SHE'S GONE!
AHH
I CAN'T SEE WASHU! IT'S LIKE SHE'S THIN AIR!
VERY COOL.
THANK YOU! I INVENTED THIS PORTABLE CAMOUFLAGE SHEET. THE THEORY BEHIND IT IS...
...THAT... YOU'RE NOT LISTENING TO ME AT ALL.
YAY!
WOW! OH, BOY! ♡
THAT SORT OF THING IS FINE, IF YOU NEED IT!
I'LL JUST FADE OUT.
WSSH
TMP
TMP
TMP
TMP
TMP

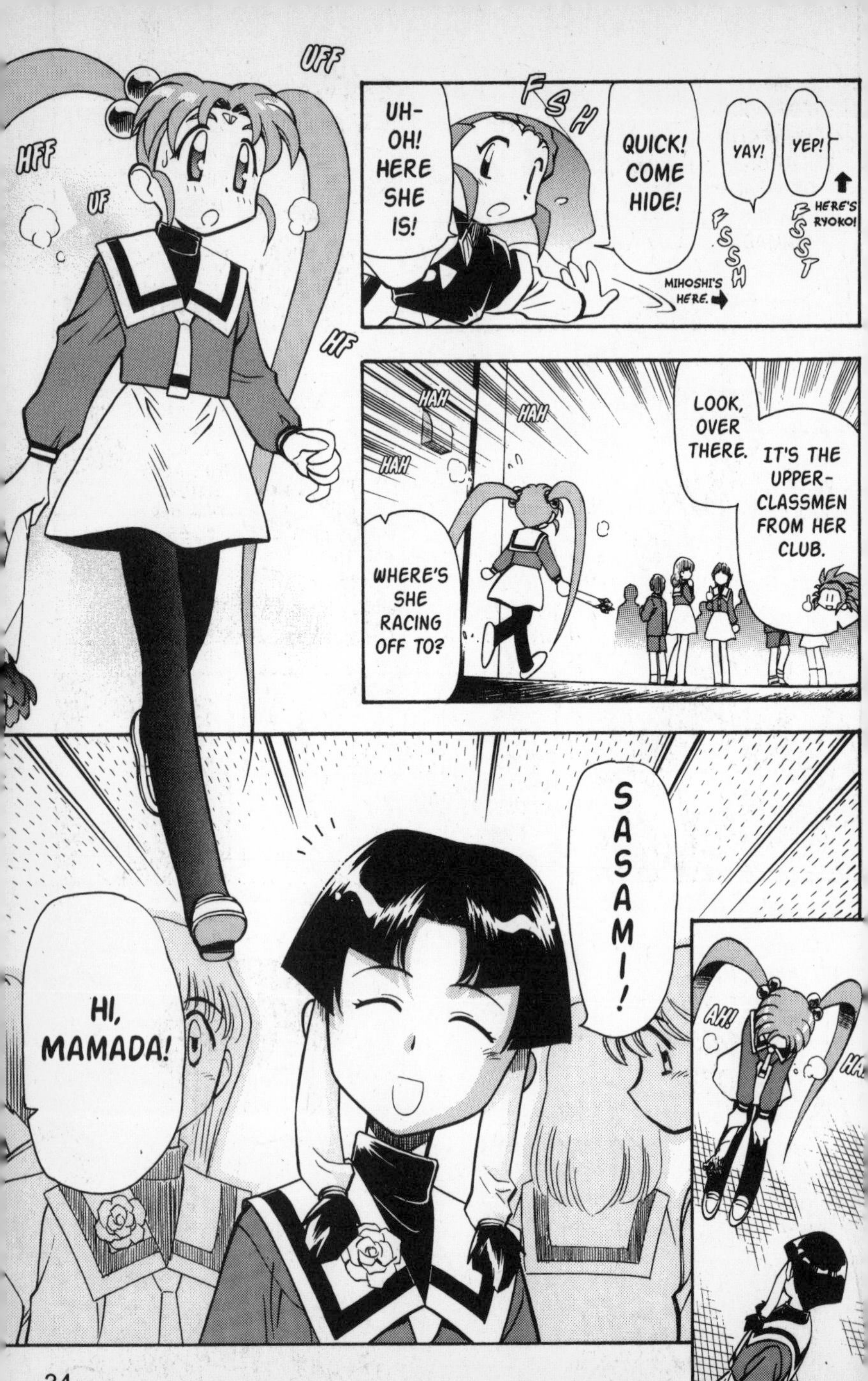
HFF
UF
UFF
HF
UH-OH! HERE SHE IS!
FSH
QUICK! COME HIDE!
YAY!
YEP!
FSSH
FSST
MIHOSHI'S HERE.
HERE'S RYOKO!
HAH
HAH
HAH
WHERE'S SHE RACING OFF TO?
LOOK, OVER THERE.
IT'S THE UPPER-CLASSMEN FROM HER CLUB.
HI, MAMADA!
SASAMI!
AH!

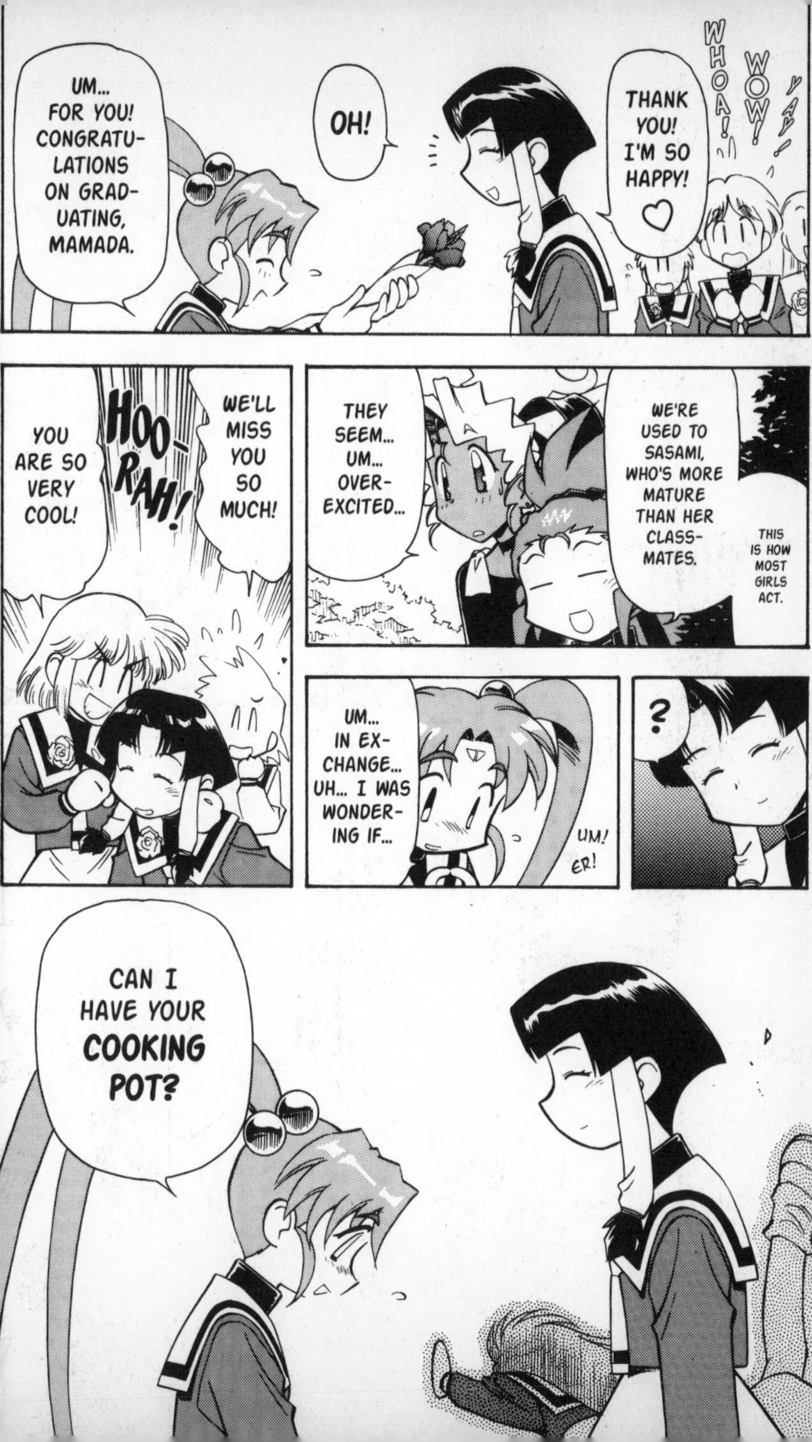

UM... FOR YOU! CONGRATULATIONS ON GRADUATING, MAMADA.
OH!
THANK YOU! I'M SO HAPPY! ♥
WHOA!
WOW!
YAY!
YOU ARE SO VERY COOL!
HOO-RAH!
WE'LL MISS YOU SO MUCH!
THEY SEEM... UM... OVER-EXCITED...
WE'RE USED TO SASAMI, WHO'S MORE MATURE THAN HER CLASSMATES.
THIS IS HOW MOST GIRLS ACT.
UM... IN EXCHANGE... UH... I WAS WONDERING IF...
UM! ER!
?
CAN I HAVE YOUR COOKING POT?

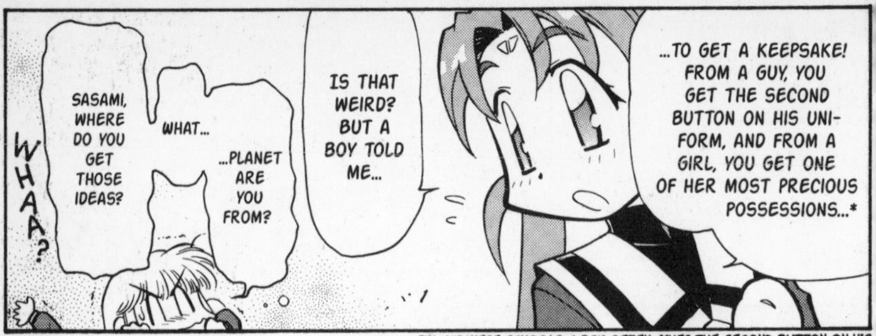
SASAMI, WHERE DO YOU GET THOSE IDEAS?
WHAA?
WHAT...
...PLANET ARE YOU FROM?
IS THAT WEIRD? BUT A BOY TOLD ME...
...TO GET A KEEPSAKE! FROM A GUY, YOU GET THE SECOND BUTTON ON HIS UNI-FORM, AND FROM A GIRL, YOU GET ONE OF HER MOST PRECIOUS POSSESSIONS...*

*IN JAPANESE SCHOOLS, A BOY OFTEN GIVES THE SECOND BUTTON ON HIS UNIFORM TO A GIRLFRIEND - LIKE CLASS RINGS IN AMERICAN SCHOOLS.

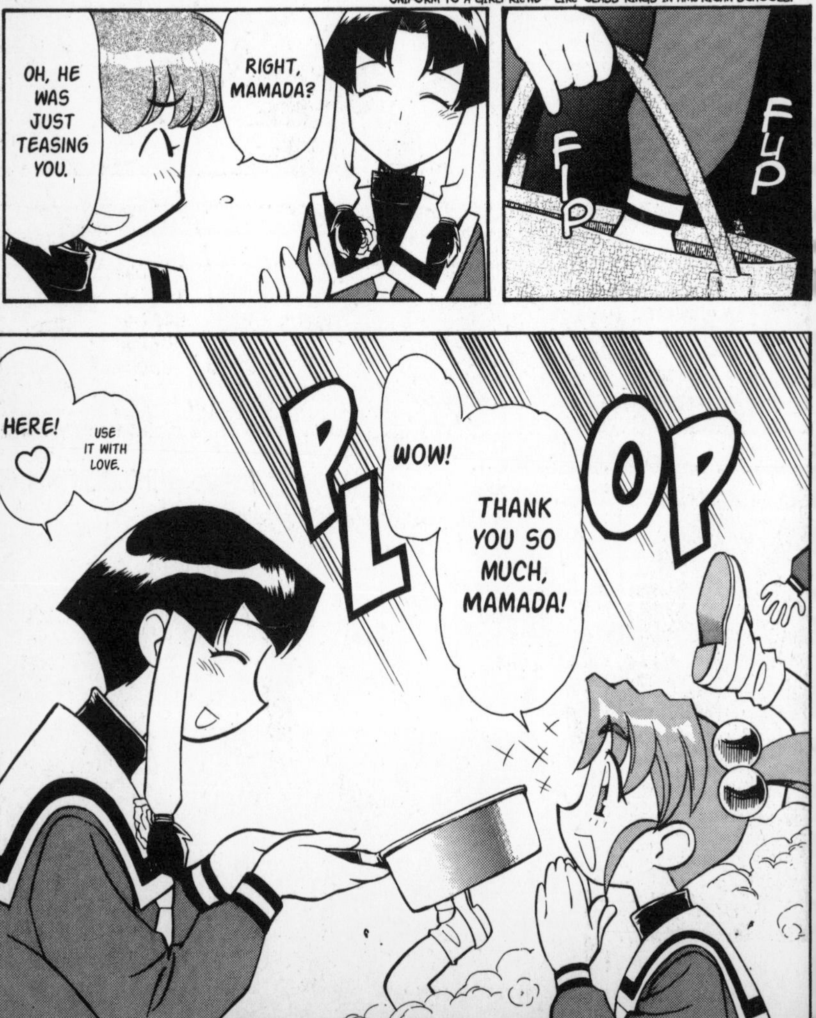
OH, HE WAS JUST TEASING YOU.
RIGHT, MAMADA?
FLIP
FLIP
HERE! ♡
USE IT WITH LOVE.
PLOP
WOW!
THANK YOU SO MUCH, MAMADA!

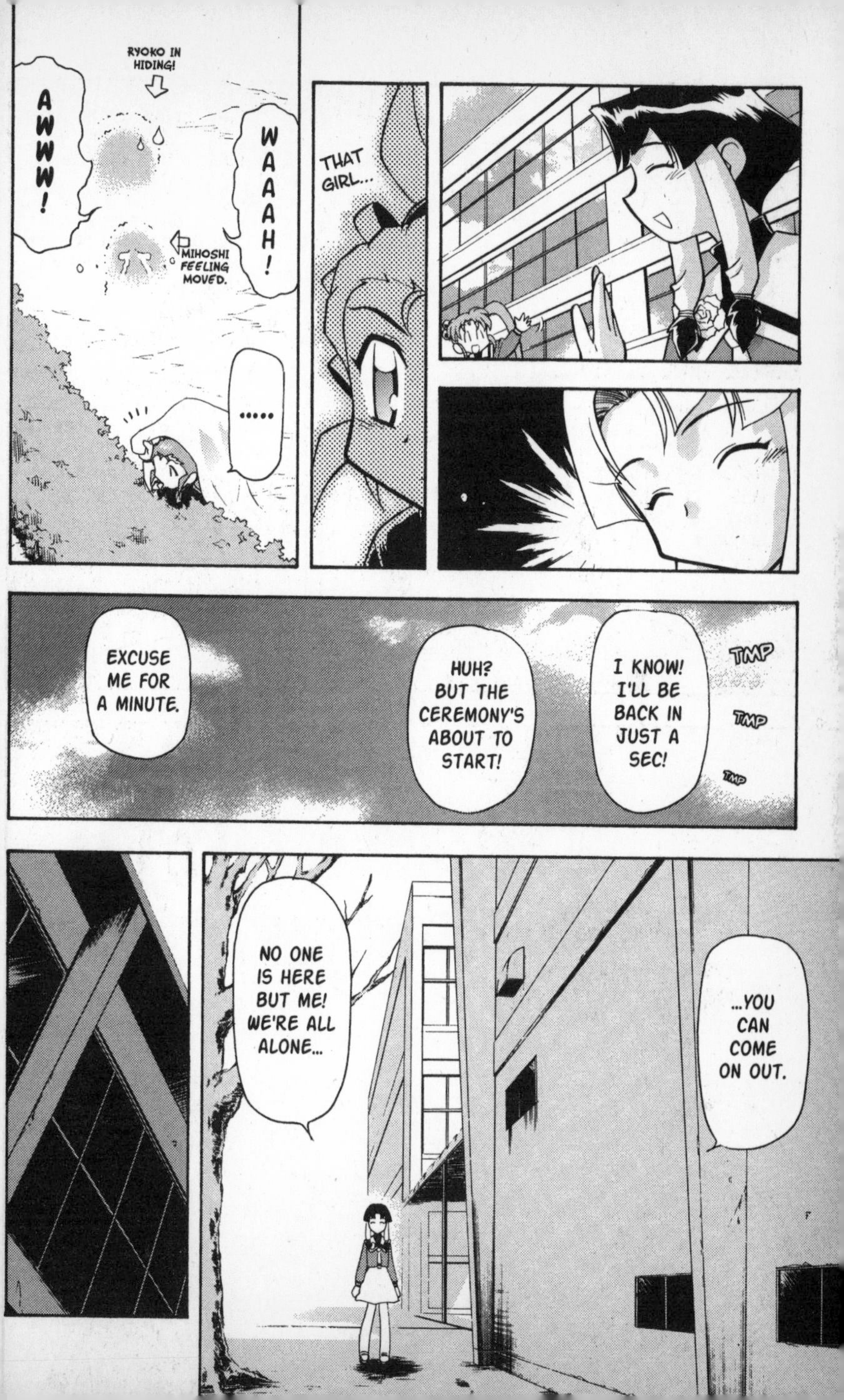

AWWW!
RYOKO IN HIDING!
MIHOSHI FEELING MOVED.
WAAAAH!
.....
THAT GIRL...
EXCUSE ME FOR A MINUTE.
HUH? BUT THE CEREMONY'S ABOUT TO START!
I KNOW! I'LL BE BACK IN JUST A SEC!
TMP
TMP
TMP
NO ONE IS HERE BUT ME! WE'RE ALL ALONE...
...YOU CAN COME ON OUT.

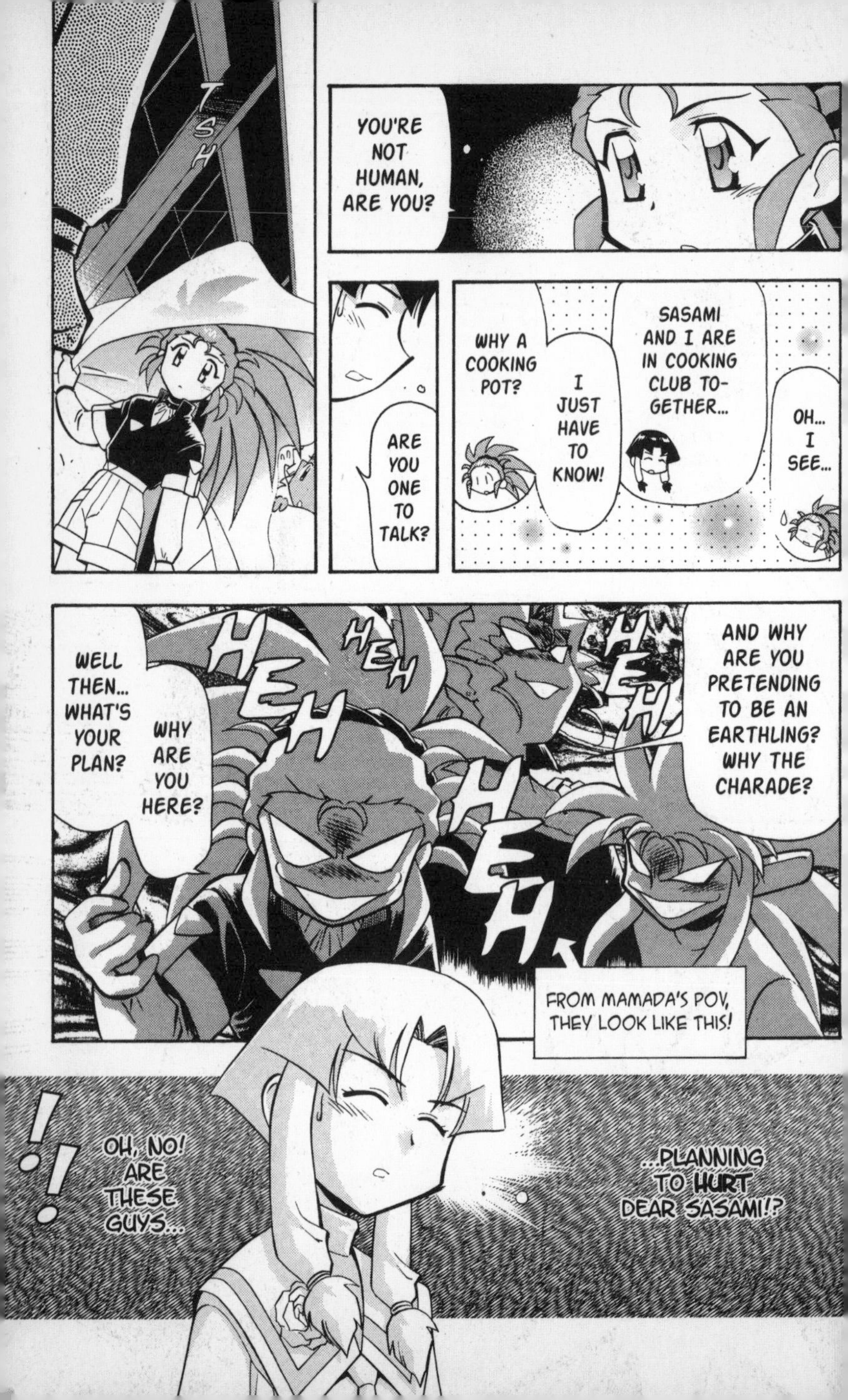
TSH
YOU'RE NOT HUMAN, ARE YOU?
ARE YOU ONE TO TALK?
WHY A COOKING POT?
I JUST HAVE TO KNOW!
SASAMI AND I ARE IN COOKING CLUB TO-GETHER...
OH... I SEE...
WELL THEN... WHAT'S YOUR PLAN?
WHY ARE YOU HERE?
HEH HEH HEH HEH HEH
AND WHY ARE YOU PRETENDING TO BE AN EARTHLING? WHY THE CHARADE?
FROM MAMADA'S POV, THEY LOOK LIKE THIS!
!!
OH, NO! ARE THESE GUYS...
...PLANNING TO HURT DEAR SASAMI!?

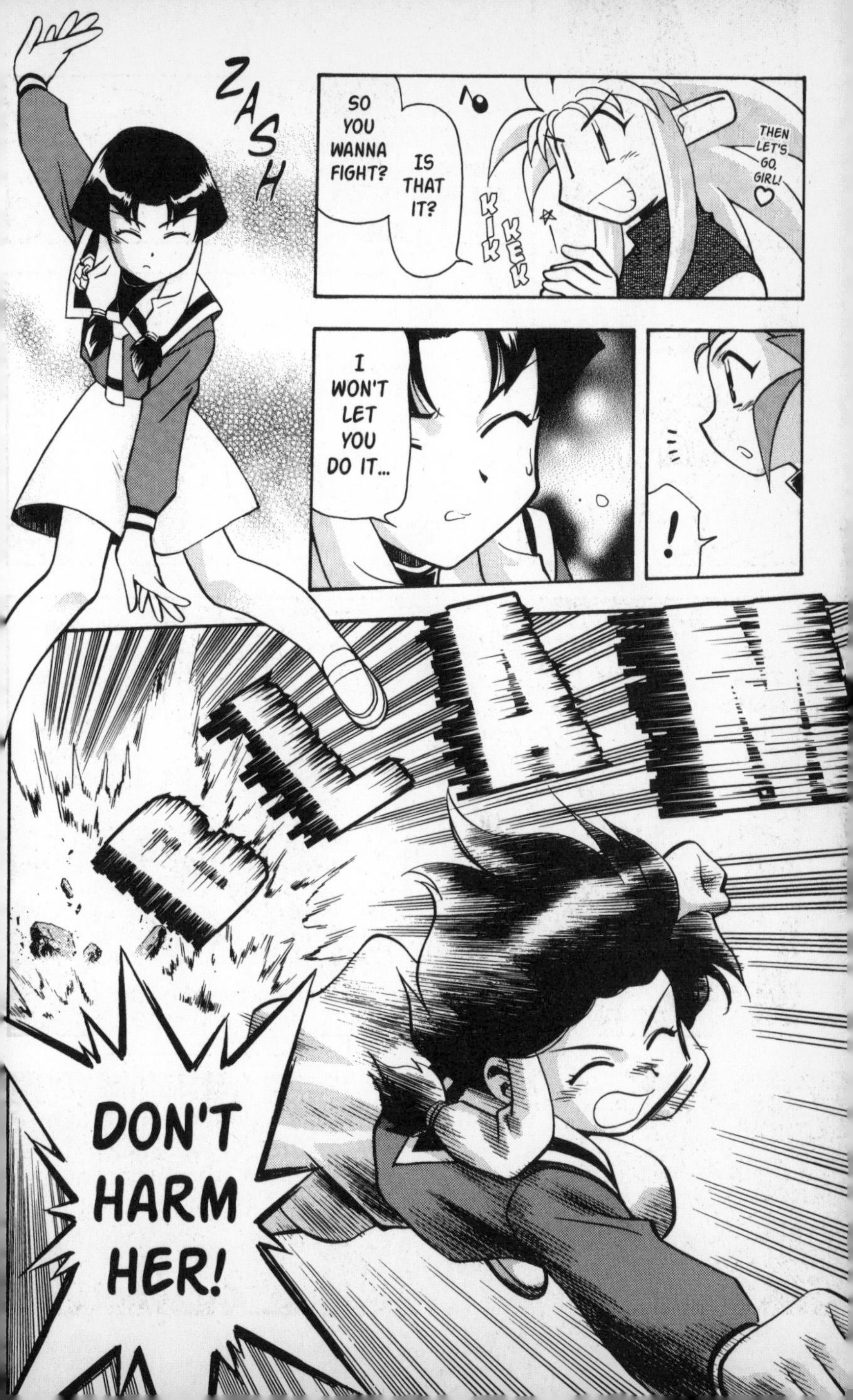
ZASH
SO YOU WANNA FIGHT?
IS THAT IT?
KIK KEK
THEN LET'S GO, GIRL! ♡
I WON'T LET YOU DO IT...
!
DON'T HARM HER!

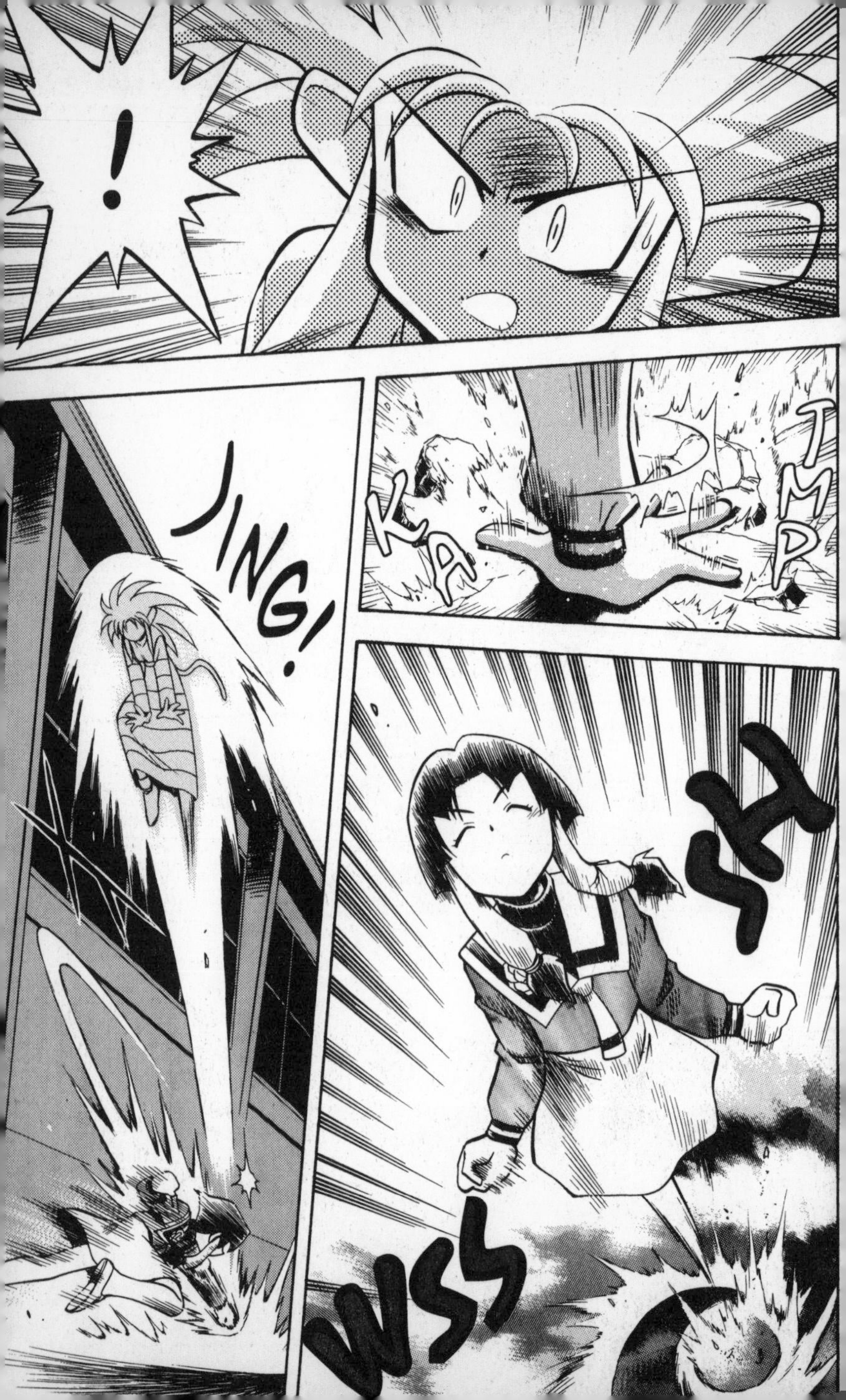
!
JING!
KA
TMP
WSS
SH

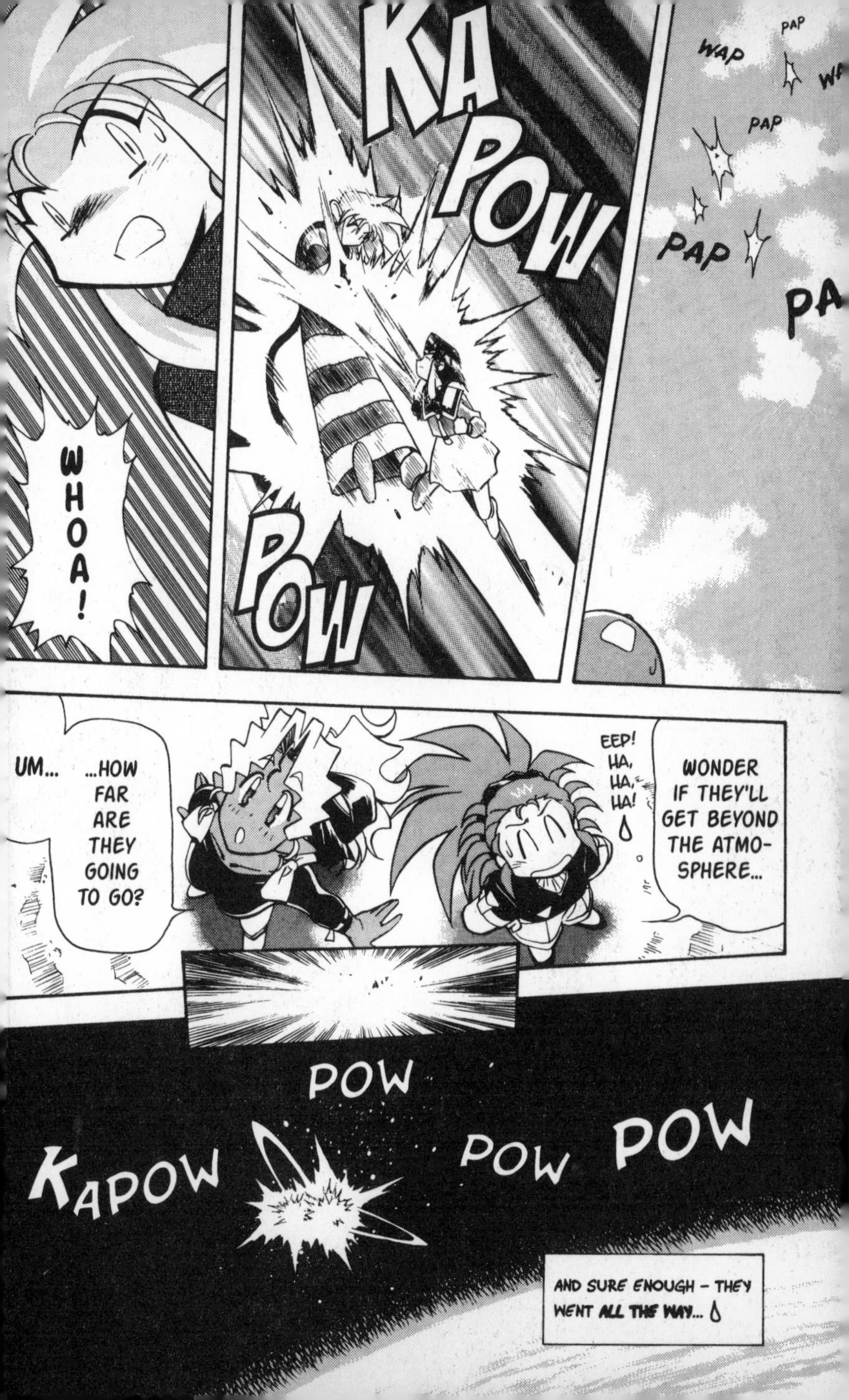
WHOA!
KA POW
POW
WAP
PAP
WA
PAP
PAP
PA
UM...
...HOW FAR ARE THEY GOING TO GO?
EEP! HA, HA, HA!
WONDER IF THEY'LL GET BEYOND THE ATMO-SPHERE...
POW
KAPOW
POW POW
AND SURE ENOUGH – THEY WENT ALL THE WAY...

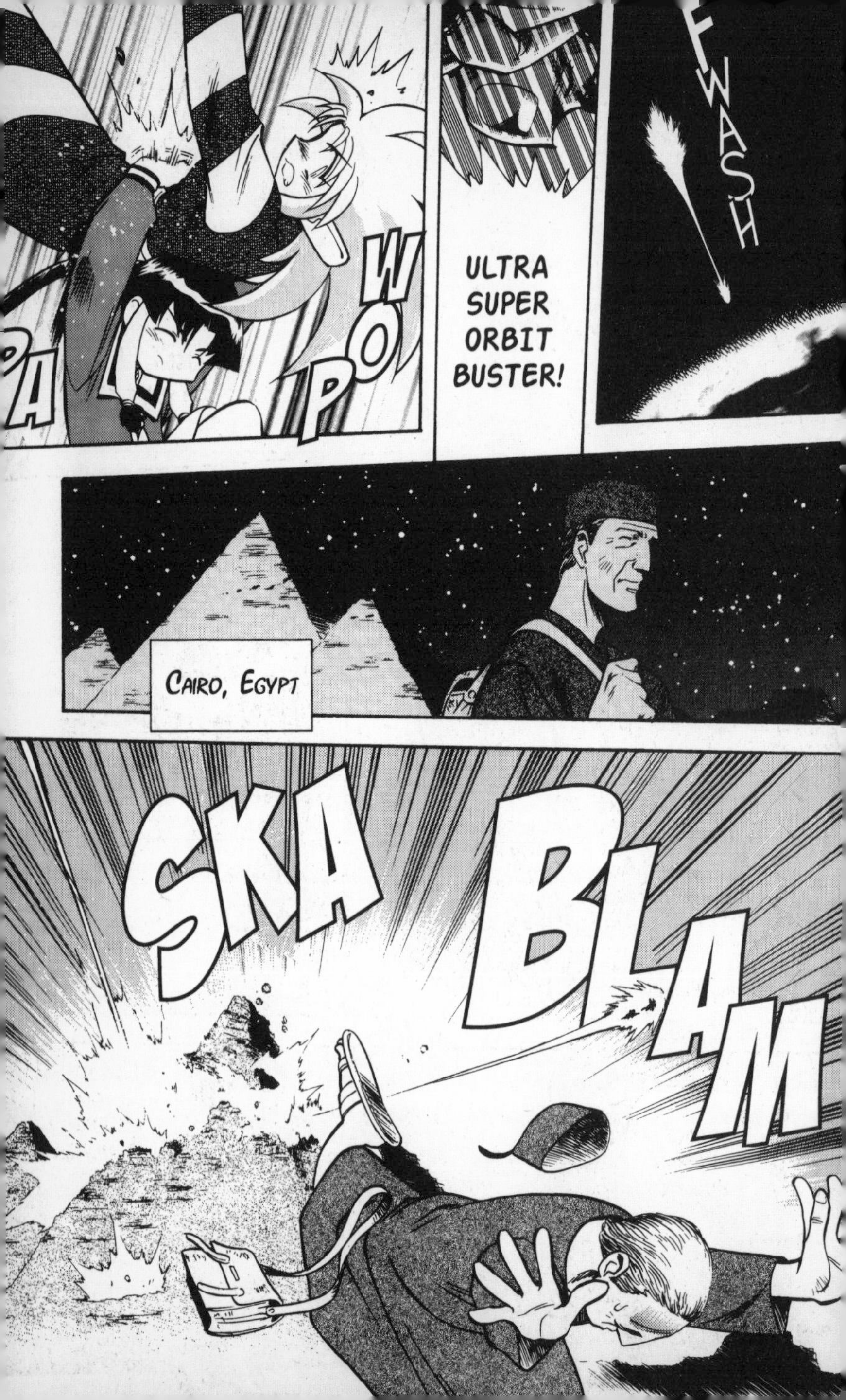
PA
POW
ULTRA SUPER ORBIT BUSTER!
FWASH
CAIRO, EGYPT
SKA BLAM

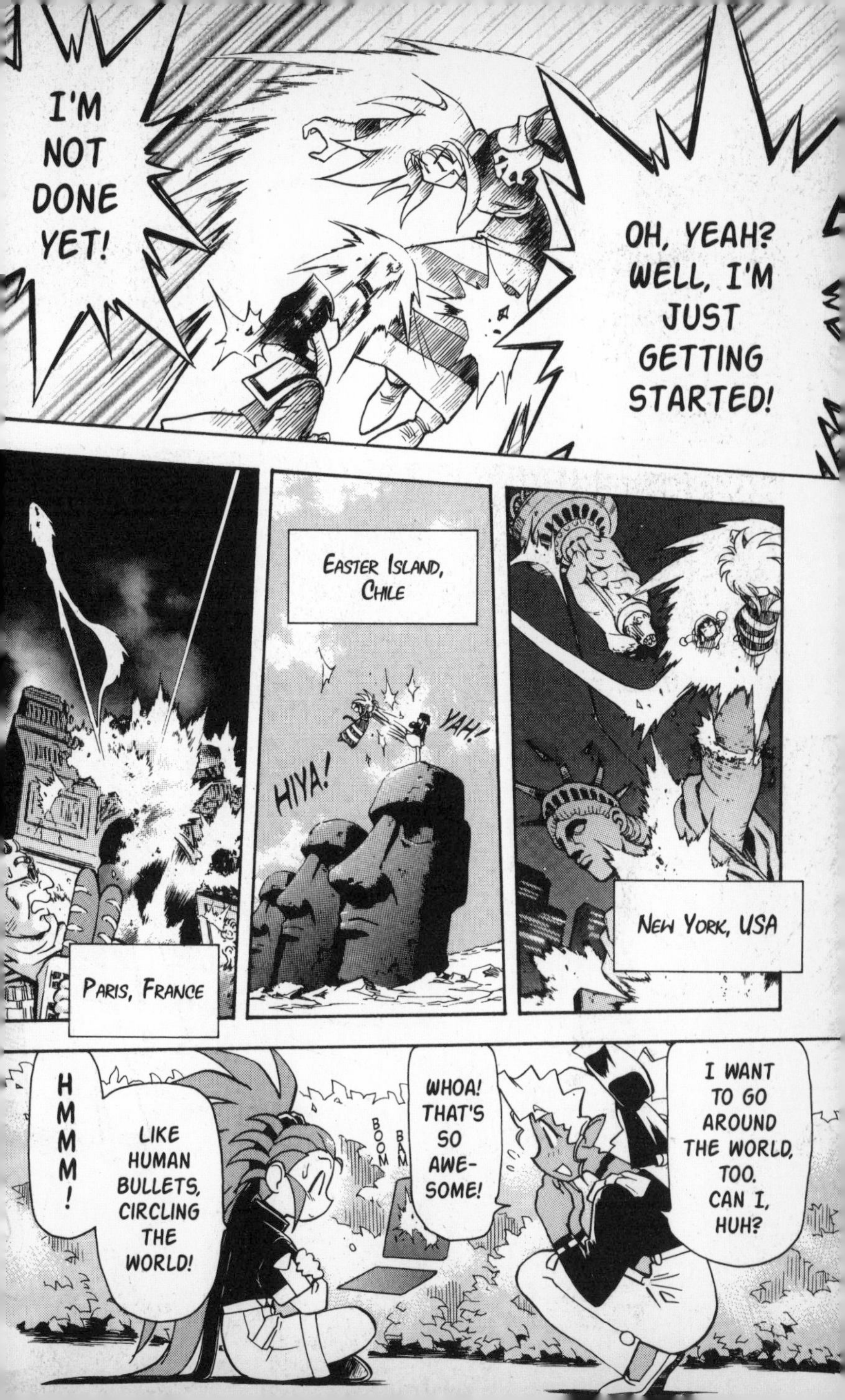
I'M NOT DONE YET!
OH, YEAH? WELL, I'M JUST GETTING STARTED!
PARIS, FRANCE
EASTER ISLAND, CHILE
YAH!
HIYA!
NEW YORK, USA
HMMM!
LIKE HUMAN BULLETS, CIRCLING THE WORLD!
BOOM
BAM
WHOA! THAT'S SO AWE-SOME!
I WANT TO GO AROUND THE WORLD, TOO. CAN I, HUH?

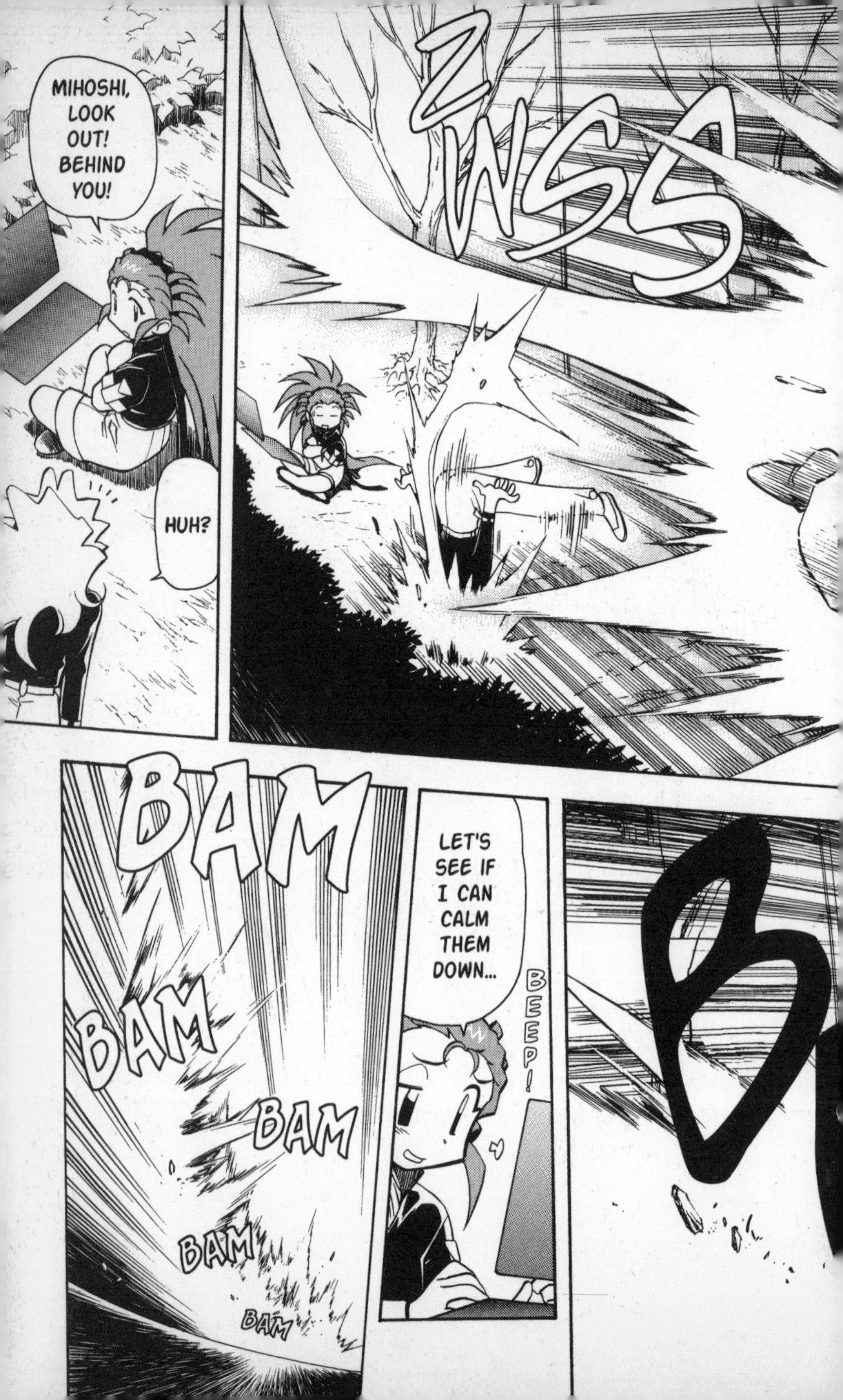
MIHOSHI, LOOK OUT! BEHIND YOU!
HUH?
ZWSSS
BAM
BAM
BAM
BAM
BAM
LET'S SEE IF I CAN CALM THEM DOWN...
BEEP!

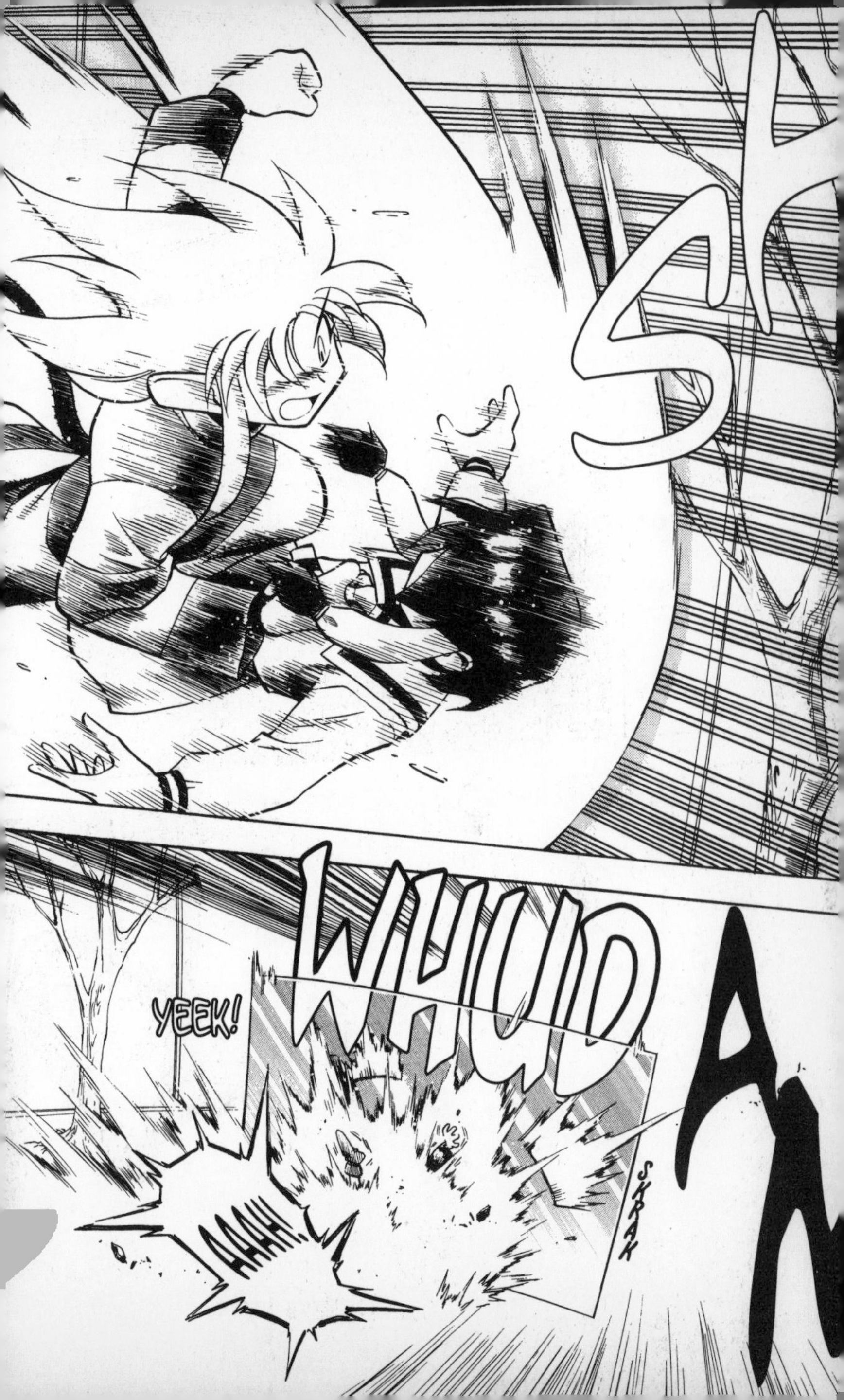
YEEK!
WHUD
AAAH!
SKRAK

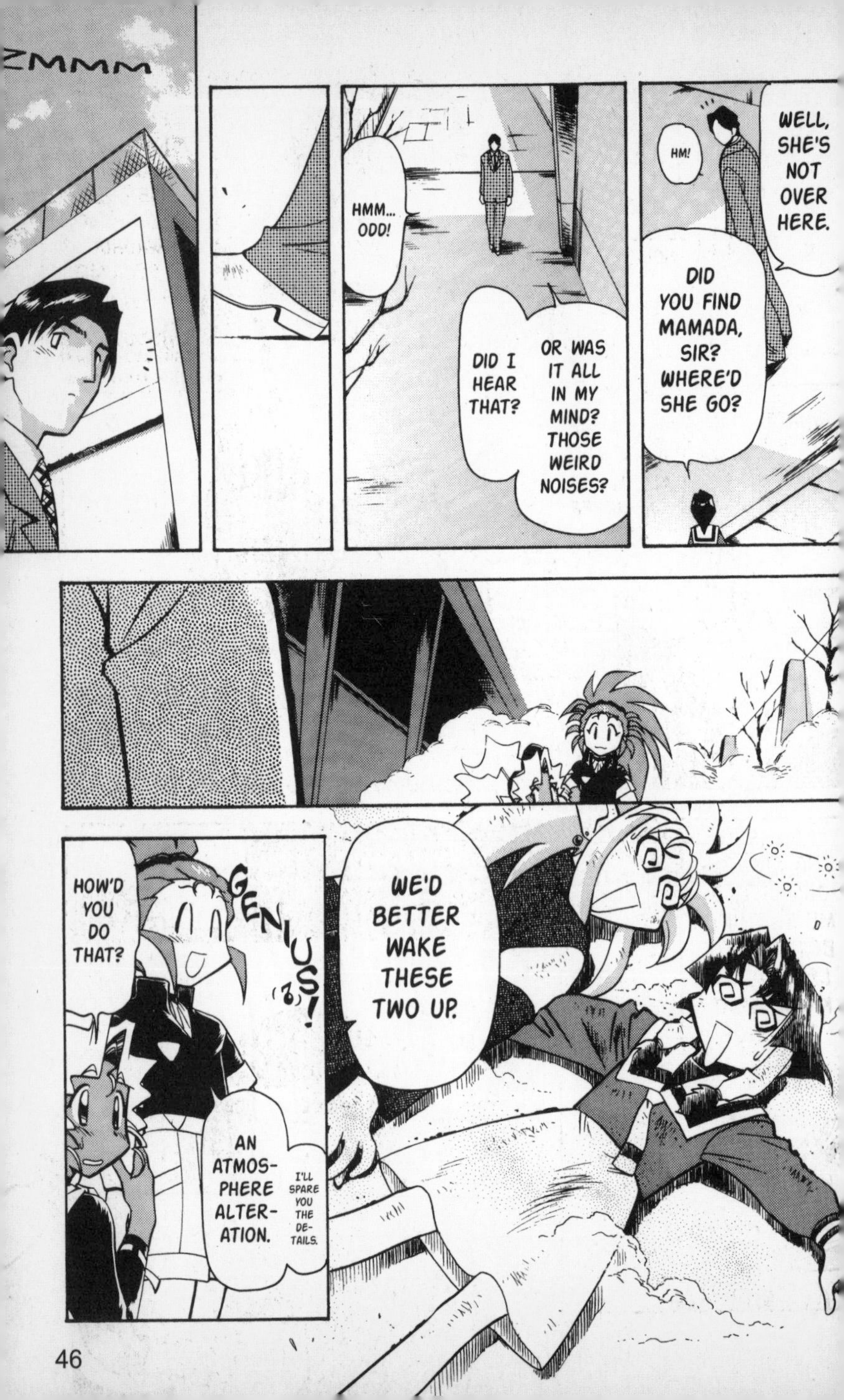
ZMMM
HMM... ODD!
DID I HEAR THAT?
OR WAS IT ALL IN MY MIND? THOSE WEIRD NOISES?
HM!
WELL, SHE'S NOT OVER HERE.
DID YOU FIND MAMADA, SIR? WHERE'D SHE GO?
HOW'D YOU DO THAT?
GENIUS!
AN ATMOSPHERE ALTERATION.
I'LL SPARE YOU THE DETAILS.
WE'D BETTER WAKE THESE TWO UP.

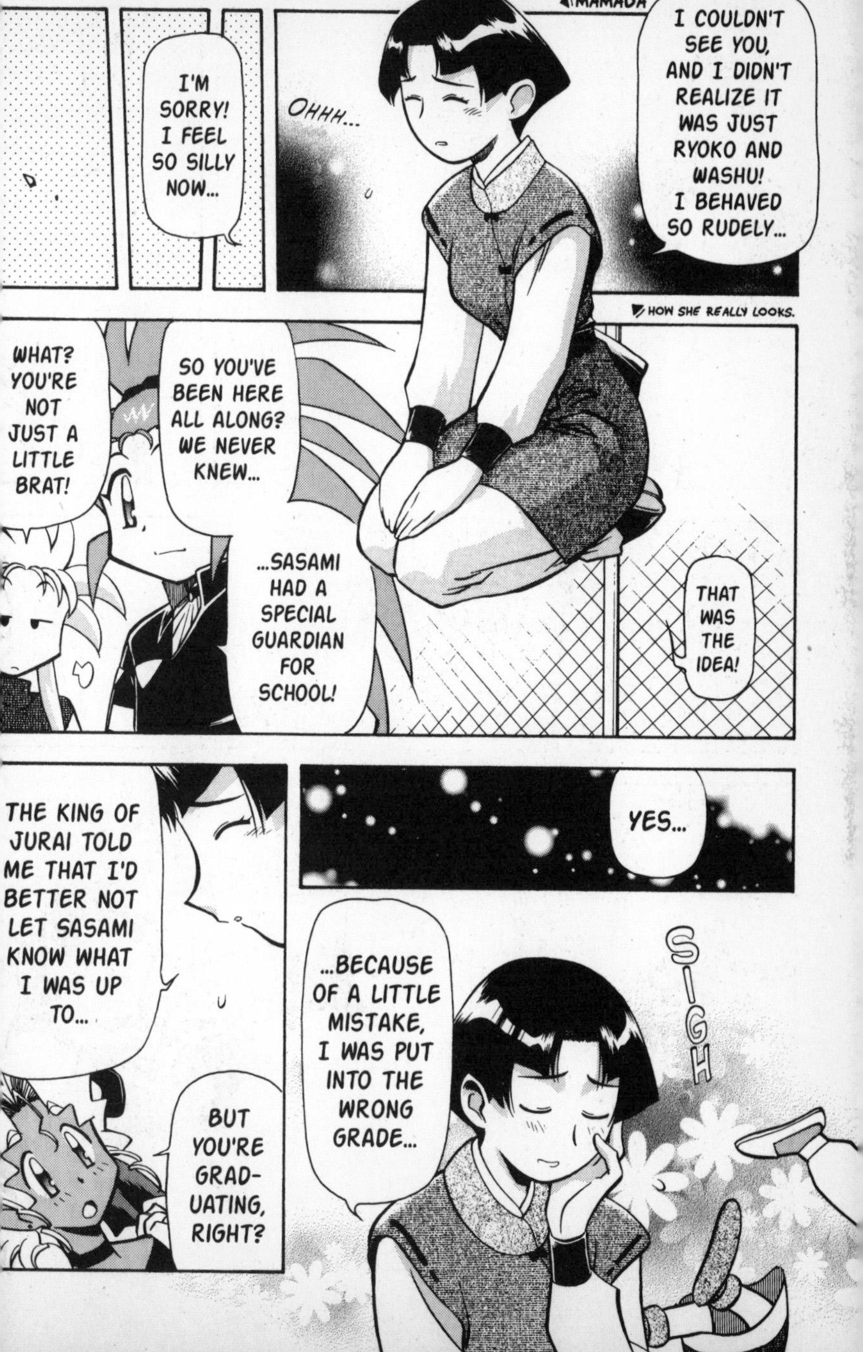
I'M SORRY! I FEEL SO SILLY NOW...
MAMADA
OHHH...
I COULDN'T SEE YOU, AND I DIDN'T REALIZE IT WAS JUST RYOKO AND WASHU! I BEHAVED SO RUDELY...
HOW SHE REALLY LOOKS.
WHAT? YOU'RE NOT JUST A LITTLE BRAT!
SO YOU'VE BEEN HERE ALL ALONG? WE NEVER KNEW...
...SASAMI HAD A SPECIAL GUARDIAN FOR SCHOOL!
THAT WAS THE IDEA!
THE KING OF JURAI TOLD ME THAT I'D BETTER NOT LET SASAMI KNOW WHAT I WAS UP TO...
BUT YOU'RE GRAD-UATING, RIGHT?
YES...
...BECAUSE OF A LITTLE MISTAKE, I WAS PUT INTO THE WRONG GRADE...
SIGH

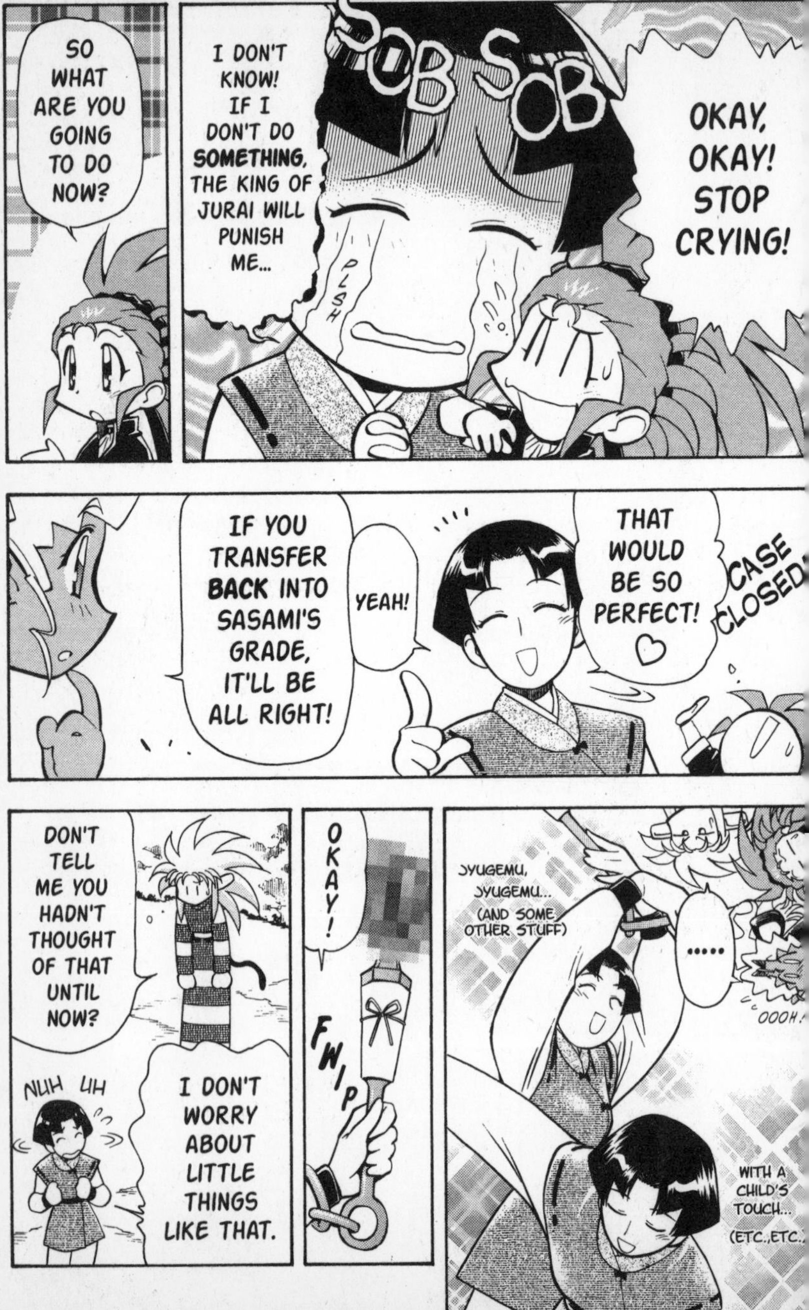
SO WHAT ARE YOU GOING TO DO NOW?
I DON'T KNOW! IF I DON'T DO SOMETHING, THE KING OF JURAI WILL PUNISH ME...
SOB SOB
PLSH
OKAY, OKAY! STOP CRYING!
IF YOU TRANSFER BACK INTO SASAMI'S GRADE, IT'LL BE ALL RIGHT!
YEAH!
THAT WOULD BE SO PERFECT!
CASE CLOSED!
DON'T TELL ME YOU HADN'T THOUGHT OF THAT UNTIL NOW?
NUH UH
I DON'T WORRY ABOUT LITTLE THINGS LIKE THAT.
OKAY!
FWIP
JYUGEMU, JYUGEMU... (AND SOME OTHER STUFF)
.....
OOOH!
WITH A CHILD'S TOUCH...
(ETC.,ETC.)

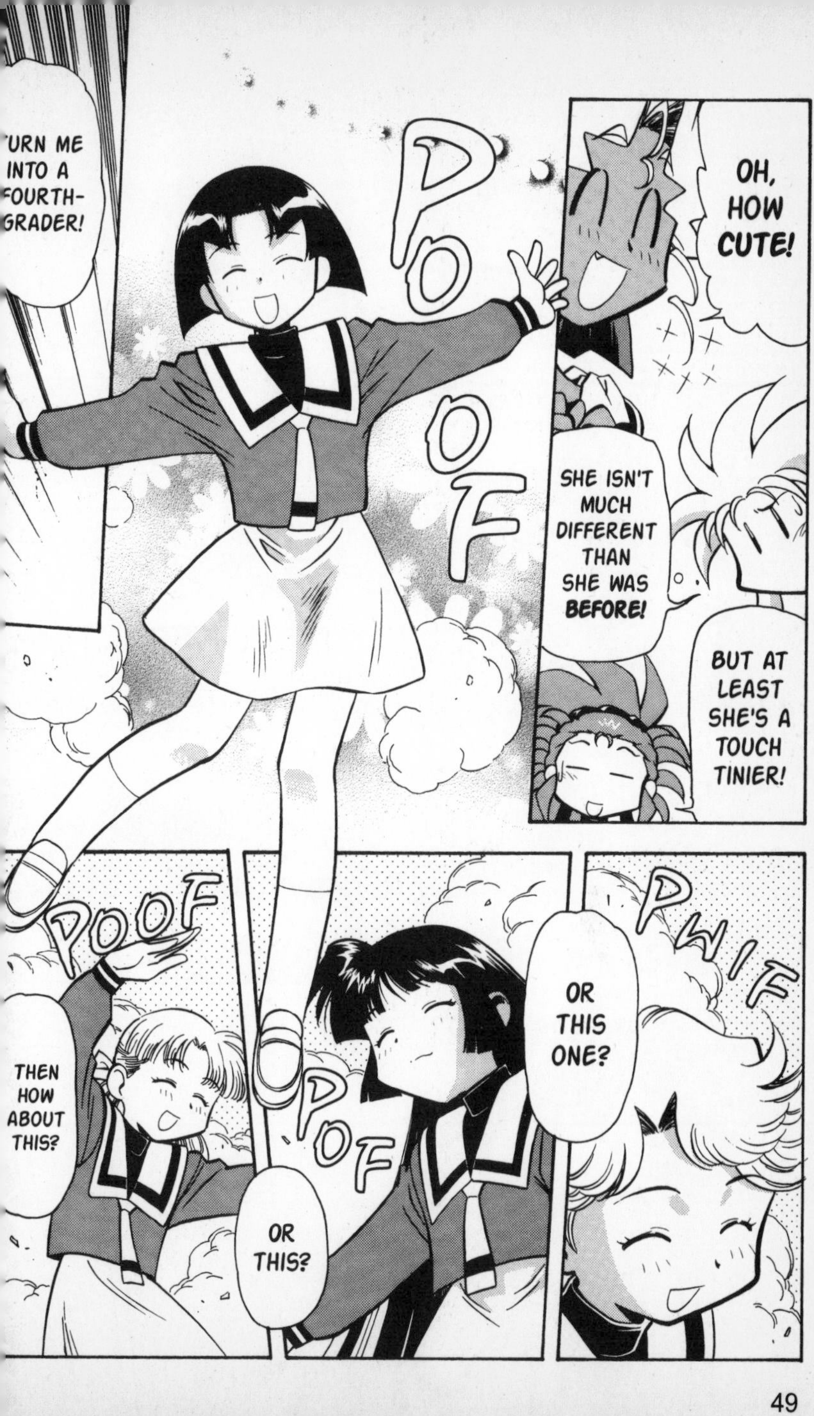

TURN ME INTO A FOURTH-GRADER!
POOF
OH, HOW CUTE!
SHE ISN'T MUCH DIFFERENT THAN SHE WAS **BEFORE!**
BUT AT LEAST SHE'S A TOUCH TINIER!
POOF
THEN HOW ABOUT THIS?
POOF
OR THIS?
PWIF
OR THIS ONE?

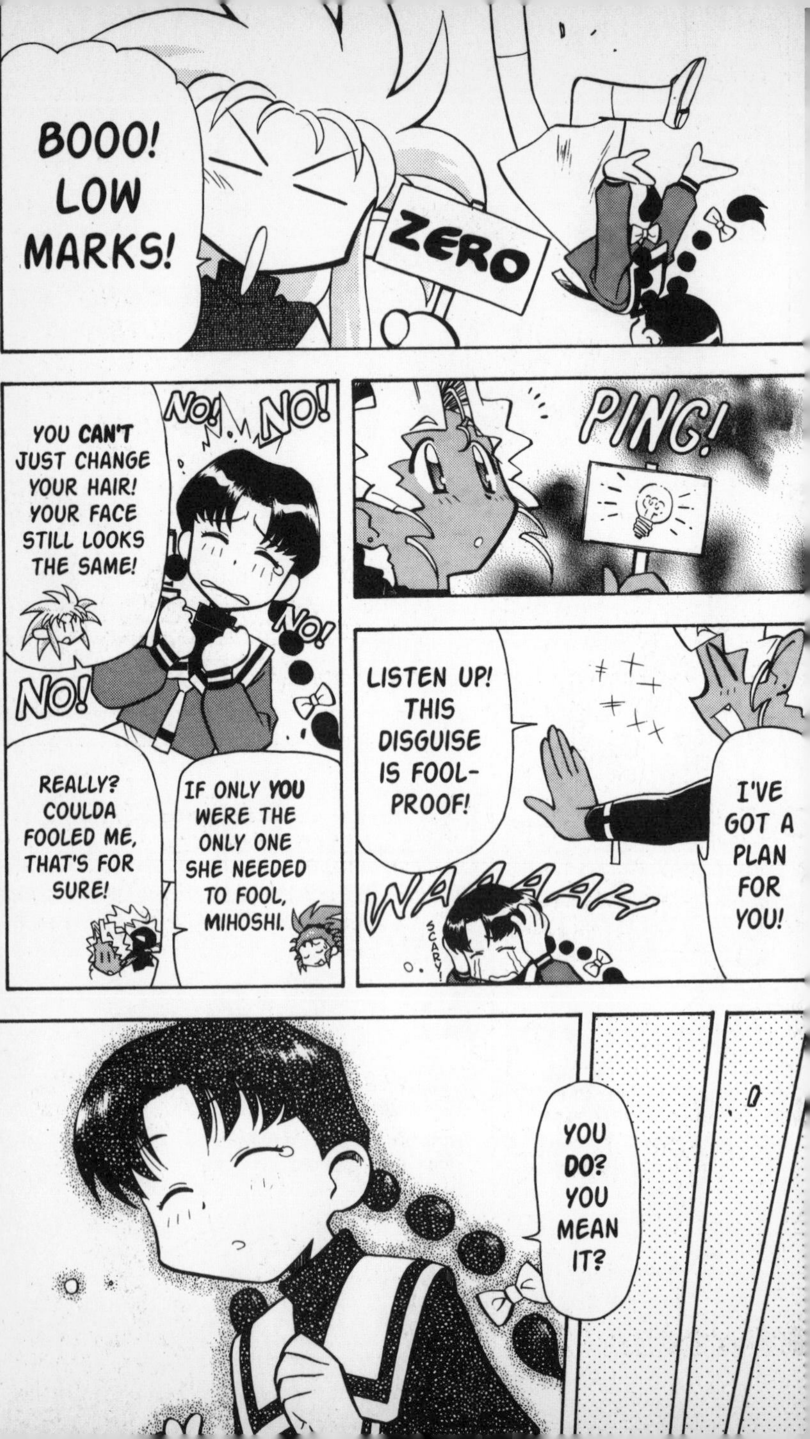
BOOO! LOW MARKS!
ZERO
YOU CAN'T JUST CHANGE YOUR HAIR! YOUR FACE STILL LOOKS THE SAME!
NO! NO!
NO!
NO!
REALLY? COULDA FOOLED ME, THAT'S FOR SURE!
IF ONLY YOU WERE THE ONLY ONE SHE NEEDED TO FOOL, MIHOSHI.
PING!
LISTEN UP! THIS DISGUISE IS FOOL-PROOF!
I'VE GOT A PLAN FOR YOU!
WAAAAH
SCARY!
YOU DO? YOU MEAN IT?

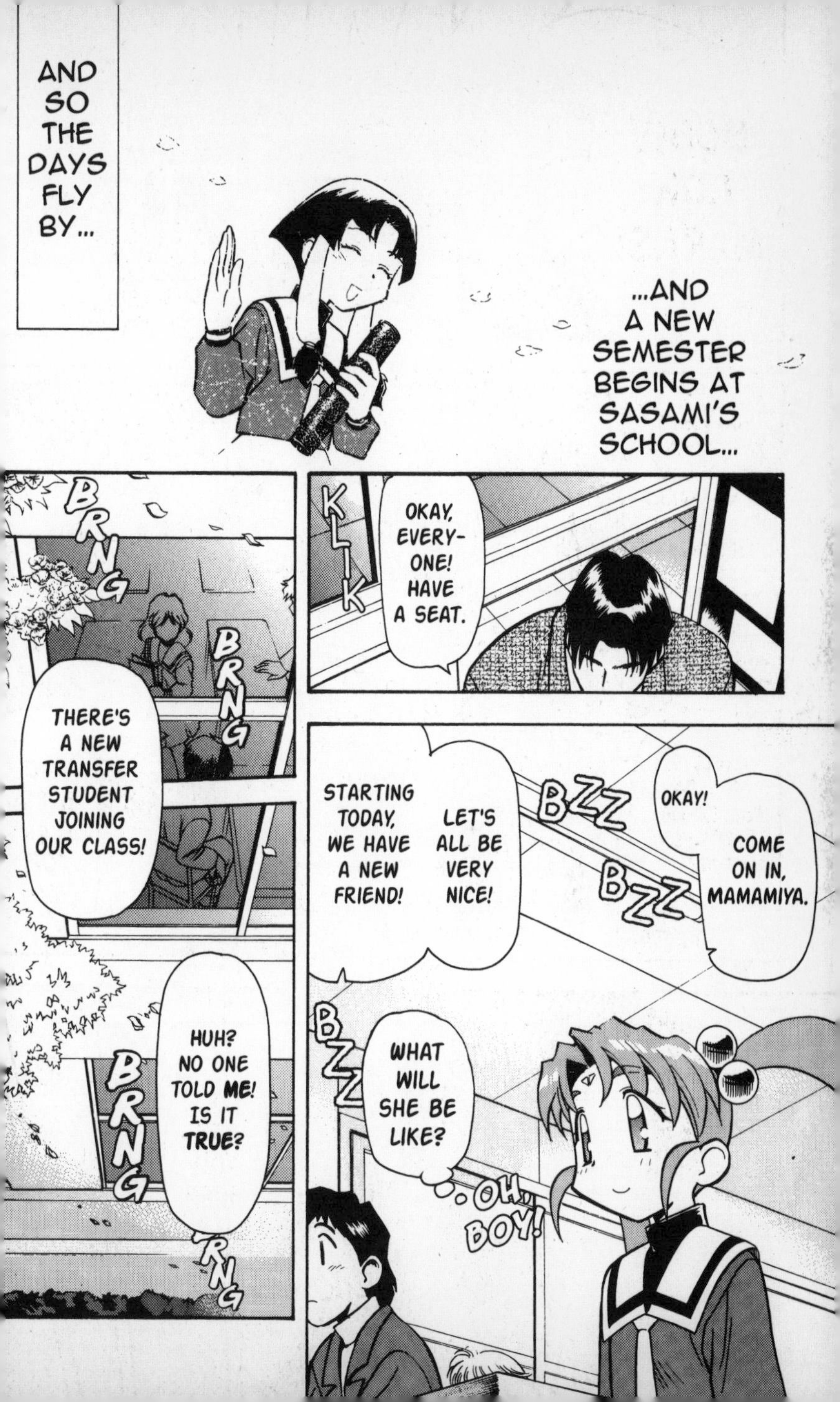
AND SO THE DAYS FLY BY...
...AND A NEW SEMESTER BEGINS AT SASAMI'S SCHOOL...
BRNG
BRNG
BRNG
THERE'S A NEW TRANSFER STUDENT JOINING OUR CLASS!
HUH? NO ONE TOLD ME! IS IT TRUE?
BRNG
RNG
KLIK
OKAY, EVERYONE! HAVE A SEAT.
STARTING TODAY, WE HAVE A NEW FRIEND!
LET'S ALL BE VERY NICE!
BZZ
BZZ
OKAY!
COME ON IN, MAMAMIYA.
BZZ
WHAT WILL SHE BE LIKE?
OH, BOY!

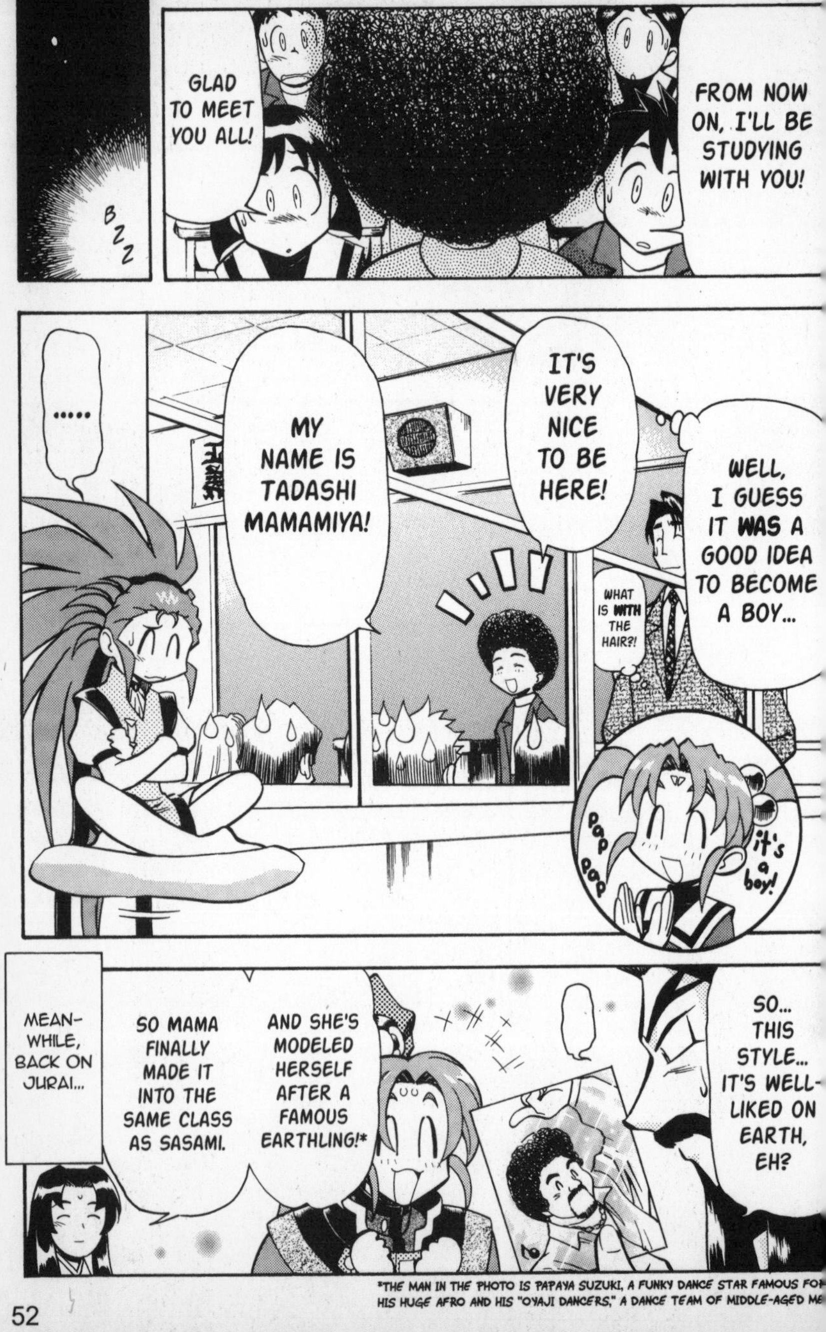
BZZ
GLAD TO MEET YOU ALL!
FROM NOW ON, I'LL BE STUDYING WITH YOU!
.....
MY NAME IS TADASHI MAMAMIYA!
IT'S VERY NICE TO BE HERE!
WHAT IS WITH THE HAIR?!
WELL, I GUESS IT WAS A GOOD IDEA TO BECOME A BOY...
pap pap
it's a boy!
MEAN-WHILE, BACK ON JURAI...
SO MAMA FINALLY MADE IT INTO THE SAME CLASS AS SASAMI.
AND SHE'S MODELED HERSELF AFTER A FAMOUS EARTHLING!*
SO... THIS STYLE... IT'S WELL-LIKED ON EARTH, EH?

*THE MAN IN THE PHOTO IS PAPAYA SUZUKI, A FUNKY DANCE STAR FAMOUS FO HIS HUGE AFRO AND HIS "OYAJI DANCERS," A DANCE TEAM OF MIDDLE-AGED ME

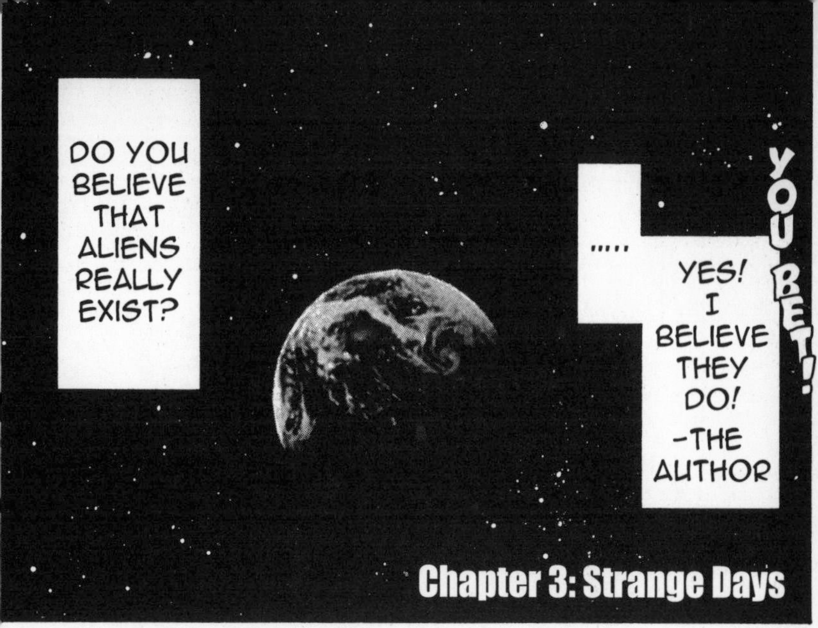
DO YOU BELIEVE THAT ALIENS REALLY EXIST?
.....
YES! I BELIEVE THEY DO! -THE AUTHOR
YOU BET!

Chapter 3: Strange Days

THEN MAY WE CONTINUE?

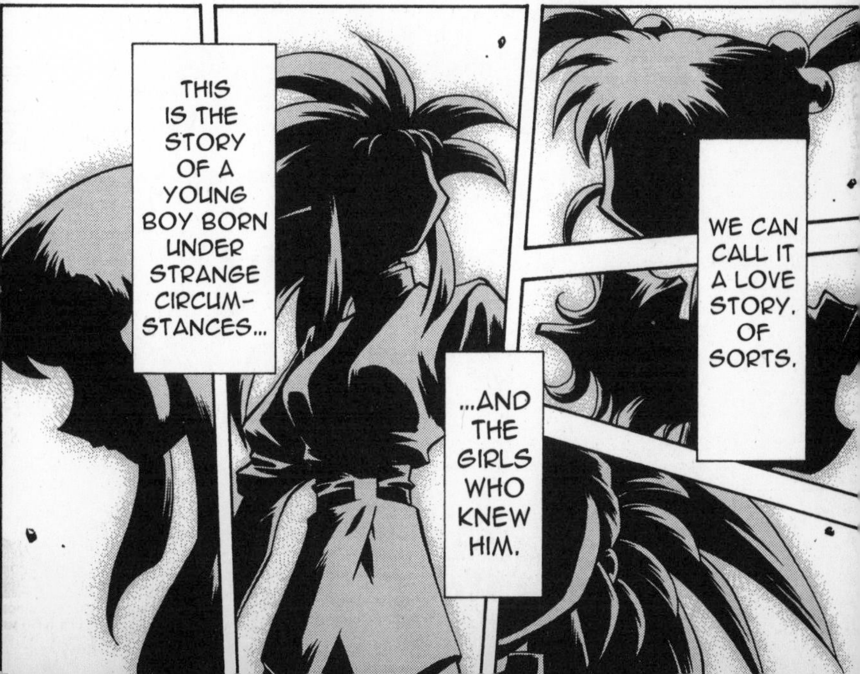
THIS IS THE STORY OF A YOUNG BOY BORN UNDER STRANGE CIRCUM-STANCES...
...AND THE GIRLS WHO KNEW HIM.
WE CAN CALL IT A LOVE STORY. OF SORTS.

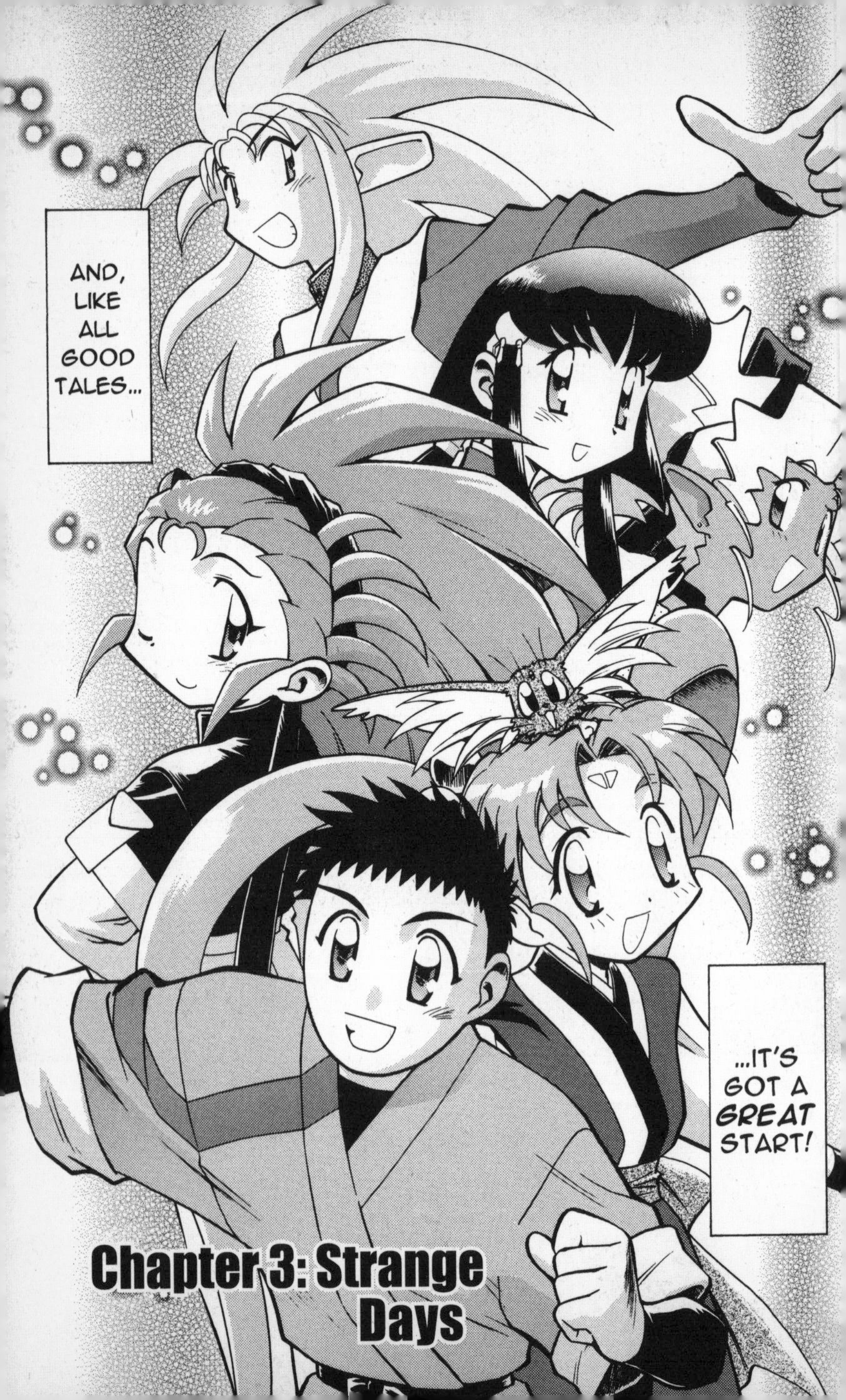
AND, LIKE ALL GOOD TALES...
...IT'S GOT A GREAT START!
Chapter 3: Strange Days

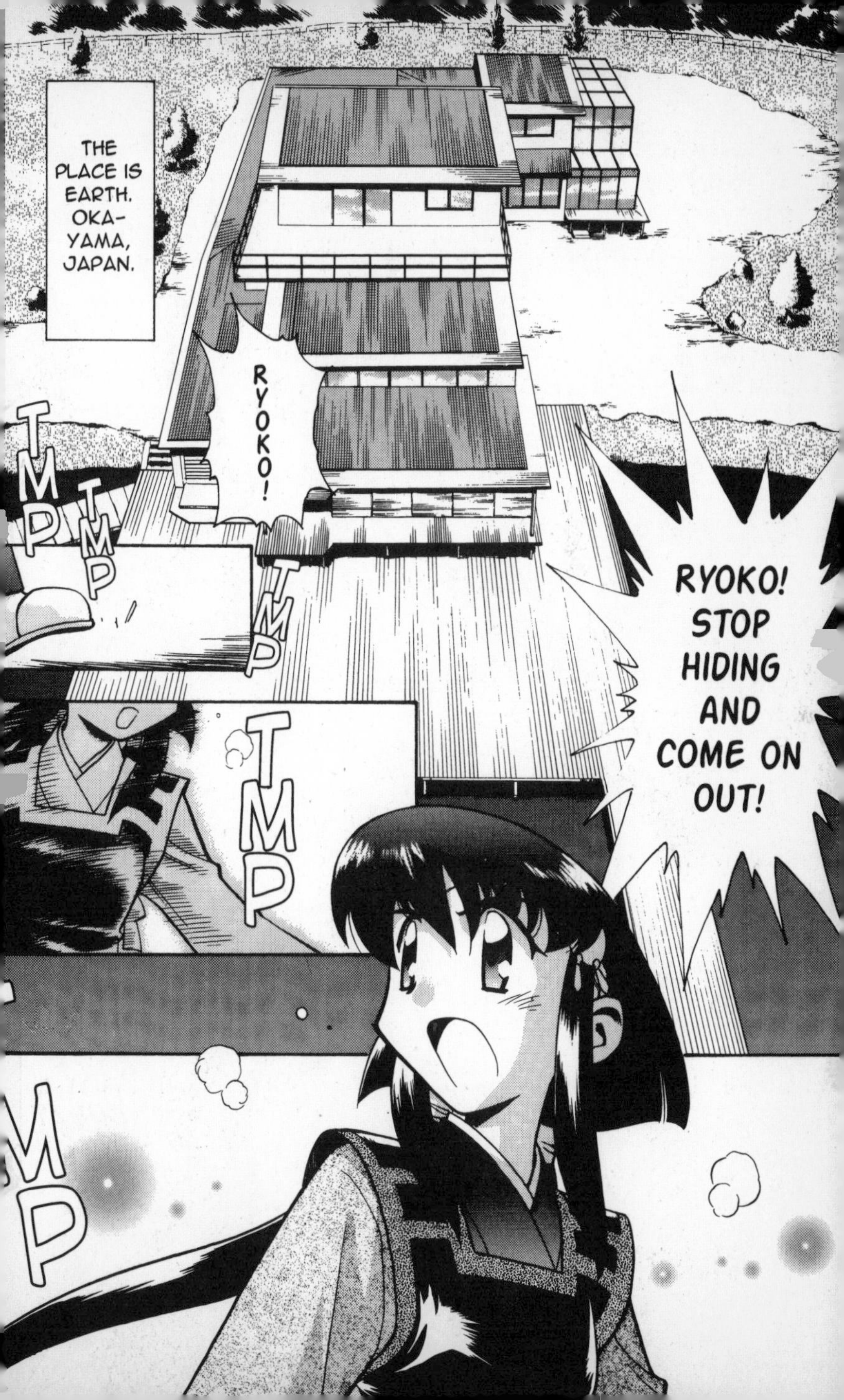
THE PLACE IS EARTH. OKA-YAMA, JAPAN.
RYOKO!
TMP
TMP
TMP
TMP
RYOKO! STOP HIDING AND COME ON OUT!
TMP

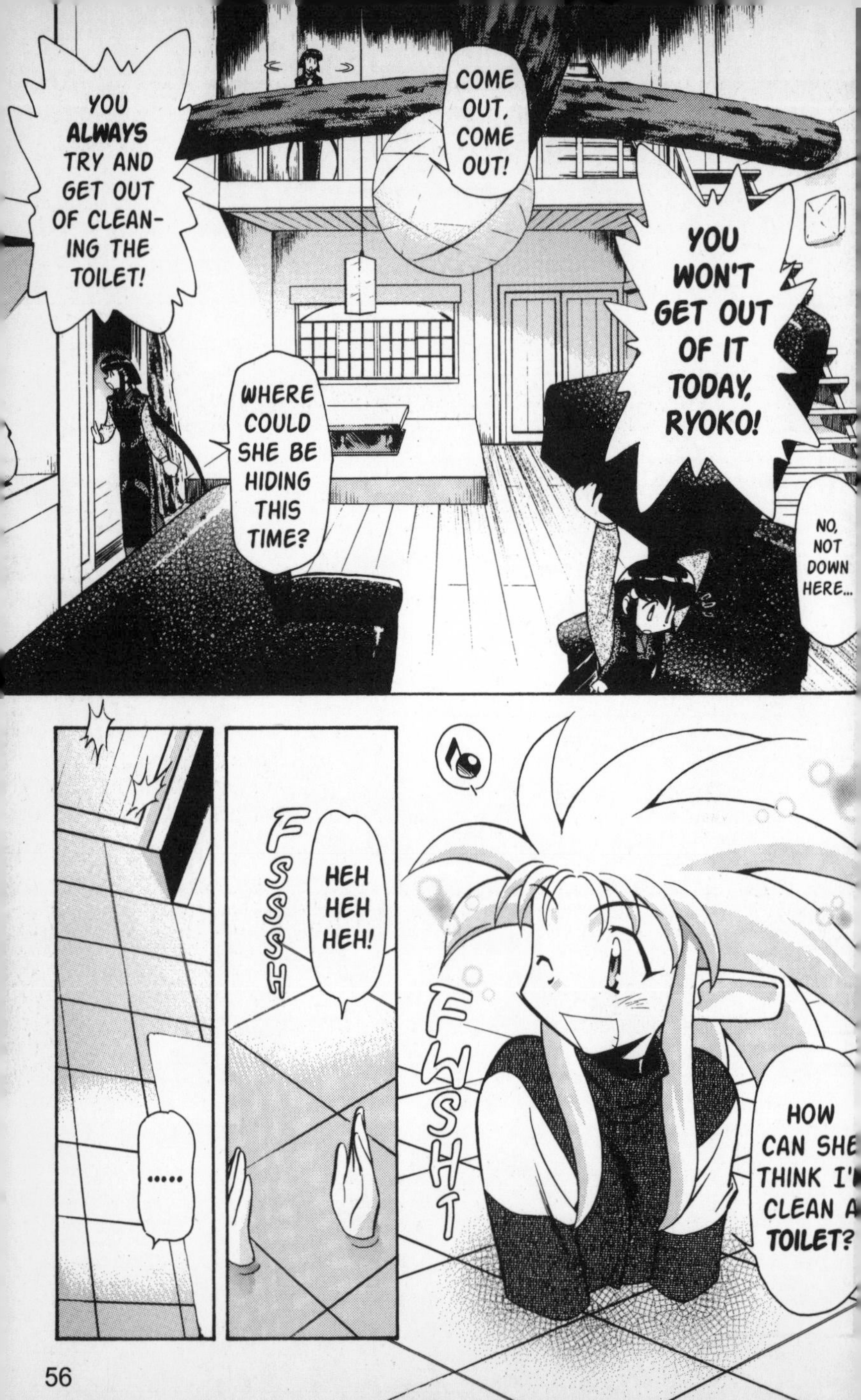
YOU ALWAYS TRY AND GET OUT OF CLEAN-ING THE TOILET!
COME OUT, COME OUT!
YOU WON'T GET OUT OF IT TODAY, RYOKO!
WHERE COULD SHE BE HIDING THIS TIME?
NO, NOT DOWN HERE...
.....
FSSSH
HEH HEH HEH!
FWSHT
HOW CAN SHE THINK I' CLEAN A TOILET?

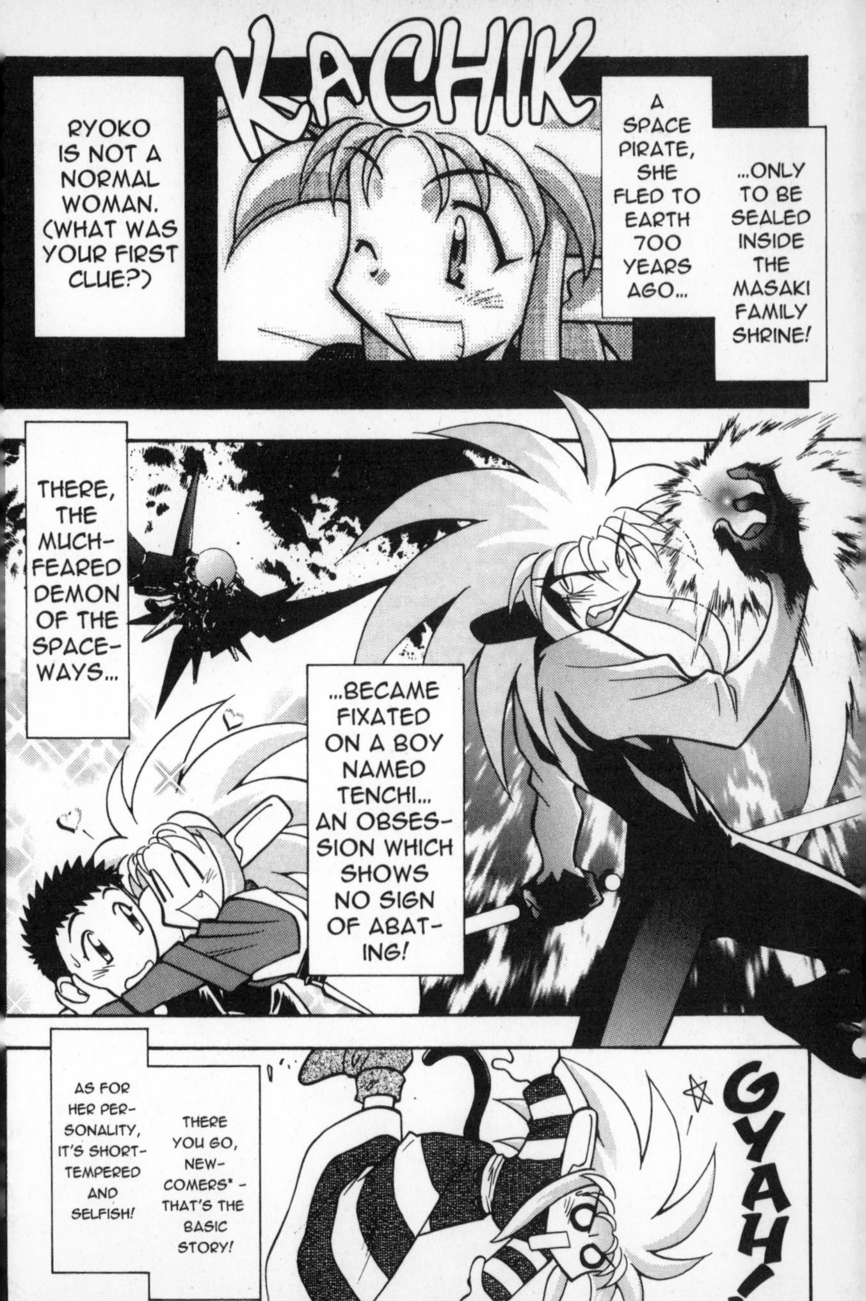
KACHIK
RYOKO IS NOT A NORMAL WOMAN. (WHAT WAS YOUR FIRST CLUE?)
A SPACE PIRATE, SHE FLED TO EARTH 700 YEARS AGO...
...ONLY TO BE SEALED INSIDE THE MASAKI FAMILY SHRINE!
THERE, THE MUCH-FEARED DEMON OF THE SPACE-WAYS...
...BECAME FIXATED ON A BOY NAMED TENCHI... AN OBSESSION WHICH SHOWS NO SIGN OF ABATING!
AS FOR HER PERSONALITY, IT'S SHORT-TEMPERED AND SELFISH!
THERE YOU GO, NEWCOMERS* - THAT'S THE BASIC STORY!
GYAH!

*THIS STORY WAS WRITTEN WHEN TENCHI MOVED FROM MONTHLY DRAGON JUNIOR MAGAZINE TO MONTHLY DRAGON AGE.

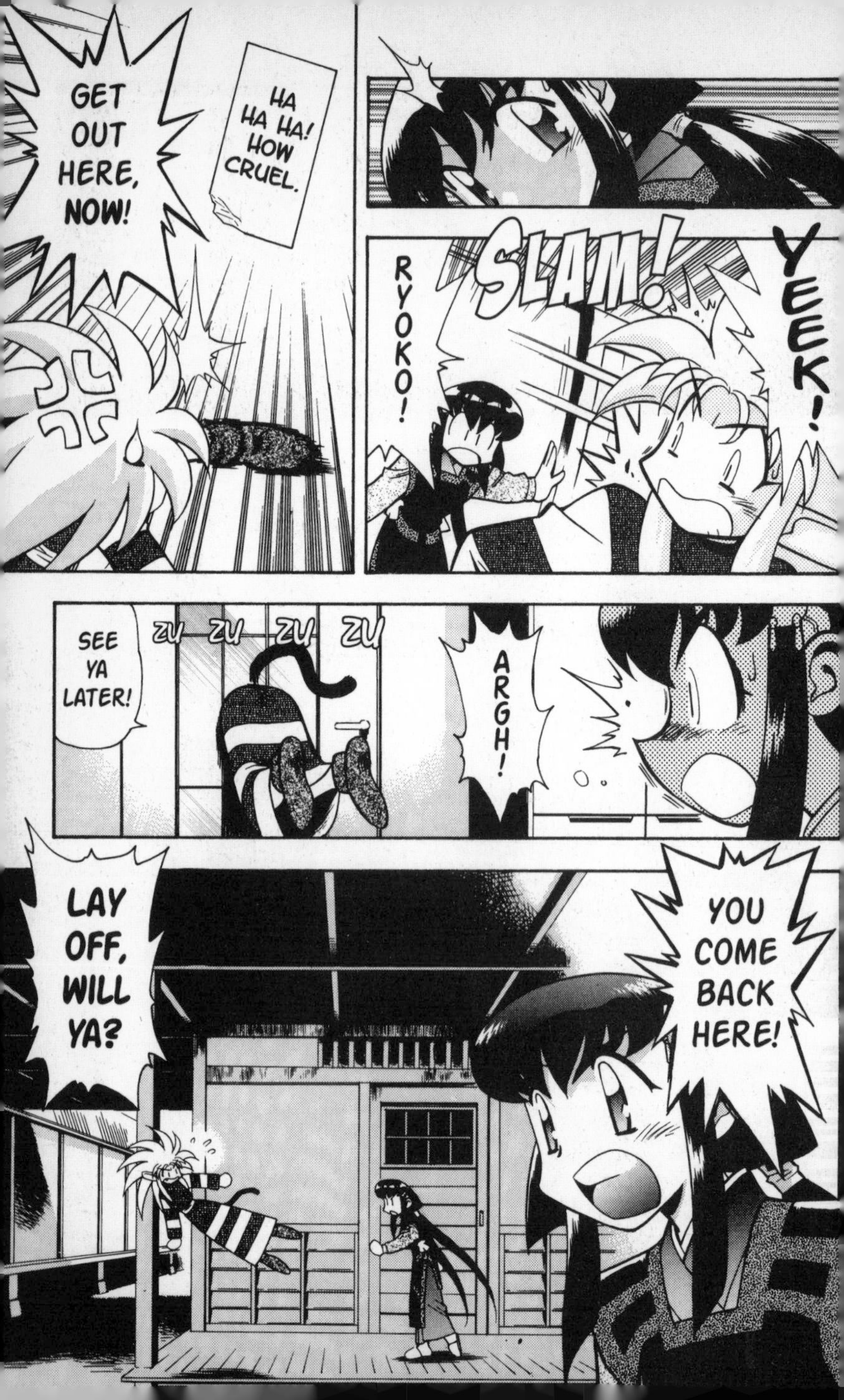
GET OUT HERE, NOW!
HA HA HA! HOW CRUEL.
RYOKO!
SLAM!
YEEK!
SEE YA LATER!
ZU ZU ZU ZU
ARGH!
LAY OFF, WILL YA?
YOU COME BACK HERE!

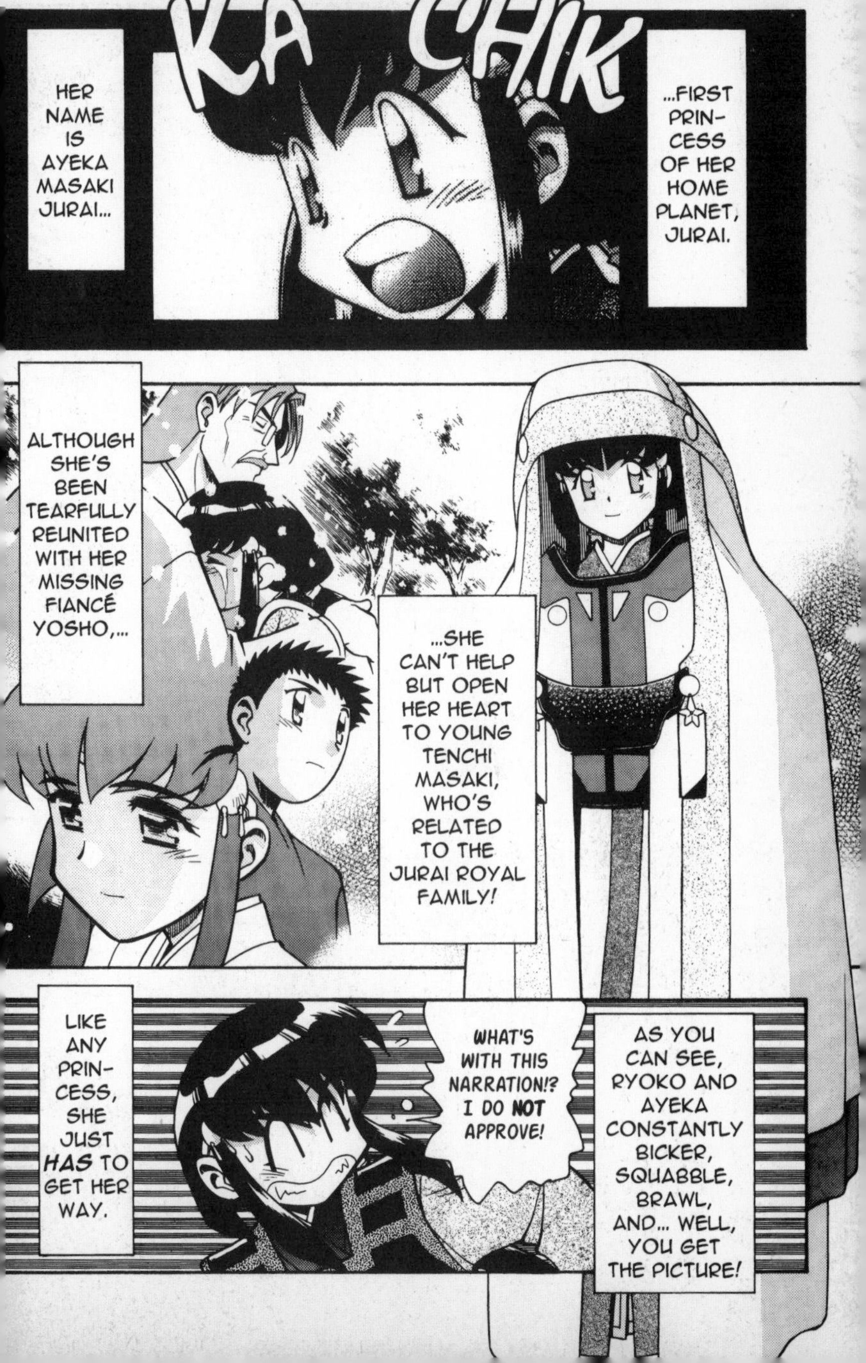
KA CHIK
HER NAME IS AYEKA MASAKI JURAI...
...FIRST PRIN-CESS OF HER HOME PLANET, JURAI.
ALTHOUGH SHE'S BEEN TEARFULLY REUNITED WITH HER MISSING FIANCÉ YOSHO,...
...SHE CAN'T HELP BUT OPEN HER HEART TO YOUNG TENCHI MASAKI, WHO'S RELATED TO THE JURAI ROYAL FAMILY!
LIKE ANY PRIN-CESS, SHE JUST **HAS** TO GET HER WAY.
WHAT'S WITH THIS NARRATION!? I DO **NOT** APPROVE!
AS YOU CAN SEE, RYOKO AND AYEKA CONSTANTLY BICKER, SQUABBLE, BRAWL, AND... WELL, YOU GET THE PICTURE!

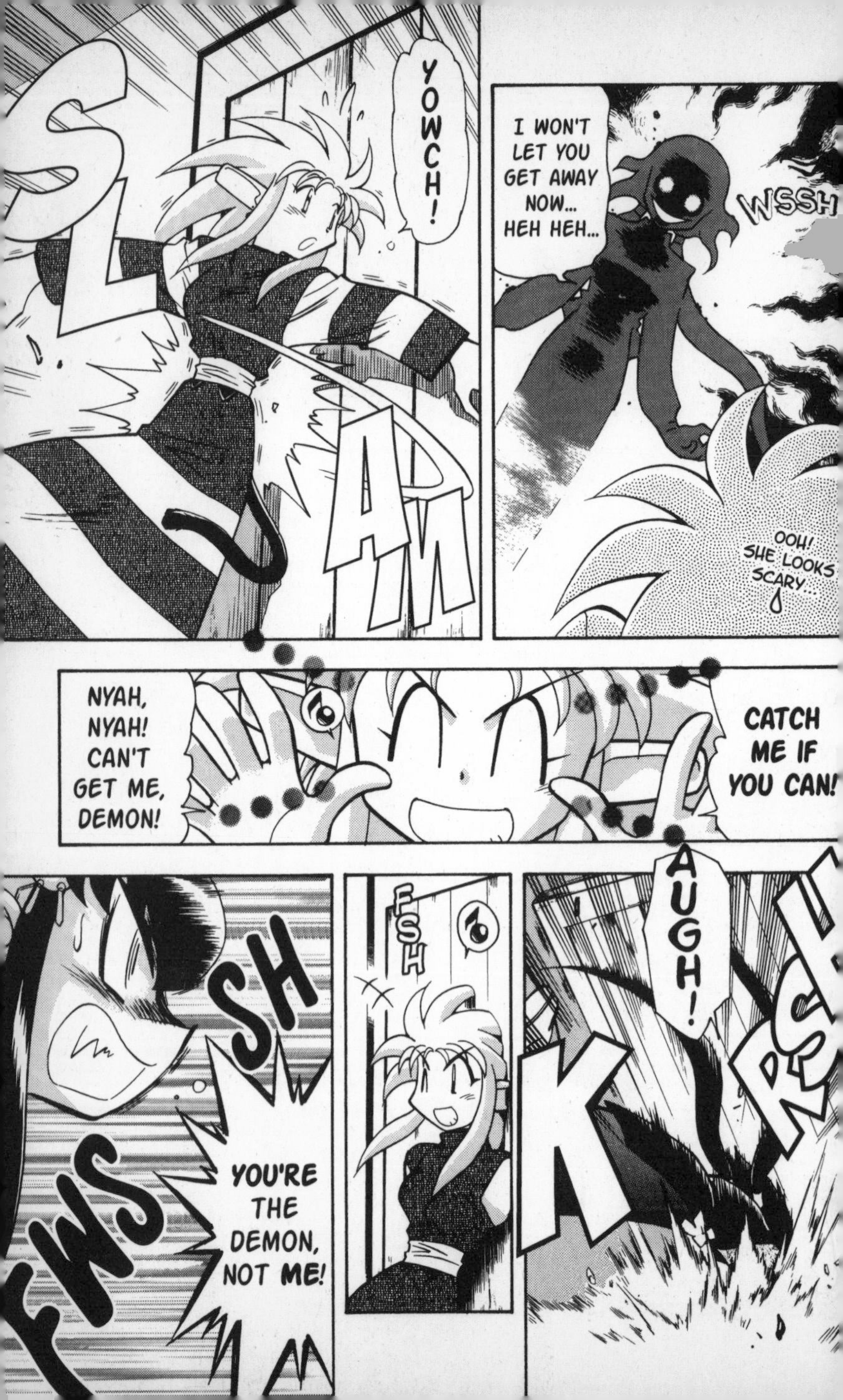
SLAM
YOWCH!
I WON'T LET YOU GET AWAY NOW... HEH HEH...
WSSH
OOH! SHE LOOKS SCARY...
NYAH, NYAH! CAN'T GET ME, DEMON!
CATCH ME IF YOU CAN!
FWSSH
YOU'RE THE DEMON, NOT ME!
FSH
AUGH!

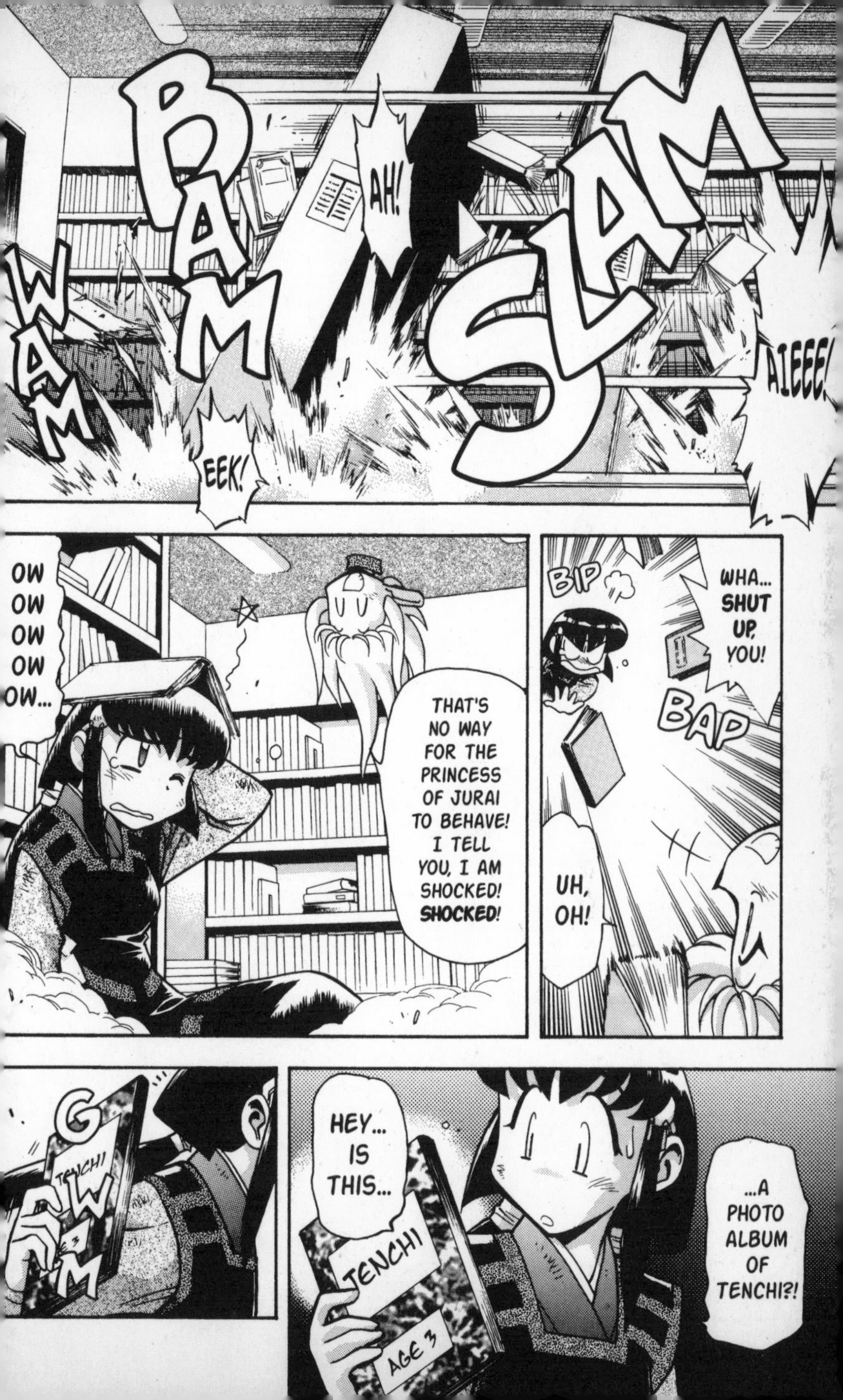
WAM
BAM
AH!
SLAM
AIEEE!
EEK!
OW OW OW OW OW...
THAT'S NO WAY FOR THE PRINCESS OF JURAI TO BEHAVE! I TELL YOU, I AM SHOCKED! SHOCKED!
BIP
WHA... SHUT UP, YOU!
BAP
UH, OH!
G
TENCHI
WWAM
HEY... IS THIS...
...A PHOTO ALBUM OF TENCHI?!
TENCHI
AGE 3

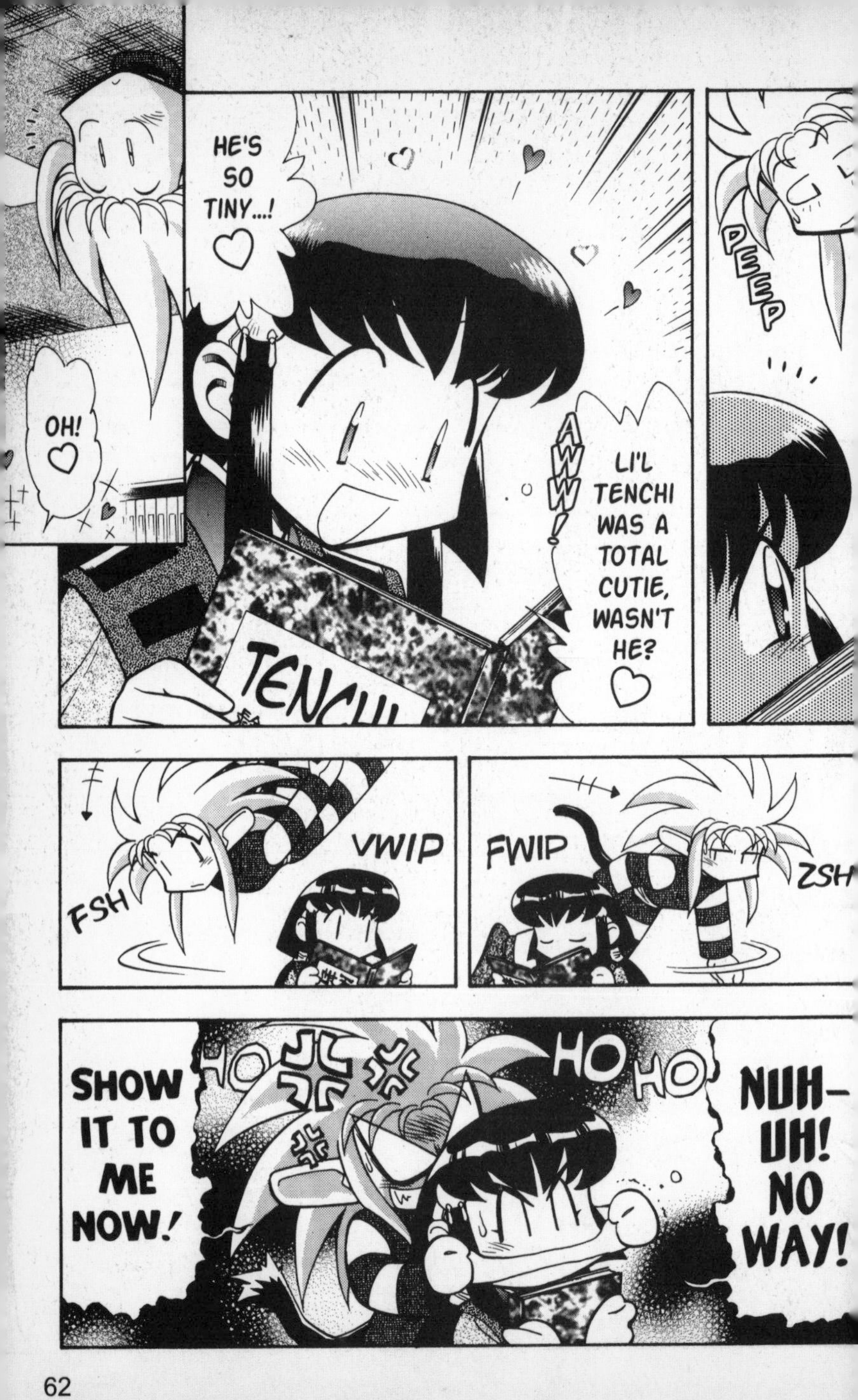
OH! ♡
HE'S SO TINY...! ♡
AWWW!
LI'L TENCHI WAS A TOTAL CUTIE, WASN'T HE? ♡
PEEP
FSH
VWIP
FWIP
ZSH
SHOW IT TO ME NOW!
HO HO HO HO
NUH-UH! NO WAY!

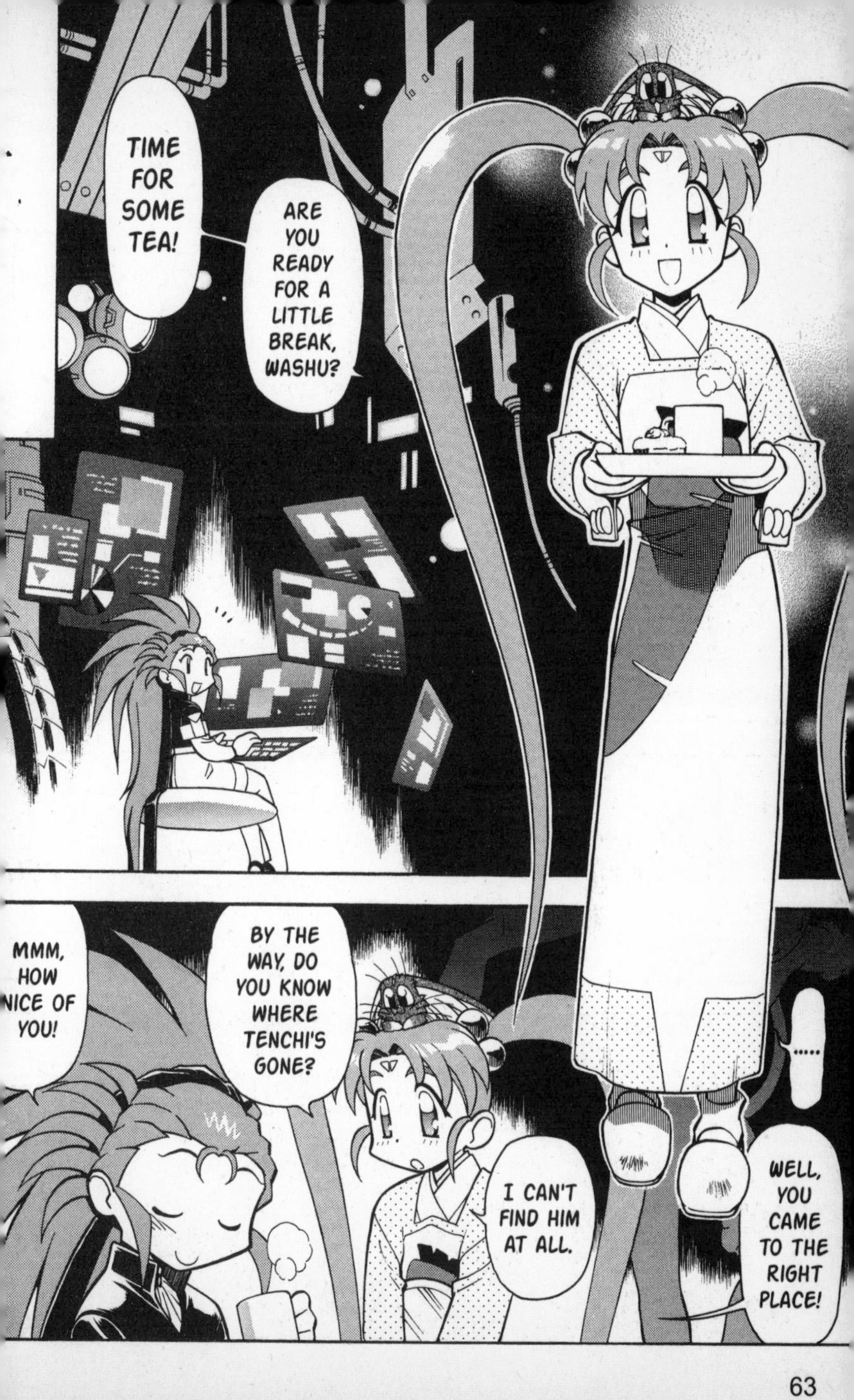
TIME FOR SOME TEA!
ARE YOU READY FOR A LITTLE BREAK, WASHU?
MMM, HOW NICE OF YOU!
BY THE WAY, DO YOU KNOW WHERE TENCHI'S GONE?
I CAN'T FIND HIM AT ALL.
......
WELL, YOU CAME TO THE RIGHT PLACE!

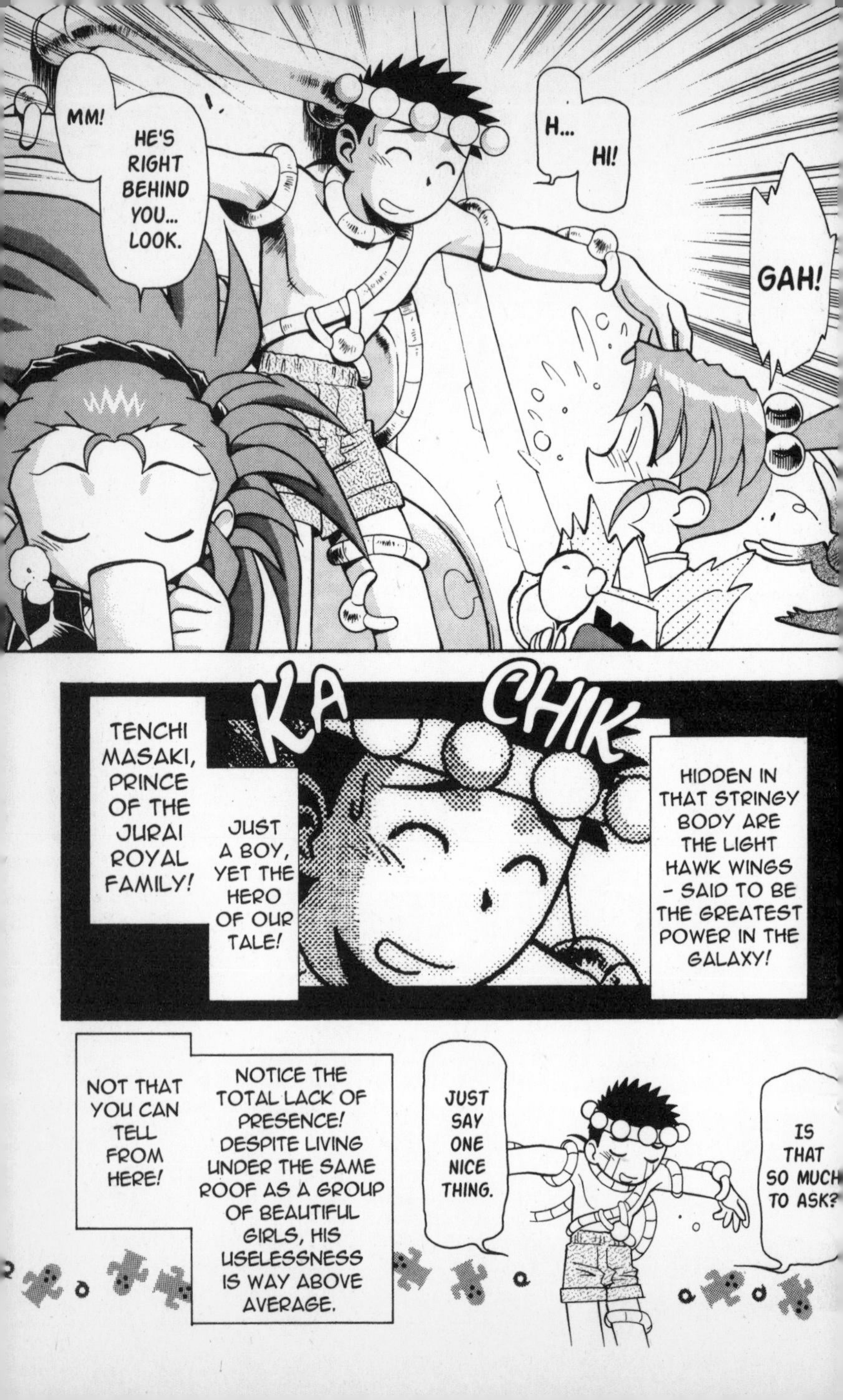
MM! HE'S RIGHT BEHIND YOU... LOOK.
H... HI!
GAH!
KA CHIK
TENCHI MASAKI, PRINCE OF THE JURAI ROYAL FAMILY!
JUST A BOY, YET THE HERO OF OUR TALE!
HIDDEN IN THAT STRINGY BODY ARE THE LIGHT HAWK WINGS - SAID TO BE THE GREATEST POWER IN THE GALAXY!
NOT THAT YOU CAN TELL FROM HERE!
NOTICE THE TOTAL LACK OF PRESENCE! DESPITE LIVING UNDER THE SAME ROOF AS A GROUP OF BEAUTIFUL GIRLS, HIS USELESSNESS IS WAY ABOVE AVERAGE.
JUST SAY ONE NICE THING.
IS THAT SO MUCH TO ASK?

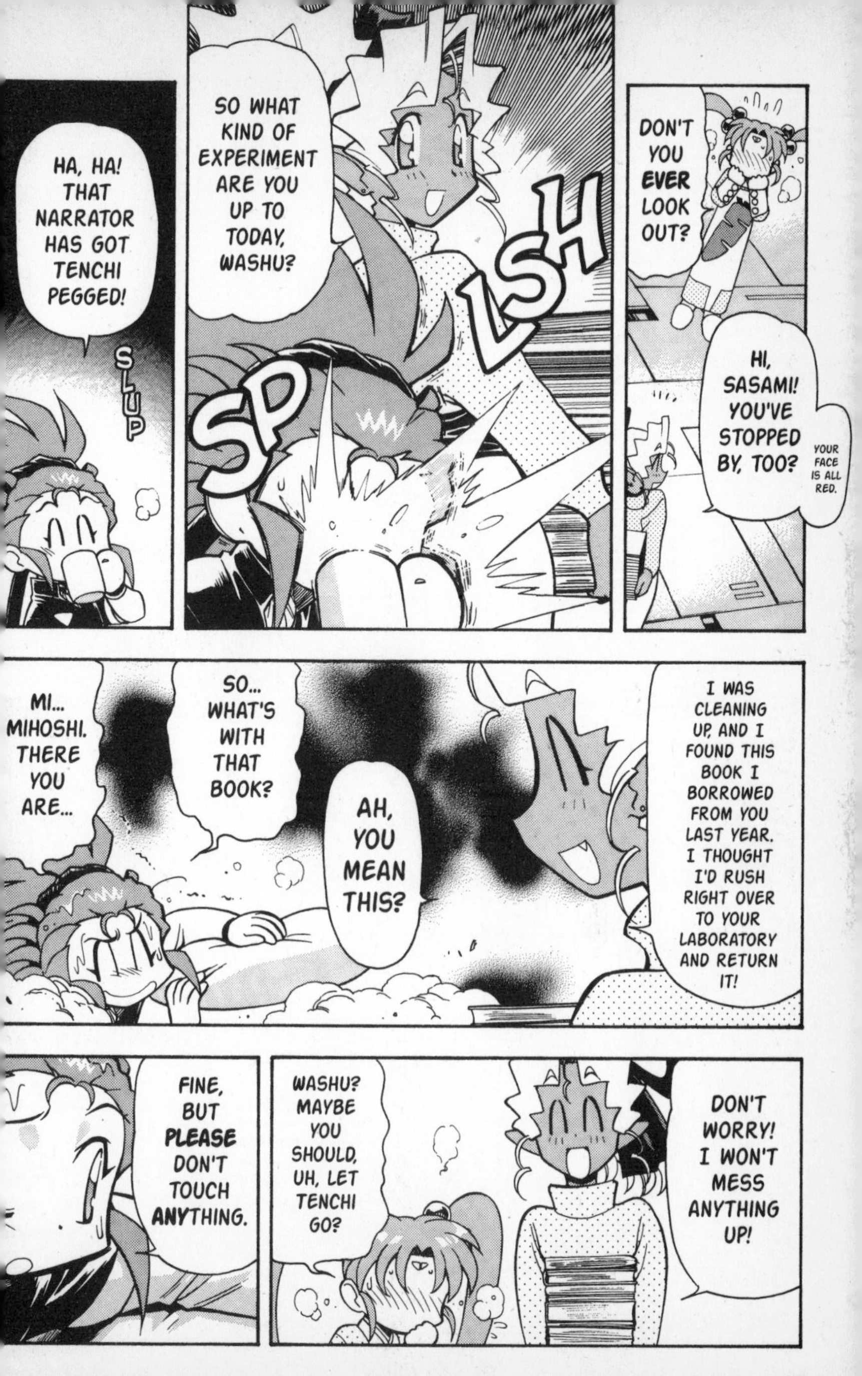
HA, HA! THAT NARRATOR HAS GOT TENCHI PEGGED!
SLUP
SO WHAT KIND OF EXPERIMENT ARE YOU UP TO TODAY, WASHU?
SPLSH
DON'T YOU EVER LOOK OUT?
HI, SASAMI! YOU'VE STOPPED BY, TOO?
YOUR FACE IS ALL RED.
MI... MIHOSHI. THERE YOU ARE...
SO... WHAT'S WITH THAT BOOK?
AH, YOU MEAN THIS?
I WAS CLEANING UP, AND I FOUND THIS BOOK I BORROWED FROM YOU LAST YEAR. I THOUGHT I'D RUSH RIGHT OVER TO YOUR LABORATORY AND RETURN IT!
FINE, BUT PLEASE DON'T TOUCH ANYTHING.
WASHU? MAYBE YOU SHOULD, UH, LET TENCHI GO?
DON'T WORRY! I WON'T MESS ANYTHING UP!

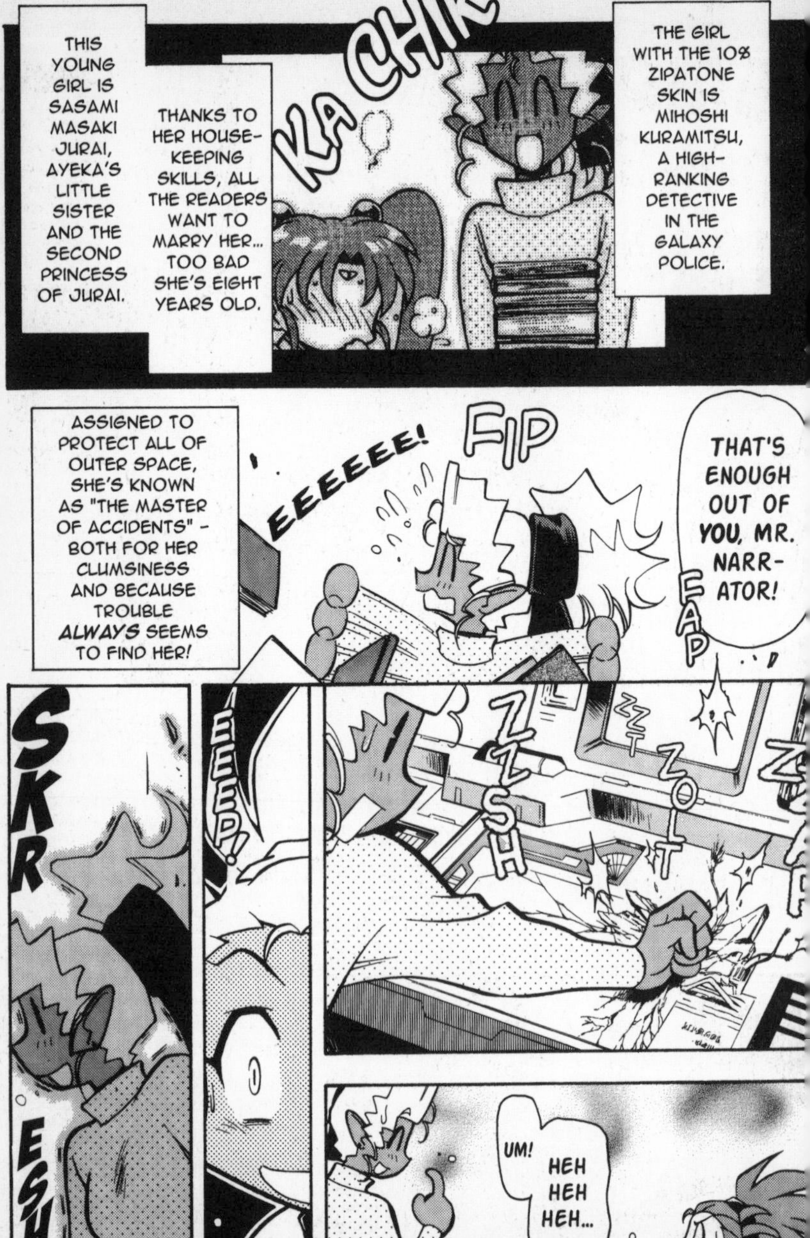

THIS YOUNG GIRL IS SASAMI MASAKI JURAI, AYEKA'S LITTLE SISTER AND THE SECOND PRINCESS OF JURAI.
THANKS TO HER HOUSE-KEEPING SKILLS, ALL THE READERS WANT TO MARRY HER... TOO BAD SHE'S EIGHT YEARS OLD.
KA CHIK
THE GIRL WITH THE 10% ZIPATONE SKIN IS MIHOSHI KURAMITSU, A HIGH-RANKING DETECTIVE IN THE GALAXY POLICE.
ASSIGNED TO PROTECT ALL OF OUTER SPACE, SHE'S KNOWN AS "THE MASTER OF ACCIDENTS" - BOTH FOR HER CLUMSINESS AND BECAUSE TROUBLE *ALWAYS* SEEMS TO FIND HER!
EEEEEEE!
FIP
FAP
THAT'S ENOUGH OUT OF **YOU**, MR. NARR-ATOR!
SKRESH
EEEP!
ZZSH
ZZT
ZOLT
UM!
HEH HEH HEH...

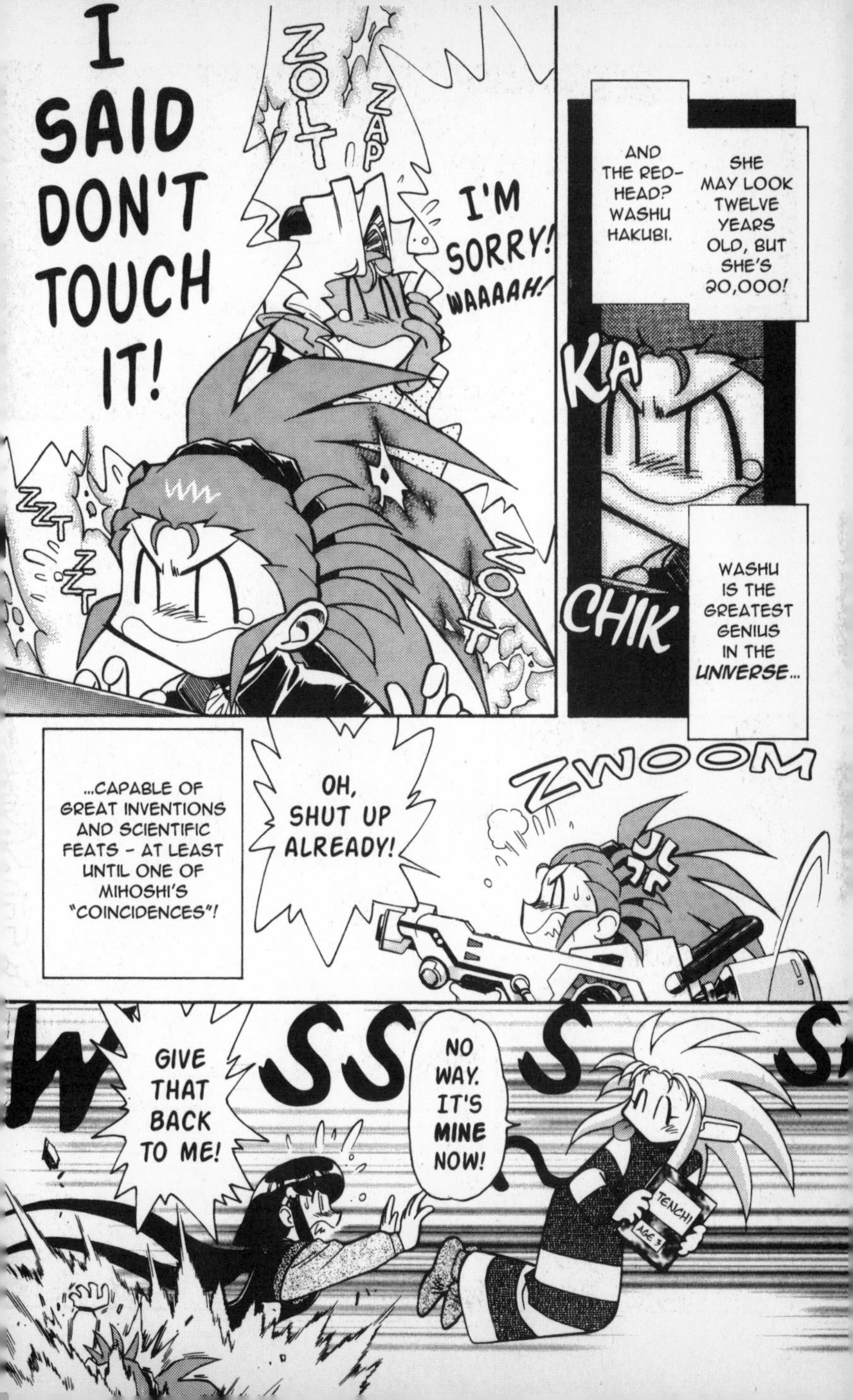

I SAID DON'T TOUCH IT!
ZOLT
ZAP
I'M SORRY!
WAAAAH!
ZZZT
ZZZT
ZOLT
AND THE RED-HEAD? WASHU HAKUBI.
SHE MAY LOOK TWELVE YEARS OLD, BUT SHE'S 20,000!
KA
CHIK
WASHU IS THE GREATEST GENIUS IN THE UNIVERSE...
...CAPABLE OF GREAT INVENTIONS AND SCIENTIFIC FEATS - AT LEAST UNTIL ONE OF MIHOSHI'S "COINCIDENCES"!
OH, SHUT UP ALREADY!
ZWOOM
WSSSS
GIVE THAT BACK TO ME!
NO WAY. IT'S MINE NOW!
TENCHI
AGE 3

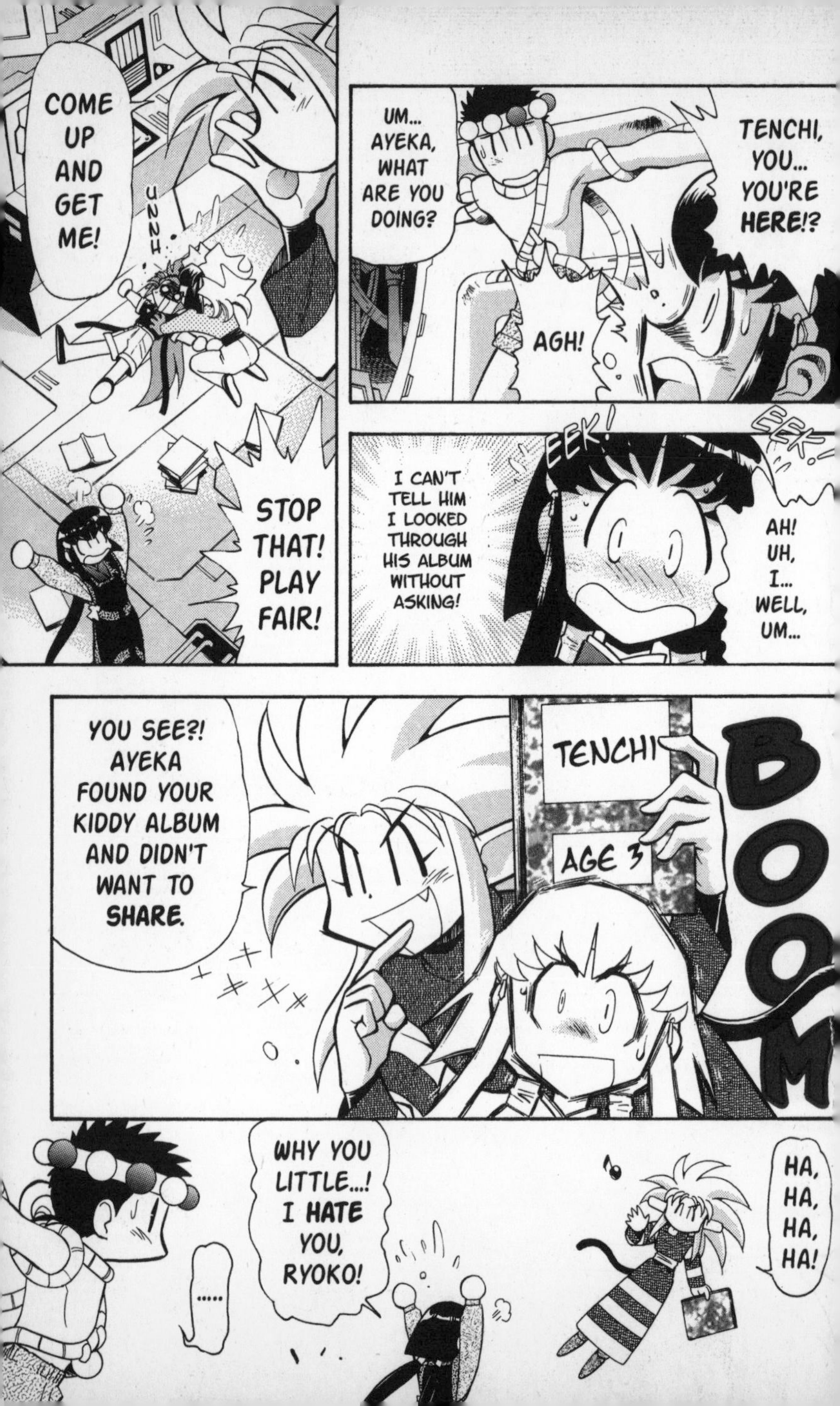
COME UP AND GET ME!
UNNH
STOP THAT! PLAY FAIR!
UM... AYEKA, WHAT ARE YOU DOING?
TENCHI, YOU... YOU'RE HERE!?
AGH!
EEK!
EEK!
I CAN'T TELL HIM I LOOKED THROUGH HIS ALBUM WITHOUT ASKING!
AH! UH, I... WELL, UM...
YOU SEE?! AYEKA FOUND YOUR KIDDY ALBUM AND DIDN'T WANT TO SHARE.
TENCHI
AGE 3
BOOM
.....
WHY YOU LITTLE...! I HATE YOU, RYOKO!
HA, HA, HA, HA!

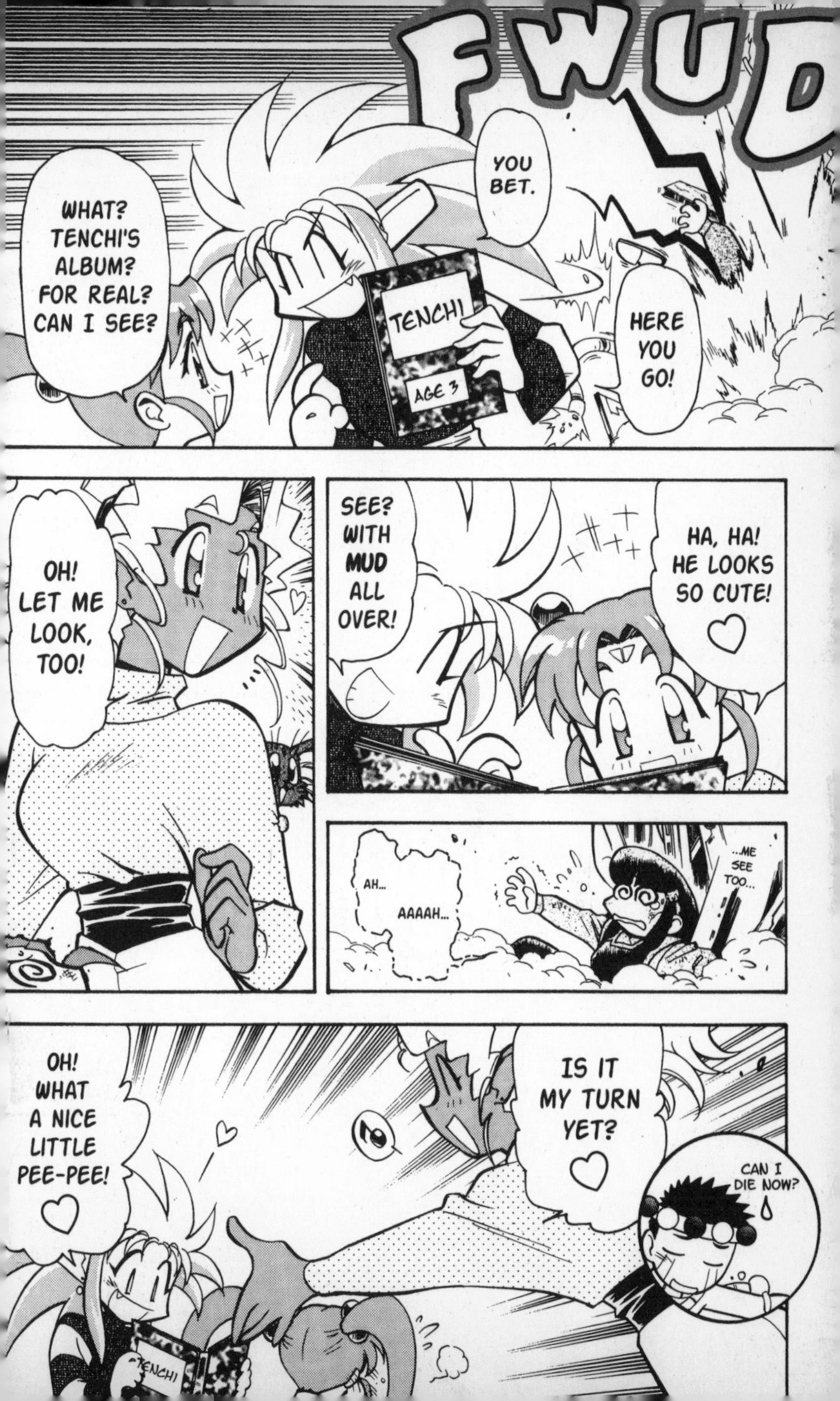

FWUD
WHAT? TENCHI'S ALBUM? FOR REAL? CAN I SEE?
YOU BET.
TENCHI
AGE 3
HERE YOU GO!
OH! LET ME LOOK, TOO!
SEE? WITH **MUD** ALL OVER!
HA, HA! HE LOOKS SO CUTE!
AH...
AAAAH...
...ME SEE TOO...
OH! WHAT A NICE LITTLE PEE-PEE!
IS IT MY TURN YET?
CAN I DIE NOW?
TENCHI

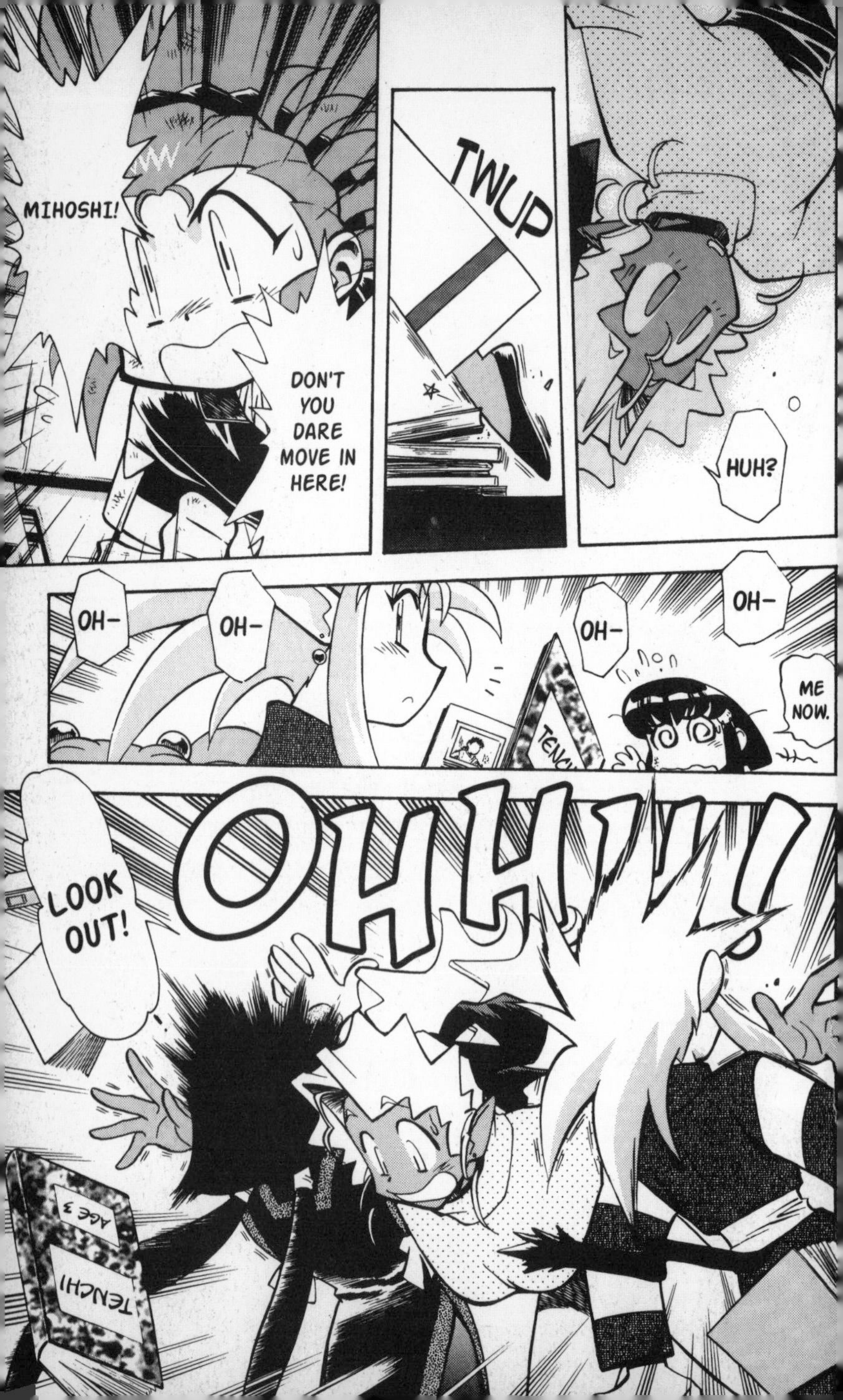

MIHOSHI!
DON'T YOU DARE MOVE IN HERE!
TWUP
HUH?
OH-
OH-
OH-
OH-
ME NOW.
LOOK OUT!
OHH!!!!
TENCHI AGE 3

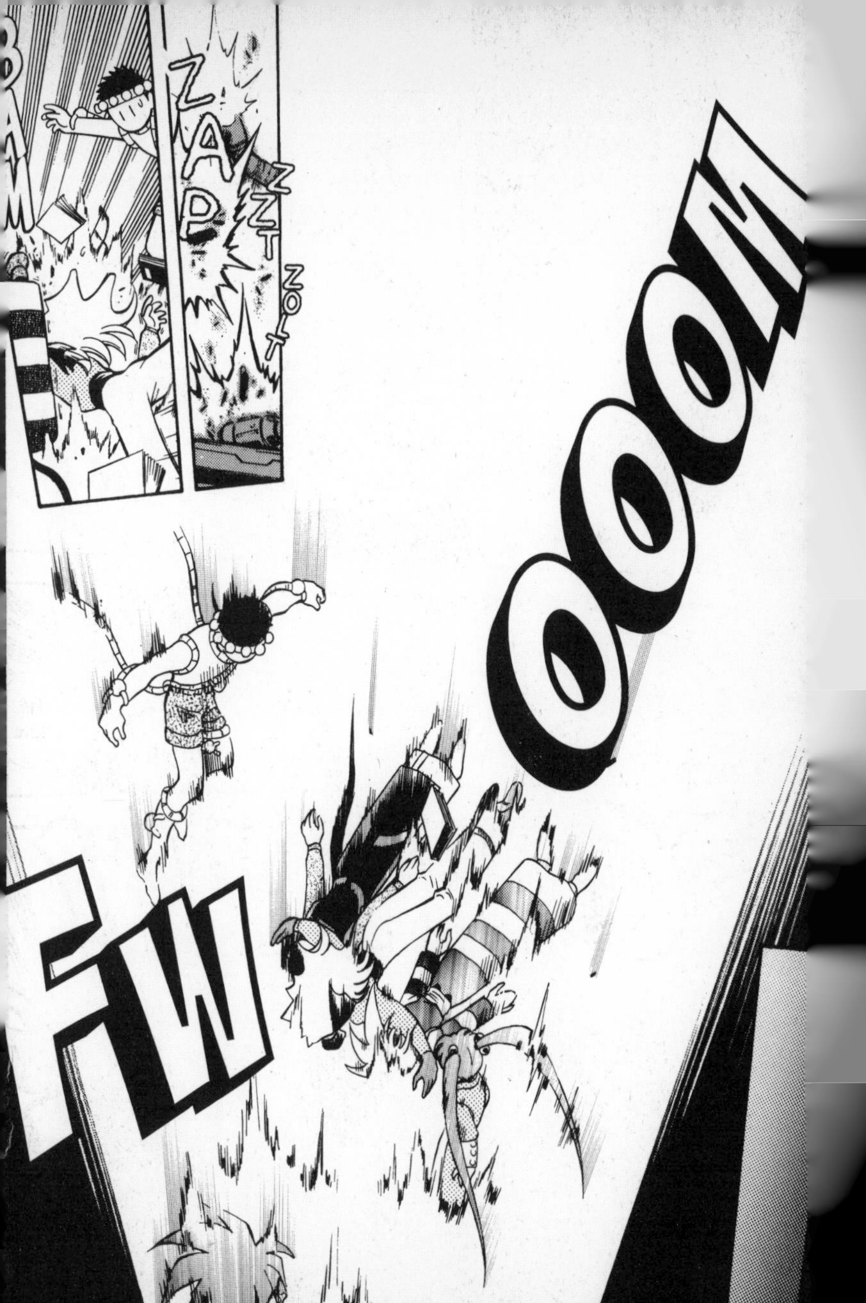
BAM
ZAP
ZZZT
ZOLT
FW
OOOM

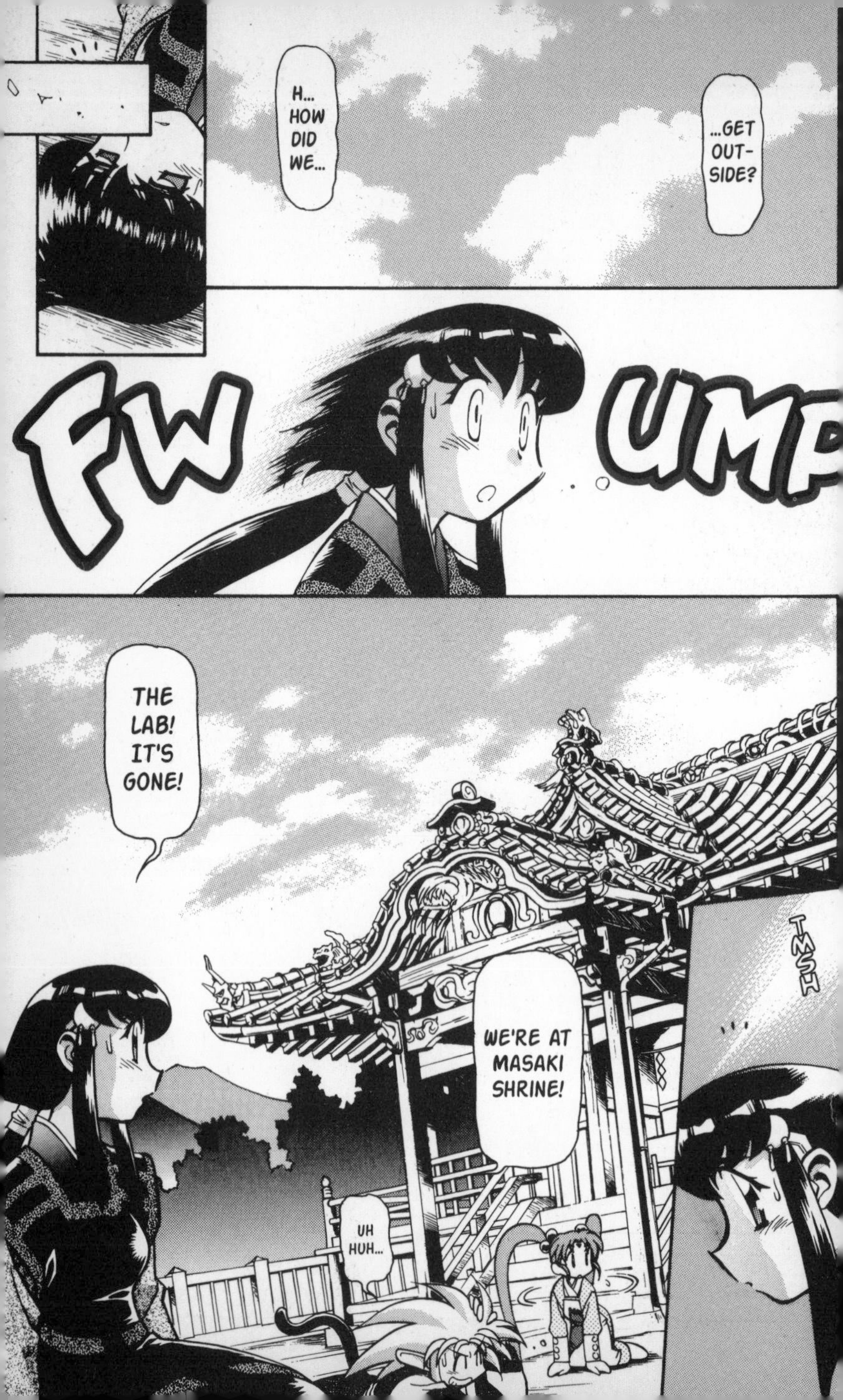
H... HOW DID WE...
...GET OUT-SIDE?
FWUMP
THE LAB! IT'S GONE!
WE'RE AT MASAKI SHRINE!
UH HUH...
TMSH

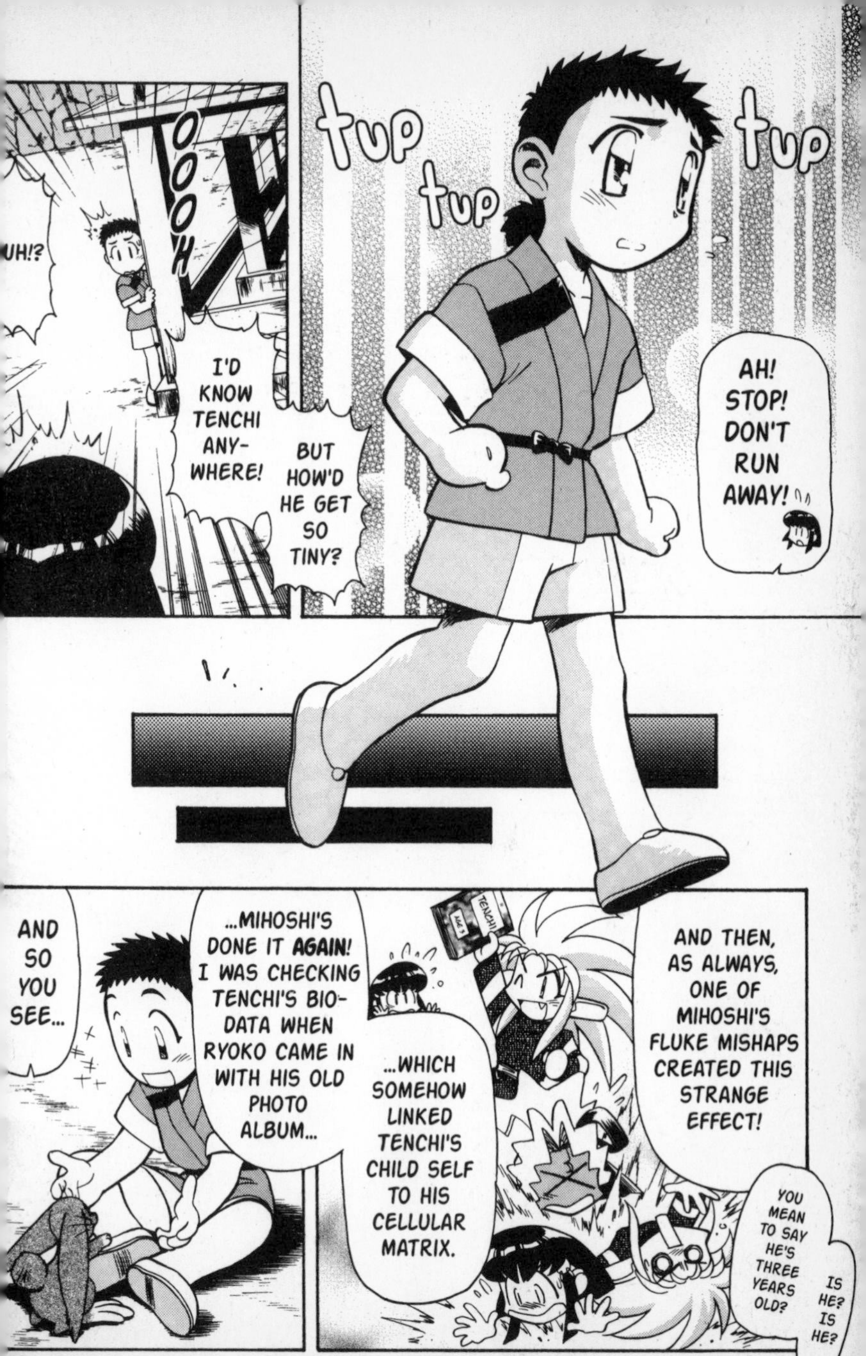
UH!?
OOOOH
I'D KNOW TENCHI ANY-WHERE!
BUT HOW'D HE GET SO TINY?
tup
tup
tup
AH! STOP! DON'T RUN AWAY!
AND SO YOU SEE...
...MIHOSHI'S DONE IT **AGAIN**! I WAS CHECKING TENCHI'S BIO-DATA WHEN RYOKO CAME IN WITH HIS OLD PHOTO ALBUM...
TENCHI
...WHICH SOMEHOW LINKED TENCHI'S CHILD SELF TO HIS CELLULAR MATRIX.
AND THEN, AS ALWAYS, ONE OF MIHOSHI'S FLUKE MISHAPS CREATED THIS STRANGE EFFECT!
YOU MEAN TO SAY HE'S THREE YEARS OLD?
IS HE? IS HE?

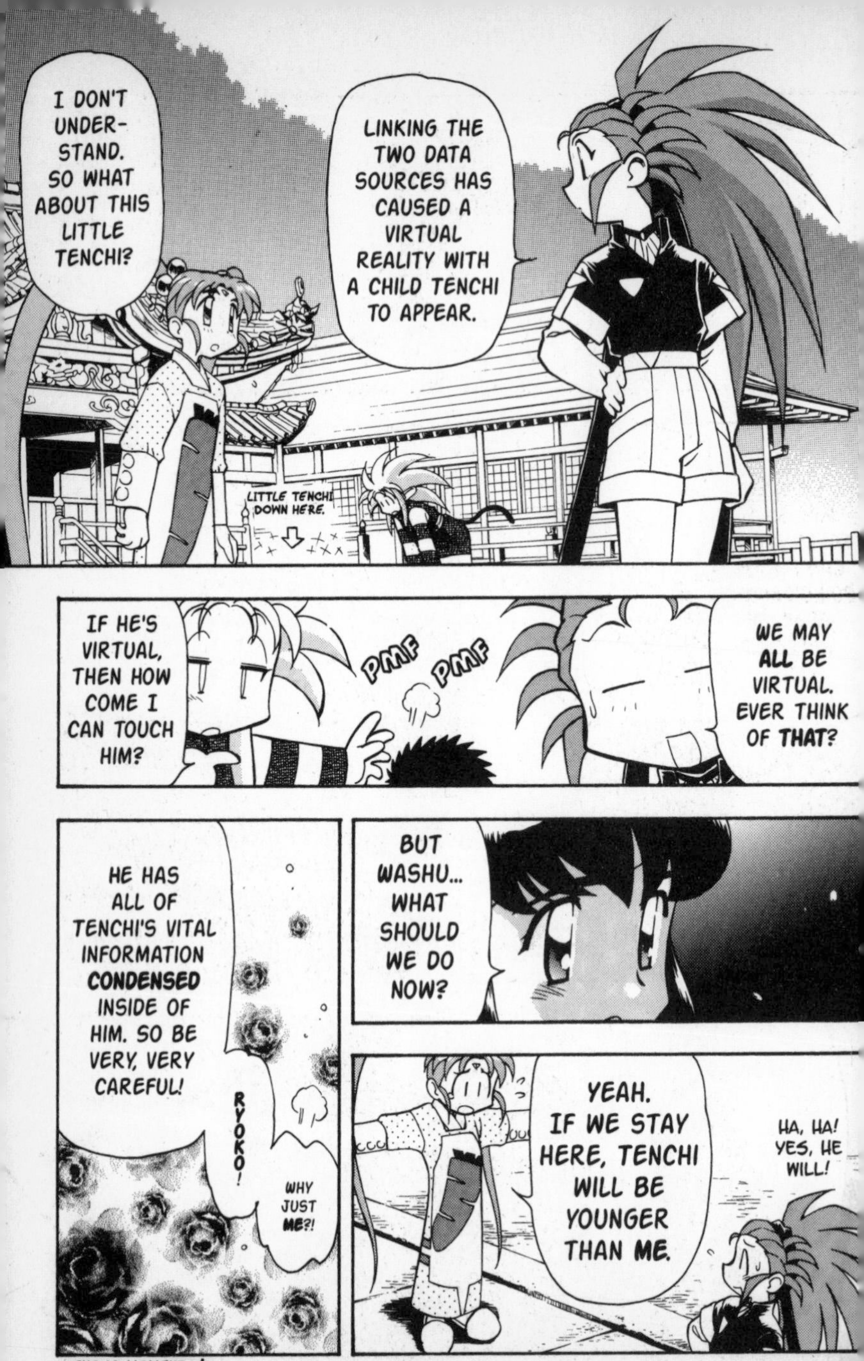
I DON'T UNDER-STAND. SO WHAT ABOUT THIS LITTLE TENCHI?
LINKING THE TWO DATA SOURCES HAS CAUSED A VIRTUAL REALITY WITH A CHILD TENCHI TO APPEAR.
LITTLE TENCHI DOWN HERE.
IF HE'S VIRTUAL, THEN HOW COME I CAN TOUCH HIM?
PMF
PMF
WE MAY **ALL** BE VIRTUAL. EVER THINK OF **THAT**?
HE HAS ALL OF TENCHI'S VITAL INFORMATION **CONDENSED** INSIDE OF HIM. SO BE VERY, VERY CAREFUL!
RYOKO!
WHY JUST **ME**?!
BUT WASHU... WHAT SHOULD WE DO NOW?
YEAH. IF WE STAY HERE, TENCHI WILL BE YOUNGER THAN **ME**.
HA, HA! YES, HE WILL!
SHOJO MOMENT...

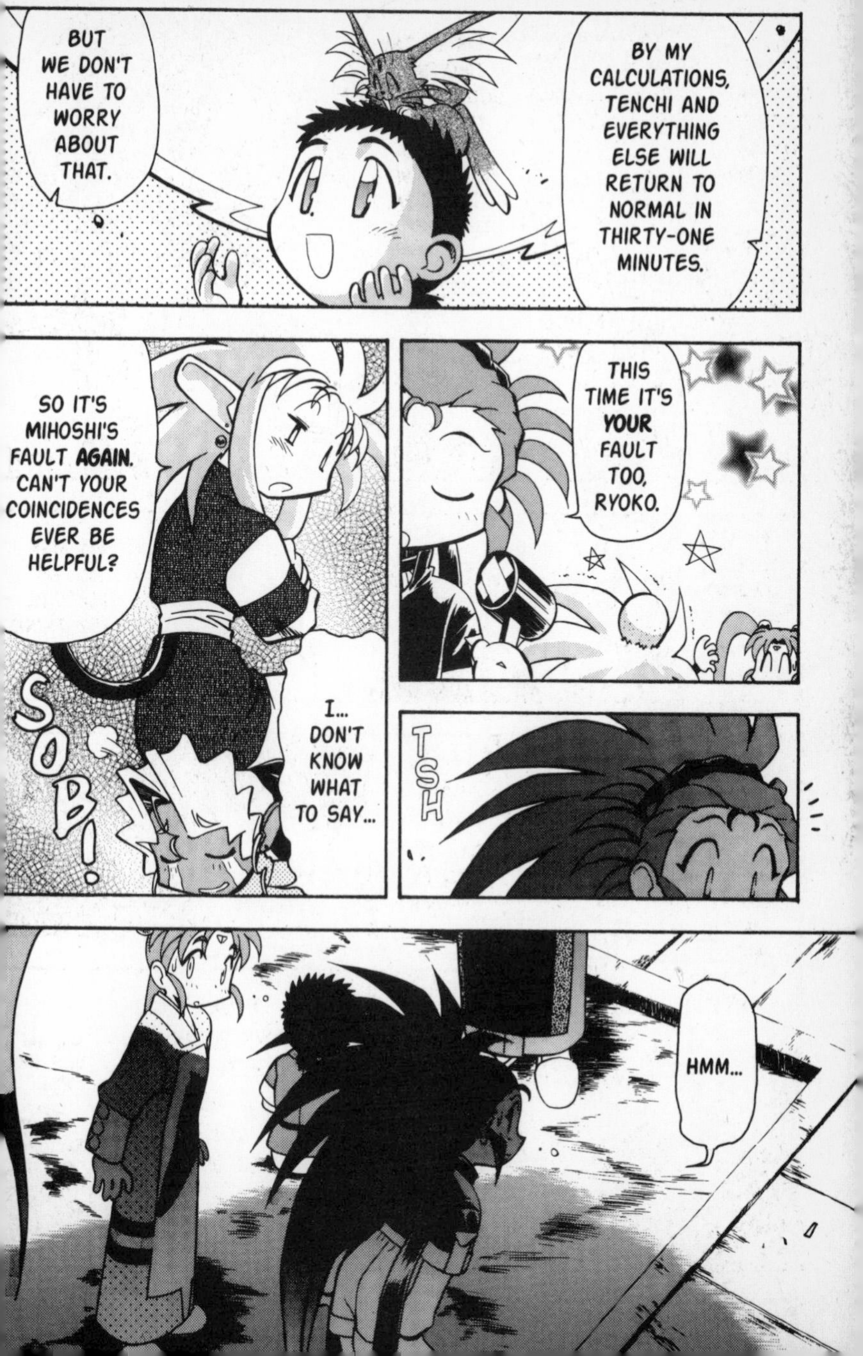
BUT WE DON'T HAVE TO WORRY ABOUT THAT.
BY MY CALCULATIONS, TENCHI AND EVERYTHING ELSE WILL RETURN TO NORMAL IN THIRTY-ONE MINUTES.
SO IT'S MIHOSHI'S FAULT AGAIN. CAN'T YOUR COINCIDENCES EVER BE HELPFUL?
SOB!
I... DON'T KNOW WHAT TO SAY...
THIS TIME IT'S YOUR FAULT TOO, RYOKO.
TSH
HMM...

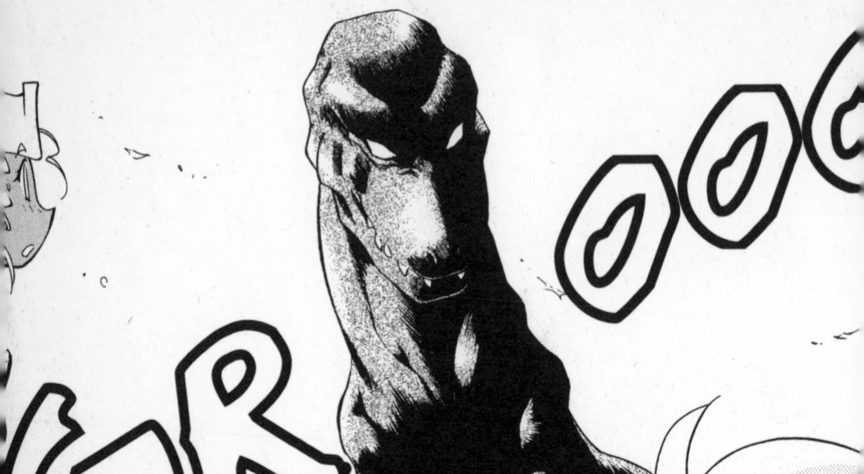
GROOO

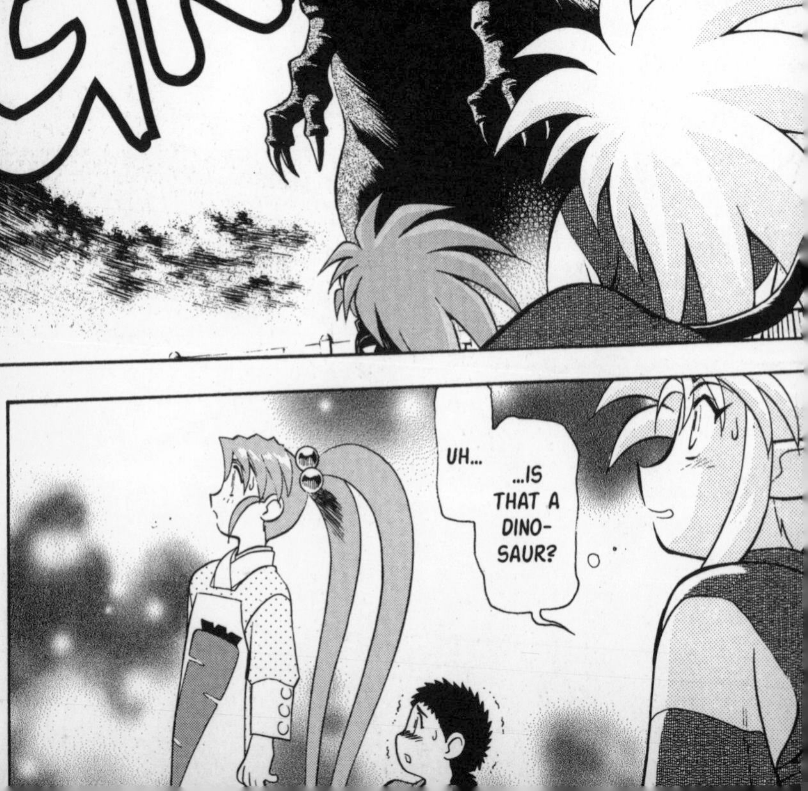
UH... ...IS THAT A DINO-SAUR?

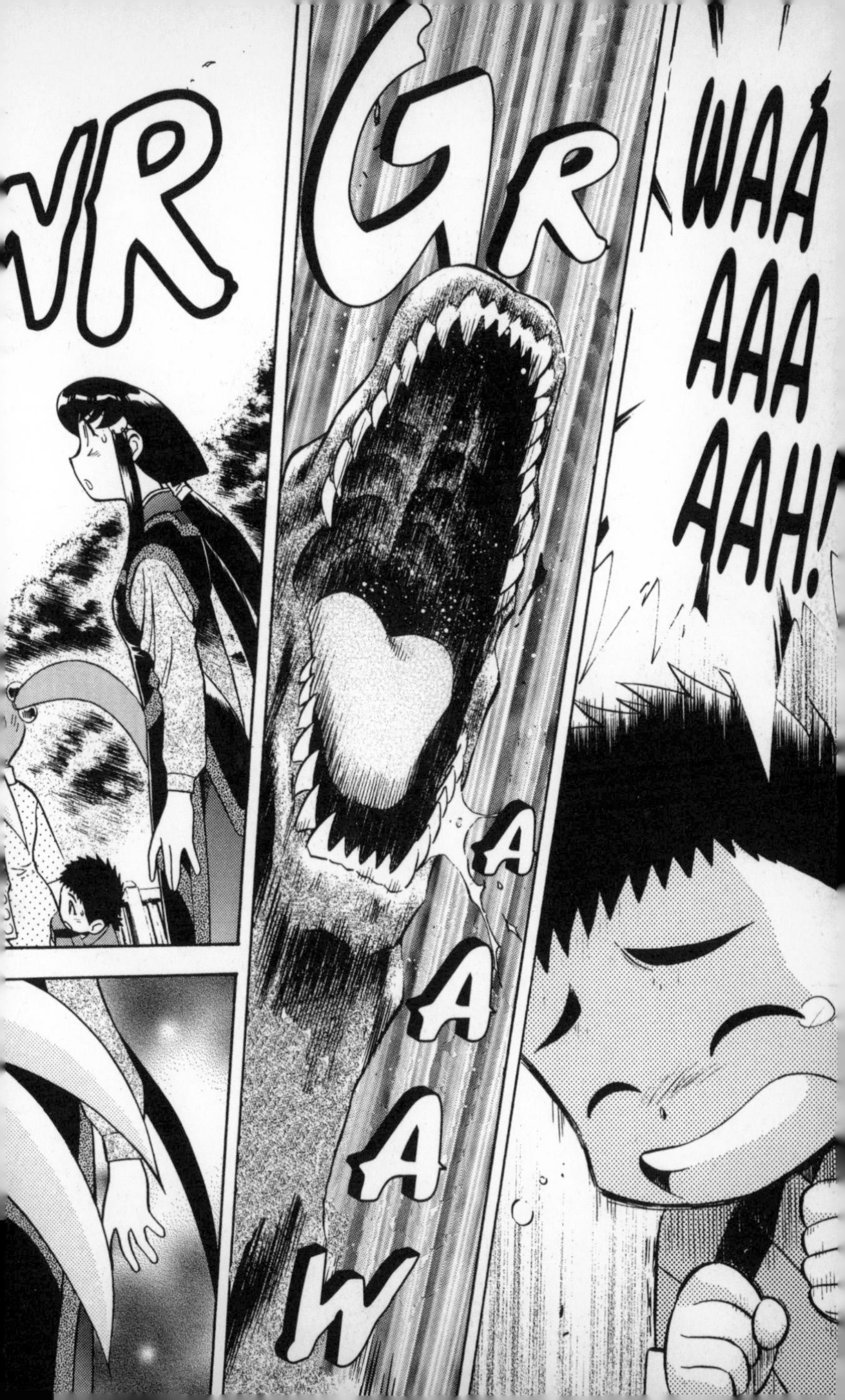
VR
GR
AAAW
WAAAAAAAAH!

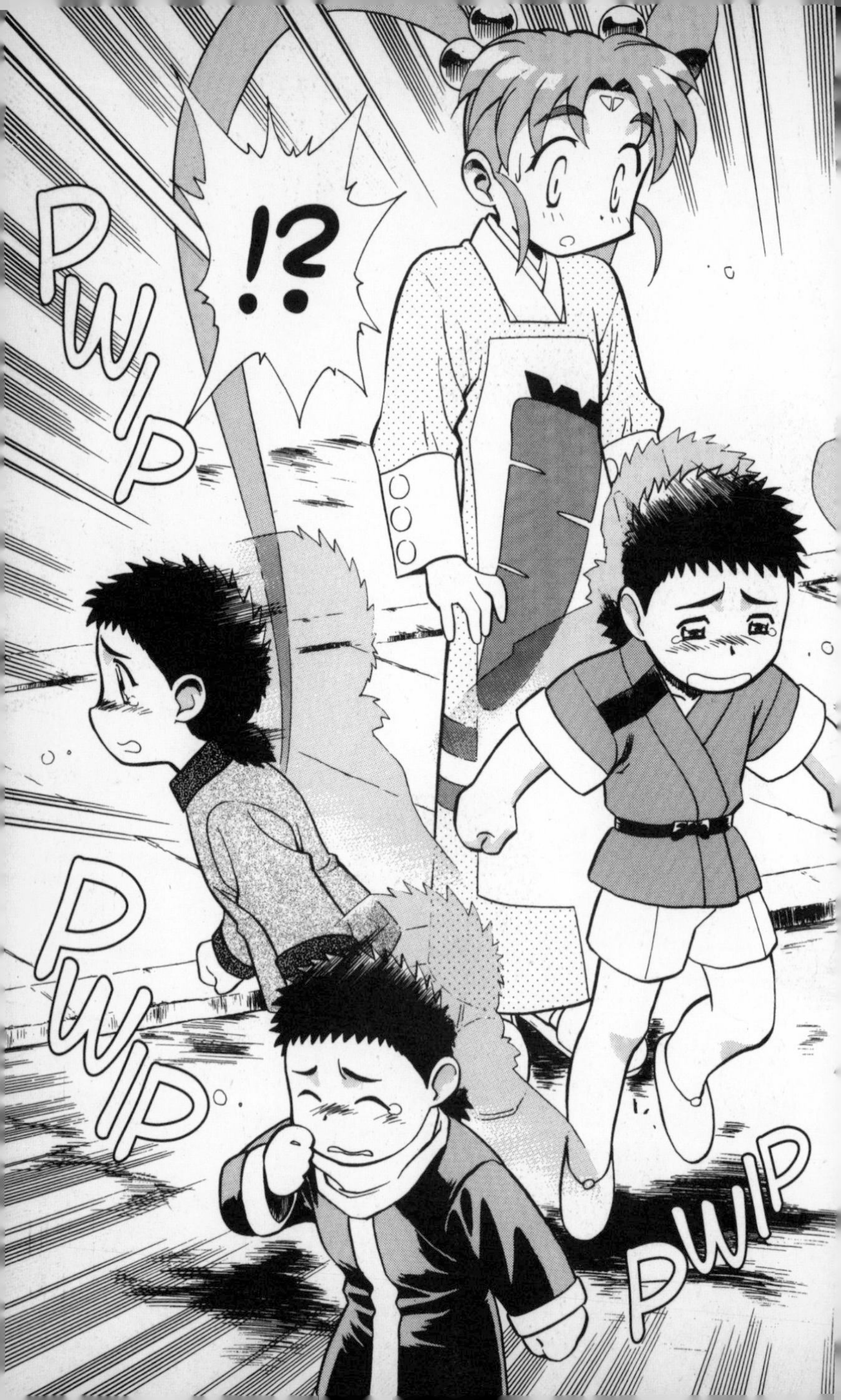
PWIP
!?
PWIP
PWIP

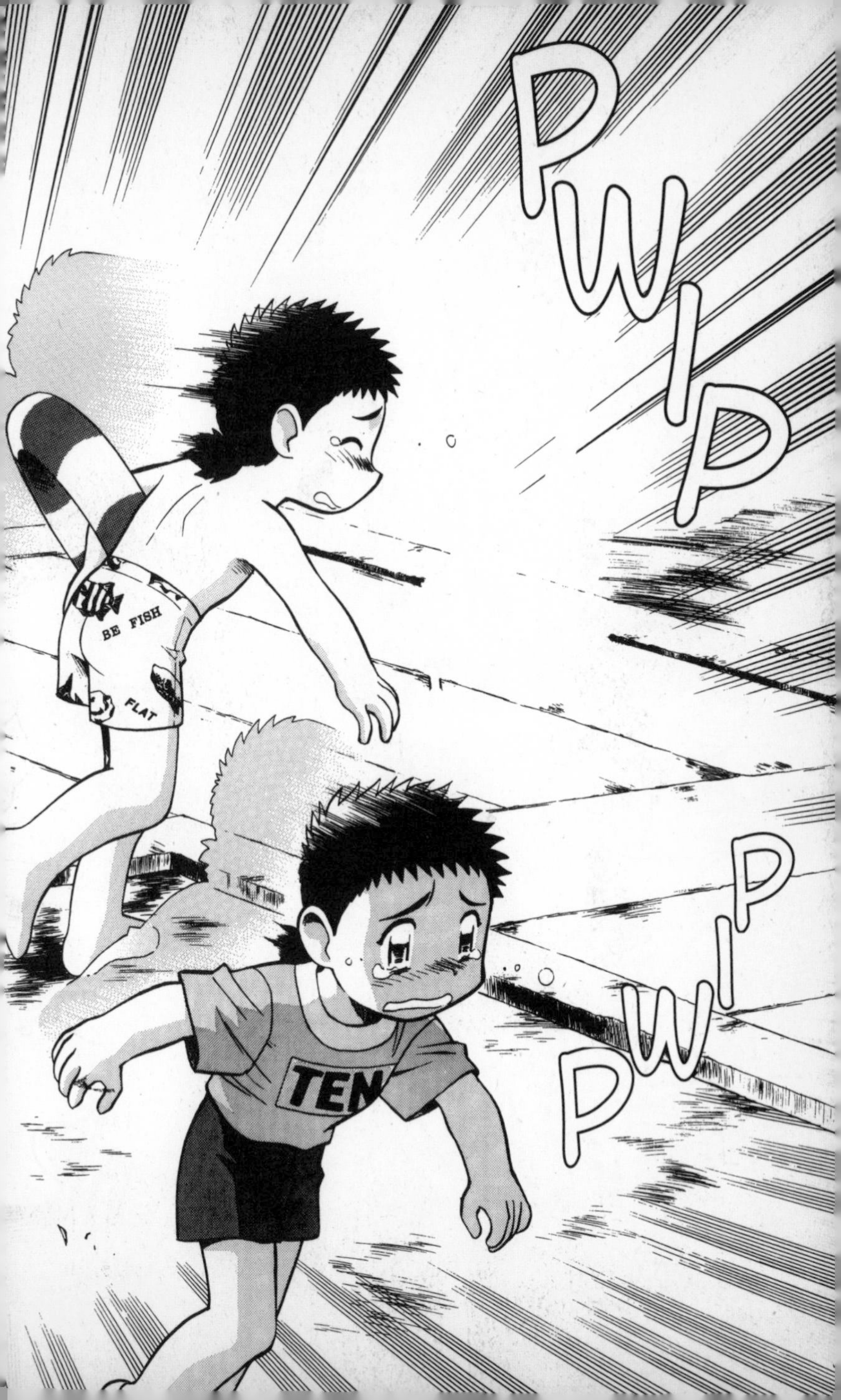
PWIP
BE FISH
FLAT
TEN
PWIP

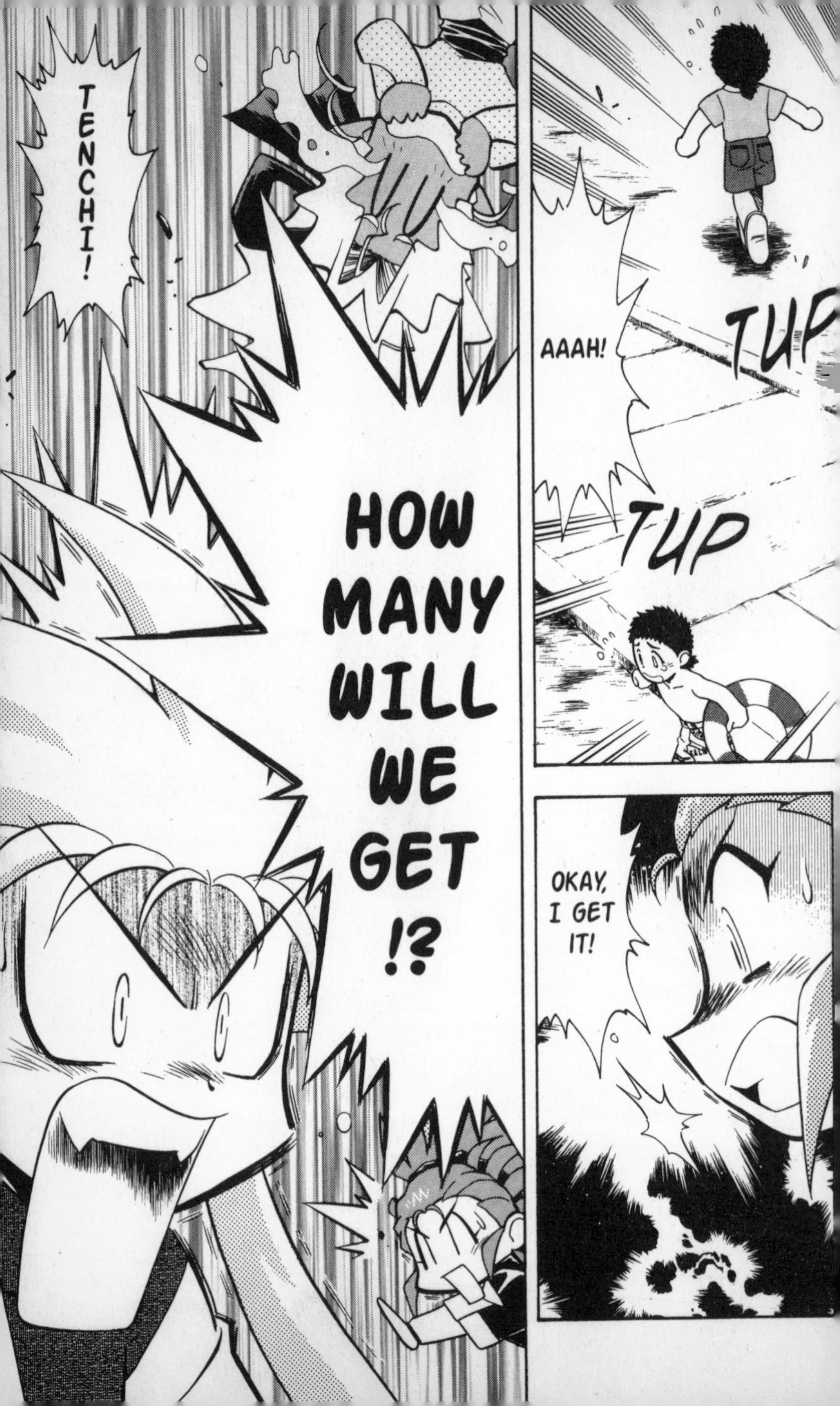
TENCHI!
HOW MANY WILL WE GET !?
AAAH!
TUP
TUP
OKAY, I GET IT!

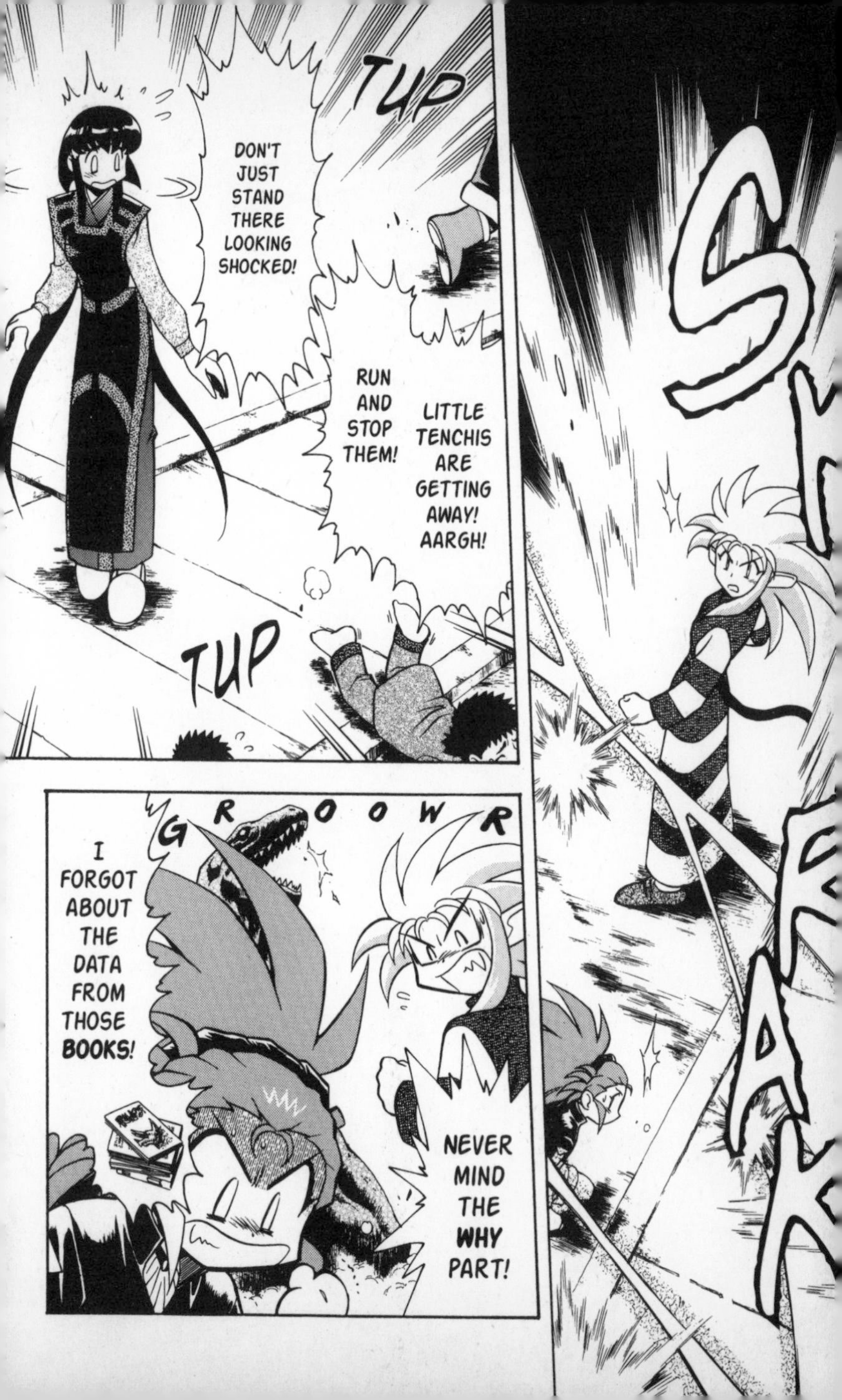

DON'T JUST STAND THERE LOOKING SHOCKED!
TUP
RUN AND STOP THEM!
LITTLE TENCHIS ARE GETTING AWAY! AARGH!
TUP
G R O O W R
I FORGOT ABOUT THE DATA FROM THOSE **BOOKS!**
NEVER MIND THE **WHY** PART!

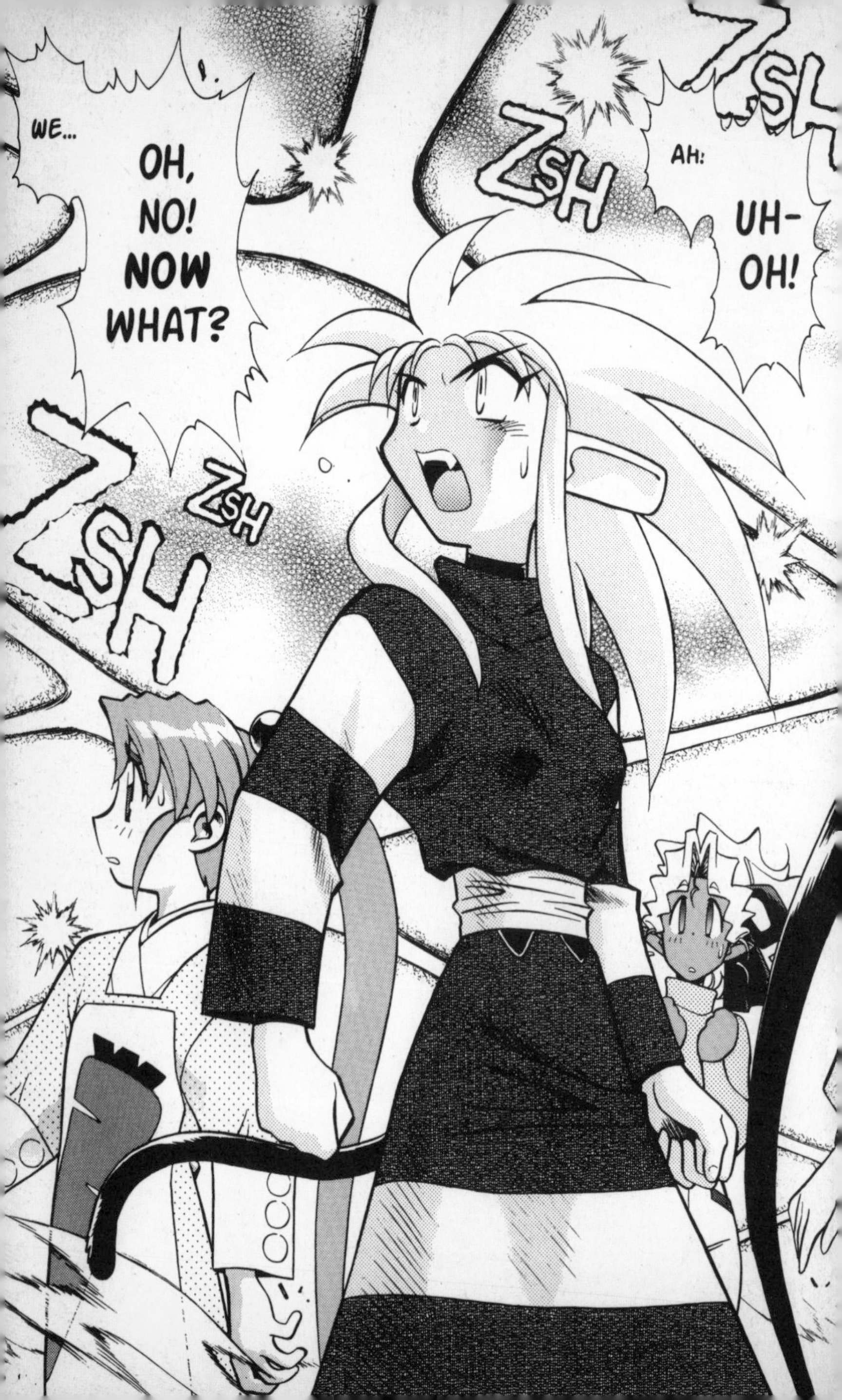
WE...
OH, NO! NOW WHAT?
ZSH
ZSH
AH:
UH-OH!
ZSH
ZSH

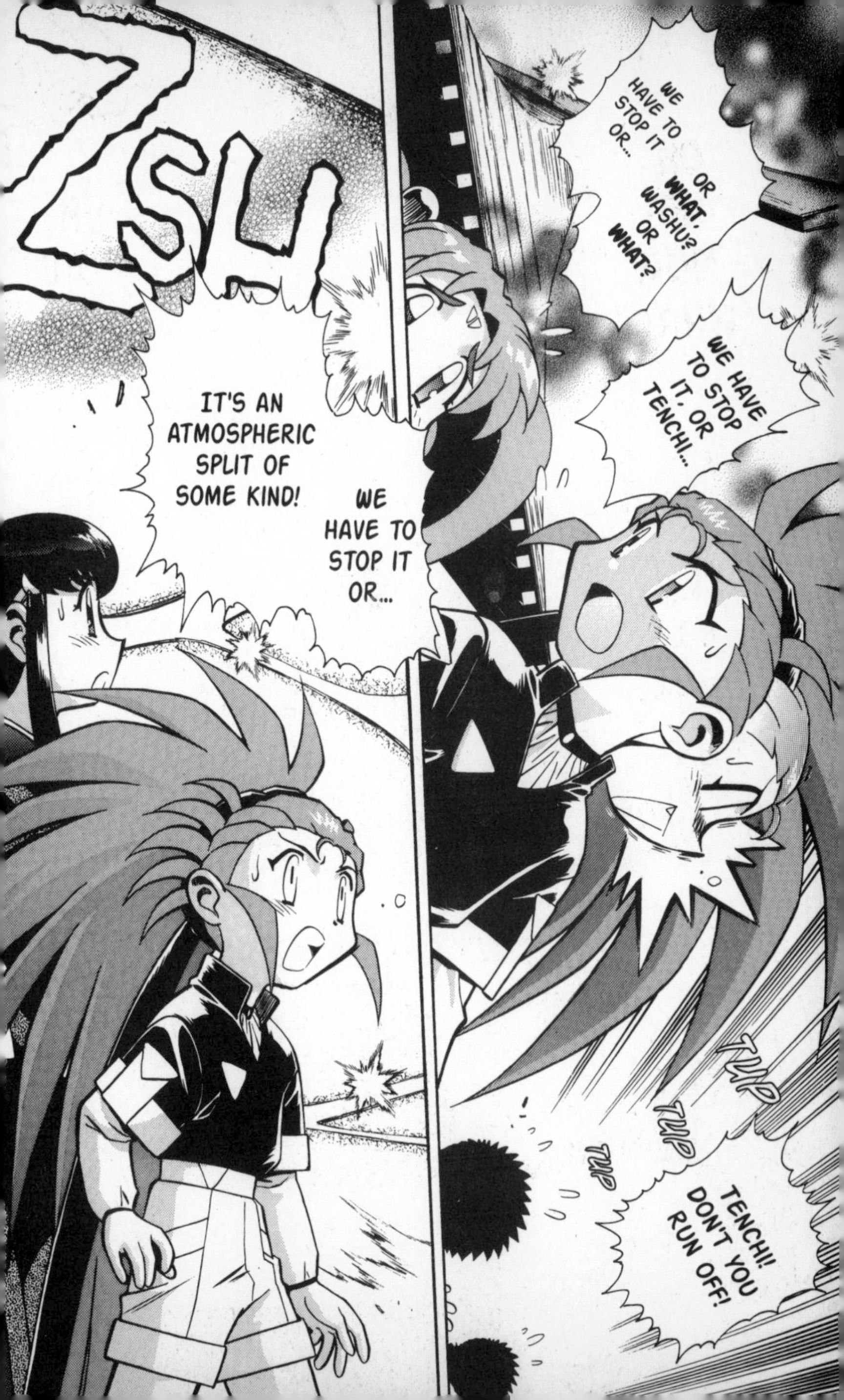
ZSLI
IT'S AN ATMOSPHERIC SPLIT OF SOME KIND!
WE HAVE TO STOP IT OR...
WE HAVE TO STOP IT OR...
OR WHAT, WASHU? OR WHAT?
WE HAVE TO STOP IT, OR TENCHI...
TUP
TUP
TUP
TENCHI!! DON'T YOU RUN OFF!

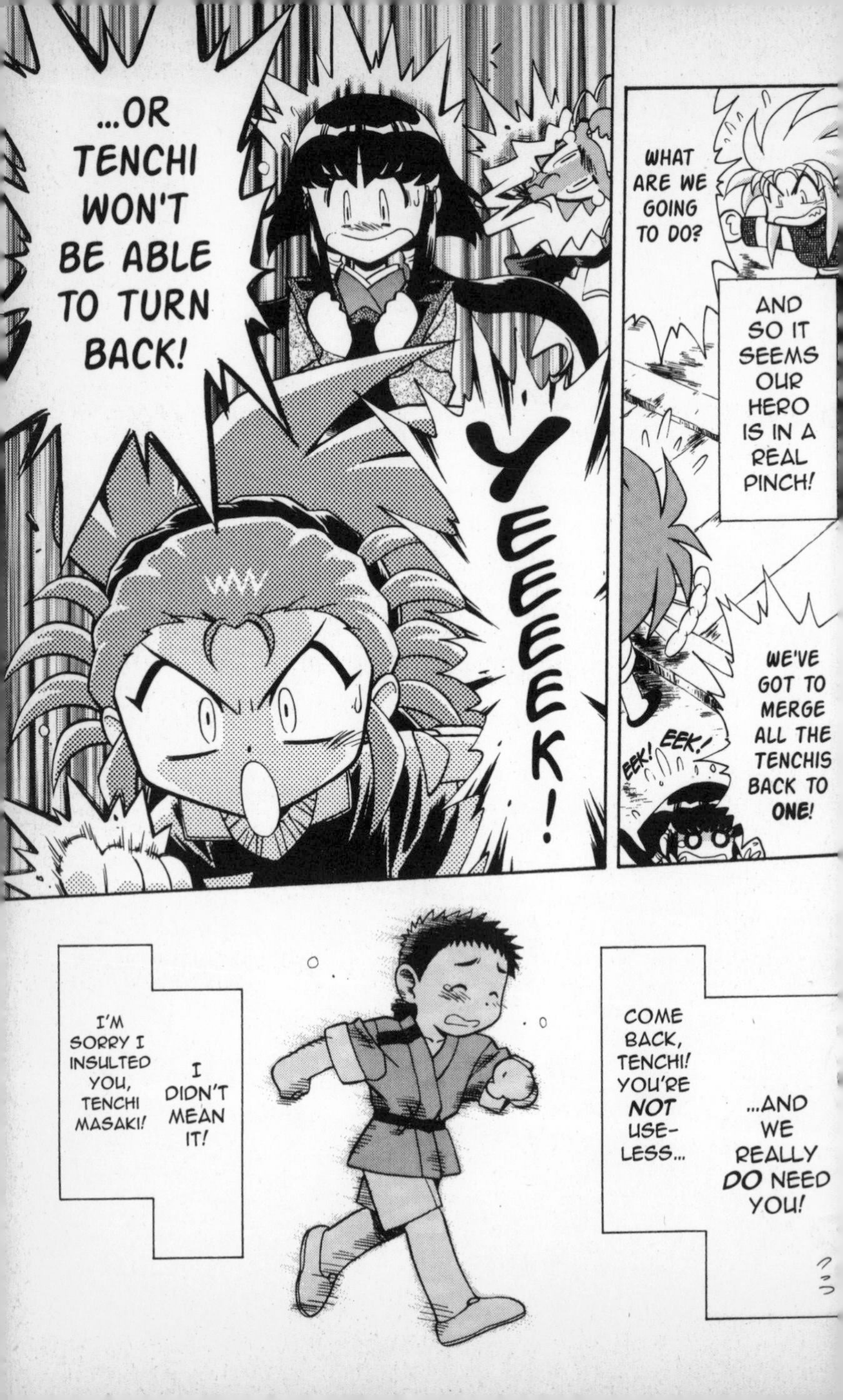
...OR TENCHI WON'T BE ABLE TO TURN BACK!
YEEEEK!
WHAT ARE WE GOING TO DO?
AND SO IT SEEMS OUR HERO IS IN A REAL PINCH!
EEK! EEK!
WE'VE GOT TO MERGE ALL THE TENCHIS BACK TO ONE!
I'M SORRY I INSULTED YOU, TENCHI MASAKI!
I DIDN'T MEAN IT!
COME BACK, TENCHI! YOU'RE NOT USELESS...
...AND WE REALLY DO NEED YOU!

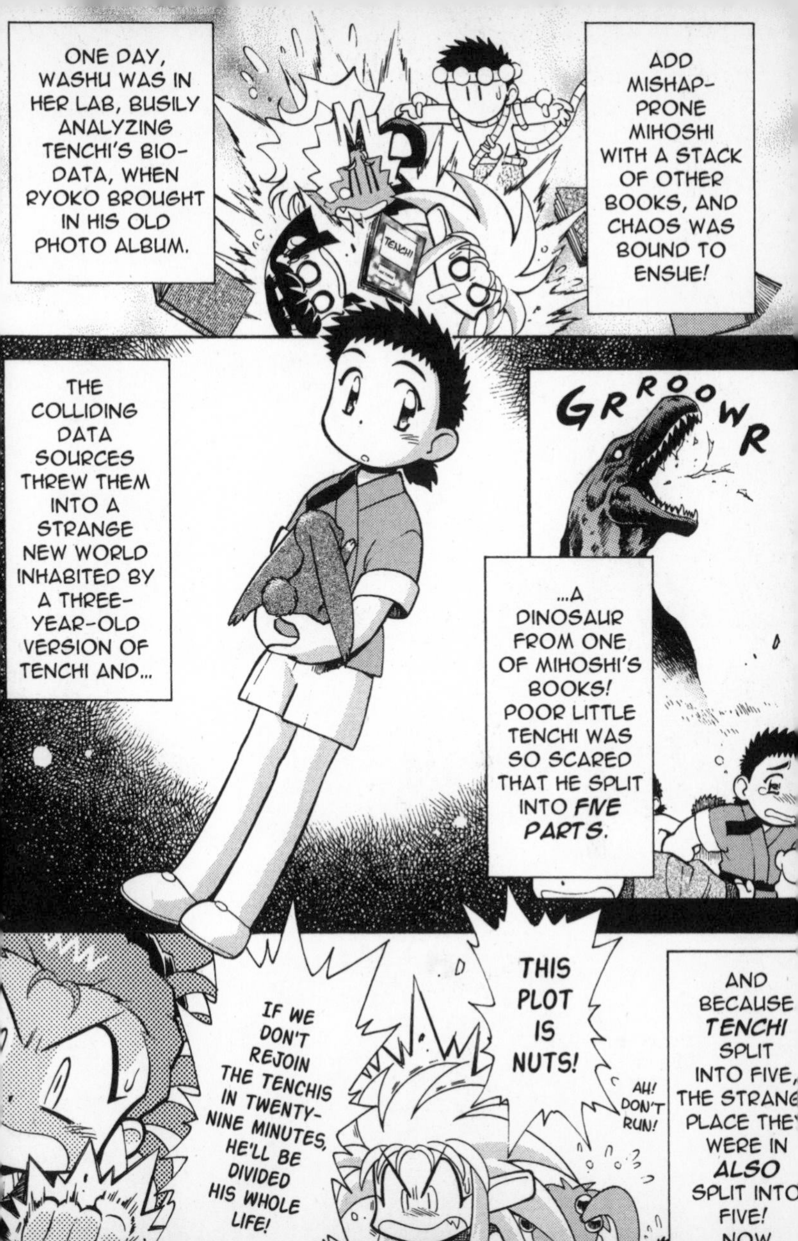
ONE DAY, WASHU WAS IN HER LAB, BUSILY ANALYZING TENCHI'S BIO-DATA, WHEN RYOKO BROUGHT IN HIS OLD PHOTO ALBUM.
TENCHI
ADD MISHAP-PRONE MIHOSHI WITH A STACK OF OTHER BOOKS, AND CHAOS WAS BOUND TO ENSUE!
THE COLLIDING DATA SOURCES THREW THEM INTO A STRANGE NEW WORLD INHABITED BY A THREE-YEAR-OLD VERSION OF TENCHI AND...
GRROOWR
...A DINOSAUR FROM ONE OF MIHOSHI'S BOOKS! POOR LITTLE TENCHI WAS SO SCARED THAT HE SPLIT INTO FIVE PARTS.
IF WE DON'T REJOIN THE TENCHIS IN TWENTY-NINE MINUTES, HE'LL BE DIVIDED HIS WHOLE LIFE!
THIS PLOT IS NUTS!
AH! DON'T RUN!
AND BECAUSE TENCHI SPLIT INTO FIVE, THE STRANG PLACE THE WERE IN ALSO SPLIT INTO FIVE! NOW

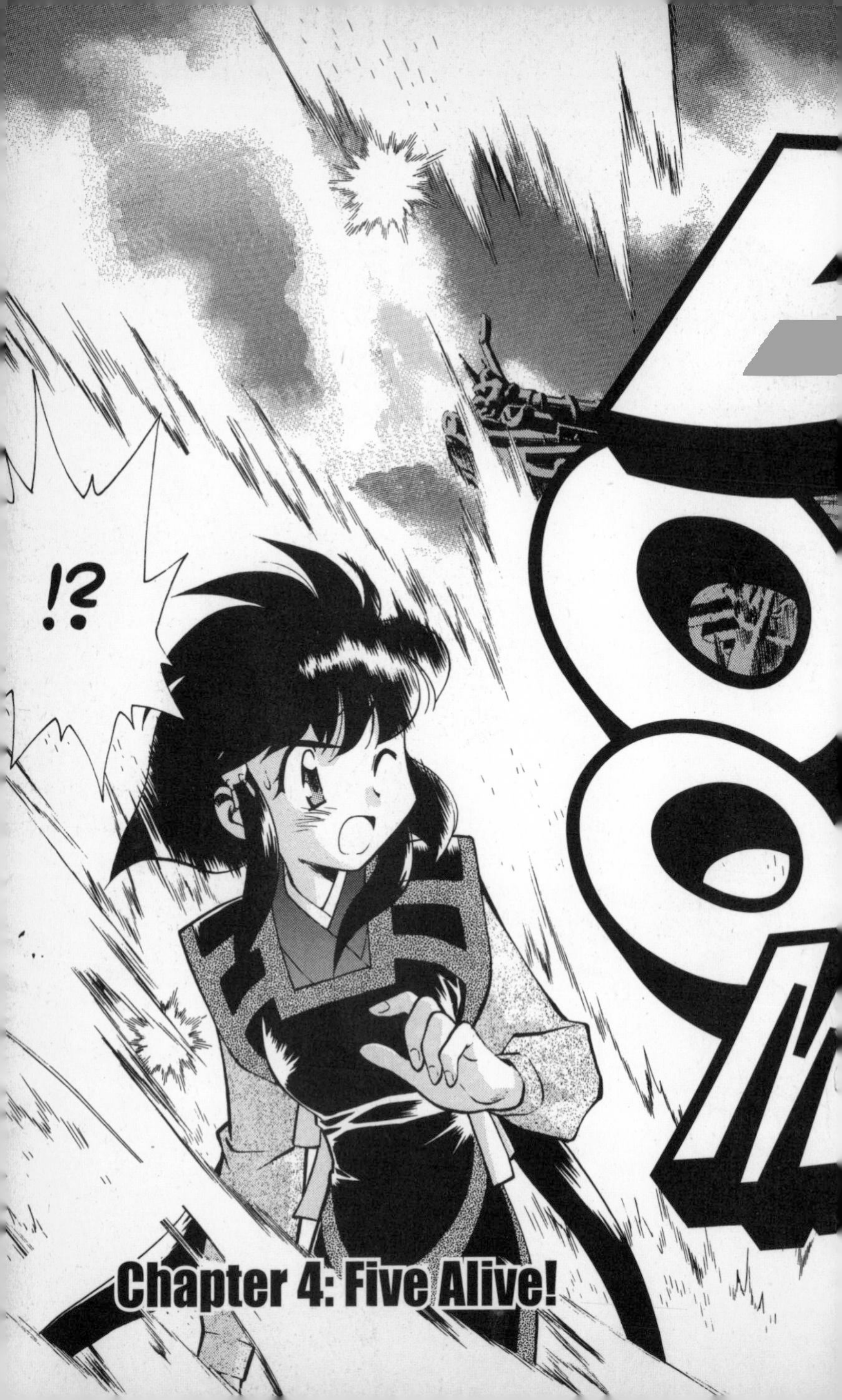
!?

Chapter 4: Five Alive!

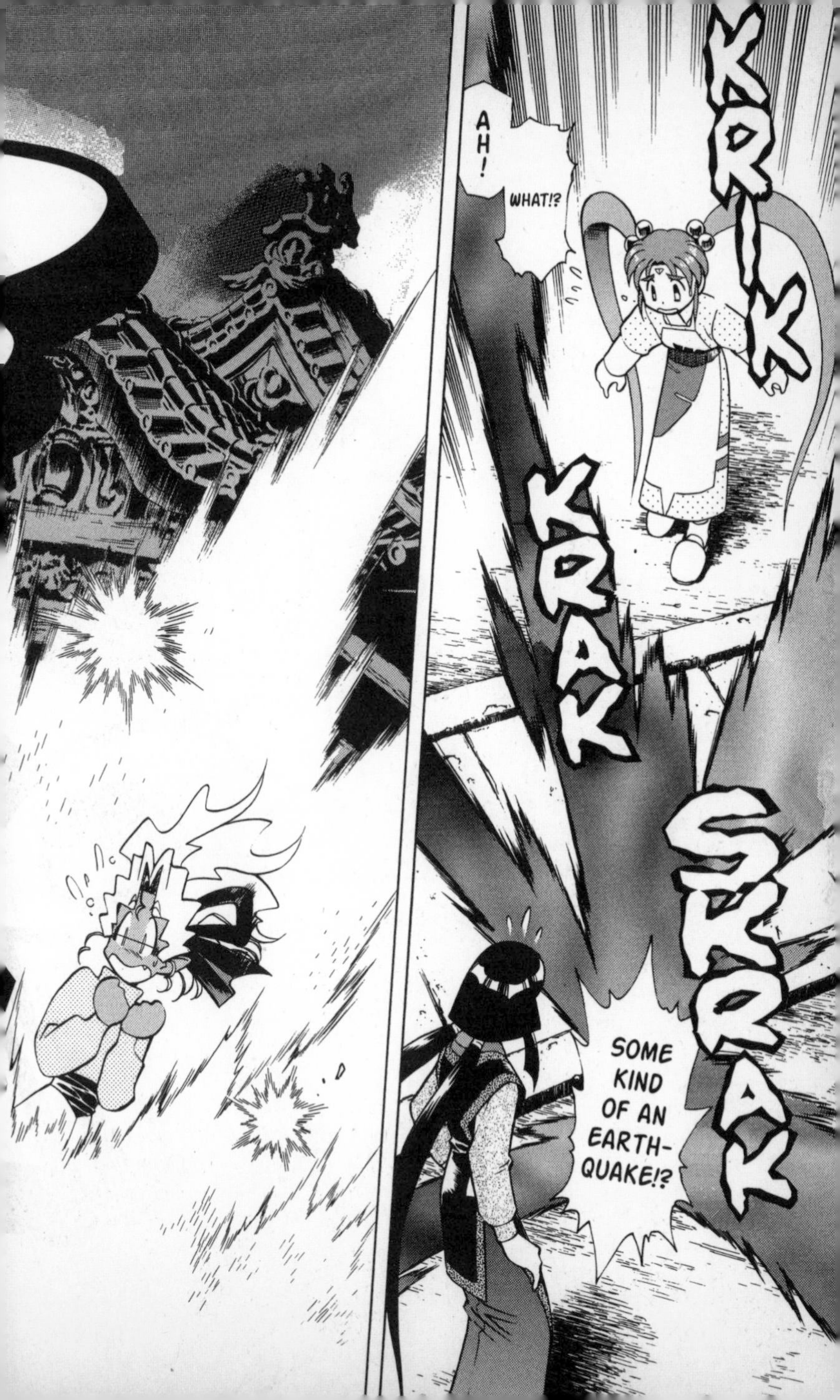
AH!
WHAT!?
KRIK
KRAK
SKRAK
SOME KIND OF AN EARTH-QUAKE!?

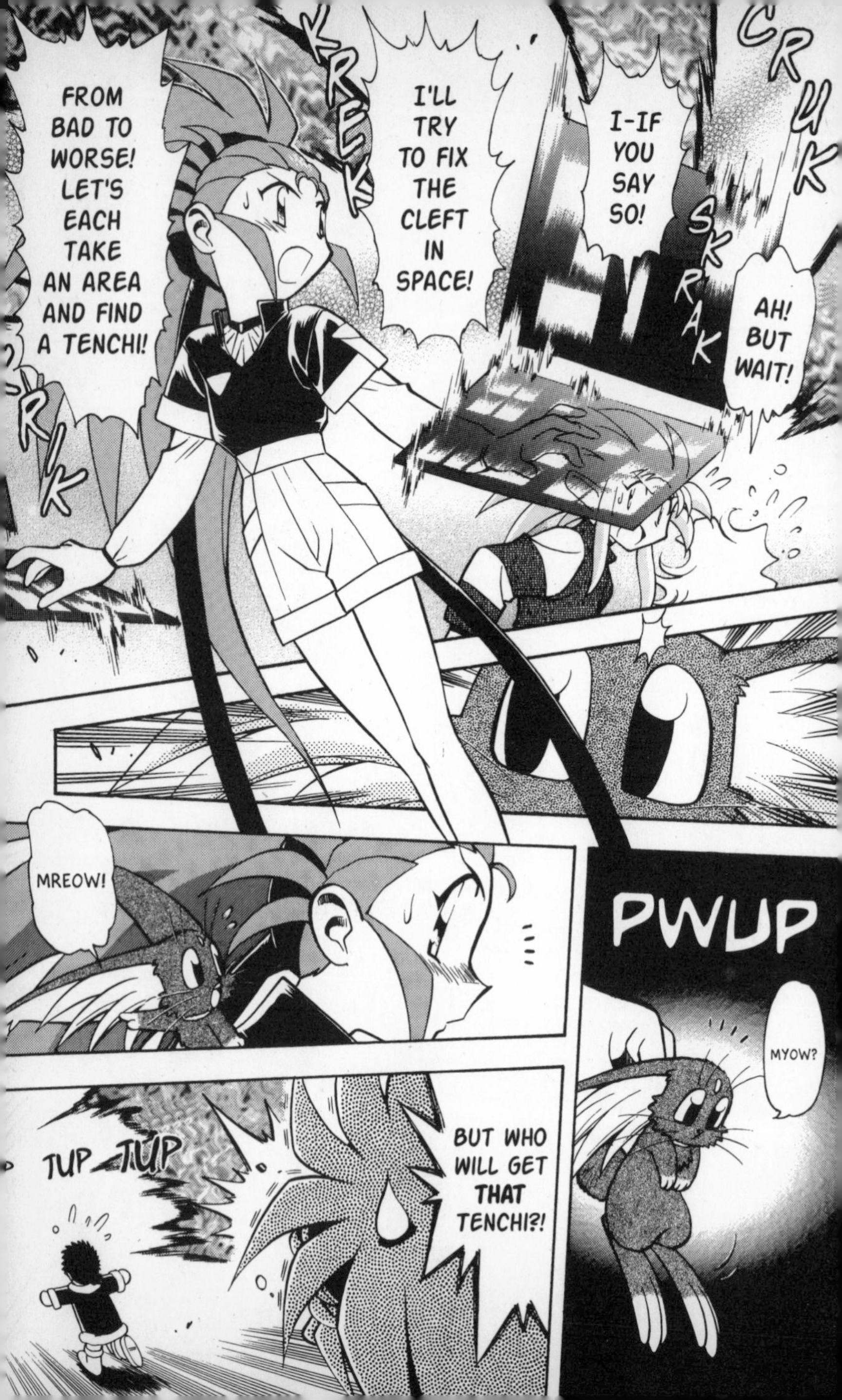
FROM BAD TO WORSE! LET'S EACH TAKE AN AREA AND FIND A TENCHI!
KREK
I'LL TRY TO FIX THE CLEFT IN SPACE!
I-IF YOU SAY SO!
CRUK
SKRAK
AH! BUT WAIT!
RIK
MREOW!
PWUP
MYOW?
TUP TUP
BUT WHO WILL GET THAT TENCHI?!

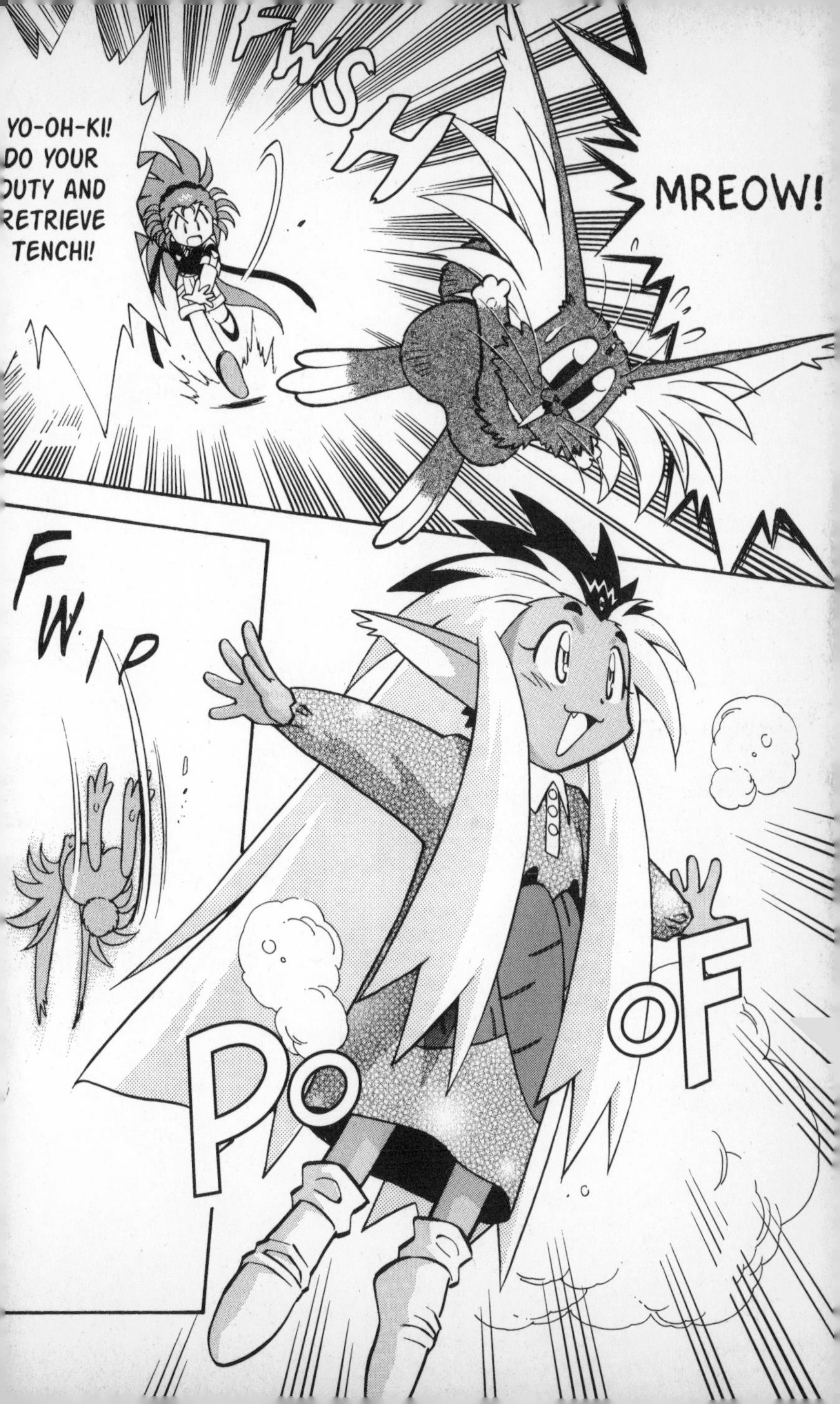

FWSH
YO-OH-KI! DO YOUR DUTY AND RETRIEVE TENCHI!
MREOW!
FWIP
POOF

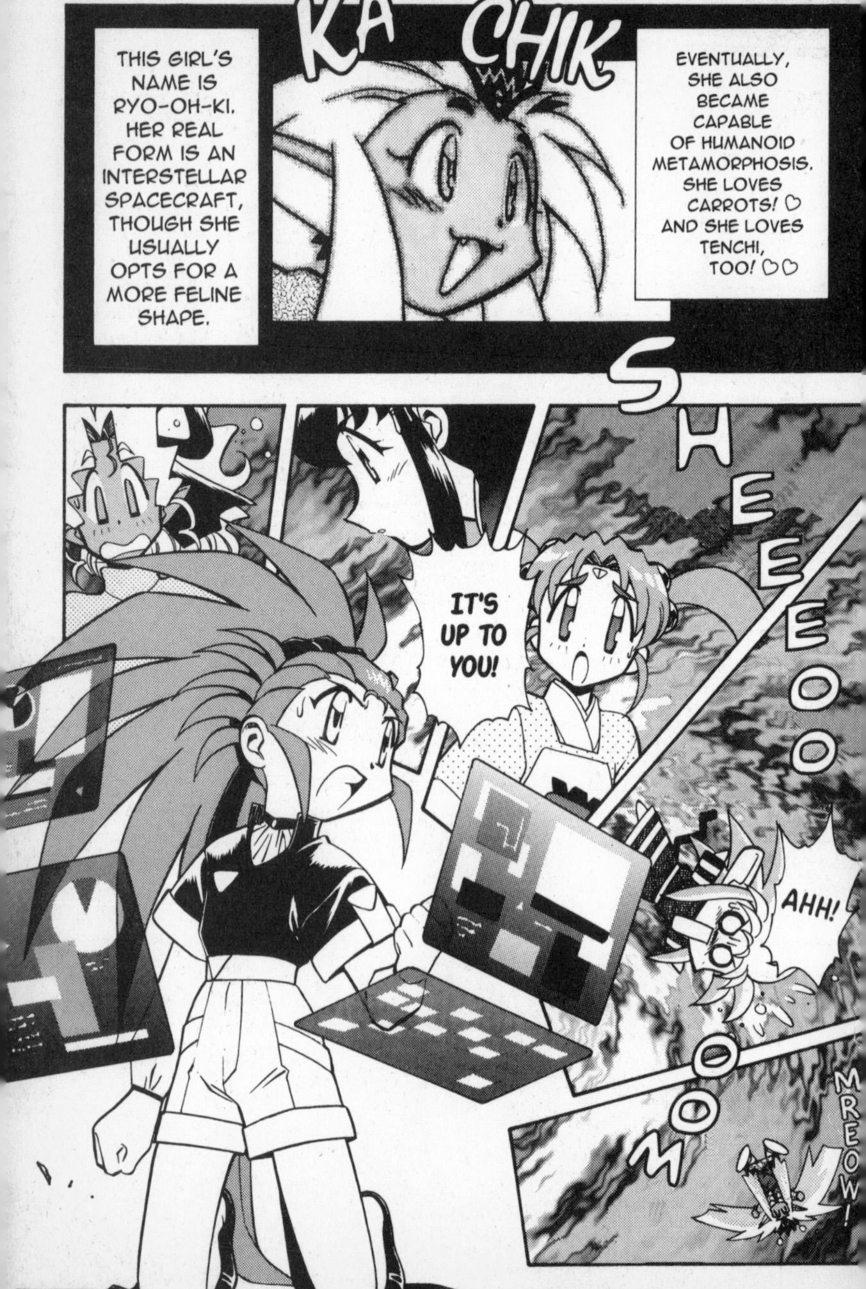

THIS GIRL'S NAME IS RYO-OH-KI. HER REAL FORM IS AN INTERSTELLAR SPACECRAFT, THOUGH SHE USUALLY OPTS FOR A MORE FELINE SHAPE.
KA CHIK
EVENTUALLY, SHE ALSO BECAME CAPABLE OF HUMANOID METAMORPHOSIS. SHE LOVES CARROTS! ♡ AND SHE LOVES TENCHI, TOO! ♡♡
IT'S UP TO YOU!
SSHEEEEOOOOOM
AHH!
MREOW!

R

RM

RMB

RMB

RMB

!?

PTERODACTYL
PTERODACTYL

WHOA!

HMMM... MUST BE THE WORLD FROM THAT DINOSAUR BOOK.

I CAN'T BELIEVE MIHOSHI DID IT TO US AGAIN!

THE WORLD OF DINOSAURS

UH-OH! I HAVE TO FIND TENCHI FAST!

TENCHI?

RRRMSH

BIRDS

BIRDS

BIRDS

AH !?

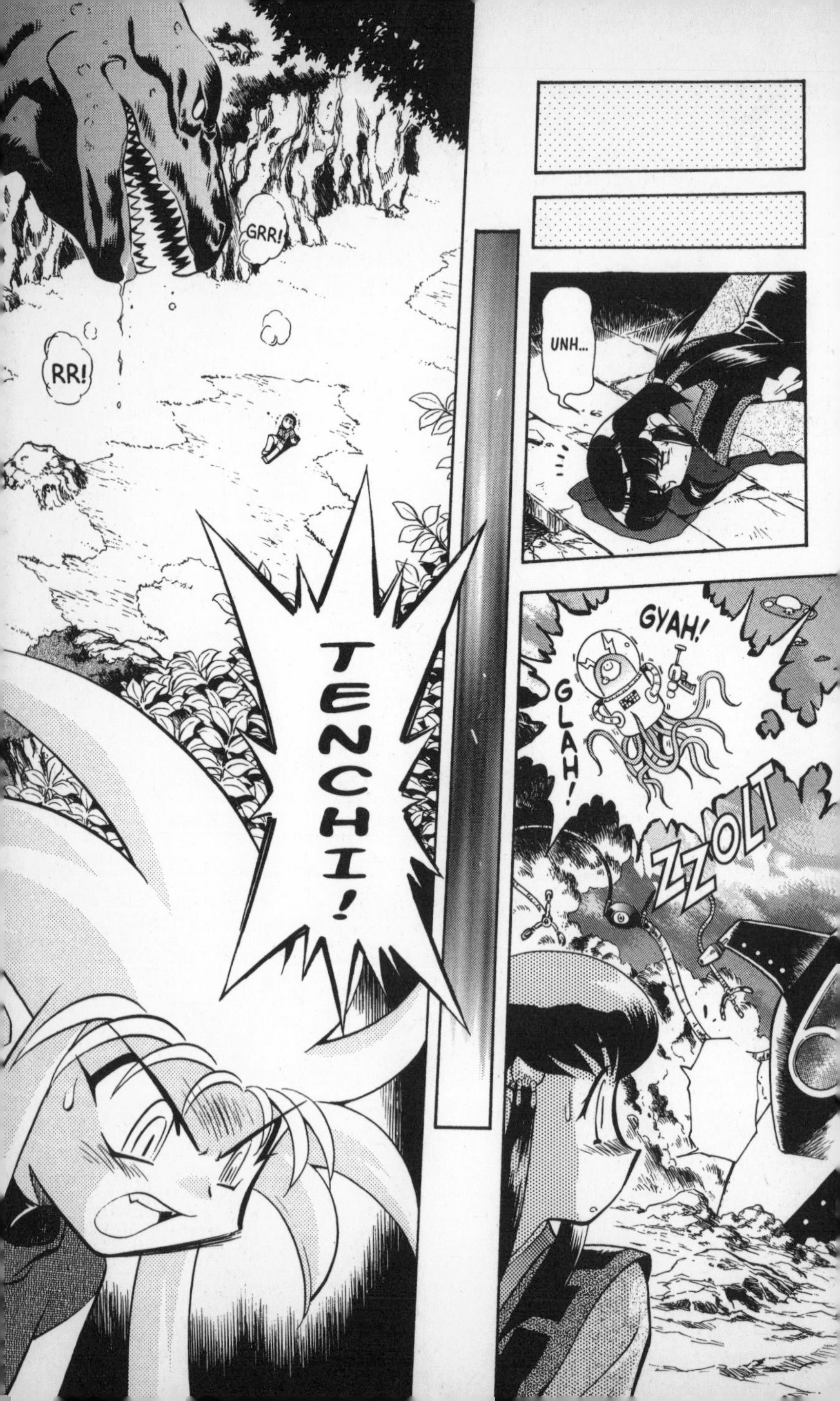
GRR!
RR!
TENCHI!
UNH...
GYAH!
GLAH!
ZZOLT

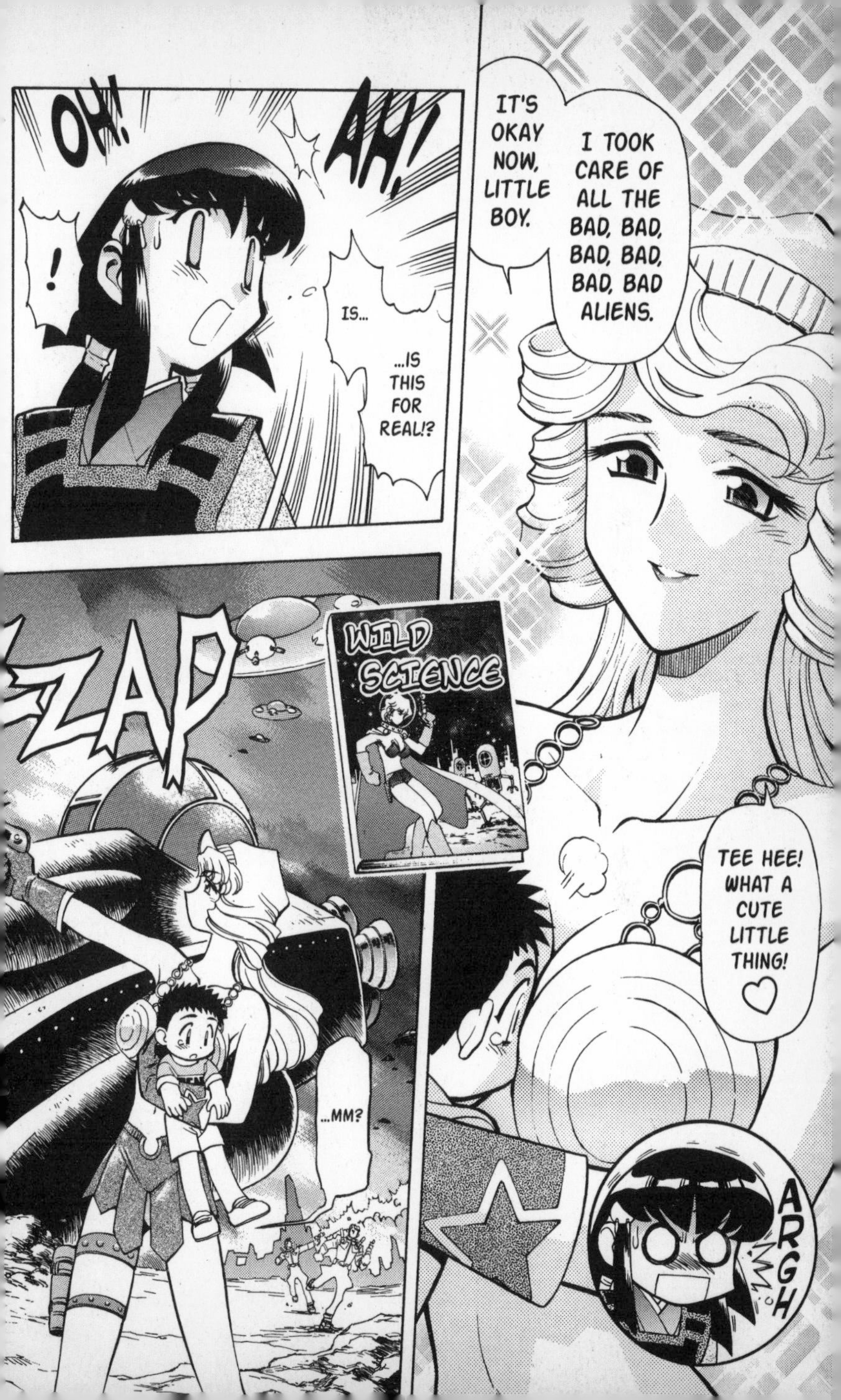
OH!
AH!
!
IS...
...IS THIS FOR REAL!?
ZAP
WILD SCIENCE
...MM?
IT'S OKAY NOW, LITTLE BOY.
I TOOK CARE OF ALL THE BAD, BAD, BAD, BAD, BAD, BAD ALIENS.
TEE HEE! WHAT A CUTE LITTLE THING! ♡
ARGH

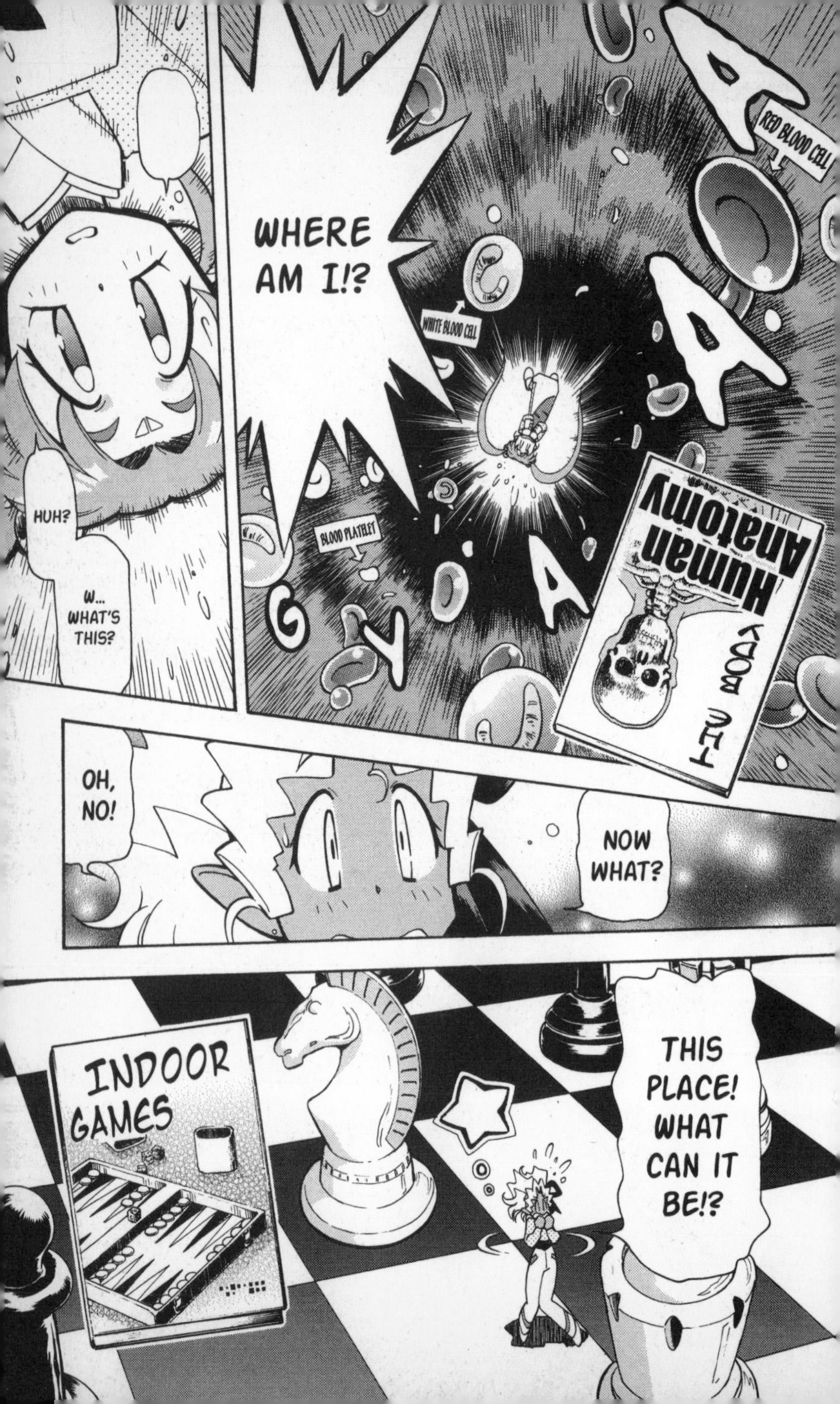
HUH?
W... WHAT'S THIS?
WHERE AM I!?
GYAAAA
RED BLOOD CELL
WHITE BLOOD CELL
BLOOD PLATELET
THE BODY
Human Anatomy
OH, NO!
NOW WHAT?
INDOOR GAMES
THIS PLACE! WHAT CAN IT BE!?

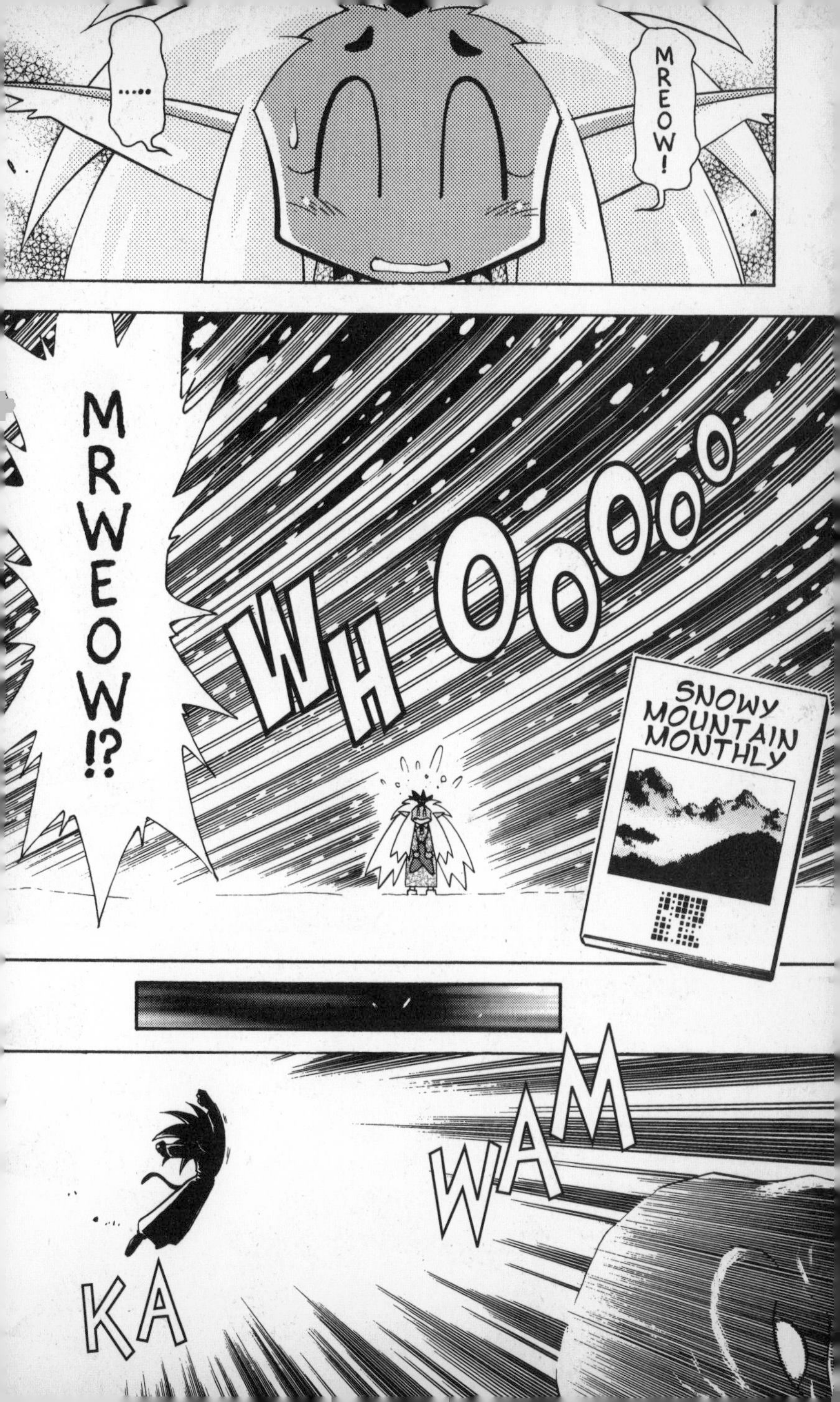
......
MREOW!
MRWEOW!?
WHOOOOOO
SNOWY MOUNTAIN MONTHLY
KA
WAM

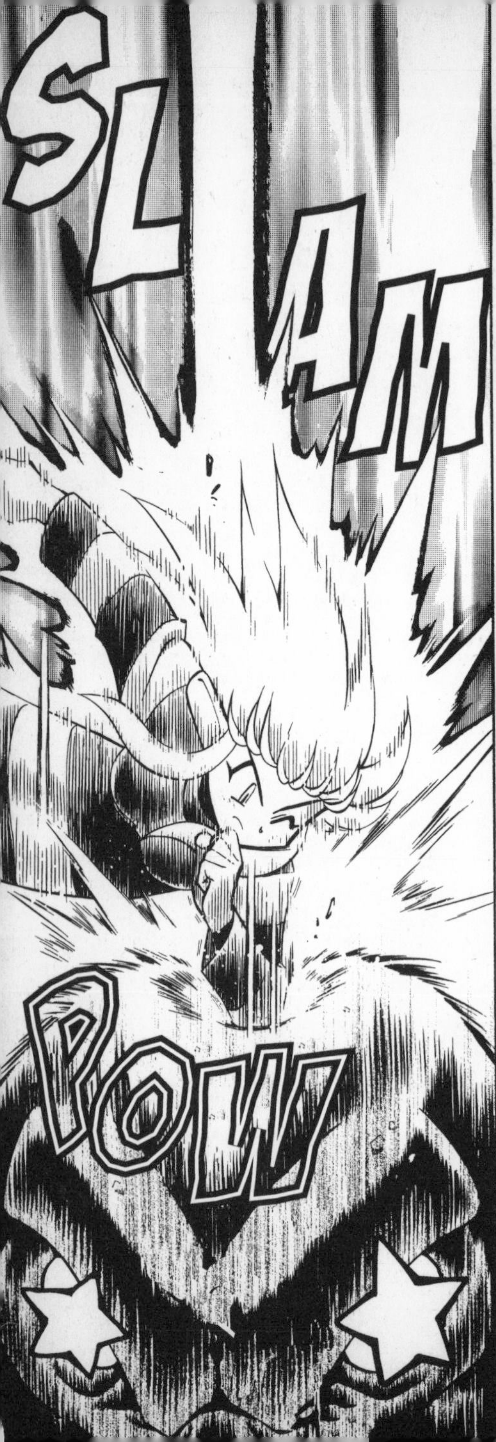
SLAM
POW
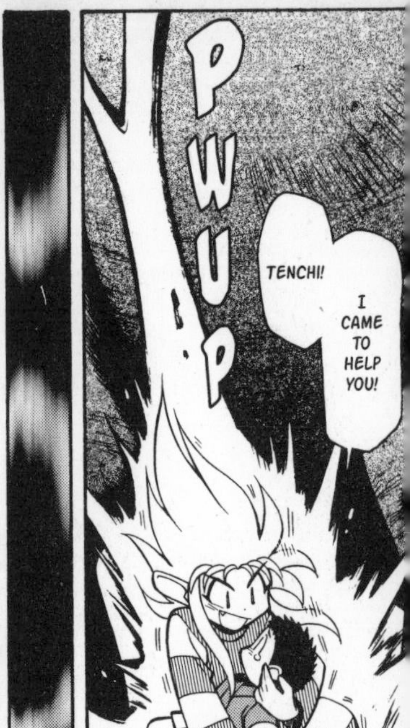
PWUP
TENCHI!
I CAME TO HELP YOU!
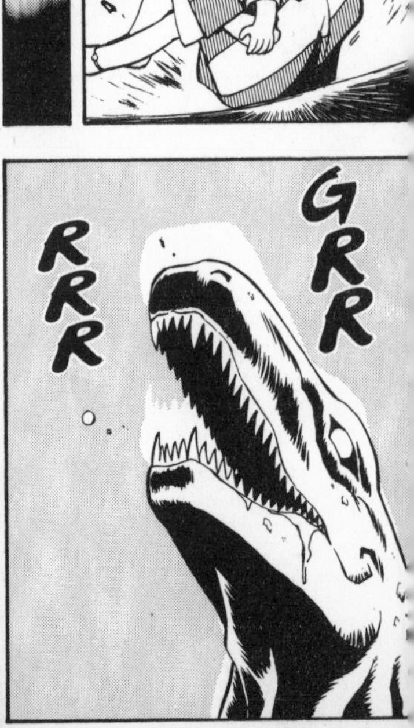
RRR
GRR

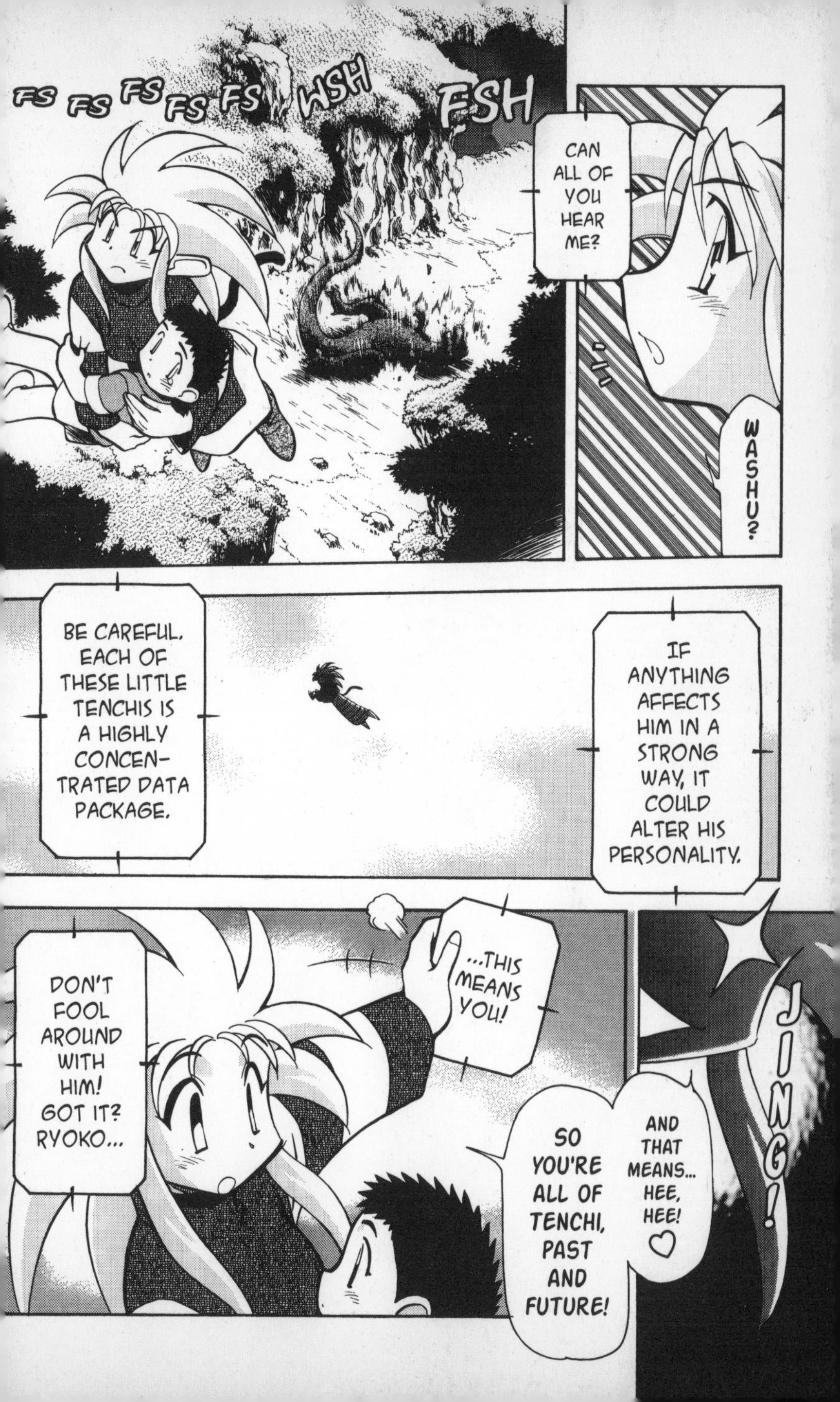

FS FS FS FS FS
WSH
FSH
CAN ALL OF YOU HEAR ME?
WASHU?
BE CAREFUL. EACH OF THESE LITTLE TENCHIS IS A HIGHLY CONCENTRATED DATA PACKAGE.
IF ANYTHING AFFECTS HIM IN A STRONG WAY, IT COULD ALTER HIS PERSONALITY.
DON'T FOOL AROUND WITH HIM! GOT IT? RYOKO...
...THIS MEANS YOU!
SO YOU'RE ALL OF TENCHI, PAST AND FUTURE!
AND THAT MEANS... HEE, HEE! ♡
JING!

PWOP

HOW ABOUT **THAT**, TENCHI? RYOKO SAVED YOU! DID YOU SEE?

TIME TO TRAIN HIM! ♡

YES!

YOU GET IT, HUH?

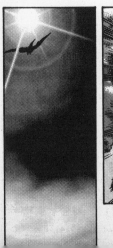

HEY! WHAT'S WRONG NOW?

WAP

?

KIK

IT'S FINE! HOLD STILL! BE GOOD!

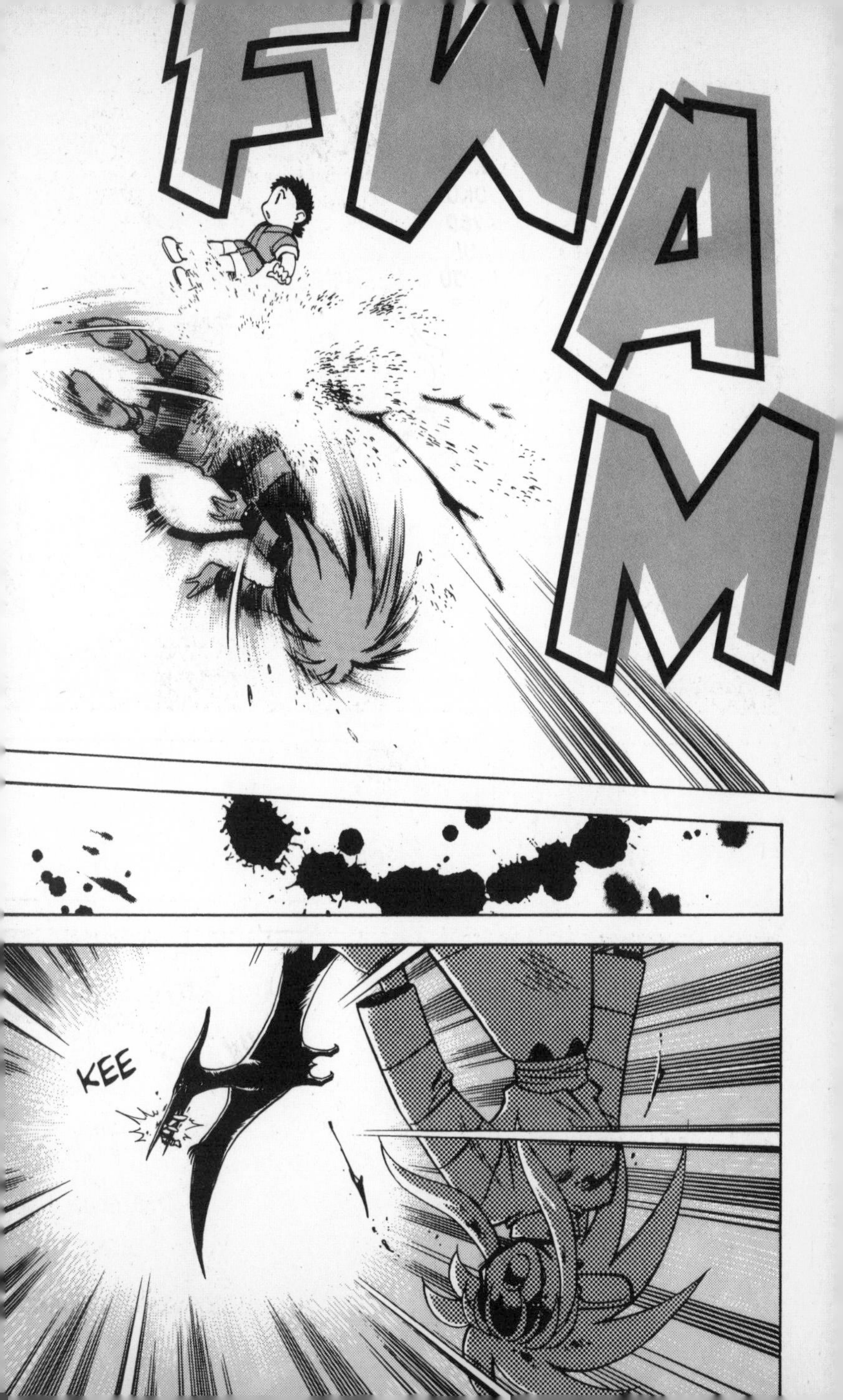
FWAM
KEE

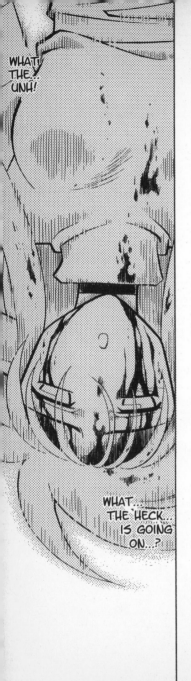

WHAT
THE...
UNH!

WHAT...
THE HECK...
IS GOING
ON...?

HEY,
TENCHI'S
GOING TO
SUFFO-
CATE!

UM...
ARE
YOU
OKAY?

HAND
HIM
OVER!

FAP

THANKS.
NO DANGER
OF SUFFO-
CATION IF
HE'S WITH
YOU! ♥

JIGGA

GRRR

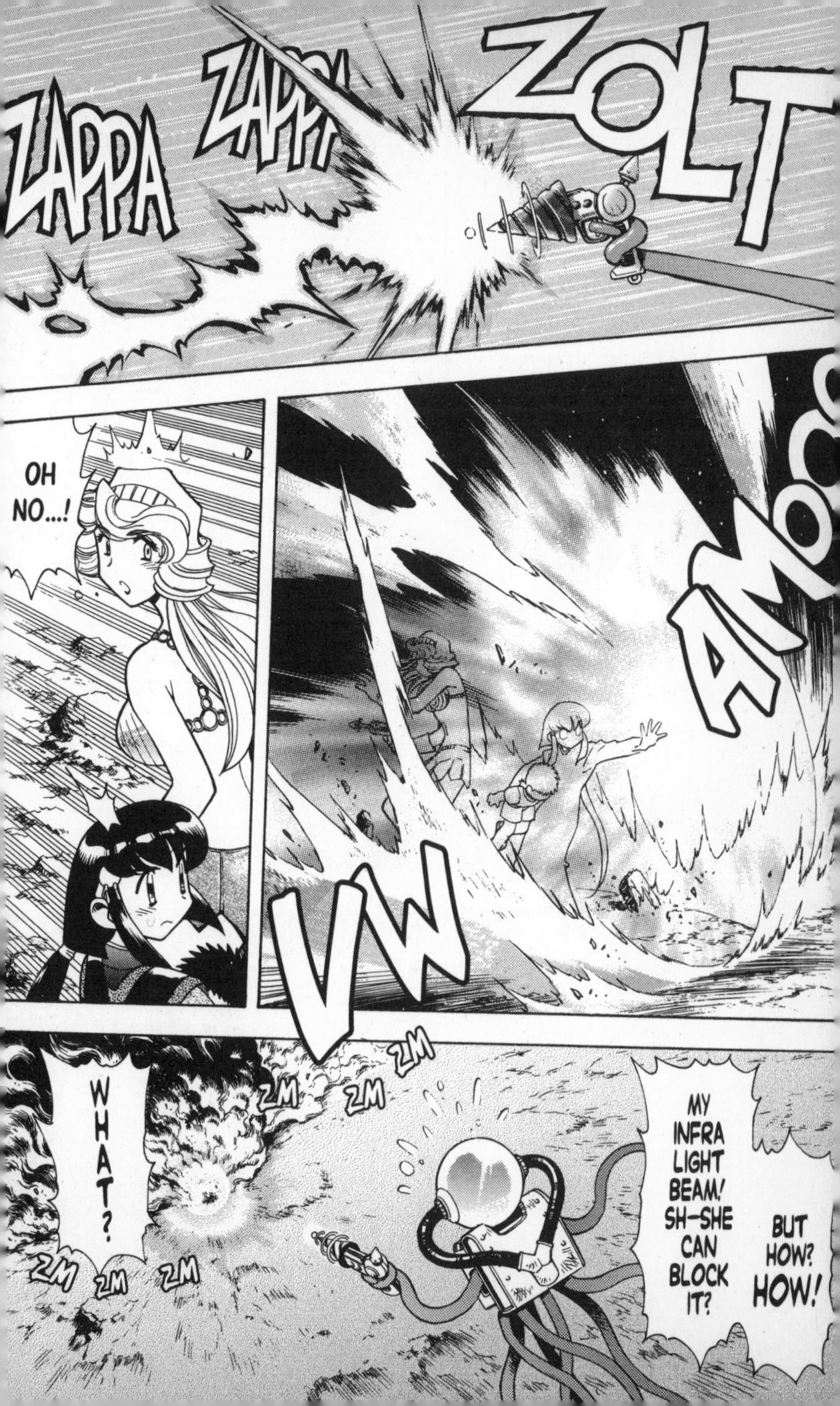
ZAPPA
ZAPPA
ZOLT
OH NO...!
AMOO
VW
ZM ZM ZM
WHAT?
ZM ZM ZM
MY INFRA LIGHT BEAM! SH-SHE CAN BLOCK IT?
BUT HOW? HOW!

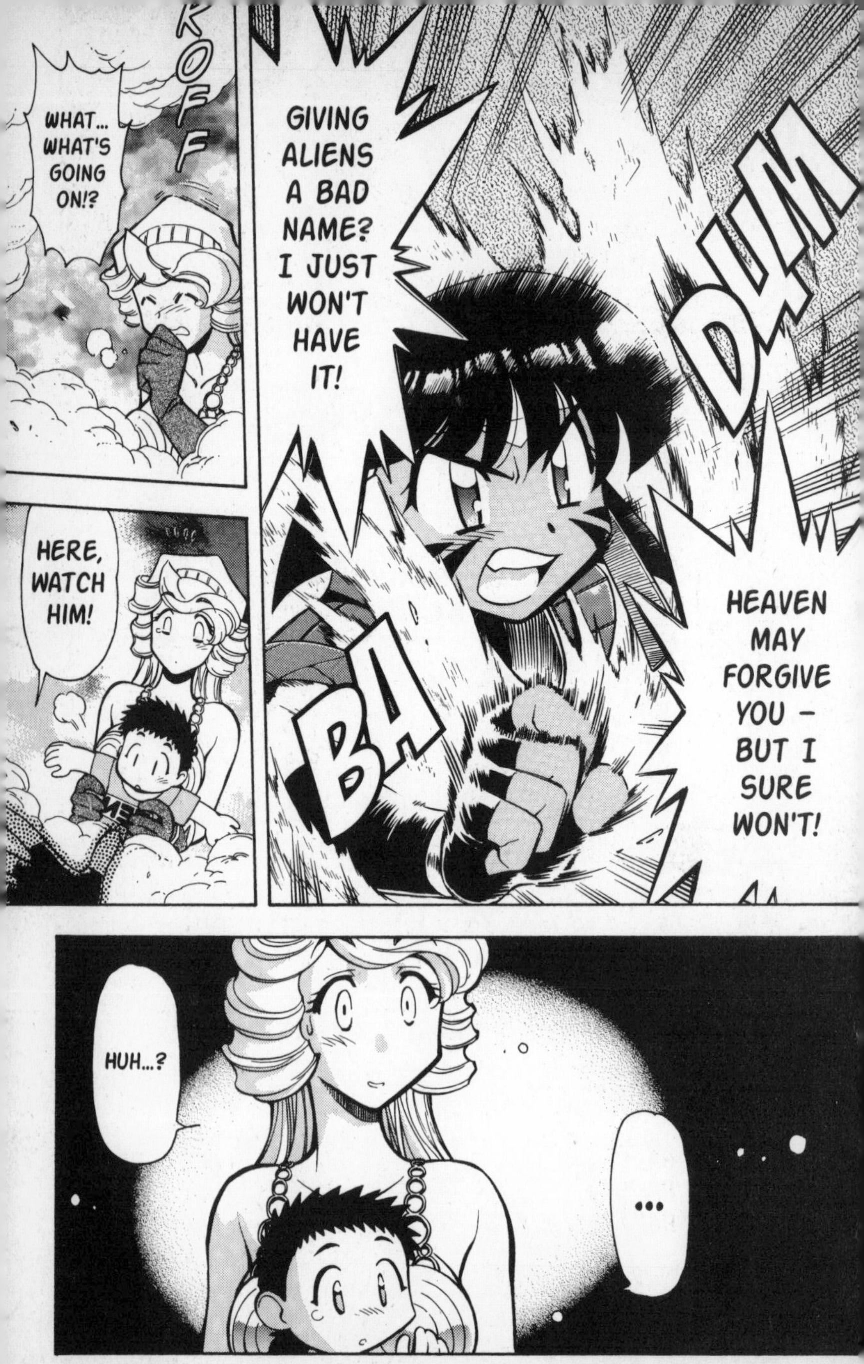
KOFF
WHAT... WHAT'S GOING ON!?
HERE, WATCH HIM!
GIVING ALIENS A BAD NAME? I JUST WON'T HAVE IT!
DUM
BA
HEAVEN MAY FORGIVE YOU – BUT I SURE WON'T!
HUH...?
...

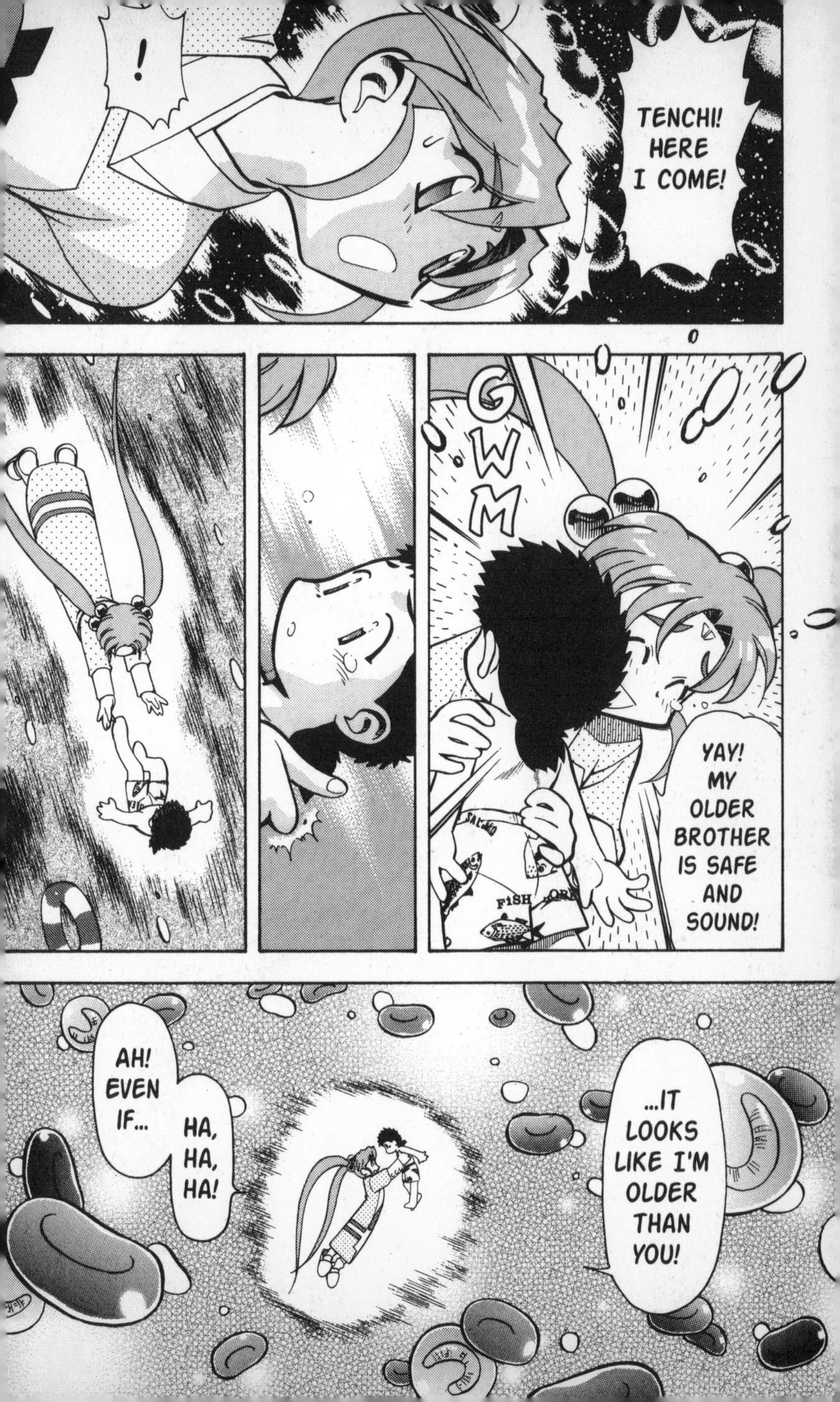
!
TENCHI! HERE I COME!
GWM
YAY! MY OLDER BROTHER IS SAFE AND SOUND!
FISH
AH! EVEN IF...
HA, HA, HA!
...IT LOOKS LIKE I'M OLDER THAN YOU!

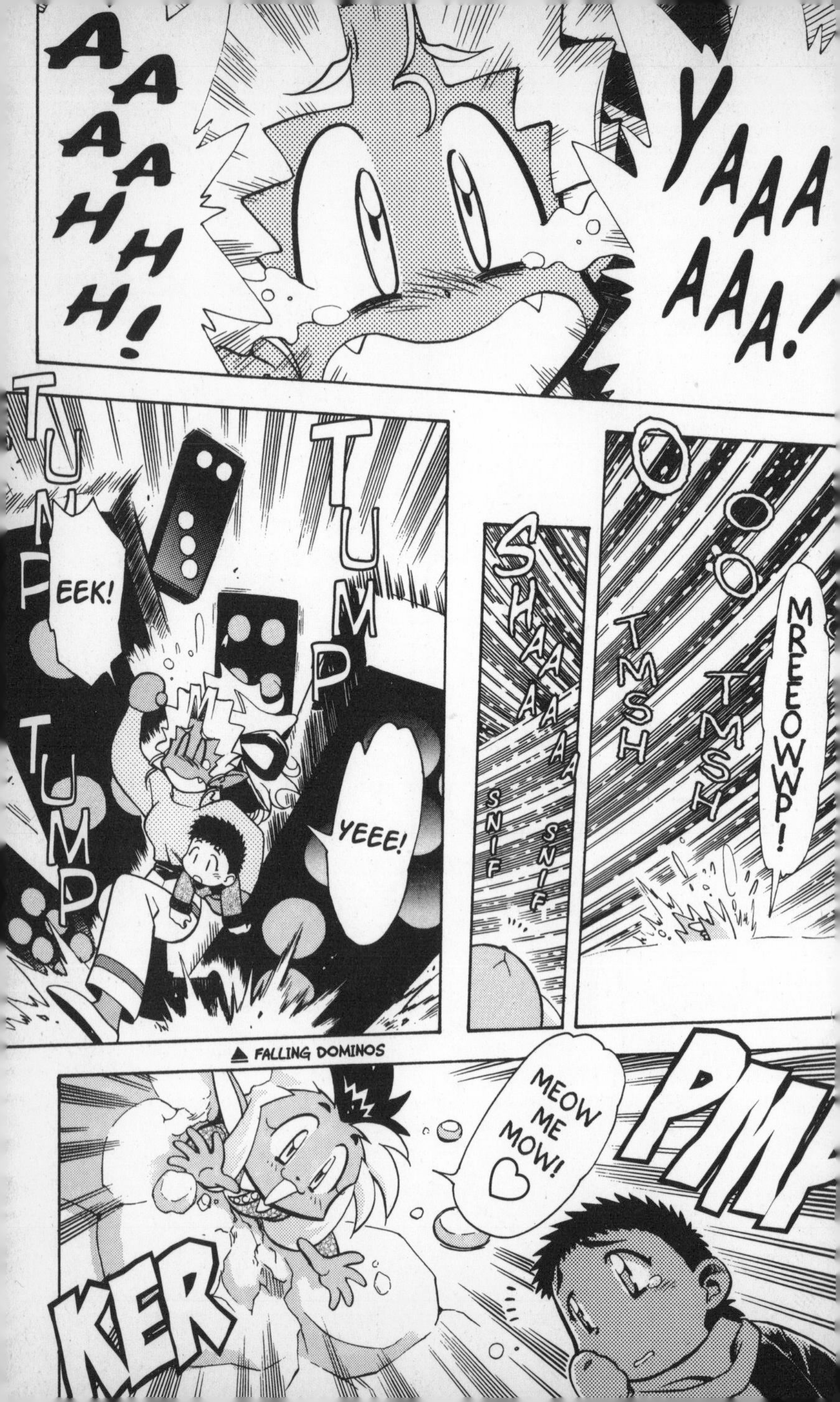
AAAAHHHH!
YAAAAAAA!
TUMP
EEK!
TUMP
TUMP
YEEE!
SHAAAAAA
SNIF SNIF
OOO
TMSH TMSH
MREEOWWP!
▲ FALLING DOMINOS
MEOW ME MOW! ♥
PM
KER

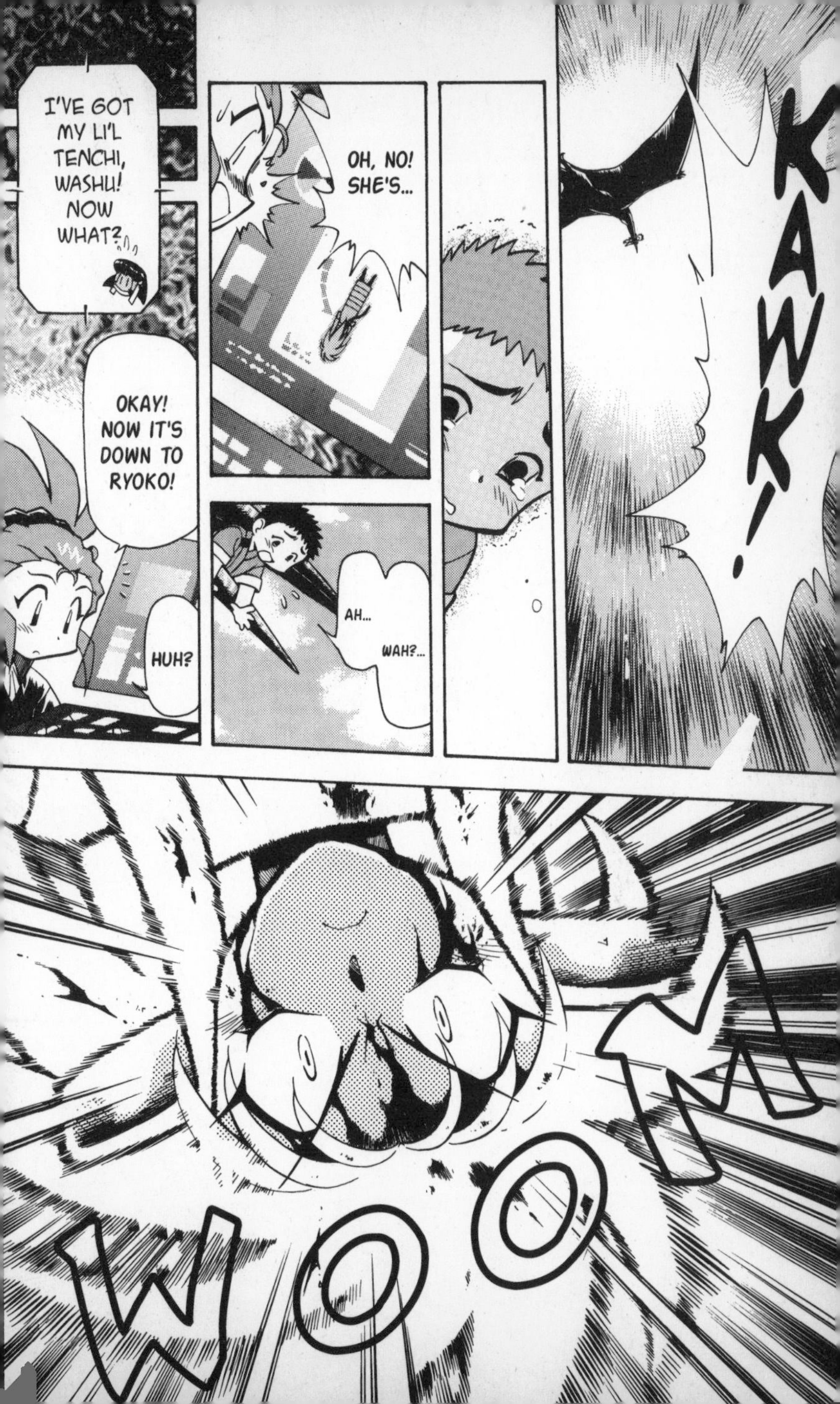
I'VE GOT MY LI'L TENCHI, WASHU! NOW WHAT?
OKAY! NOW IT'S DOWN TO RYOKO!
HUH?
OH, NO! SHE'S...
AH...
WAH?...
KAWK!
WOOOM

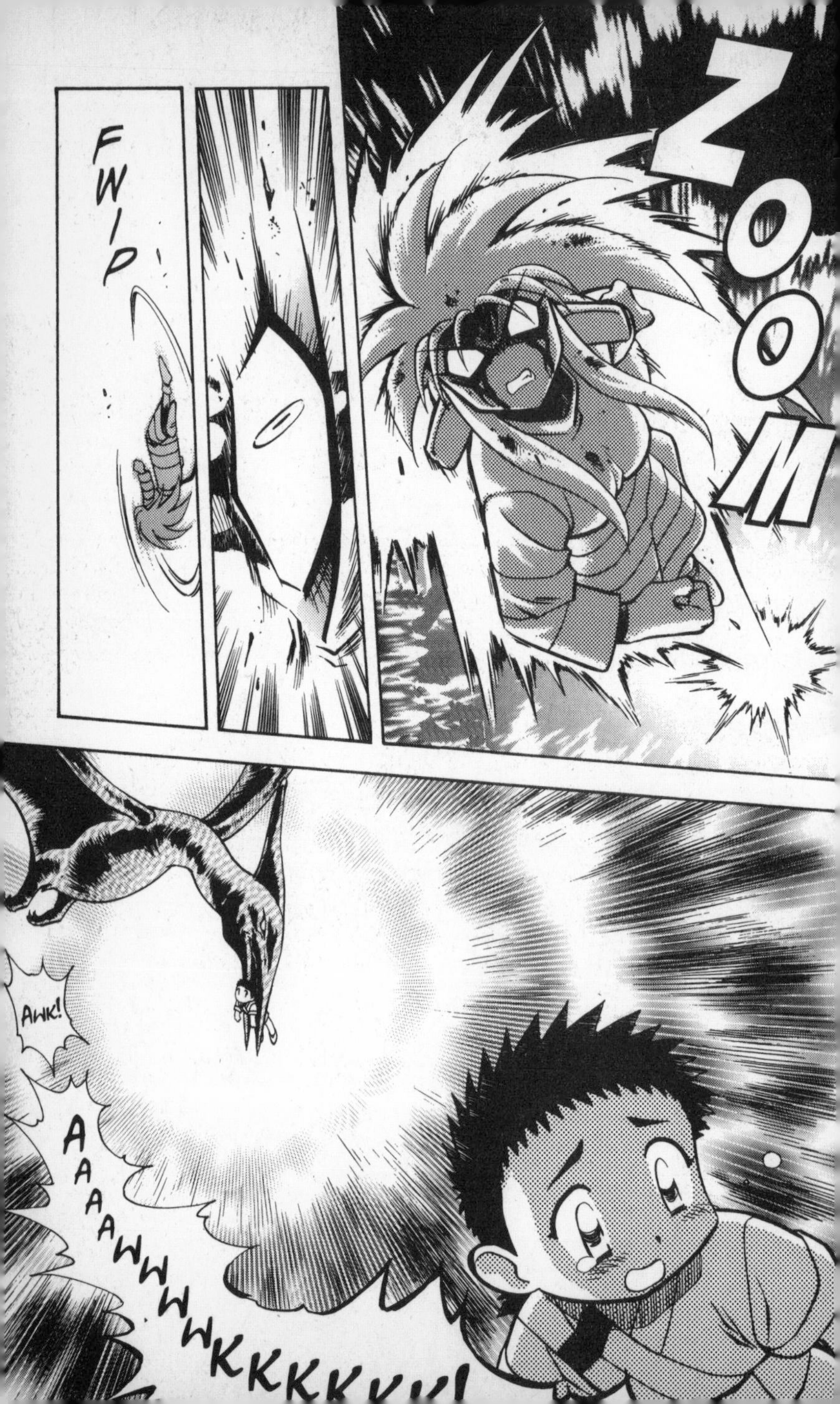

FWIP
ZOOM
AWK!
AAAAWWWWKKKKKK!!

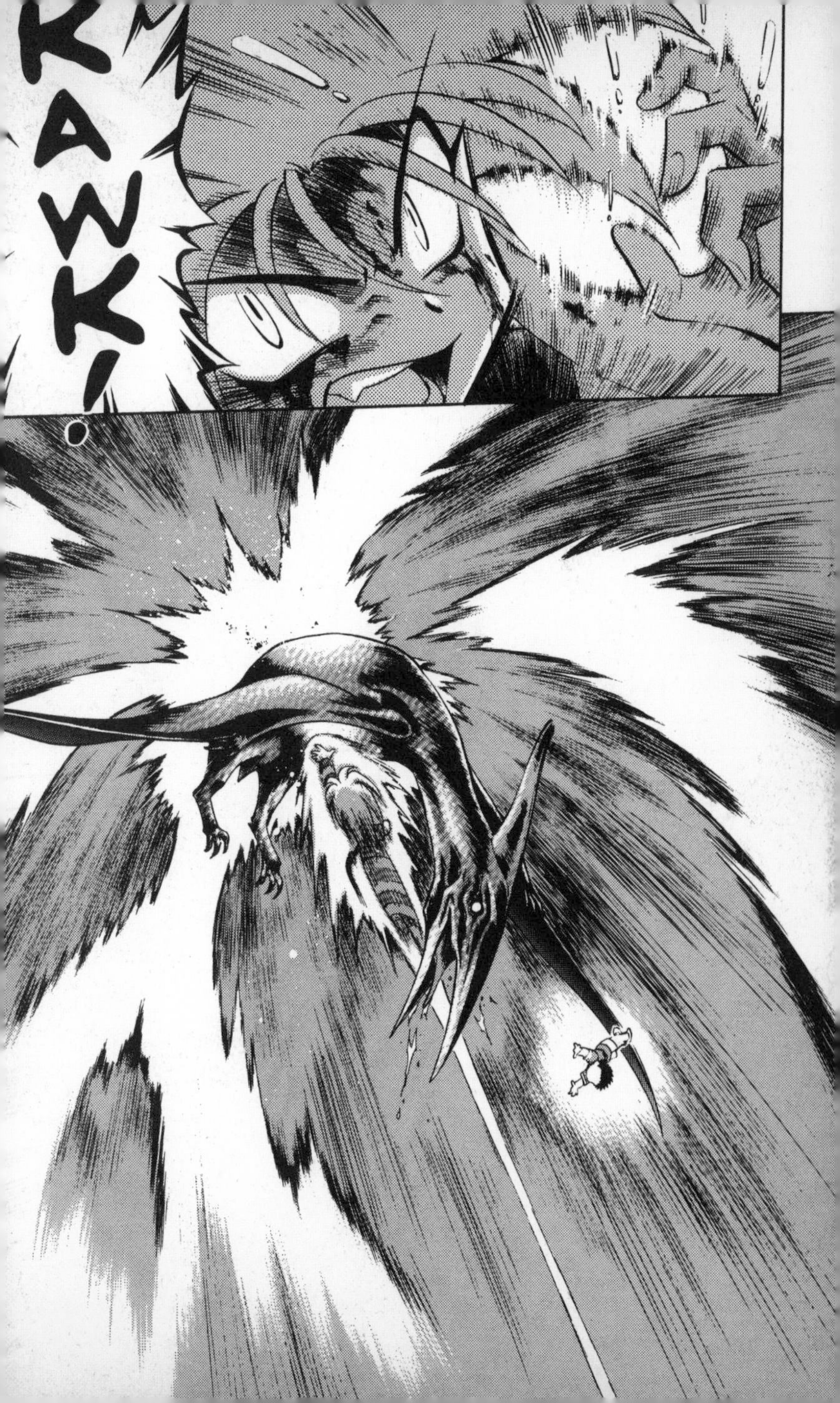
KAWK!

WUMP

KA

KEE

EEE

TAKE THIS!
I WON'T LET
YOU HURT
TENCHI!

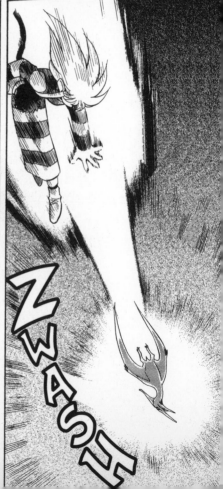

ZWASH

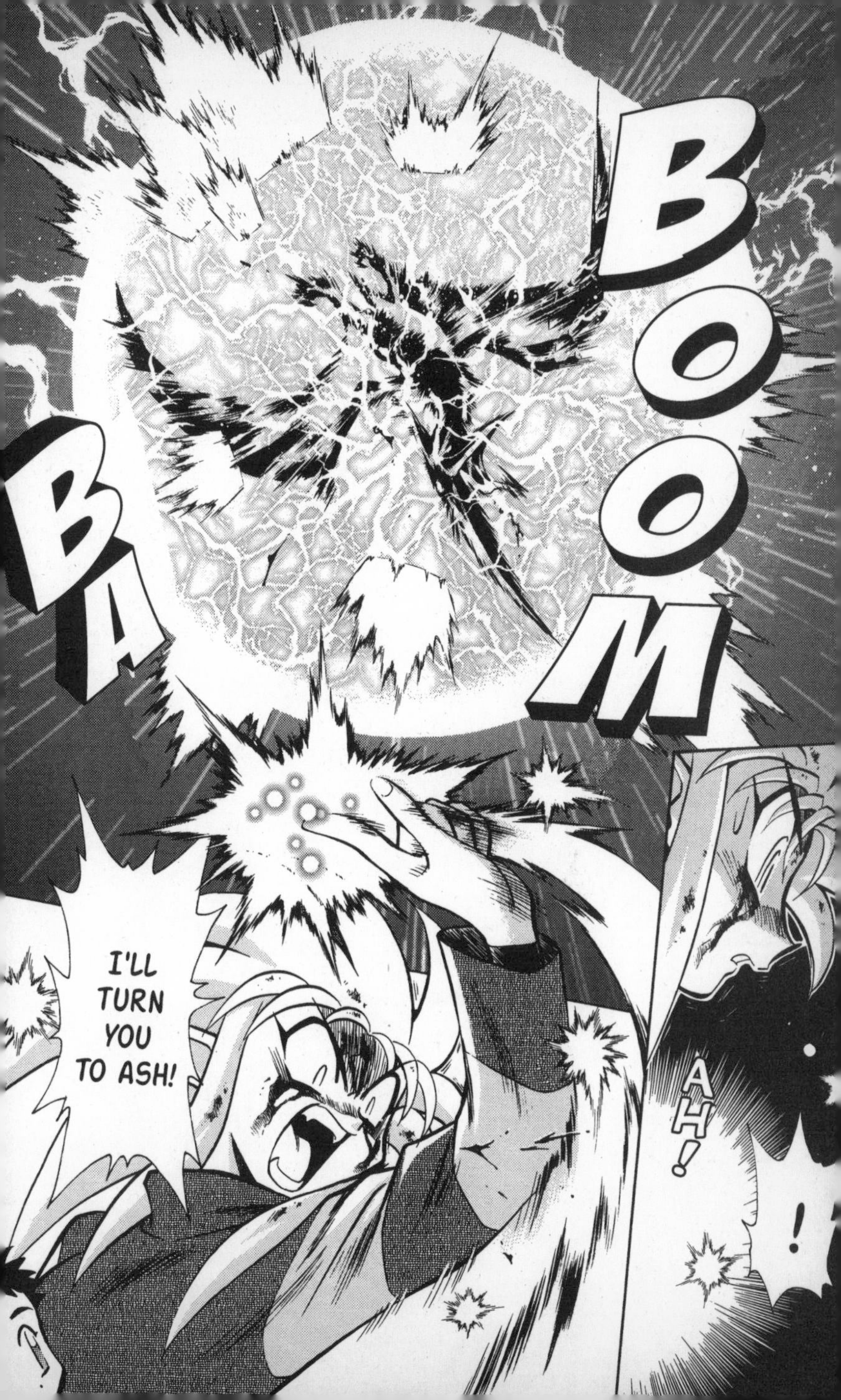
BA
BOOM
I'LL TURN YOU TO ASH!
AH!
!

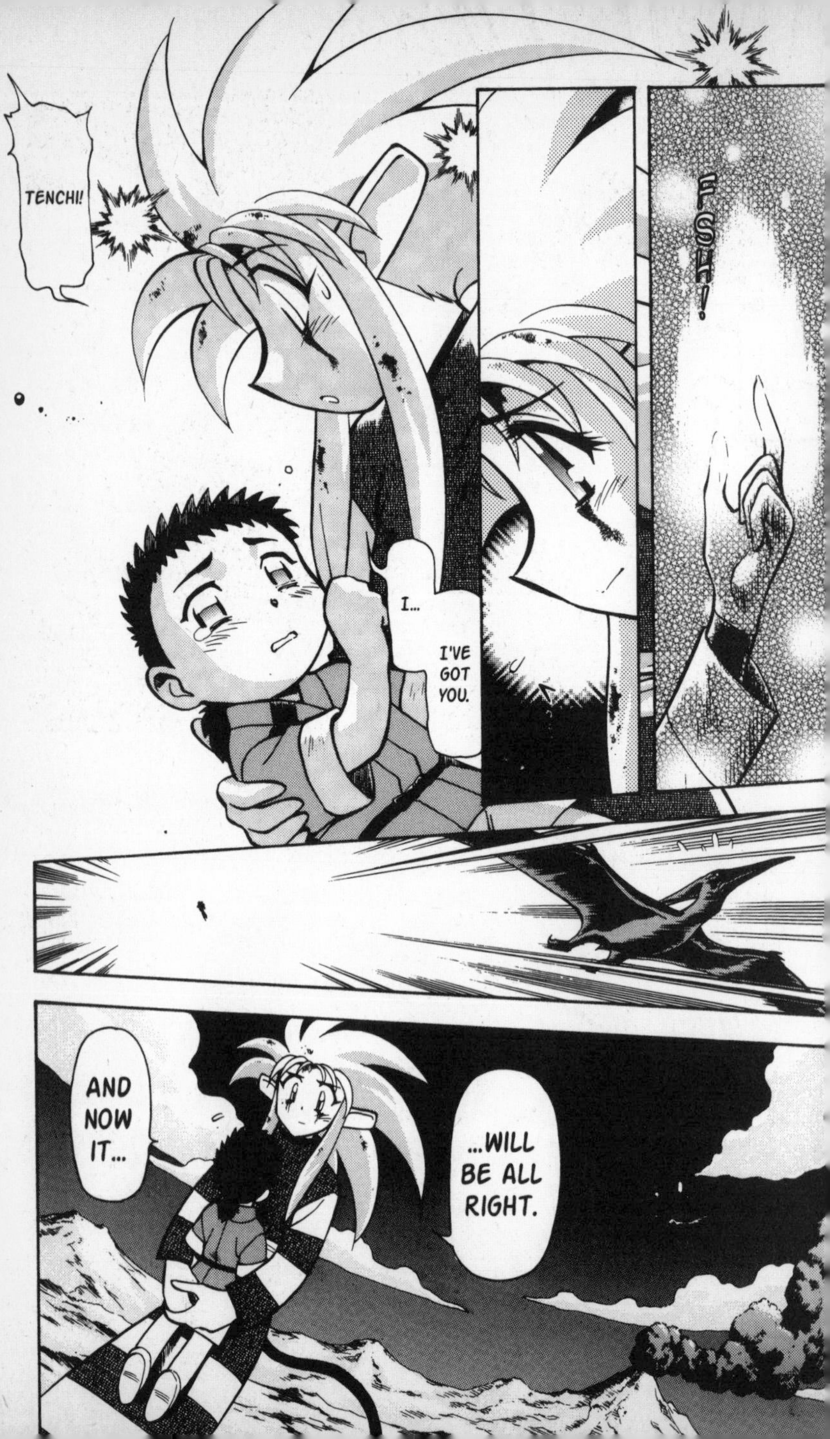
TENCHI!
I...
I'VE GOT YOU.
FSH!
AND NOW IT...
...WILL BE ALL RIGHT.

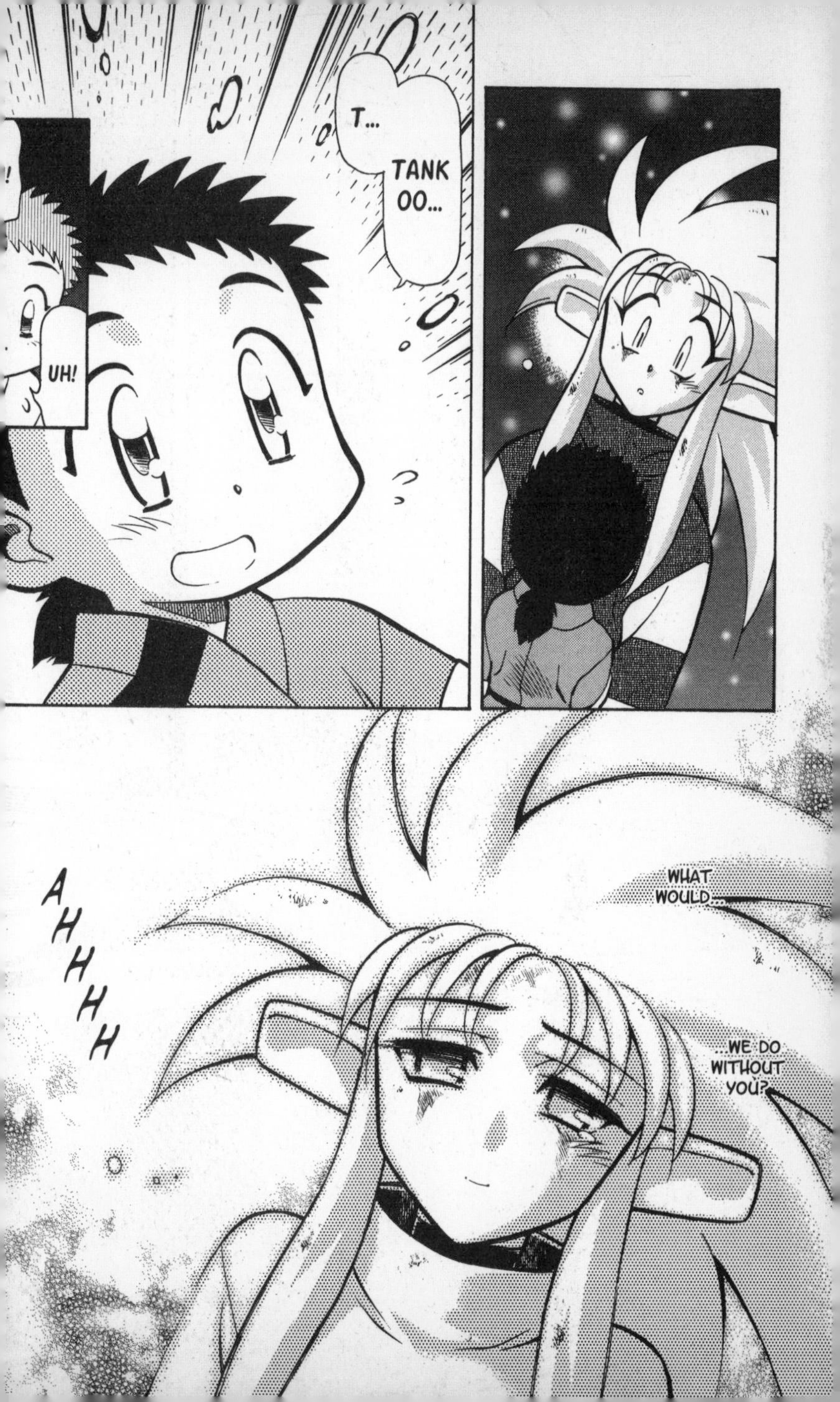
UH!
T... TANK OO...
AHHHH
WHAT WOULD...
...WE DO WITHOUT YOU?

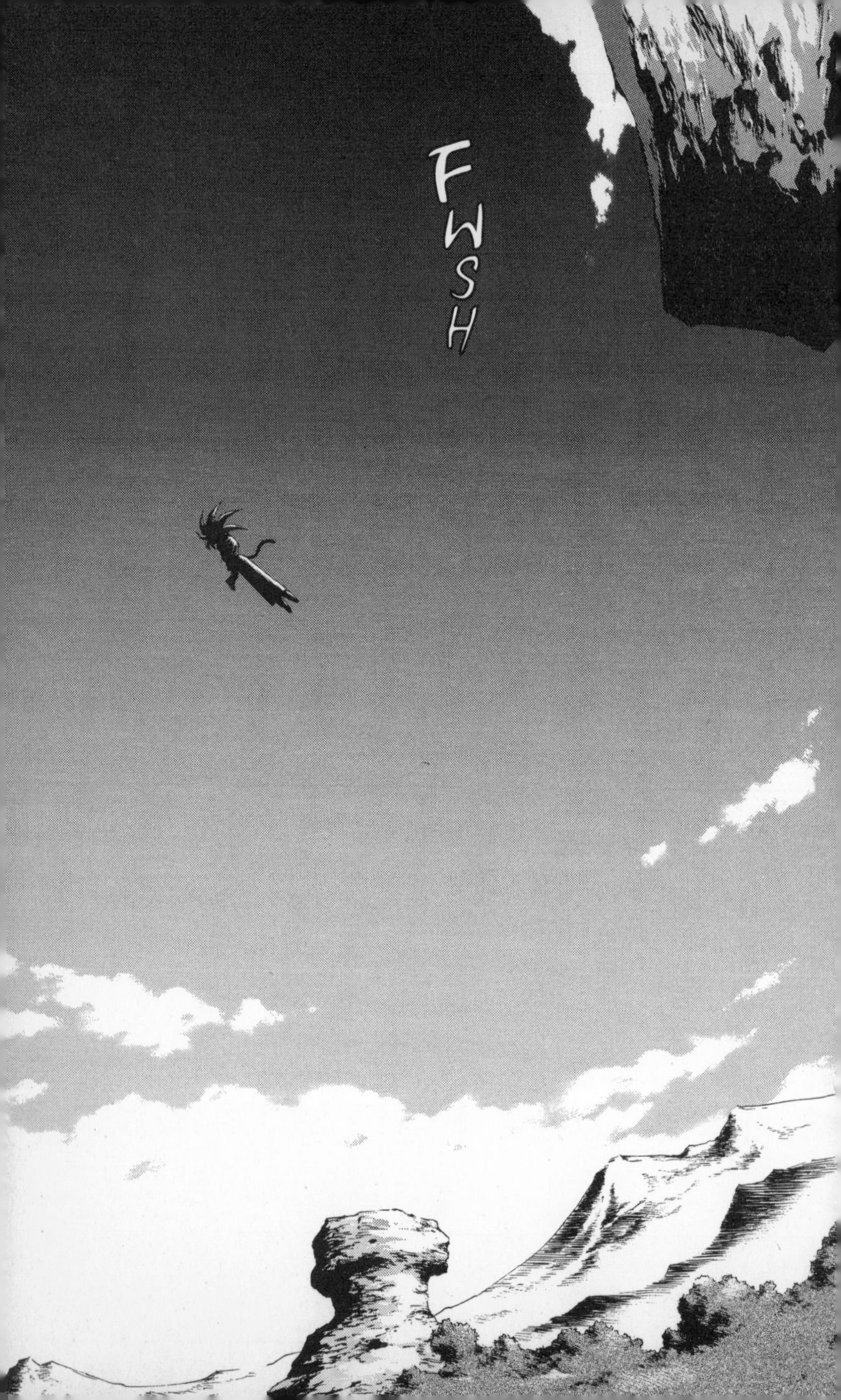
FWSH

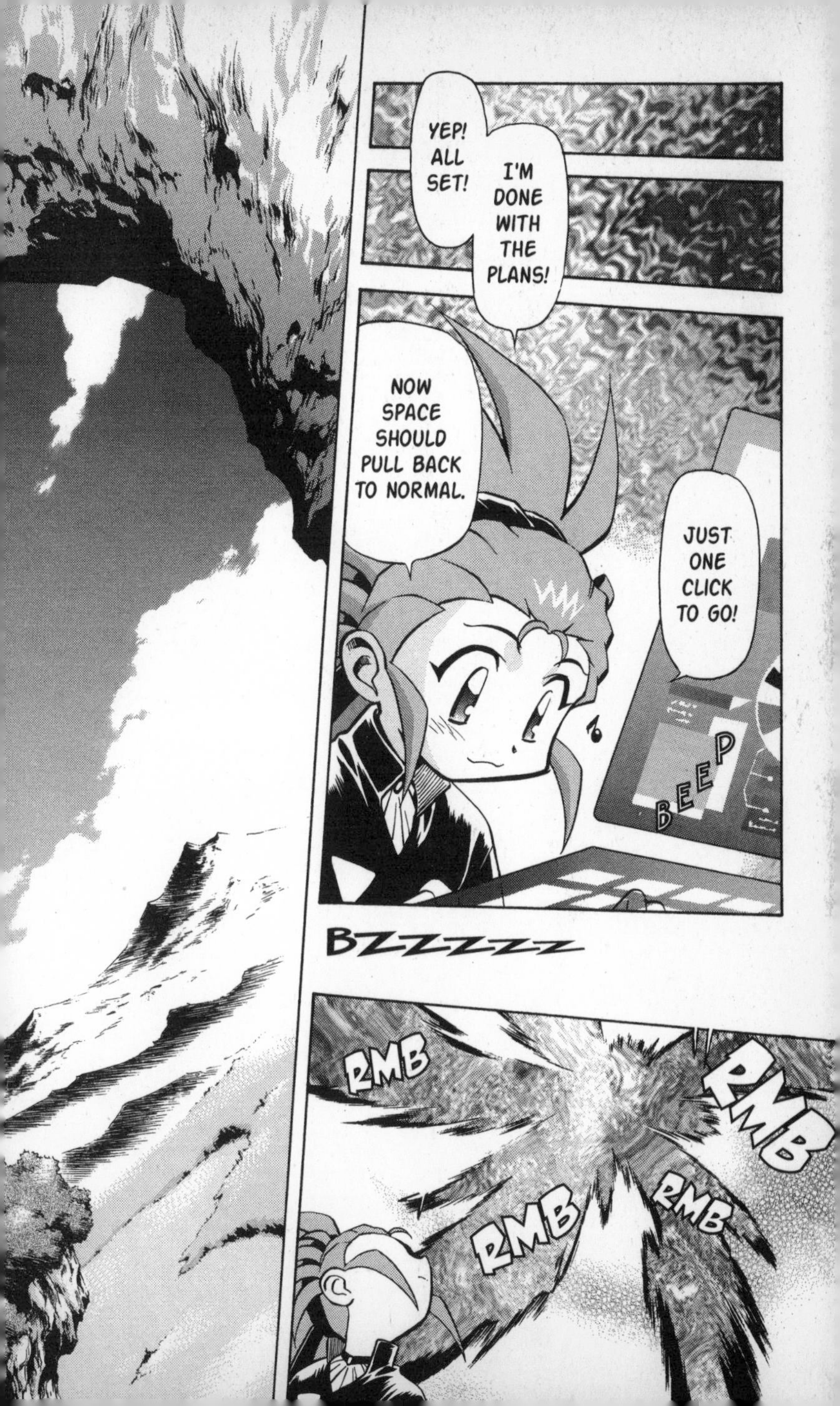
YEP! ALL SET!
I'M DONE WITH THE PLANS!
NOW SPACE SHOULD PULL BACK TO NORMAL.
JUST ONE CLICK TO GO!
BEEP
BZZZZZZ
RMB
RMB
RMB
RMB
RMB

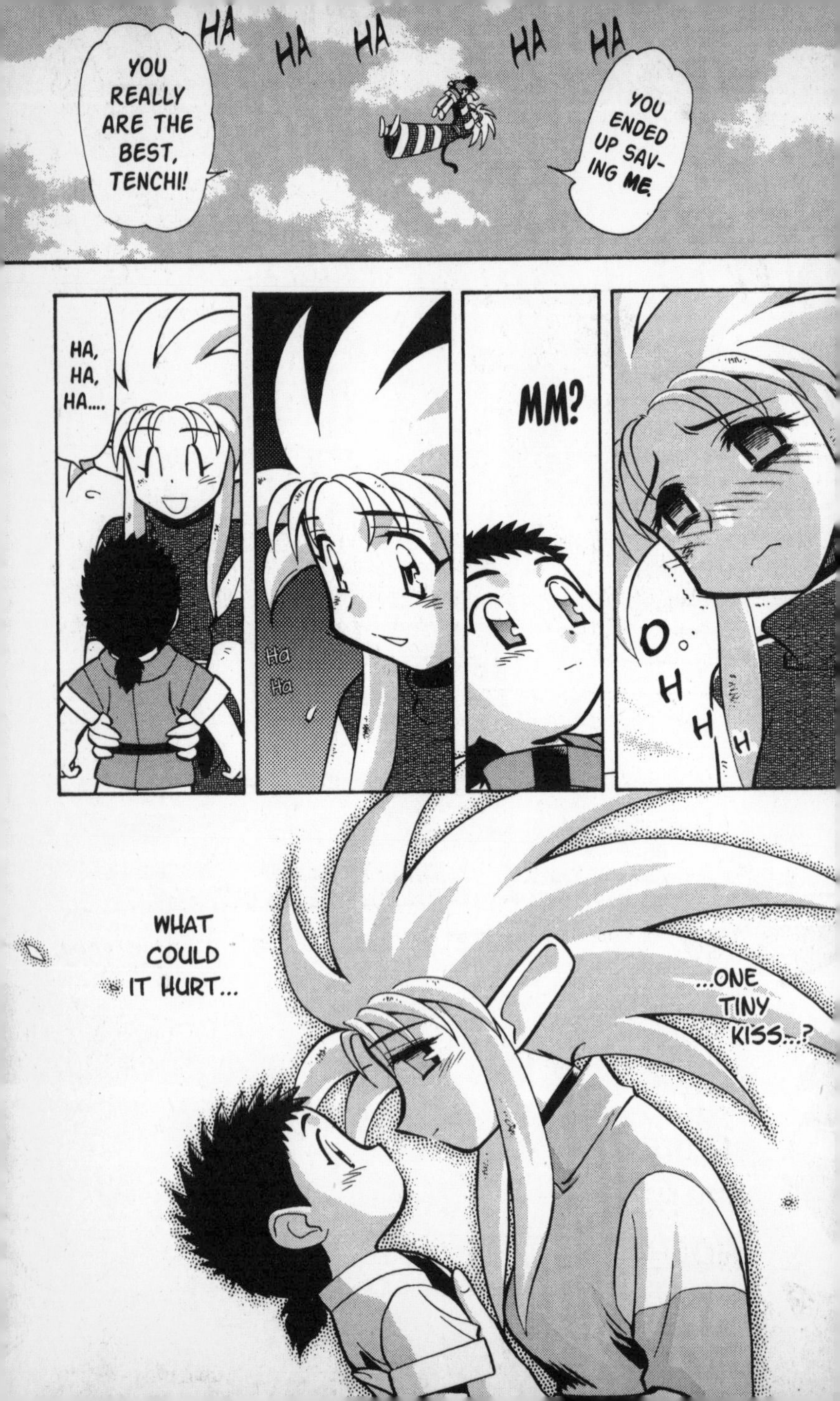
YOU REALLY ARE THE BEST, TENCHI!
HA HA HA HA HA
YOU ENDED UP SAV-ING ME.
HA, HA, HA....
Ha Ha
MM?
O O H H H H
WHAT COULD IT HURT...
...ONE TINY KISS...?

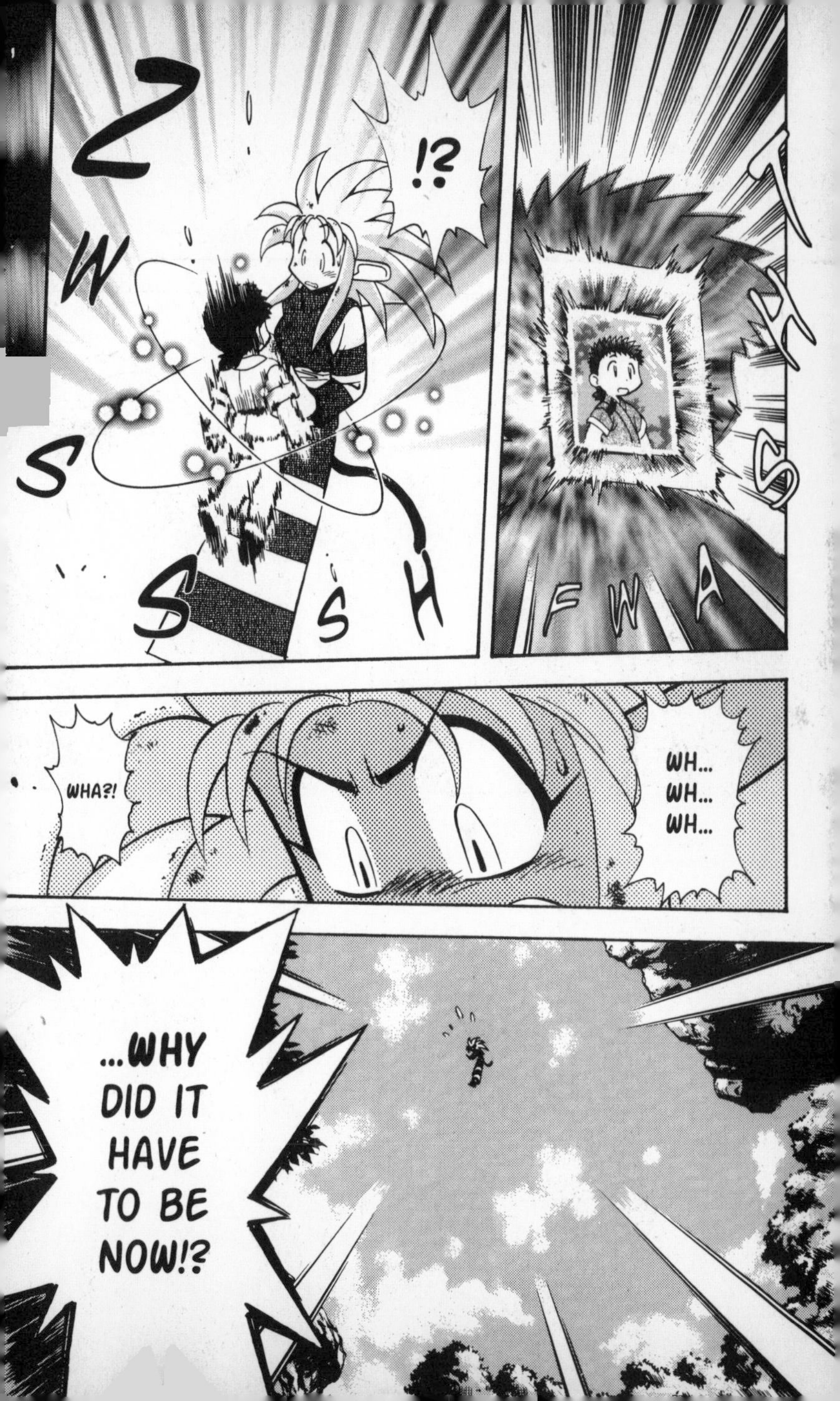
!?
WHA?!
WH... WH... WH...
...WHY DID IT HAVE TO BE NOW!?

YOU ALL DID A GOOD JOB! EVERYTHING WILL BE BACK TO NORMAL SOON...

BUT WASHU...

...TENCHI TURNED INTO A PHOTOGRAPH!

THAT'S FINE. I TOLD YOU THE DATA FROM THE PHOTOS WAS LINKED TO HIM, DIDN'T I?

FIRST EACH TENCHI IS CONDENSED, THEN ALL OF THEM WILL BE FUSED. AFTER THAT, WE'LL THAW HIM OUT.

SO GET THE DATA BACK HERE SAFELY!

YOU GOT IT?

DRAT!

I WAS SO CLOSE! SO VERY...

YOU'RE SAYING THERE'S NO TIME LEFT, EH, WASHU?

THAT'S RIGHT. THE SPACE RIFT IS CLOSING QUICKLY, SO HURRY BACK.

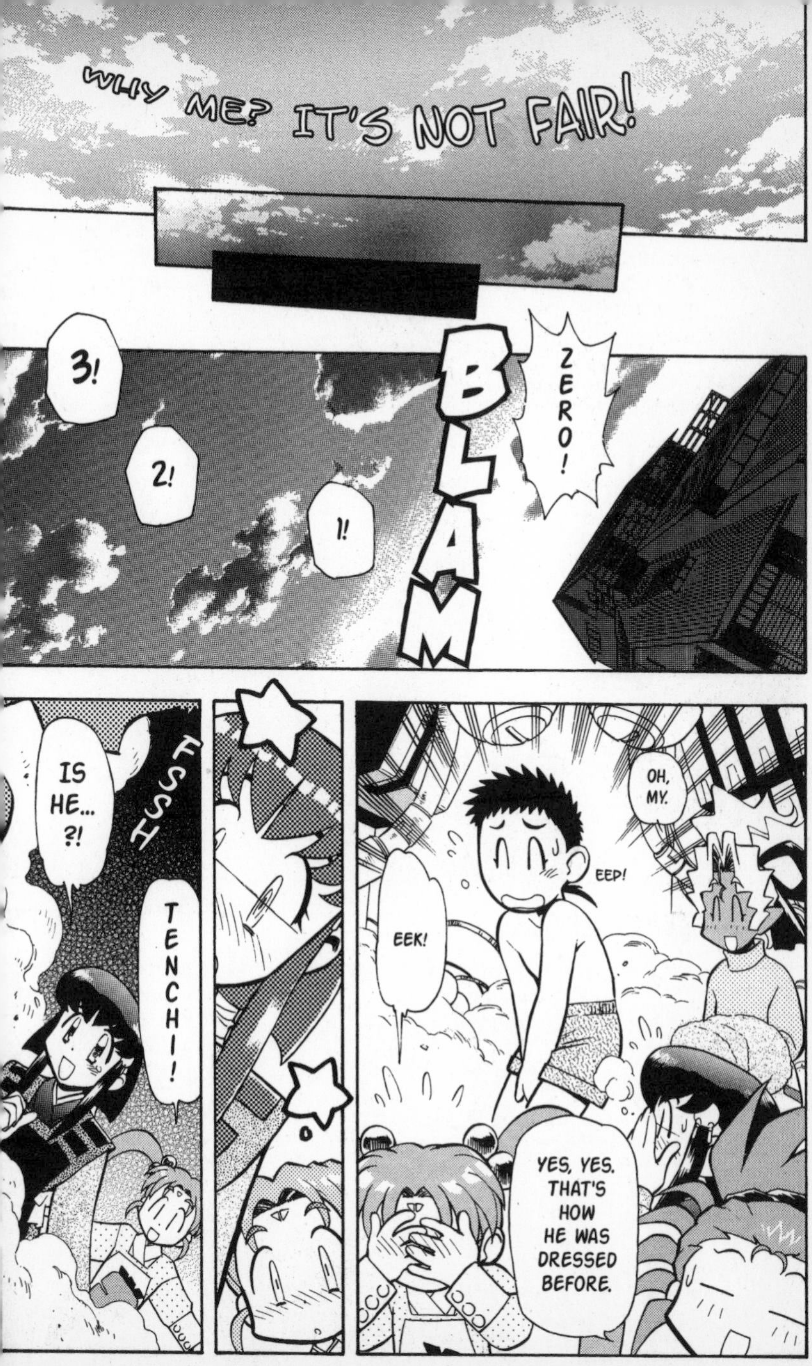
WHY ME? IT'S NOT FAIR!
3!
2!
1!
BLAM
ZERO!
IS HE...?!
FSSH
TENCHI!
EEK!
OH, MY.
EEP!
YES, YES. THAT'S HOW HE WAS DRESSED BEFORE.

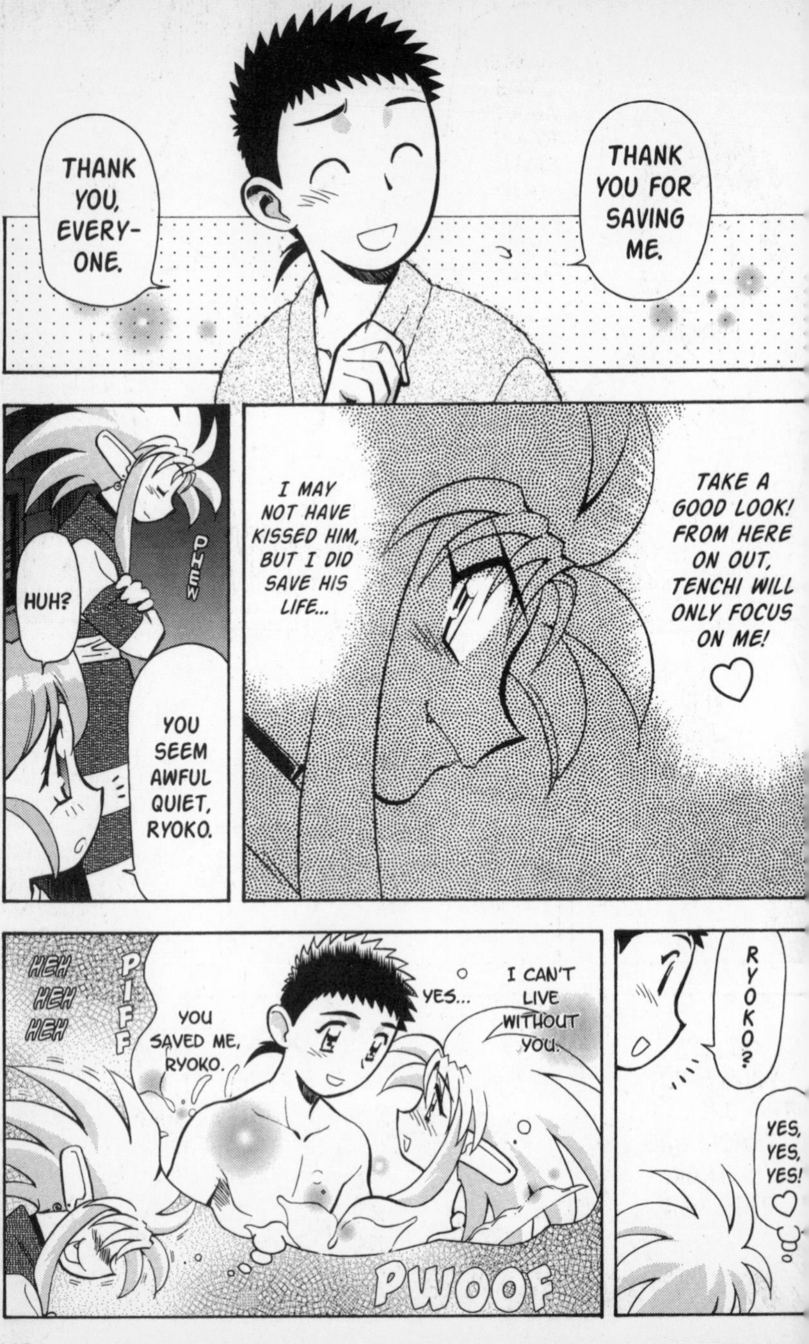
THANK YOU, EVERY-ONE.
THANK YOU FOR SAVING ME.
PHEW
HUH?
YOU SEEM AWFUL QUIET, RYOKO.
I MAY NOT HAVE KISSED HIM, BUT I DID SAVE HIS LIFE...
TAKE A GOOD LOOK! FROM HERE ON OUT, TENCHI WILL ONLY FOCUS ON ME!
HEH HEH HEH
PIFF
YOU SAVED ME, RYOKO.
YES...
I CAN'T LIVE WITHOUT YOU.
PWOOF
RYOKO?
YES, YES, YES!

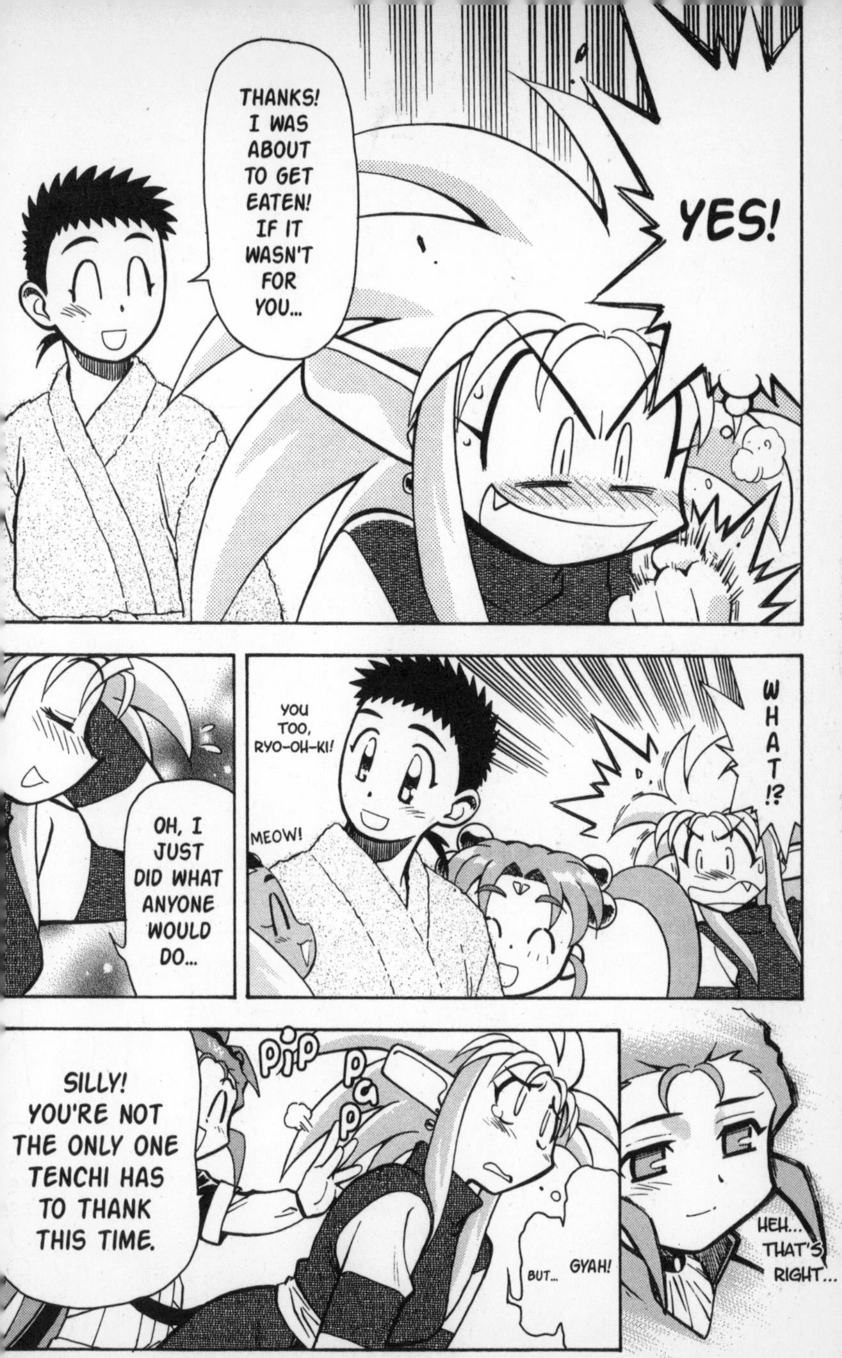
THANKS! I WAS ABOUT TO GET EATEN! IF IT WASN'T FOR YOU...
YES!
OH, I JUST DID WHAT ANYONE WOULD DO...
YOU TOO, RYO-OH-KI!
MEOW!
WHAT!?
SILLY! YOU'RE NOT THE ONLY ONE TENCHI HAS TO THANK THIS TIME.
PIP
PAP
BUT...
GYAH!
HEH... THAT'S RIGHT...

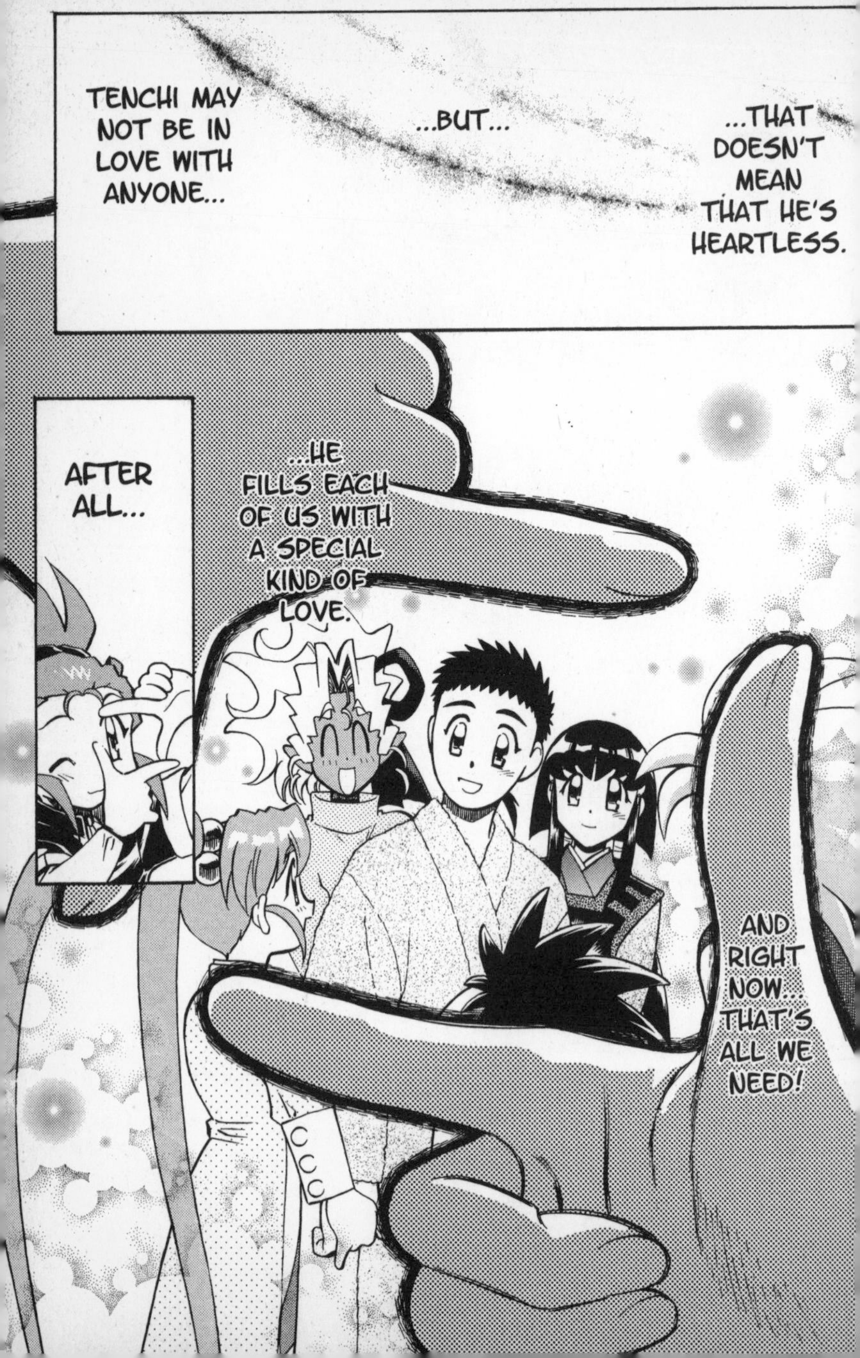
TENCHI MAY NOT BE IN LOVE WITH ANYONE...
...BUT...
...THAT DOESN'T MEAN THAT HE'S HEARTLESS.
AFTER ALL...
...HE FILLS EACH OF US WITH A SPECIAL KIND OF LOVE.
AND RIGHT NOW... THAT'S ALL WE NEED!

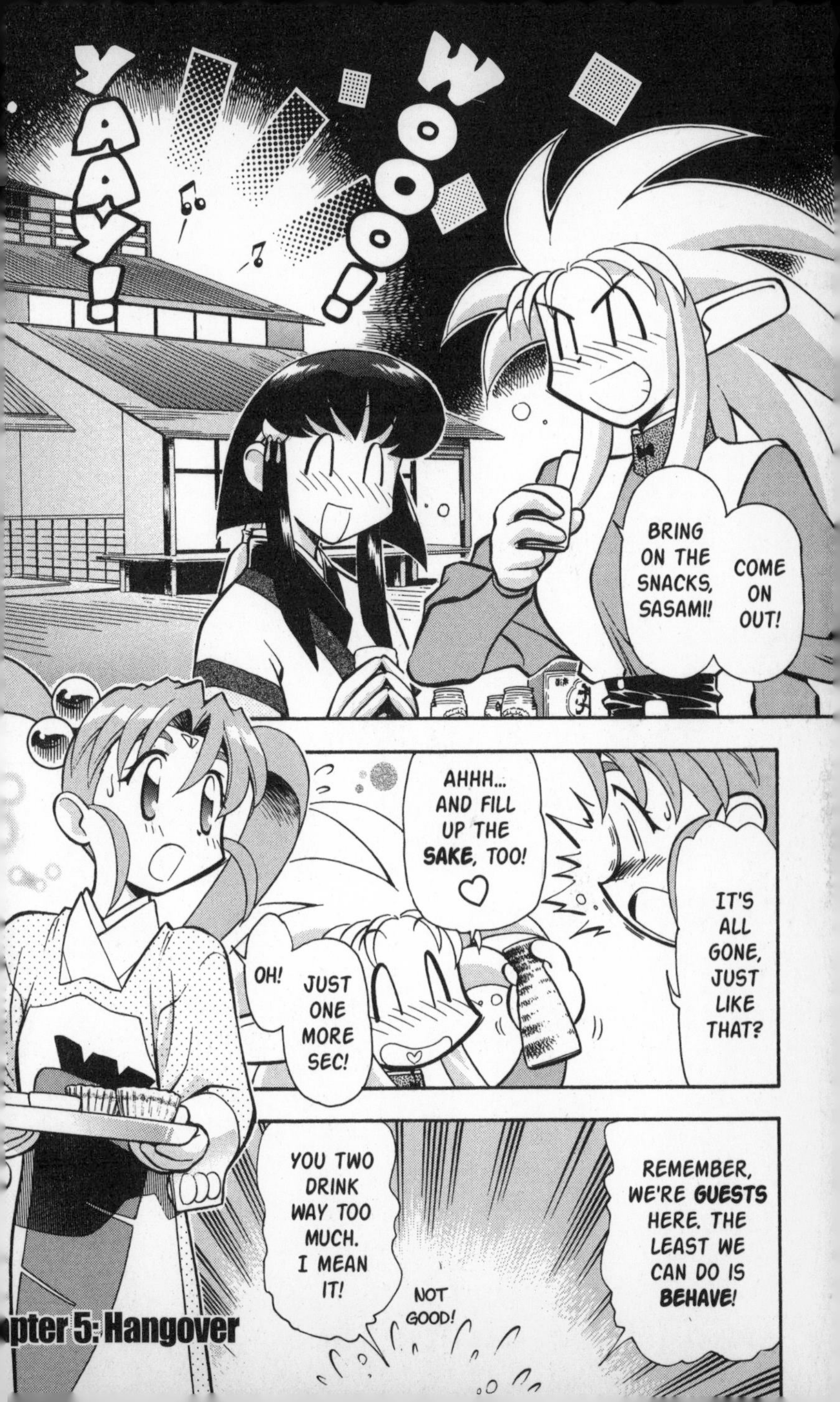
YAAAY!
WOOOO!
BRING ON THE SNACKS, SASAMI!
COME ON OUT!
pter 5: Hangover
AHHH... AND FILL UP THE **SAKE**, TOO!
OH!
JUST ONE MORE SEC!
IT'S ALL GONE, JUST LIKE THAT?
YOU TWO DRINK WAY TOO MUCH. I MEAN IT!
NOT GOOD!
REMEMBER, WE'RE **GUESTS** HERE. THE LEAST WE CAN DO IS **BEHAVE**!

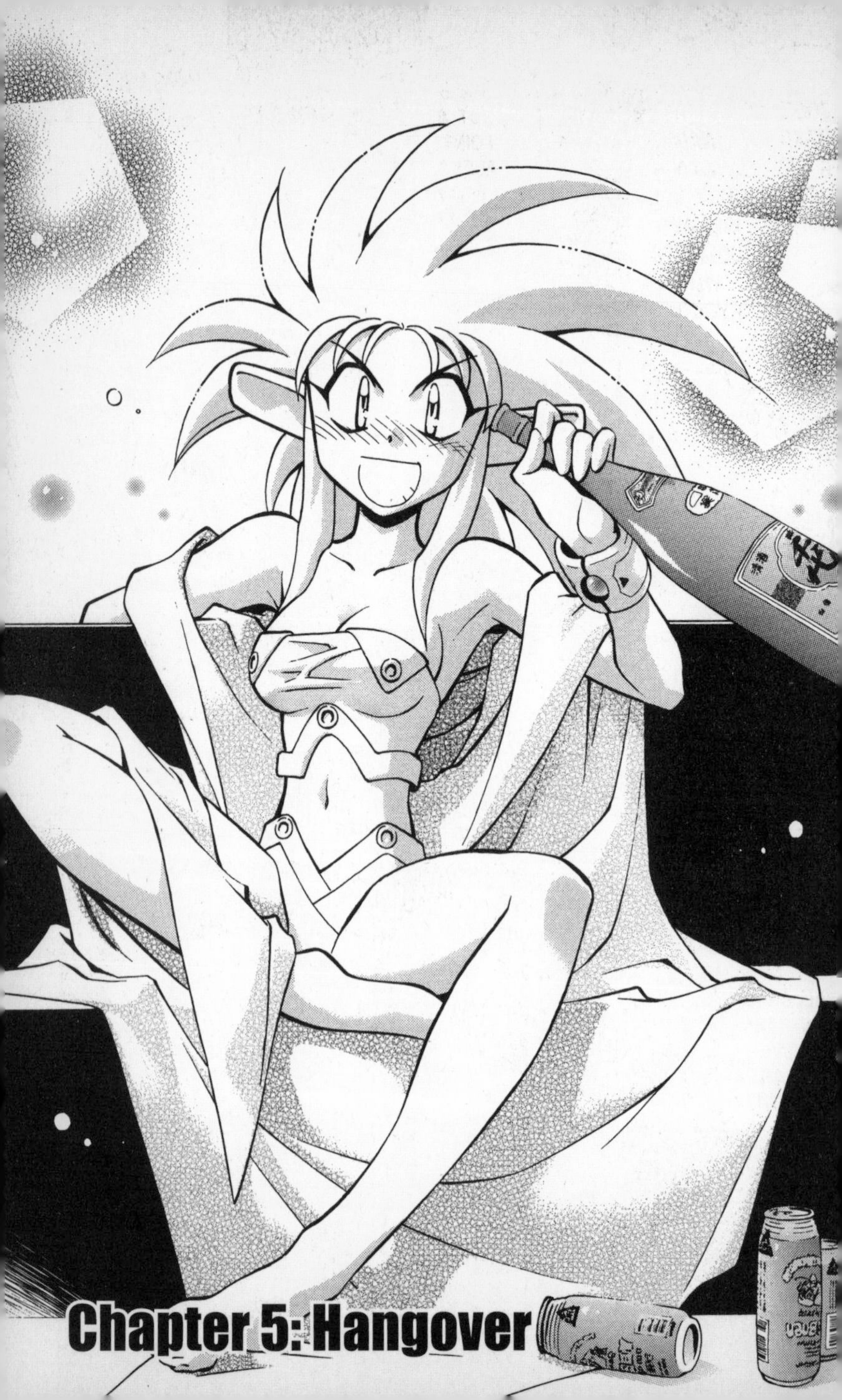

Chapter 5: Hangover

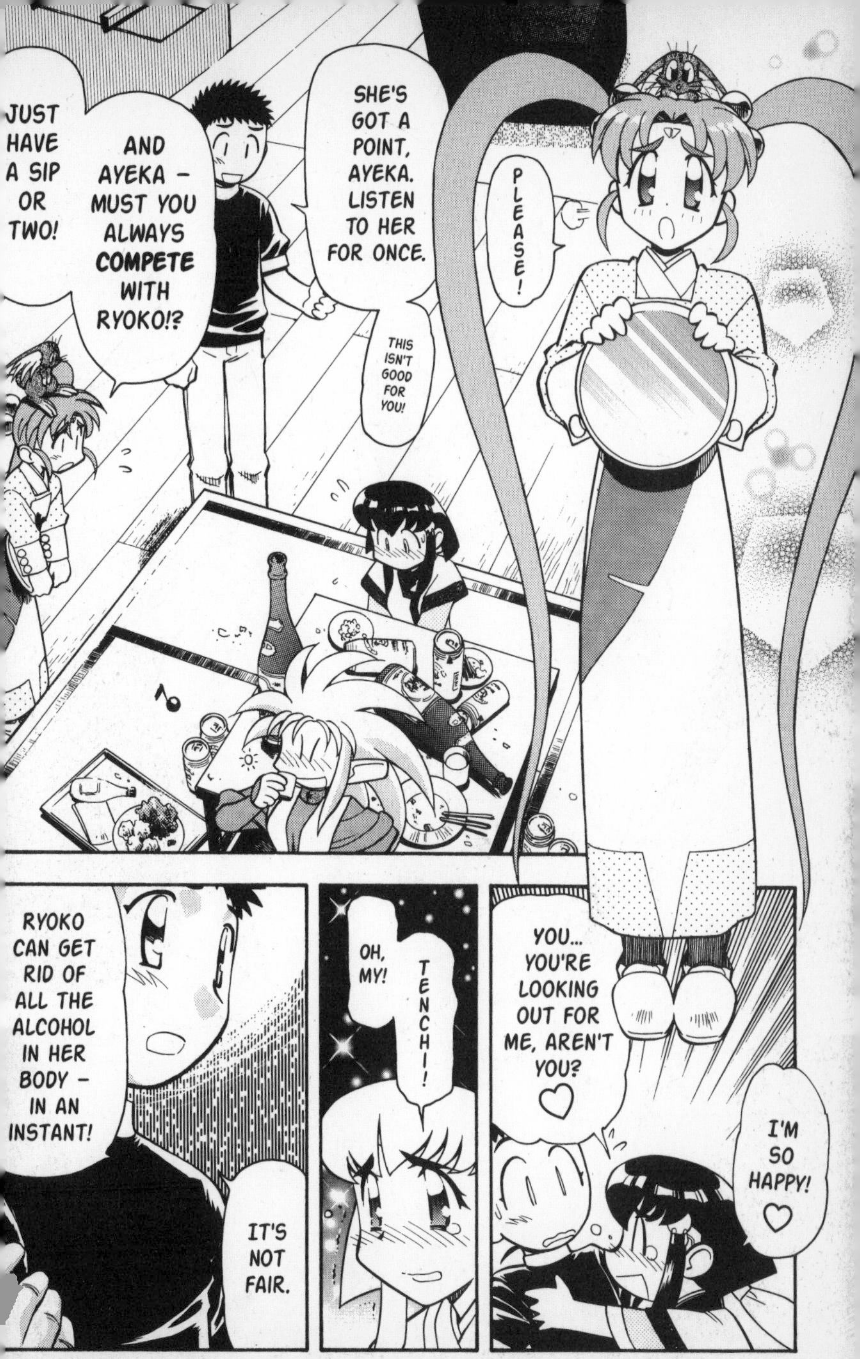
JUST HAVE A SIP OR TWO!
AND AYEKA – MUST YOU ALWAYS **COMPETE** WITH RYOKO!?
SHE'S GOT A POINT, AYEKA. LISTEN TO HER FOR ONCE.
THIS ISN'T GOOD FOR YOU!
PLEASE!
RYOKO CAN GET RID OF ALL THE ALCOHOL IN HER BODY – IN AN INSTANT!
IT'S NOT FAIR.
OH, MY!
TENCHI!
YOU... YOU'RE LOOKING OUT FOR ME, AREN'T YOU? ♥
I'M SO HAPPY! ♥

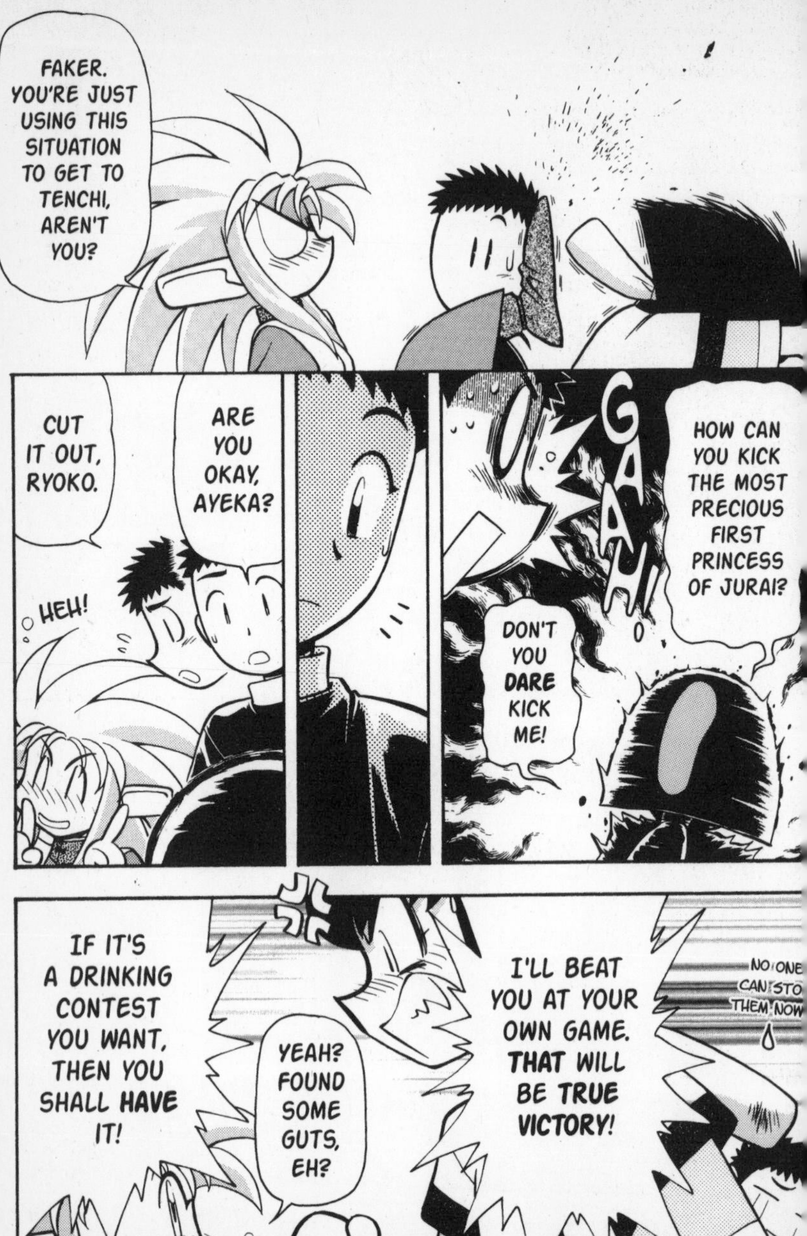
FAKER. YOU'RE JUST USING THIS SITUATION TO GET TO TENCHI, AREN'T YOU?
CUT IT OUT, RYOKO.
ARE YOU OKAY, AYEKA?
HEH!
GAAH!
HOW CAN YOU KICK THE MOST PRECIOUS FIRST PRINCESS OF JURAI?
DON'T YOU DARE KICK ME!
IF IT'S A DRINKING CONTEST YOU WANT, THEN YOU SHALL HAVE IT!
YEAH? FOUND SOME GUTS, EH?
I'LL BEAT YOU AT YOUR OWN GAME. THAT WILL BE TRUE VICTORY!
NO ONE CAN STO THEM NOW

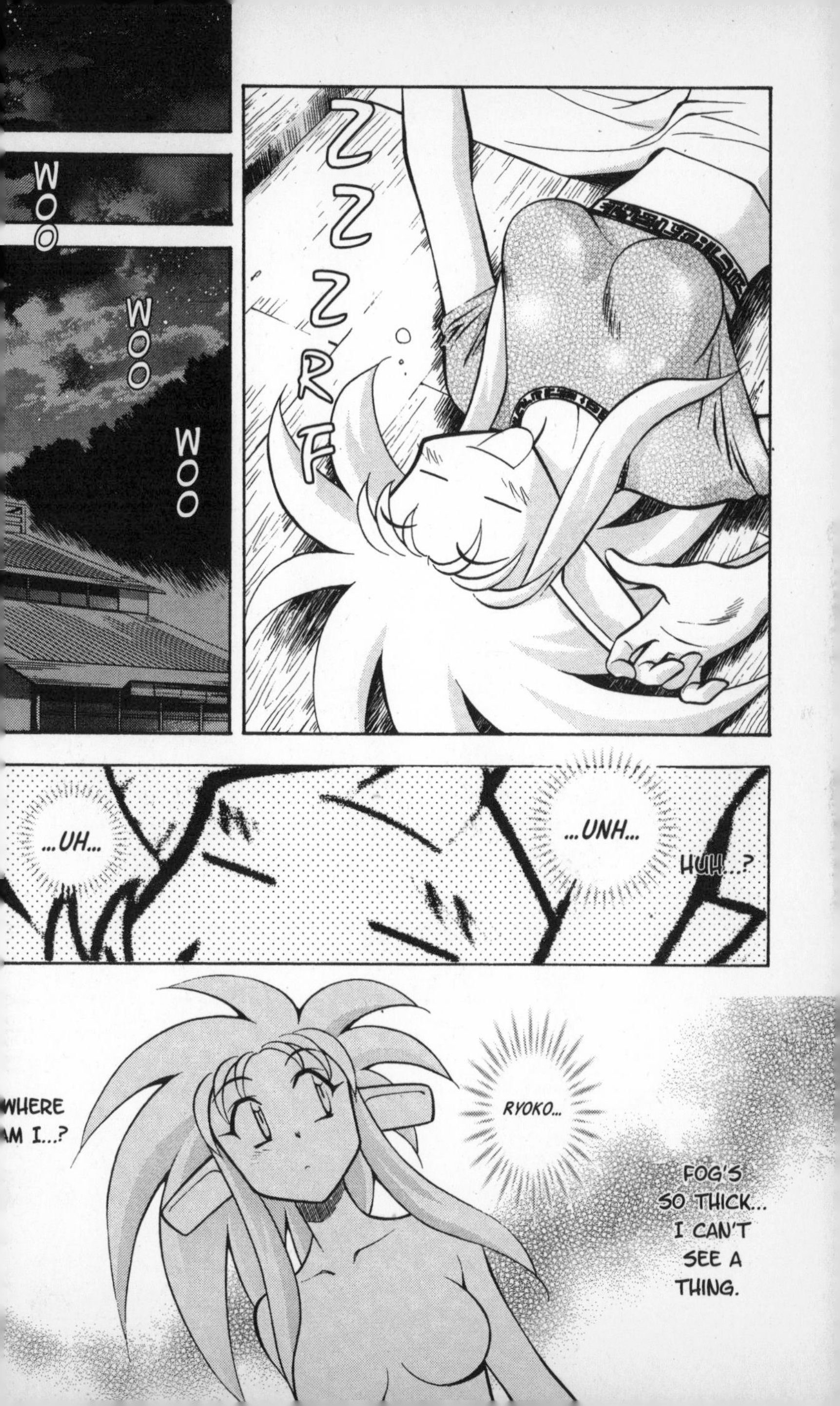
WOO
WOO
WOO
ZZZRF
...UH...
...UNH...
HUH...?
WHERE AM I...?
RYOKO...
FOG'S SO THICK... I CAN'T SEE A THING.

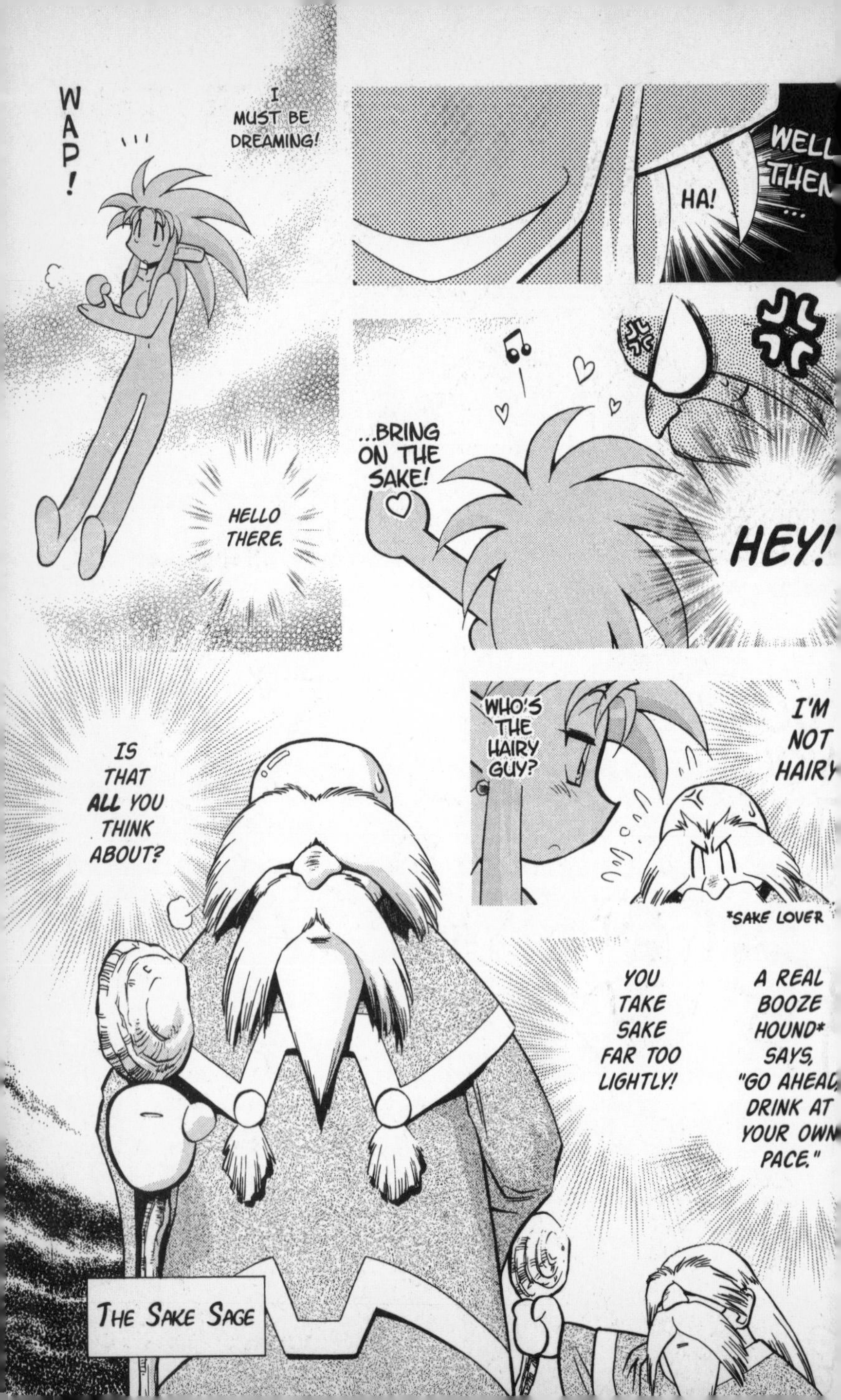
WAP!
I MUST BE DREAMING!
HELLO THERE.
HA!
WELL THEN...
...BRING ON THE SAKE!
HEY!
IS THAT ALL YOU THINK ABOUT?
WHO'S THE HAIRY GUY?
I'M NOT HAIRY
*SAKE LOVER
YOU TAKE SAKE FAR TOO LIGHTLY!
A REAL BOOZE HOUND* SAYS, "GO AHEAD, DRINK AT YOUR OWN PACE."
THE SAKE SAGE

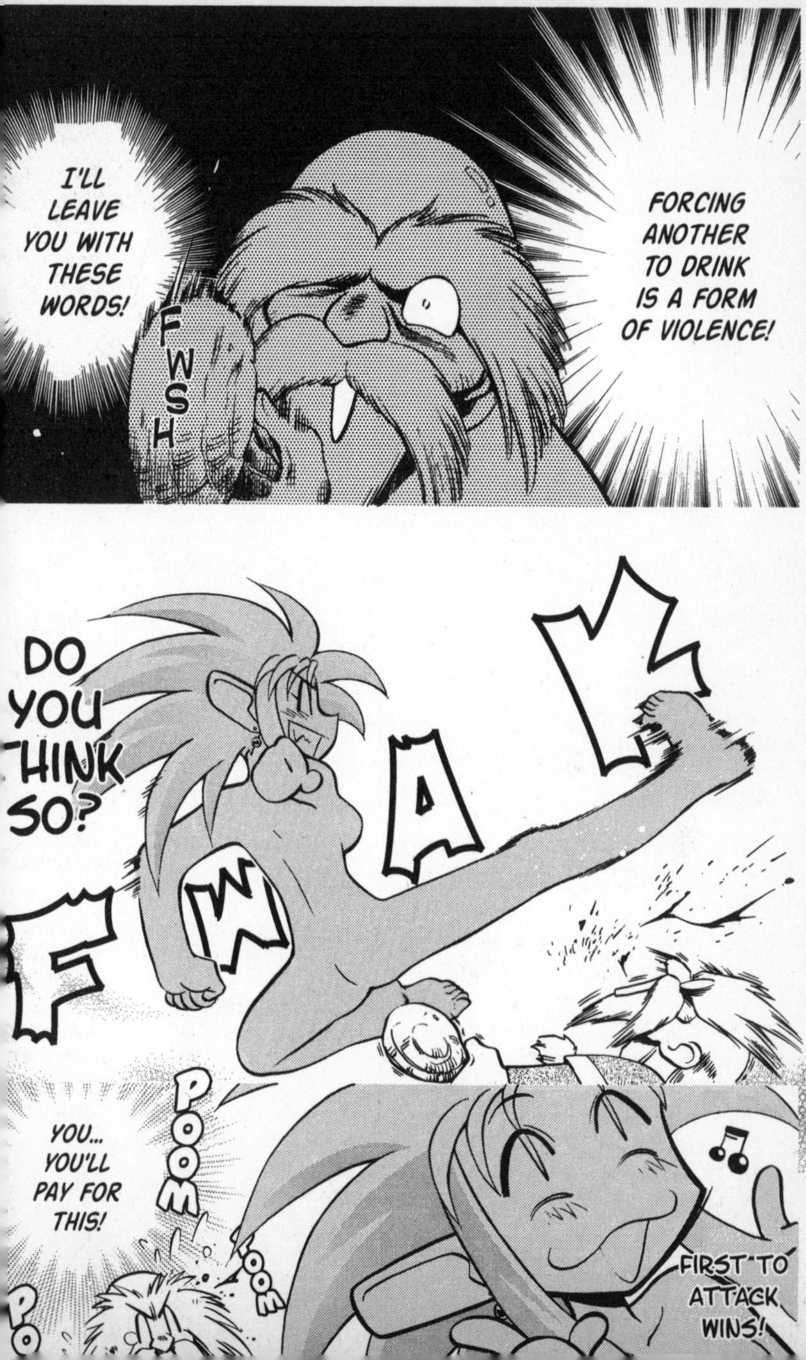
I'LL LEAVE YOU WITH THESE WORDS!
FWSH
FORCING ANOTHER TO DRINK IS A FORM OF VIOLENCE!
DO YOU THINK SO?
FWAK
YOU... YOU'LL PAY FOR THIS!
POOM
POOM
FIRST TO ATTACK WINS!

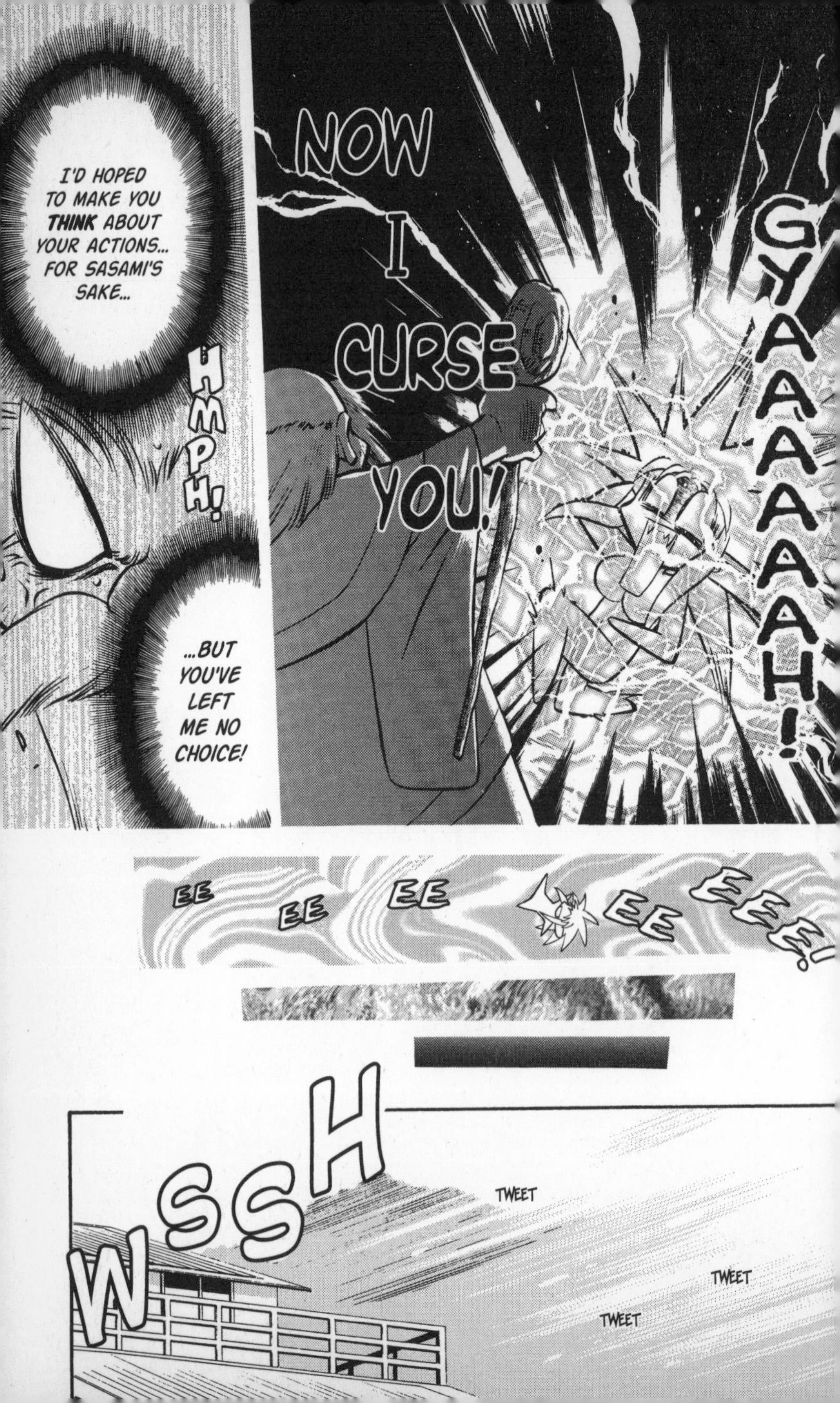
GYAAAAAAAH!
NOW I CURSE YOU!
I'D HOPED TO MAKE YOU THINK ABOUT YOUR ACTIONS... FOR SASAMI'S SAKE...
HMPH!
...BUT YOU'VE LEFT ME NO CHOICE!
EE EE EE EE EEE!
WSSH
TWEET
TWEET
TWEET

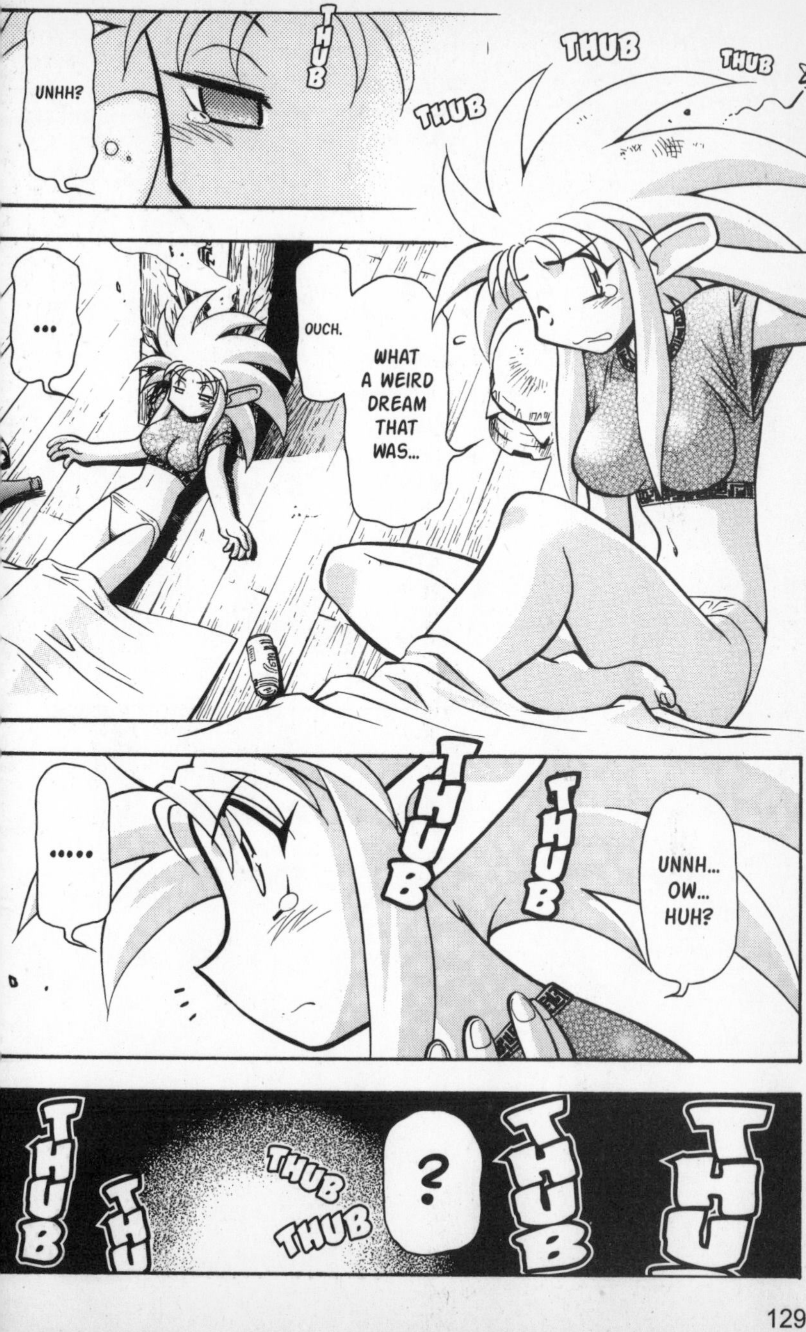
UNNH?
THUB
THUB
THUB
THUB
...
OUCH.
WHAT A WEIRD DREAM THAT WAS...
.....
THUB
THUB
UNNH... OW... HUH?
THUB
THU
THUB
THUB
?
THUB
THU

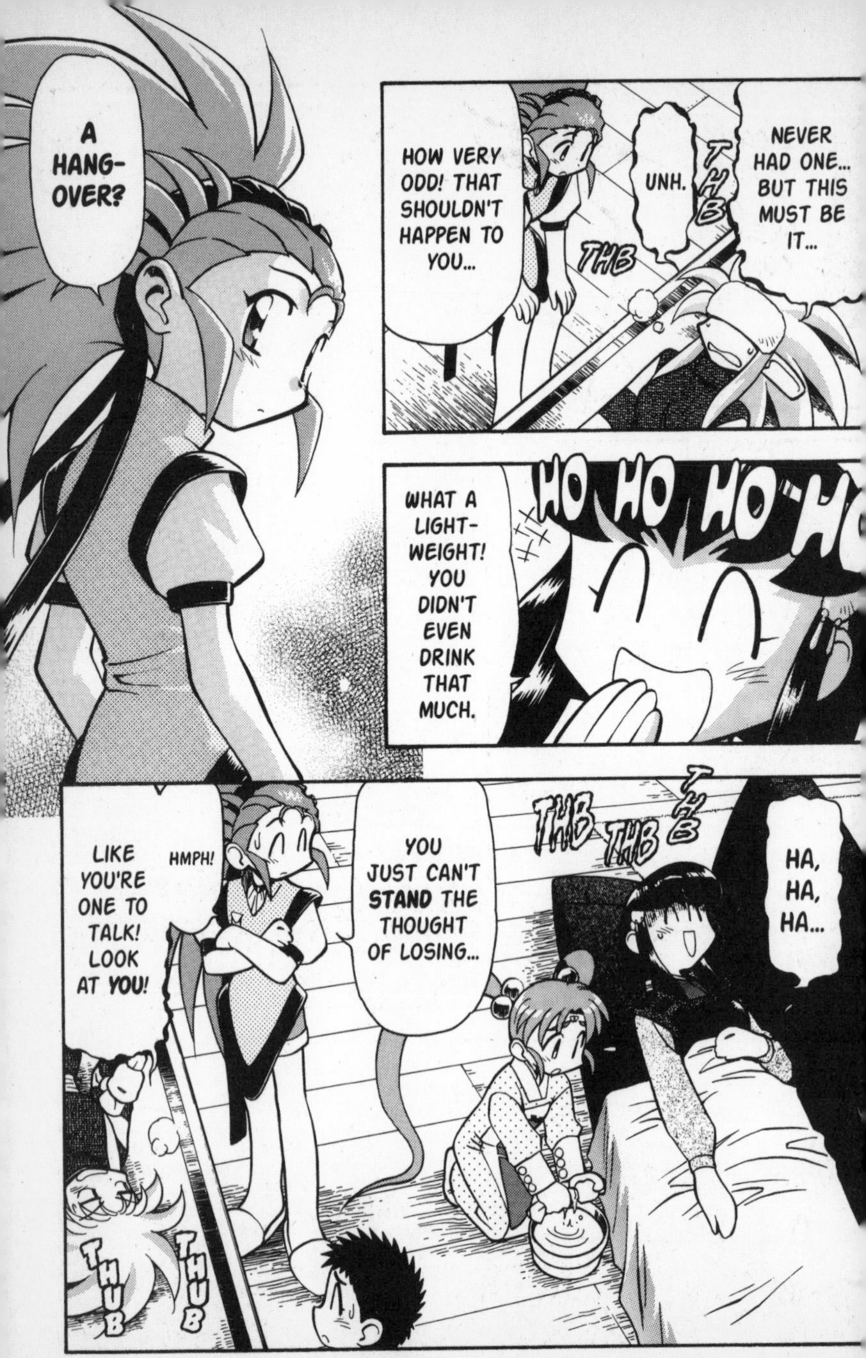
A HANG-OVER?
HOW VERY ODD! THAT SHOULDN'T HAPPEN TO YOU...
THB
UNH.
THB
NEVER HAD ONE... BUT THIS MUST BE IT...
WHAT A LIGHT-WEIGHT! YOU DIDN'T EVEN DRINK THAT MUCH.
HO HO HO HO
LIKE YOU'RE ONE TO TALK! LOOK AT YOU!
HMPH!
YOU JUST CAN'T **STAND** THE THOUGHT OF LOSING...
THB
THB
THB
HA, HA, HA...
THUB
THUB

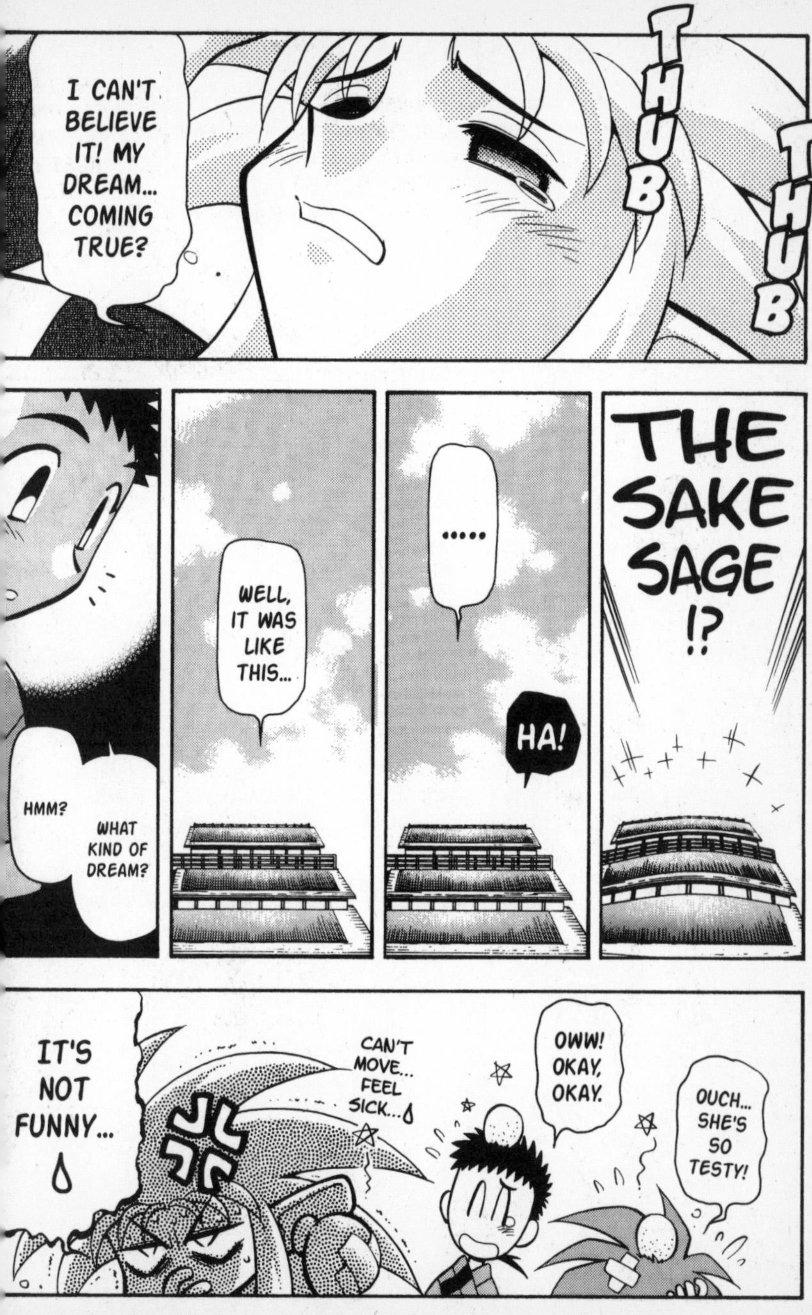
I CAN'T BELIEVE IT! MY DREAM... COMING TRUE?
THUB THUB
THUB THUB
HMM? WHAT KIND OF DREAM?
WELL, IT WAS LIKE THIS...
.....
HA!
THE SAKE SAGE !?
IT'S NOT FUNNY...
CAN'T MOVE... FEEL SICK...
OWW! OKAY, OKAY.
OUCH... SHE'S SO TESTY!

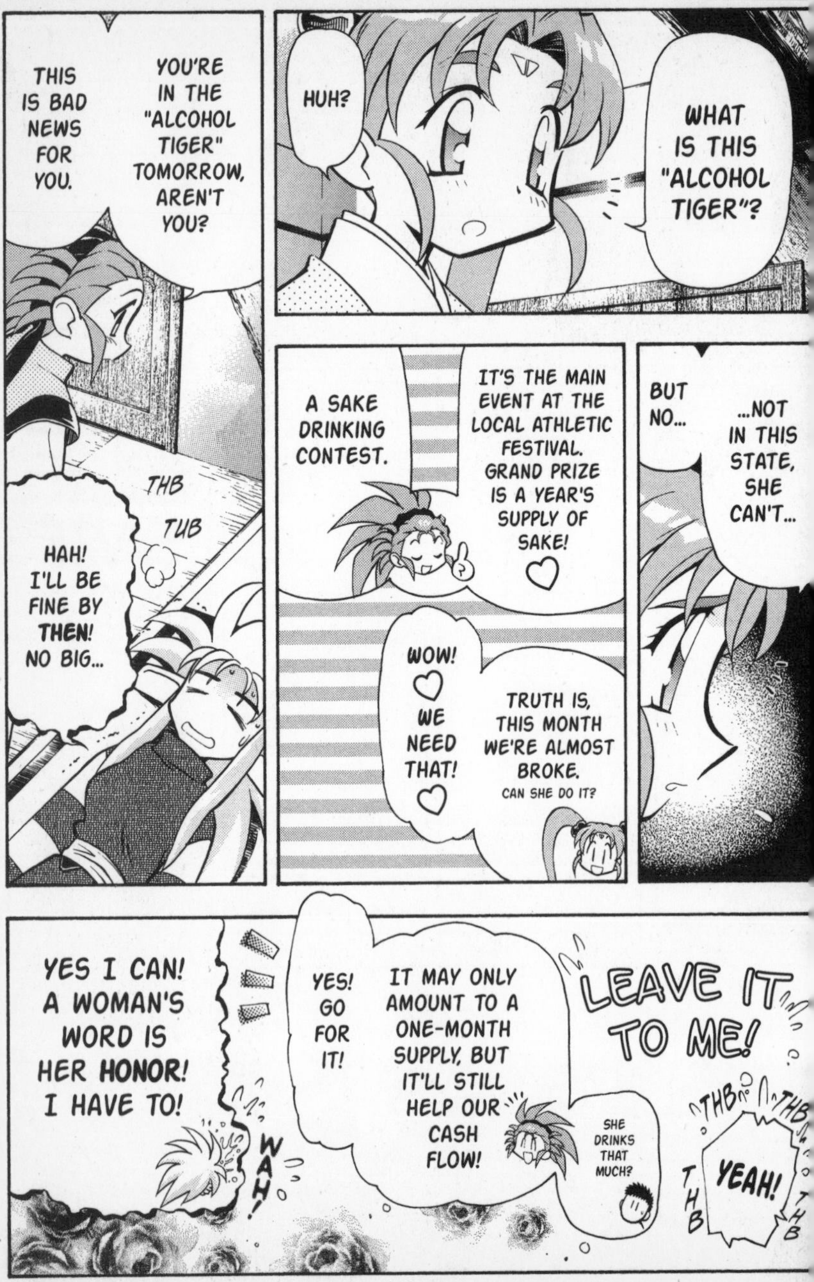

THIS IS BAD NEWS FOR YOU.
YOU'RE IN THE "ALCOHOL TIGER" TOMORROW, AREN'T YOU?
THB
TUB
HAH! I'LL BE FINE BY **THEN**! NO BIG...
HUH?
WHAT IS THIS "ALCOHOL TIGER"?
A SAKE DRINKING CONTEST.
IT'S THE MAIN EVENT AT THE LOCAL ATHLETIC FESTIVAL. GRAND PRIZE IS A YEAR'S SUPPLY OF SAKE! ♡
WOW! ♡ WE NEED THAT! ♡
TRUTH IS, THIS MONTH WE'RE ALMOST BROKE.
CAN SHE DO IT?
BUT NO...
...NOT IN THIS STATE, SHE CAN'T...
YES I CAN! A WOMAN'S WORD IS HER **HONOR**! I HAVE TO!
WAH!
YES! GO FOR IT!
IT MAY ONLY AMOUNT TO A ONE-MONTH SUPPLY, BUT IT'LL STILL HELP OUR CASH FLOW!
LEAVE IT TO ME!
SHE DRINKS THAT MUCH?
THB
THB
THB
THB
YEAH!

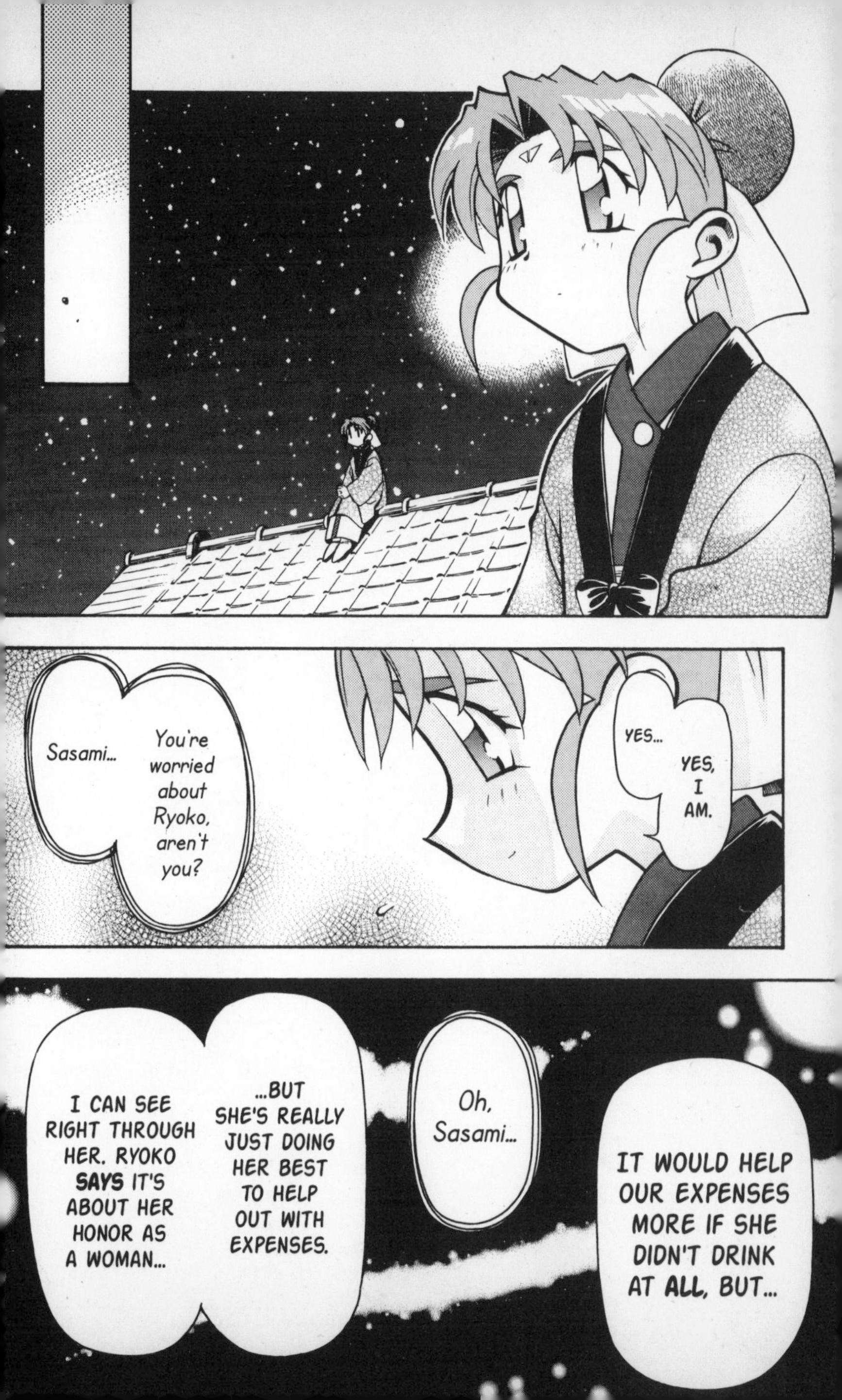
Sasami... You're worried about Ryoko, aren't you?
YES... YES, I AM.
I CAN SEE RIGHT THROUGH HER. RYOKO SAYS IT'S ABOUT HER HONOR AS A WOMAN...
...BUT SHE'S REALLY JUST DOING HER BEST TO HELP OUT WITH EXPENSES.
Oh, Sasami...
IT WOULD HELP OUR EXPENSES MORE IF SHE DIDN'T DRINK AT ALL, BUT...

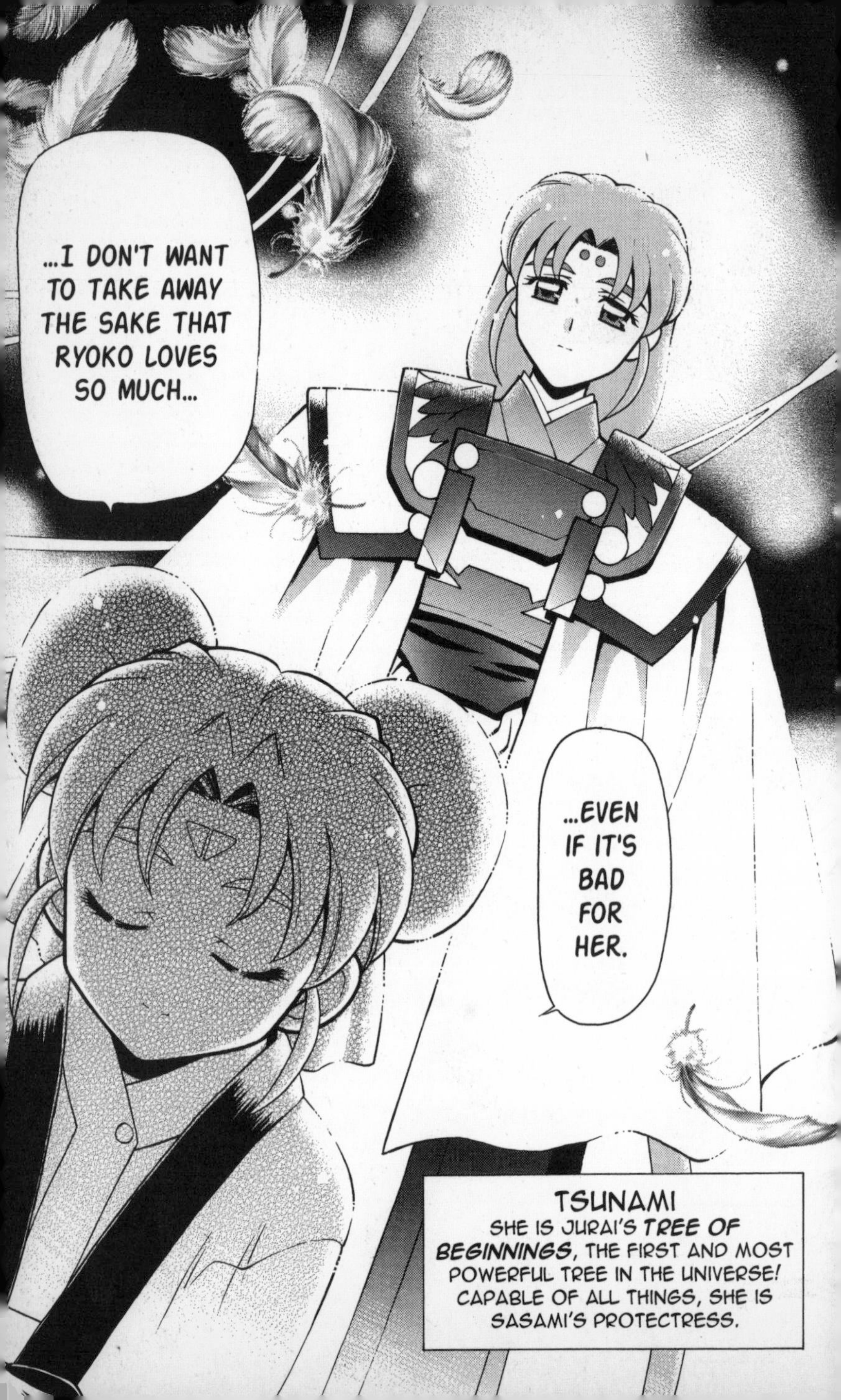
...I DON'T WANT TO TAKE AWAY THE SAKE THAT RYOKO LOVES SO MUCH...
...EVEN IF IT'S BAD FOR HER.
TSUNAMI
SHE IS JURAI'S TREE OF BEGINNINGS, THE FIRST AND MOST POWERFUL TREE IN THE UNIVERSE! CAPABLE OF ALL THINGS, SHE IS SASAMI'S PROTECTRESS.

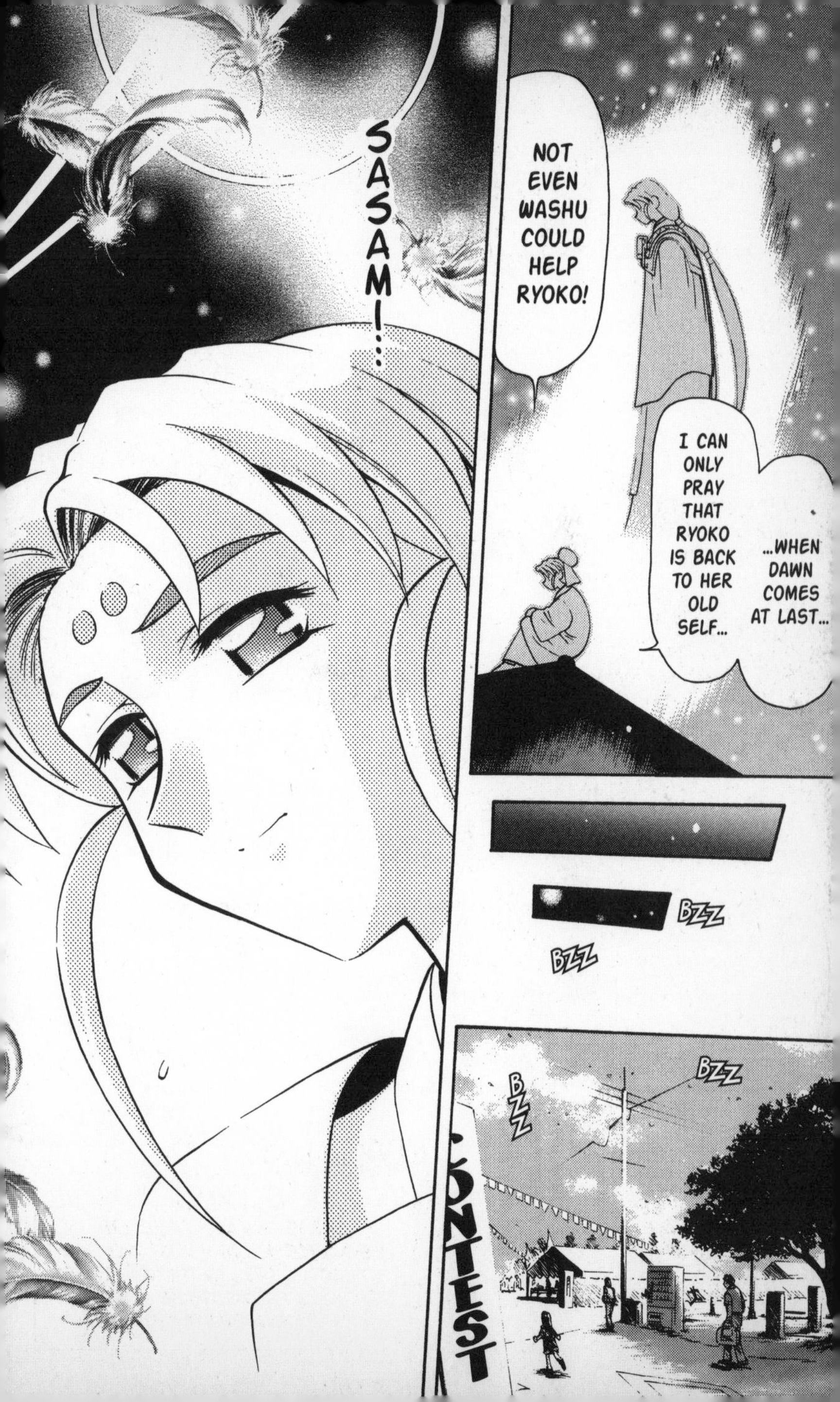
SASAMI...
NOT EVEN WASHU COULD HELP RYOKO!
I CAN ONLY PRAY THAT RYOKO IS BACK TO HER OLD SELF...
...WHEN DAWN COMES AT LAST...
BZZ
BZZ
BZZ
BZZ
CONTEST

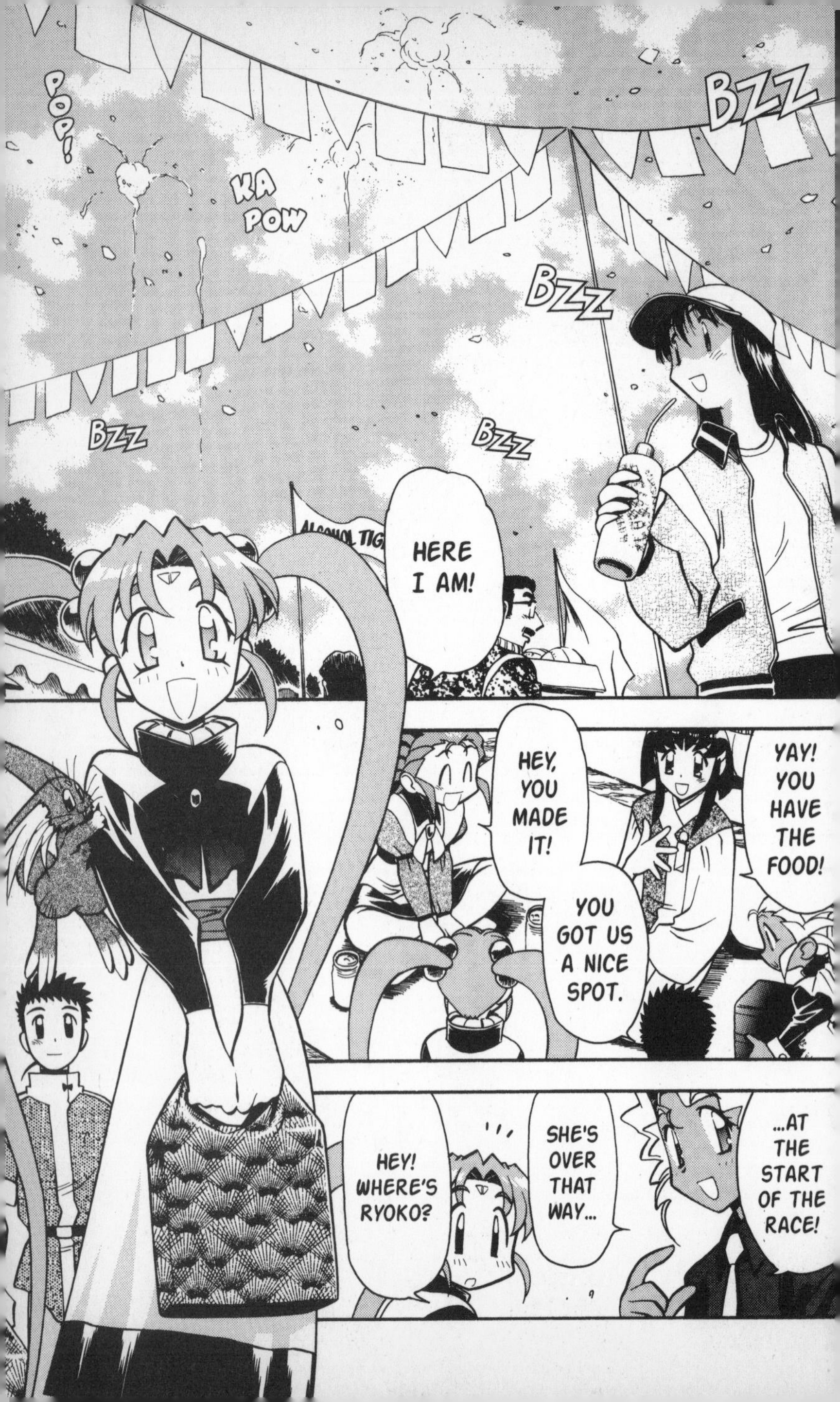

BZZ
POP!
KA POW
BZZ
BZZ
BZZ
ALCOHOL TIG
HERE I AM!
YAY! YOU HAVE THE FOOD!
HEY, YOU MADE IT!
YOU GOT US A NICE SPOT.
...AT THE START OF THE RACE!
SHE'S OVER THAT WAY...
HEY! WHERE'S RYOKO?

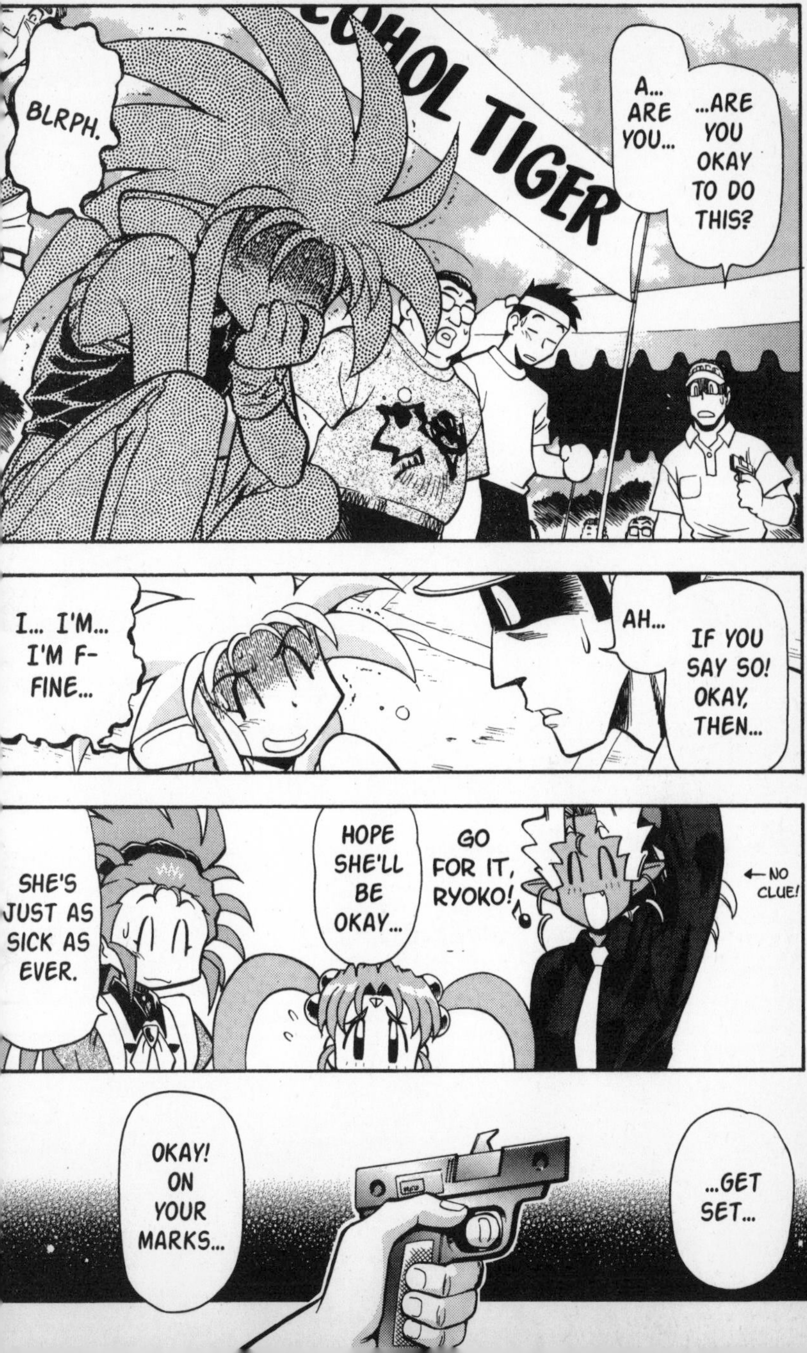
BLRPH.
COHOL TIGER
A... ARE YOU... ...ARE YOU OKAY TO DO THIS?
I... I'M... I'M F-FINE...
AH... IF YOU SAY SO! OKAY, THEN...
SHE'S JUST AS SICK AS EVER.
HOPE SHE'LL BE OKAY...
GO FOR IT, RYOKO!
← NO CLUE!
OKAY! ON YOUR MARKS...
...GET SET...

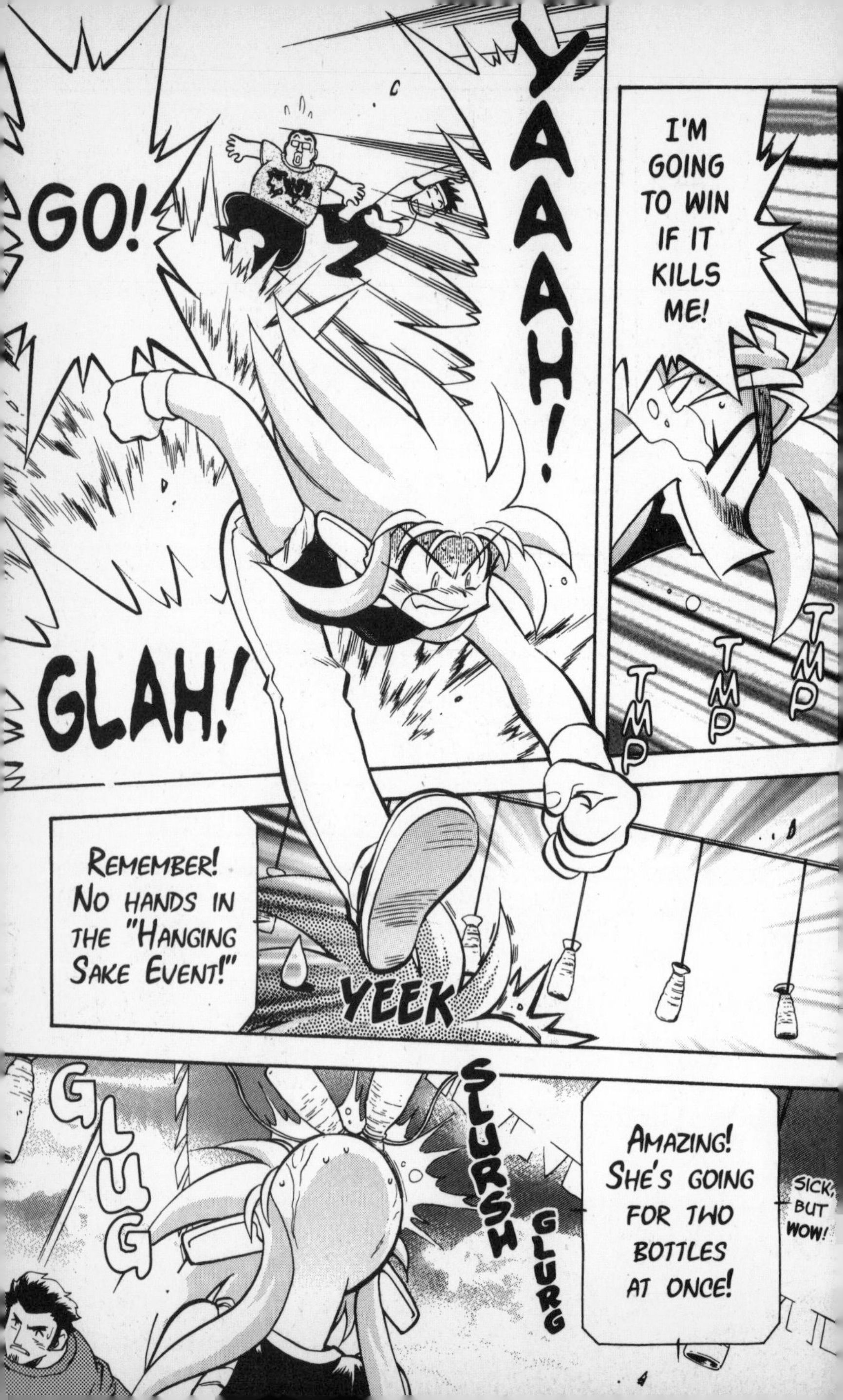
GO!
YAAAH!
GLAH!
I'M GOING TO WIN IF IT KILLS ME!
TMP TMP TMP
REMEMBER! NO HANDS IN THE "HANGING SAKE EVENT!"
YEEK
GLUG
SLURSH
GLURG
AMAZING! SHE'S GOING FOR TWO BOTTLES AT ONCE!
SICK, BUT WOW!

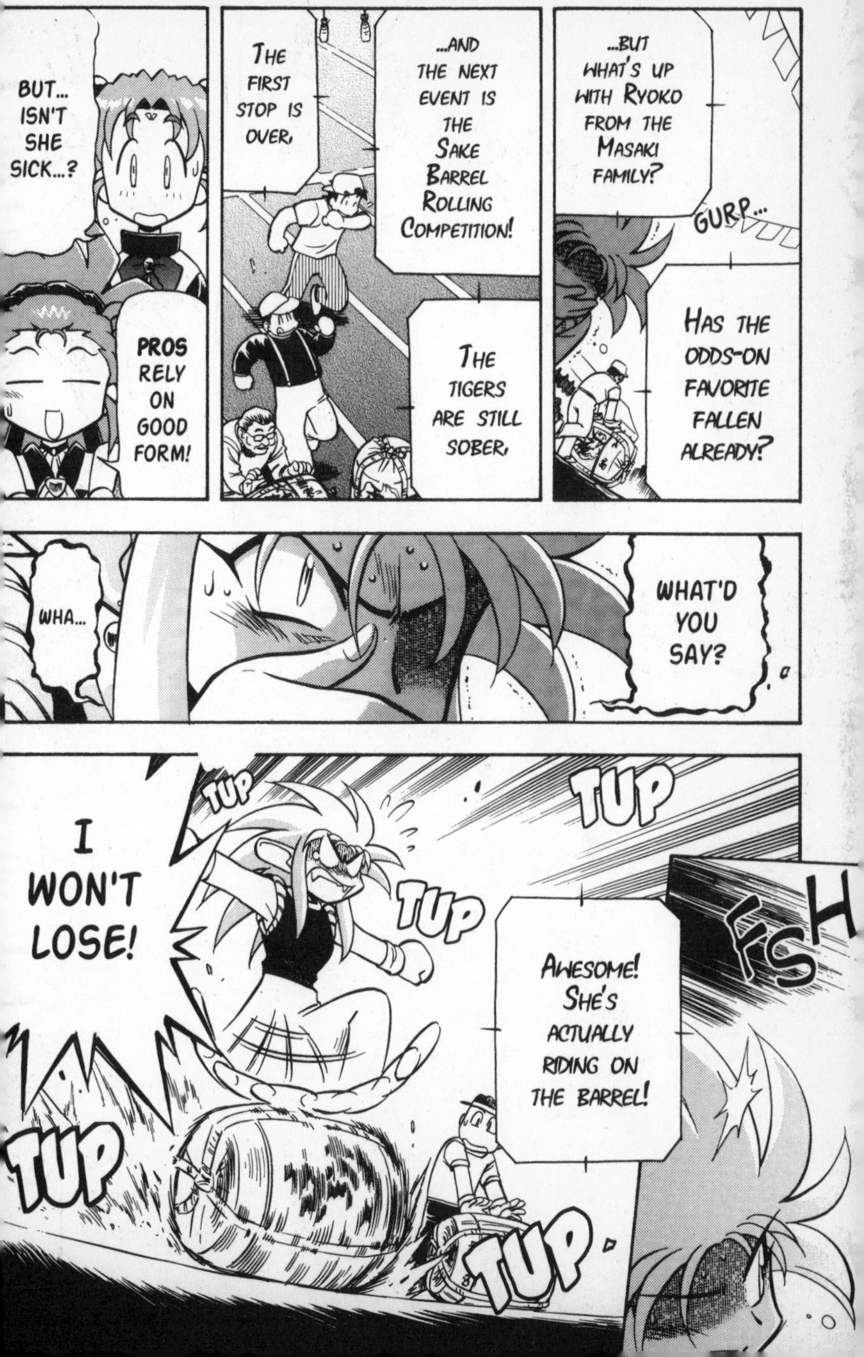

BUT... ISN'T SHE SICK...?
PROS RELY ON GOOD FORM!
THE FIRST STOP IS OVER.
...AND THE NEXT EVENT IS THE SAKE BARREL ROLLING COMPETITION!
THE TIGERS ARE STILL SOBER.
...BUT WHAT'S UP WITH RYOKO FROM THE MASAKI FAMILY?
GURP...
HAS THE ODDS-ON FAVORITE FALLEN ALREADY?
WHA...
WHAT'D YOU SAY?
TUP
TUP
I WON'T LOSE!
TUP
AWESOME! SHE'S ACTUALLY RIDING ON THE BARREL!
FSH
TUP
TUP

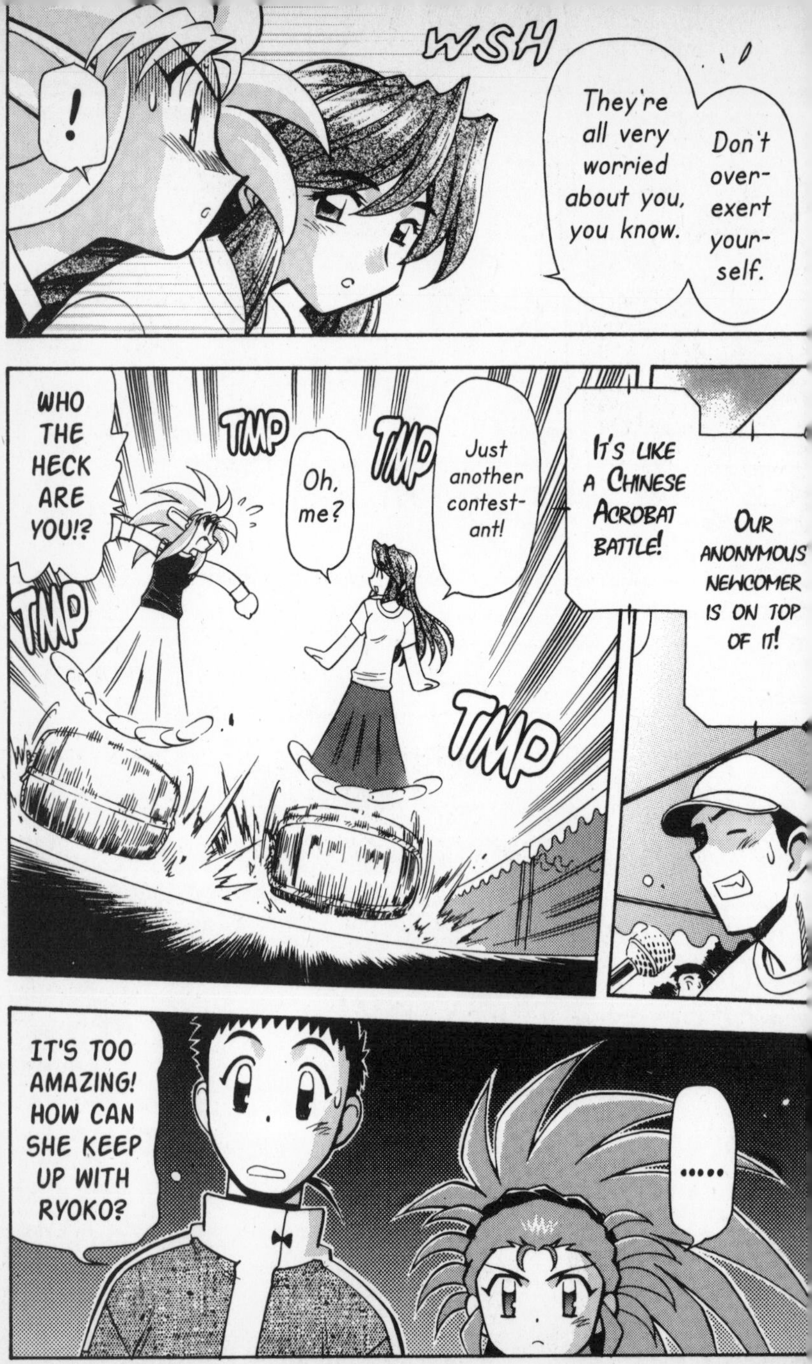
!
WSH
They're all very worried about you, you know.
Don't over-exert your-self.
WHO THE HECK ARE YOU!?
TMP
TMP
Oh, me?
TMP
Just another contest-ant!
TMP
IT'S LIKE A CHINESE ACROBAT BATTLE!
OUR ANONYMOUS NEWCOMER IS ON TOP OF IT!
IT'S TOO AMAZING! HOW CAN SHE KEEP UP WITH RYOKO?
......

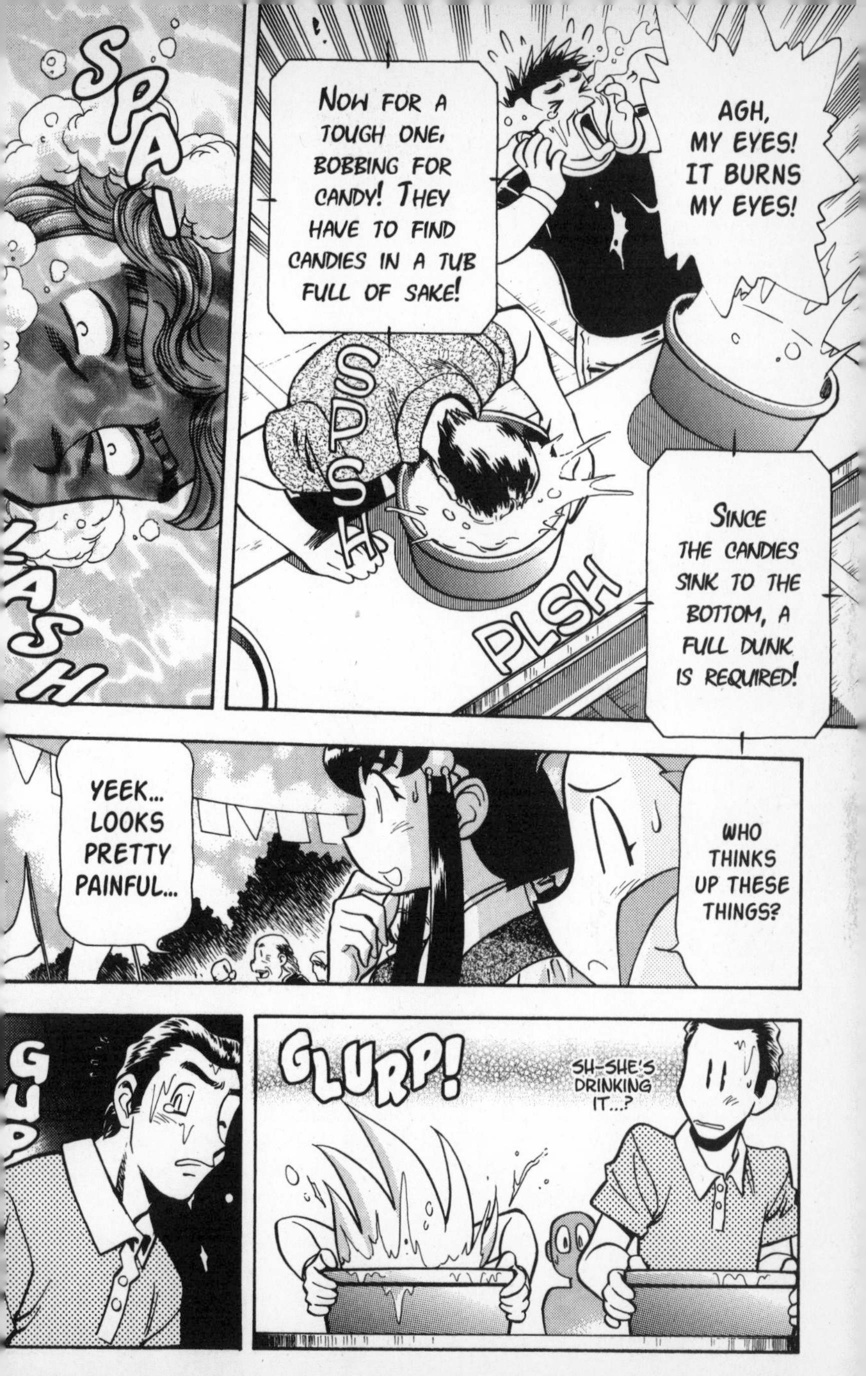
SPLASH
NOW FOR A TOUGH ONE, BOBBING FOR CANDY! THEY HAVE TO FIND CANDIES IN A TUB FULL OF SAKE!
SPSH
AGH, MY EYES! IT BURNS MY EYES!
PLSH
SINCE THE CANDIES SINK TO THE BOTTOM, A FULL DUNK IS REQUIRED!
YEEK... LOOKS PRETTY PAINFUL...
WHO THINKS UP THESE THINGS?
GULP
GLURP!
SH-SHE'S DRINKING IT...?

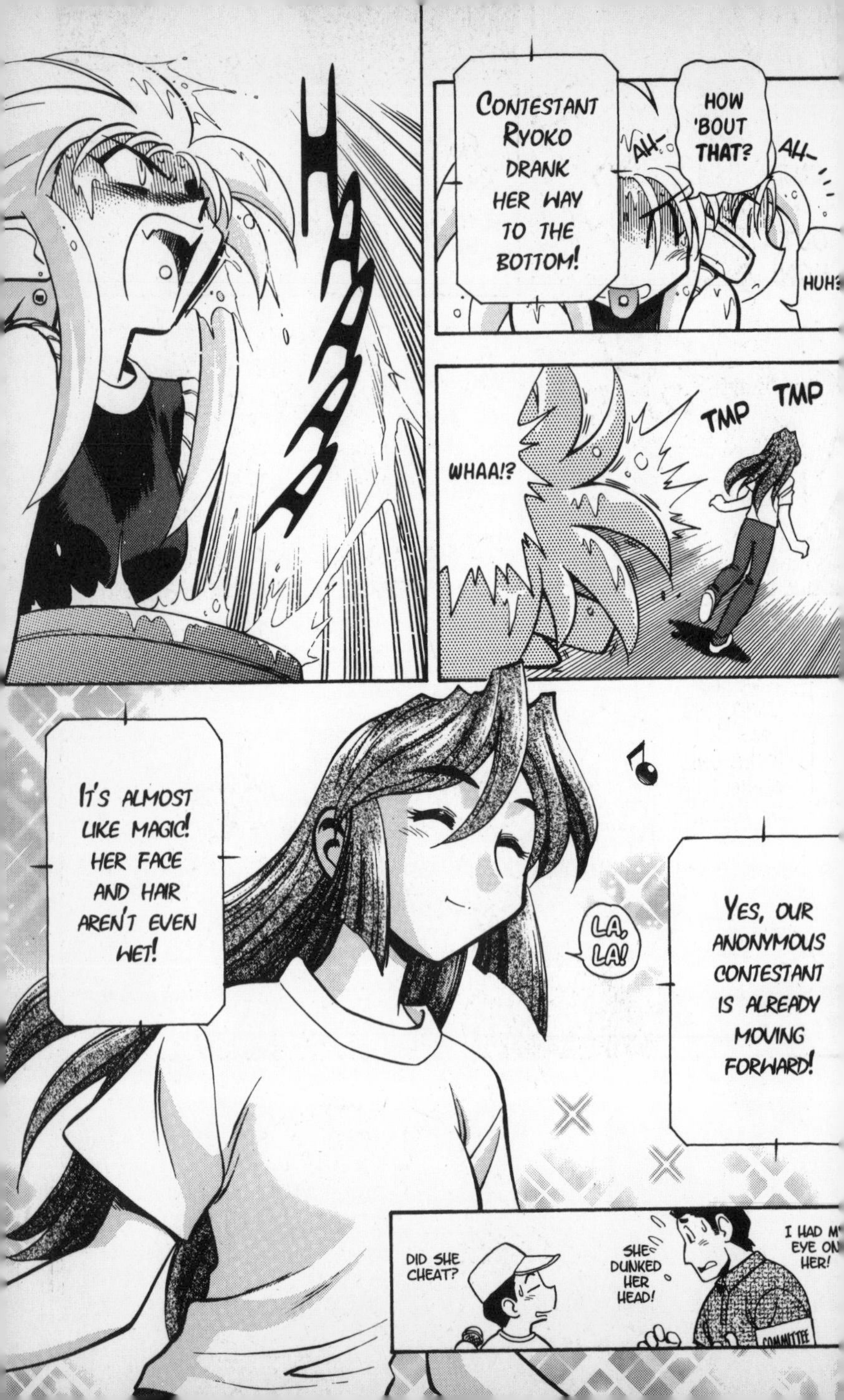
HAAAAA
CONTESTANT RYOKO DRANK HER WAY TO THE BOTTOM!
AH-
HOW 'BOUT THAT?
AH-
HUH?
WHAA!?
TMP
TMP
IT'S ALMOST LIKE MAGIC! HER FACE AND HAIR AREN'T EVEN WET!
LA, LA!
YES, OUR ANONYMOUS CONTESTANT IS ALREADY MOVING FORWARD!
DID SHE CHEAT?
SHE DUNKED HER HEAD!
I HAD MY EYE ON HER!
COMMITTEE

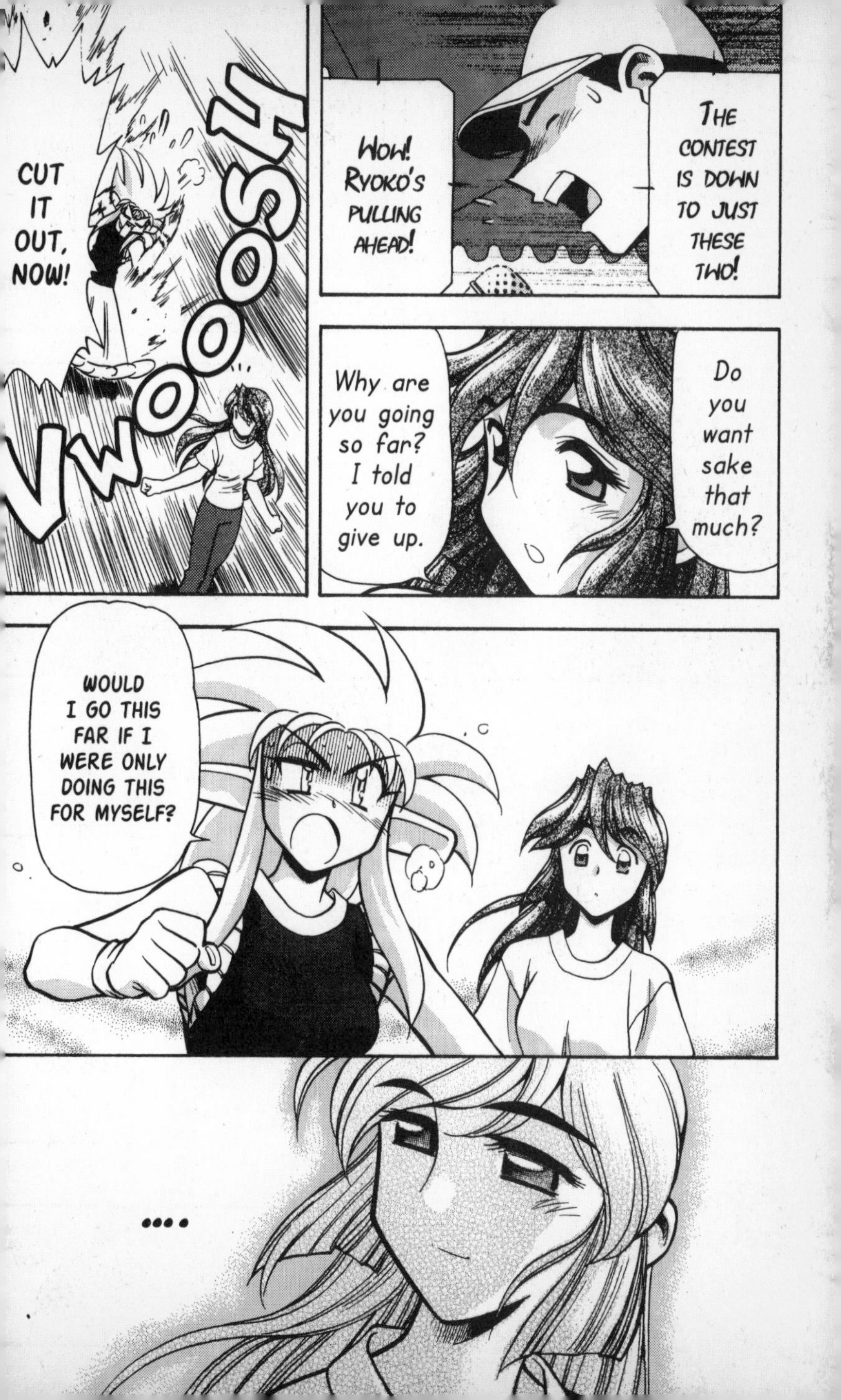
CUT IT OUT, NOW!
VWOOOOSH
WOW! RYOKO'S PULLING AHEAD!
THE CONTEST IS DOWN TO JUST THESE TWO!
Why are you going so far? I told you to give up.
Do you want sake that much?
WOULD I GO THIS FAR IF I WERE ONLY DOING THIS FOR MYSELF?
....

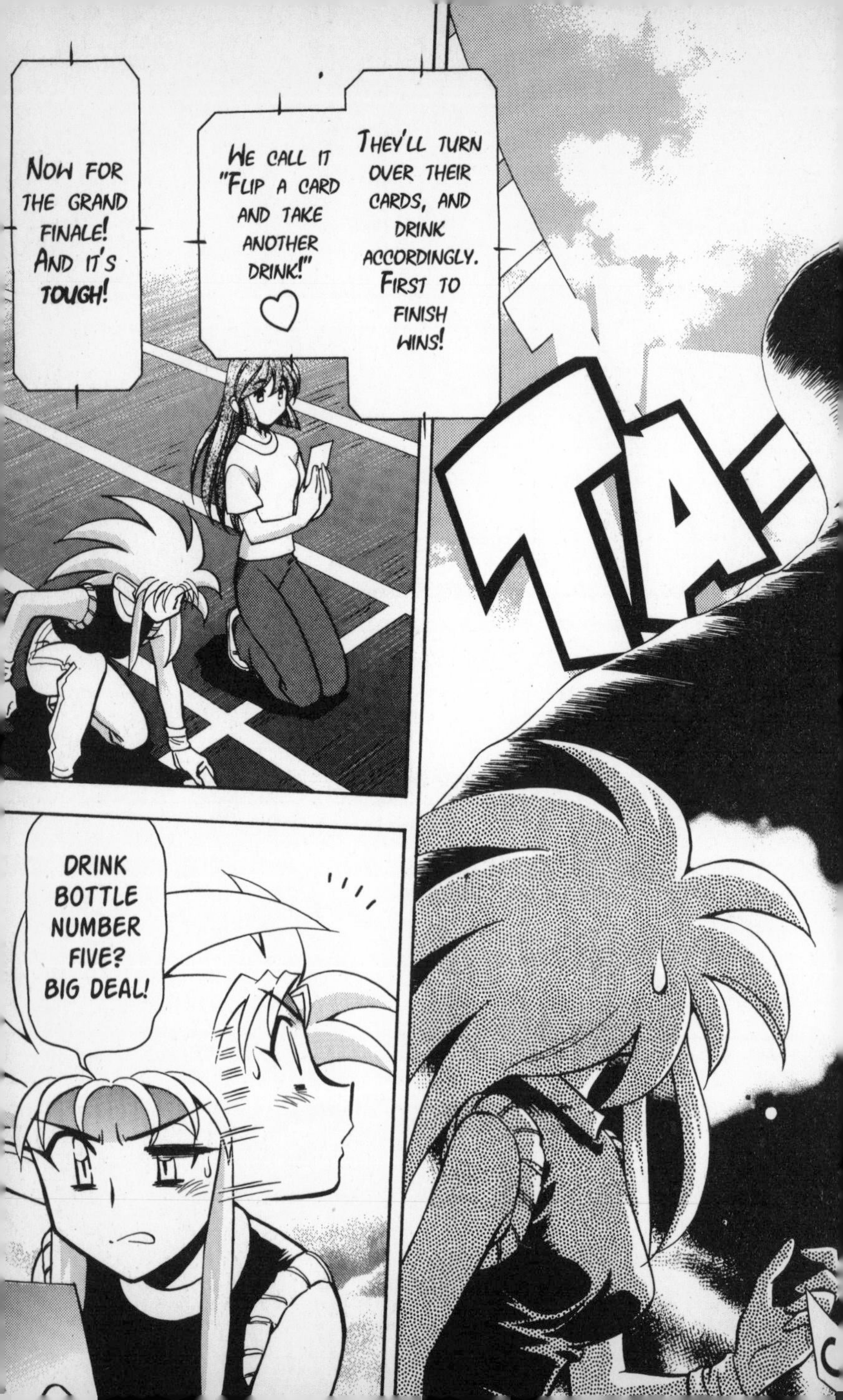

NOW FOR THE GRAND FINALE! AND IT'S TOUGH!
WE CALL IT "FLIP A CARD AND TAKE ANOTHER DRINK!" ♡
THEY'LL TURN OVER THEIR CARDS, AND DRINK ACCORDINGLY. FIRST TO FINISH WINS!
TA-
DRINK BOTTLE NUMBER FIVE? BIG DEAL!

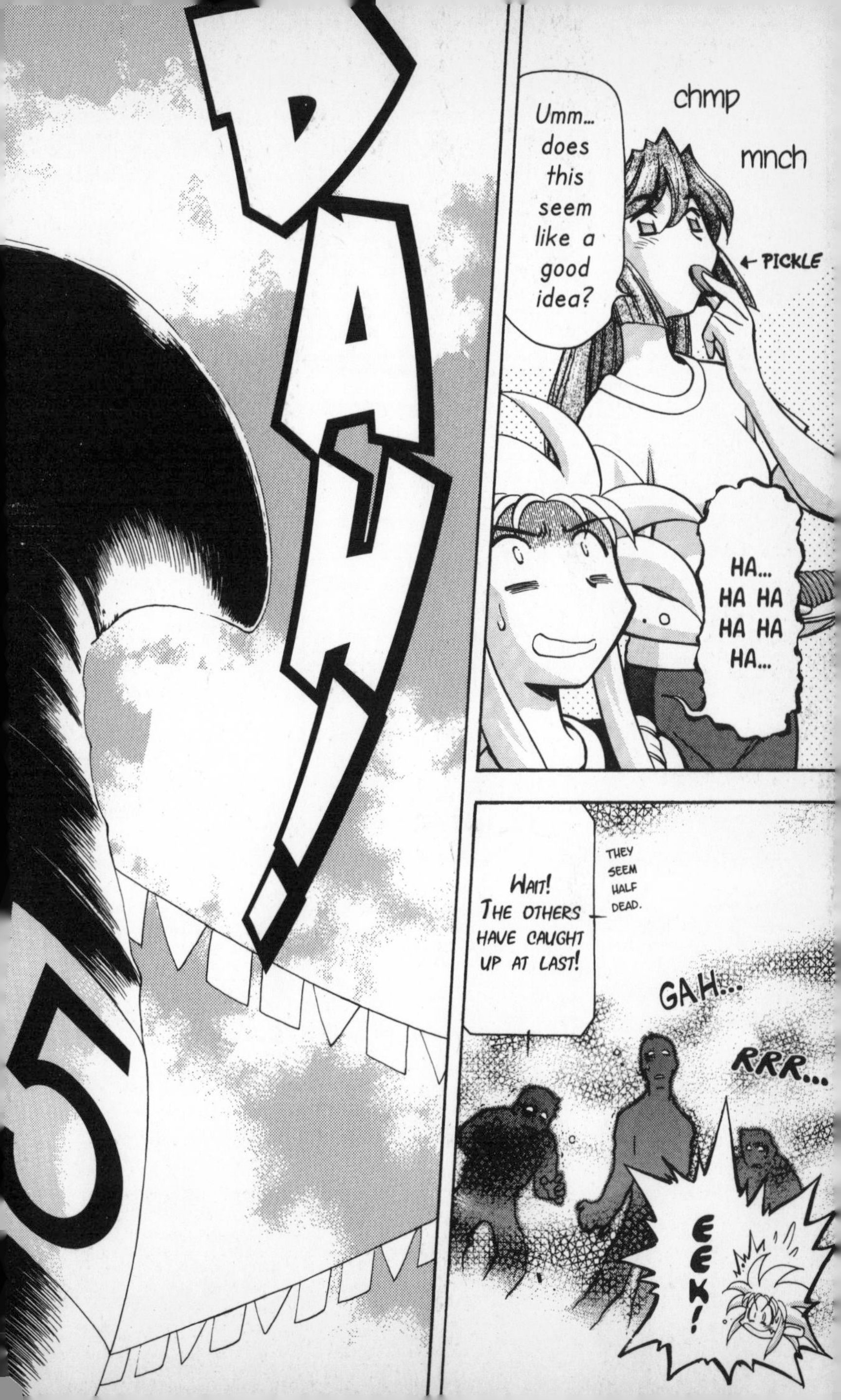
DASH!
Umm... does this seem like a good idea?
chmp
mnch
← PICKLE
HA... HA HA HA HA HA...
WAIT! THE OTHERS HAVE CAUGHT UP AT LAST!
THEY SEEM HALF DEAD.
GAH...
RRR...
EEK!

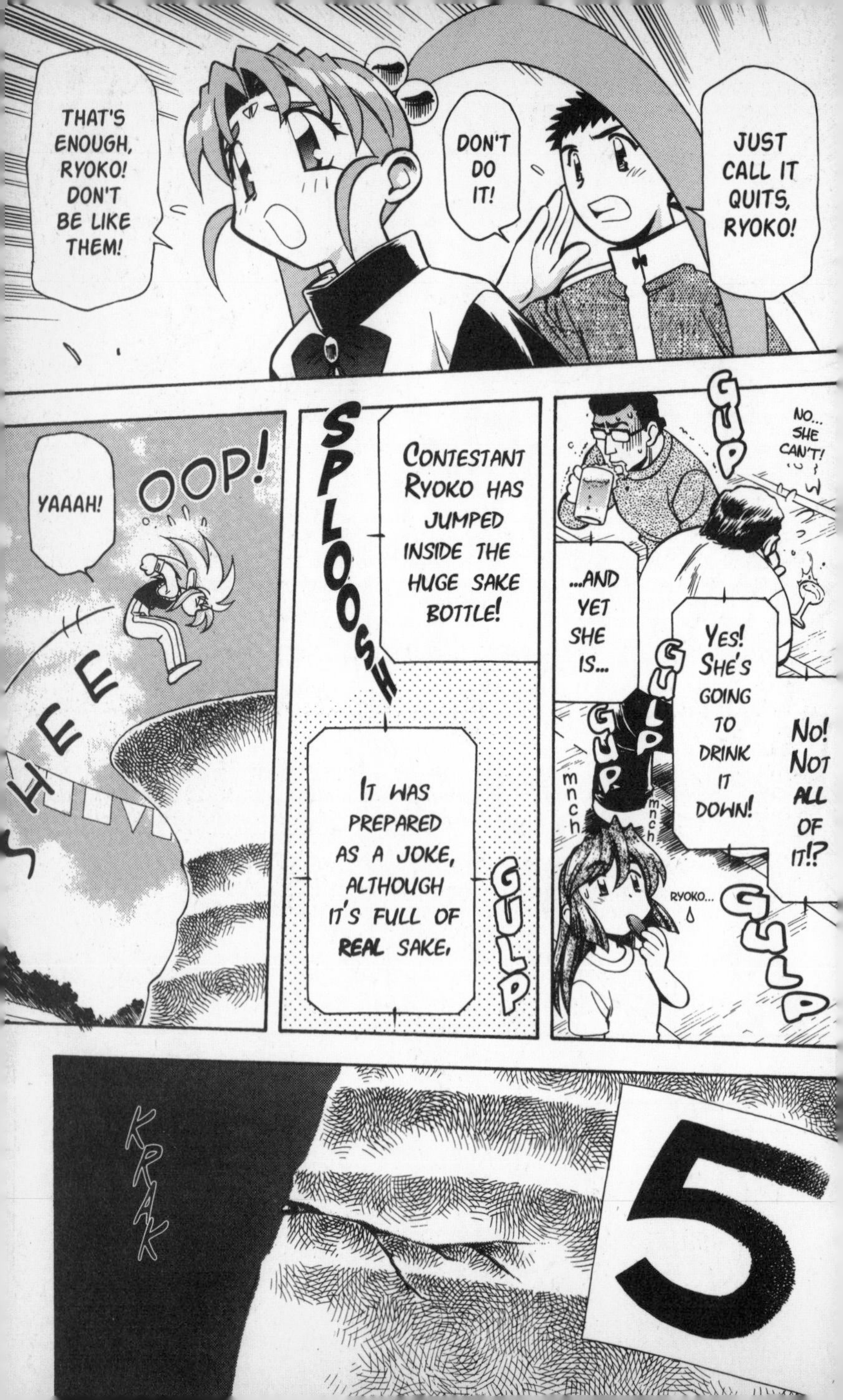
THAT'S ENOUGH, RYOKO! DON'T BE LIKE THEM!
DON'T DO IT!
JUST CALL IT QUITS, RYOKO!
YAAAH!
OOP!
SHEE
SPLOOSH
CONTESTANT RYOKO HAS JUMPED INSIDE THE HUGE SAKE BOTTLE!
IT WAS PREPARED AS A JOKE, ALTHOUGH IT'S FULL OF REAL SAKE,
GULP
GUP
NO... SHE CAN'T!
...AND YET SHE IS...
YES! SHE'S GOING TO DRINK IT DOWN!
GULP
GUP
mnch
mnch
NO! NOT ALL OF IT!?
RYOKO...
GULP
KRAK
5

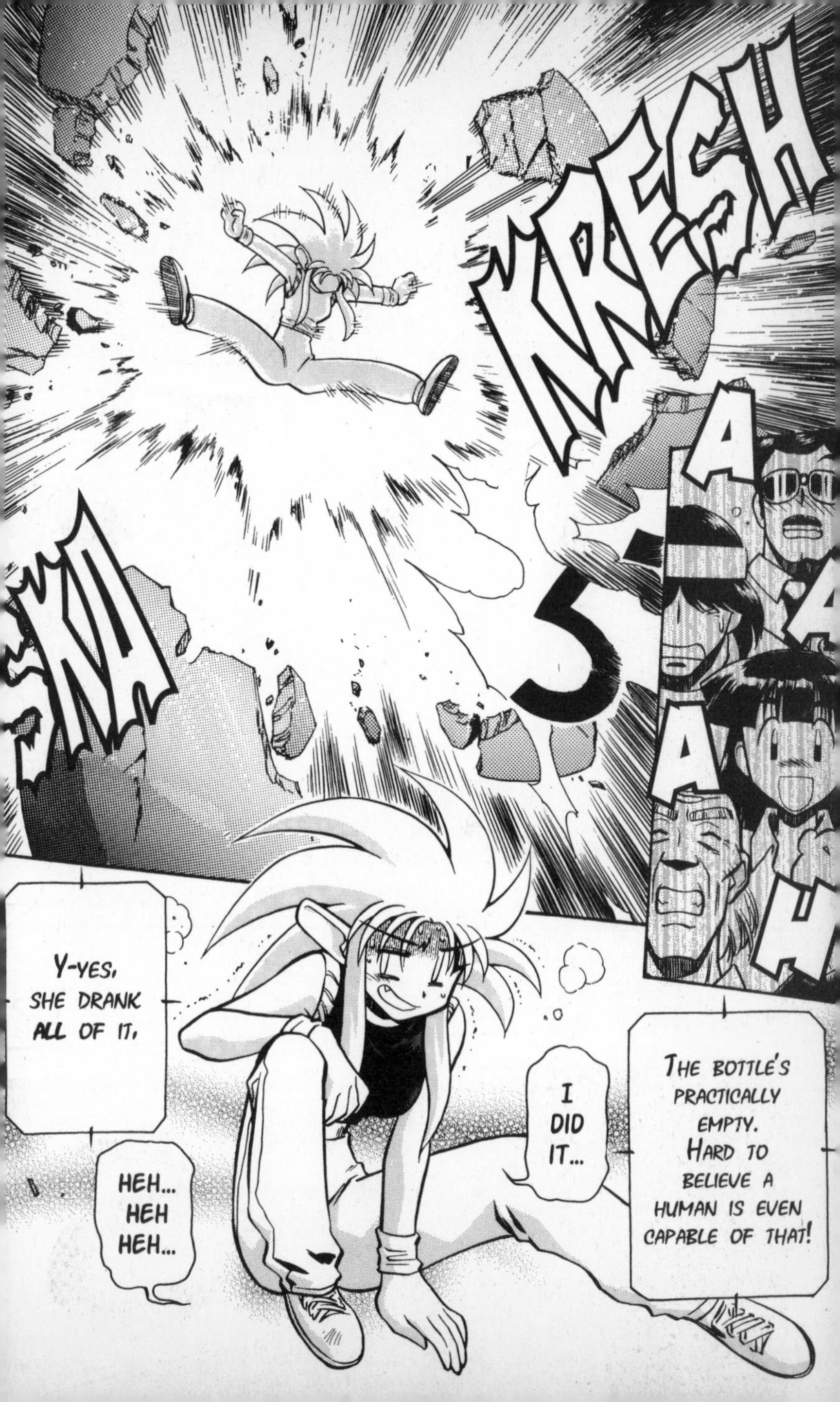
KRESCH
Y-YES, SHE DRANK ALL OF IT,
I DID IT...
THE BOTTLE'S PRACTICALLY EMPTY. HARD TO BELIEVE A HUMAN IS EVEN CAPABLE OF THAT!
HEH... HEH HEH...

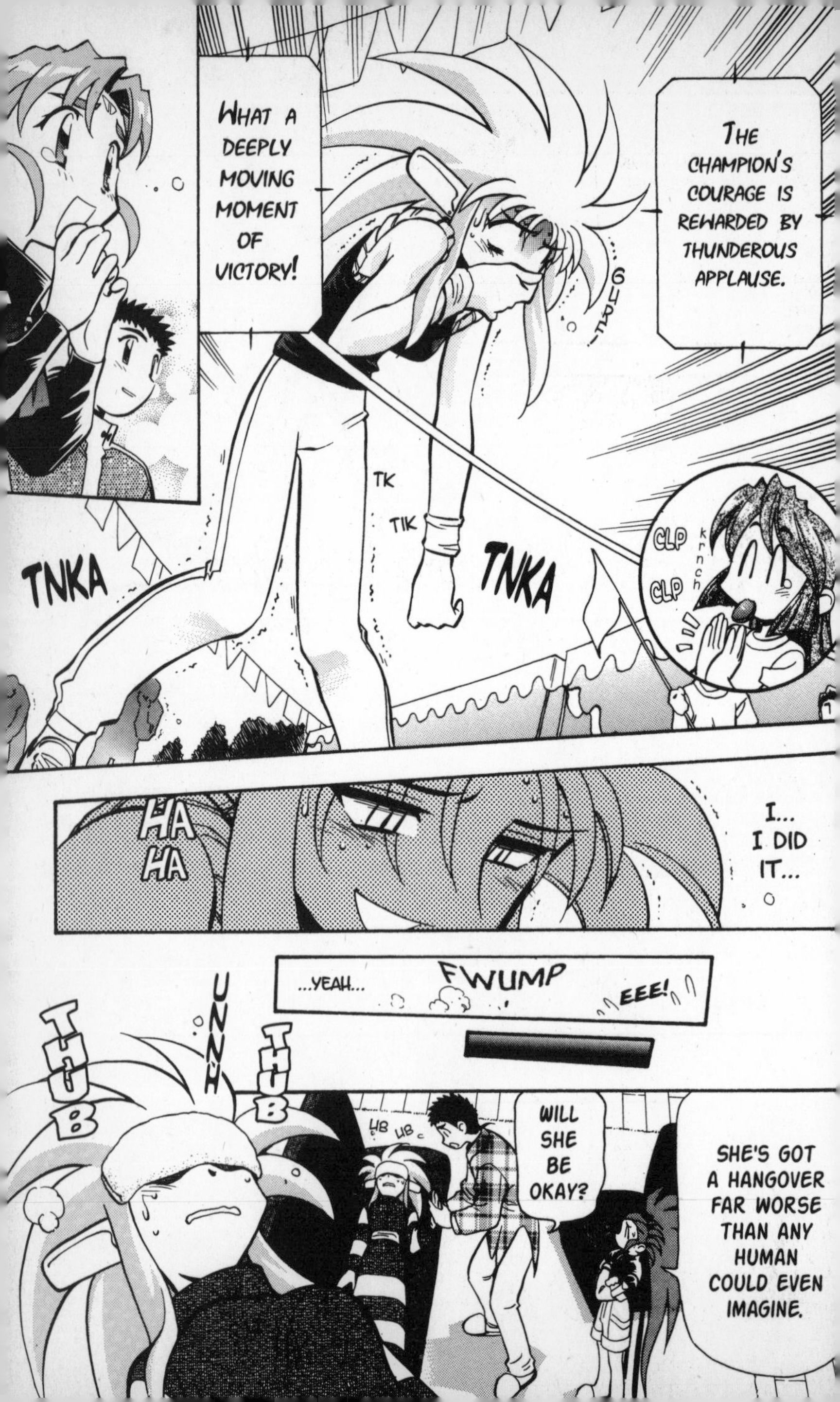

WHAT A DEEPLY MOVING MOMENT OF VICTORY!
THE CHAMPION'S COURAGE IS REWARDED BY THUNDEROUS APPLAUSE.
GURL
TK
TIK
TNKA
TNKA
CLP
krnch
CLP
HA HA
I... I DID IT...
...YEAH...
FWUMP
EEE!
THUB
UNNH
THUB
UB UB
WILL SHE BE OKAY?
SHE'S GOT A HANGOVER FAR WORSE THAN ANY HUMAN COULD EVEN IMAGINE.

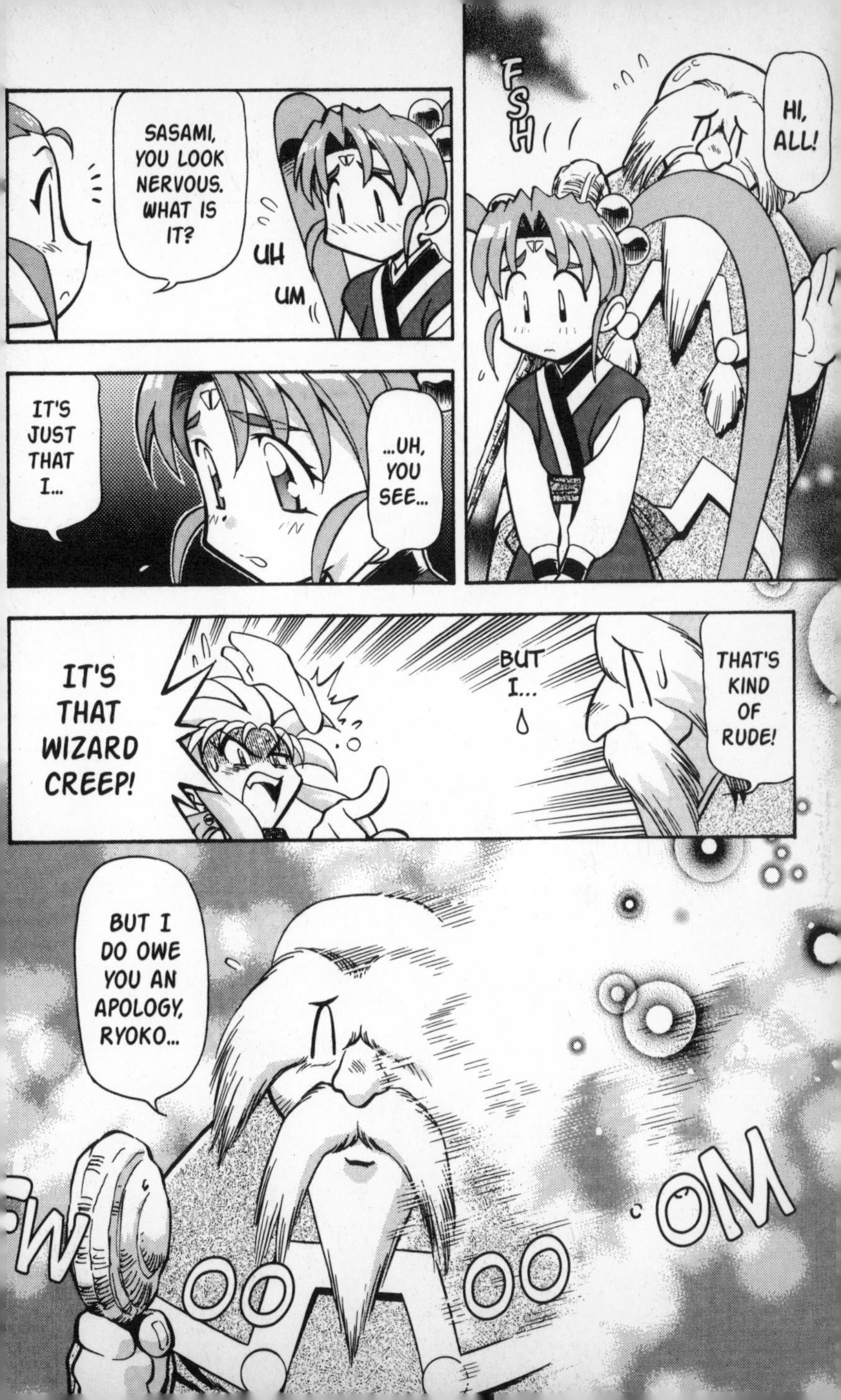
SASAMI, YOU LOOK NERVOUS. WHAT IS IT?
UH
UM
IT'S JUST THAT I...
...UH, YOU SEE...
FSH
HI, ALL!
IT'S THAT WIZARD CREEP!
BUT I...
THAT'S KIND OF RUDE!
BUT I DO OWE YOU AN APOLOGY, RYOKO...
FWOOOOOOM

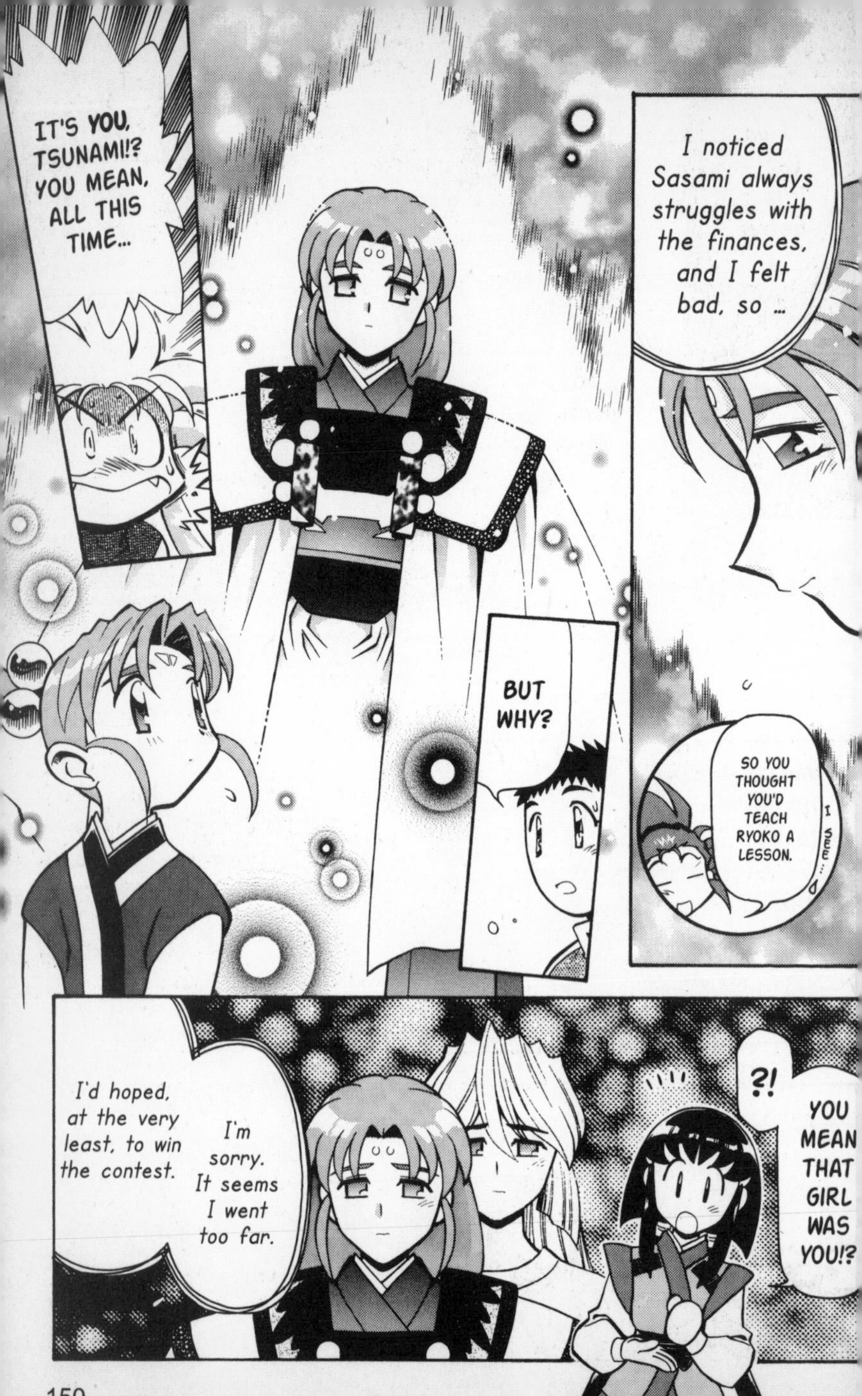
IT'S YOU, TSUNAMI!? YOU MEAN, ALL THIS TIME...
BUT WHY?
I noticed Sasami always struggles with the finances, and I felt bad, so ...
SO YOU THOUGHT YOU'D TEACH RYOKO A LESSON.
I SEE...
I'd hoped, at the very least, to win the contest.
I'm sorry. It seems I went too far.
?!
YOU MEAN THAT GIRL WAS YOU!?

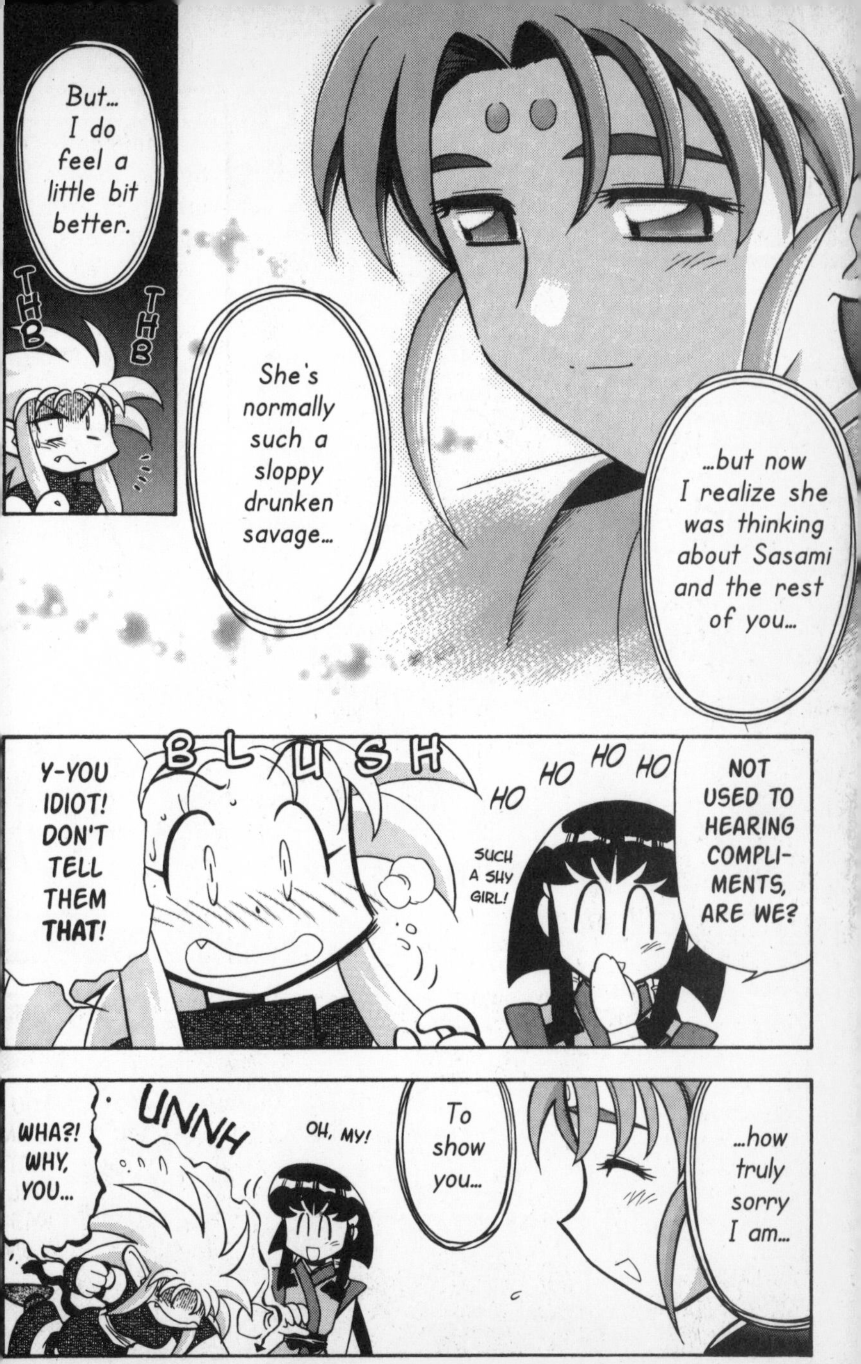

But... I do feel a little bit better.
THB THB
She's normally such a sloppy drunken savage...
...but now I realize she was thinking about Sasami and the rest of you...
Y-YOU IDIOT! DON'T TELL THEM THAT!
BLUSH
HO HO HO HO
SUCH A SHY GIRL!
NOT USED TO HEARING COMPLIMENTS, ARE WE?
WHA?! WHY, YOU...
UNNH
OH, MY!
To show you...
...how truly sorry I am...

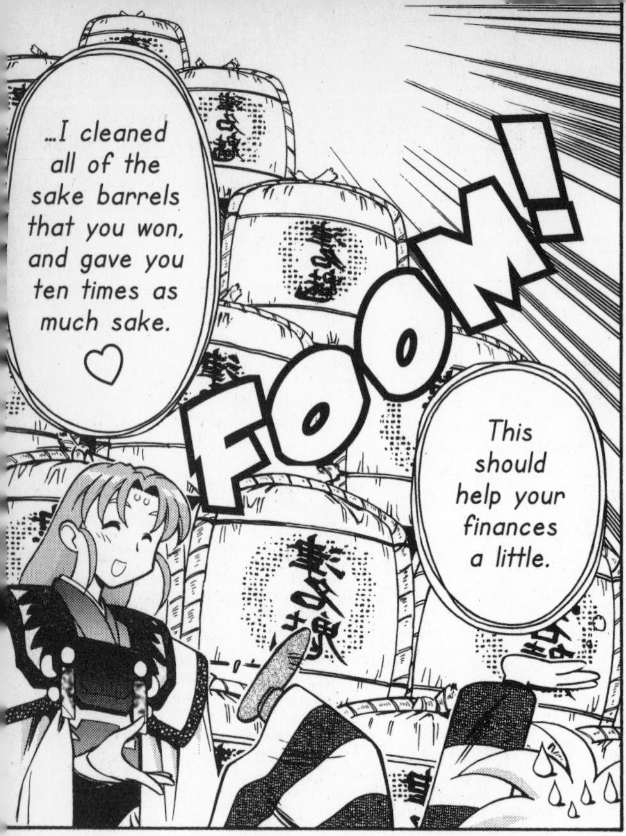
...I cleaned all of the sake barrels that you won, and gave you ten times as much sake. ♡
FOOOM!
This should help your finances a little.
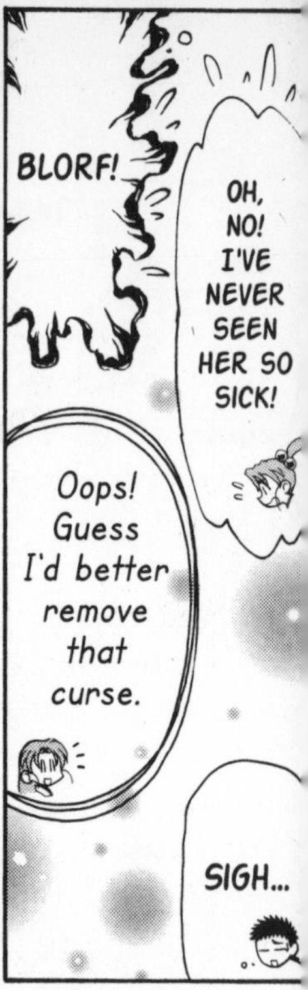
BLORF!
OH, NO! I'VE NEVER SEEN HER SO SICK!
Oops! Guess I'd better remove that curse.
SIGH...

THE FOLLOWING DAY.

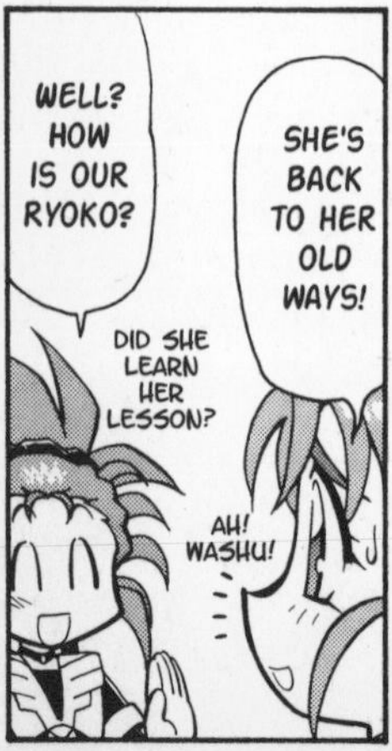
WELL? HOW IS OUR RYOKO?
SHE'S BACK TO HER OLD WAYS!
DID SHE LEARN HER LESSON?
AH! WASHU!
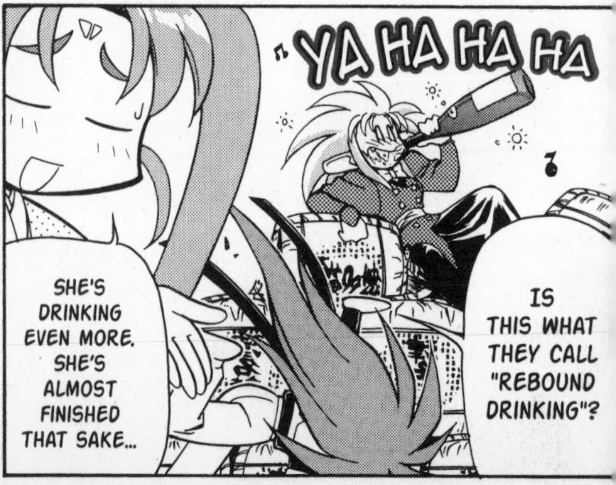
YA HA HA HA
SHE'S DRINKING EVEN MORE. SHE'S ALMOST FINISHED THAT SAKE...
IS THIS WHAT THEY CALL "REBOUND DRINKING"?

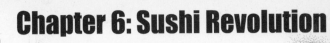

Chapter 6: Sushi Revolution

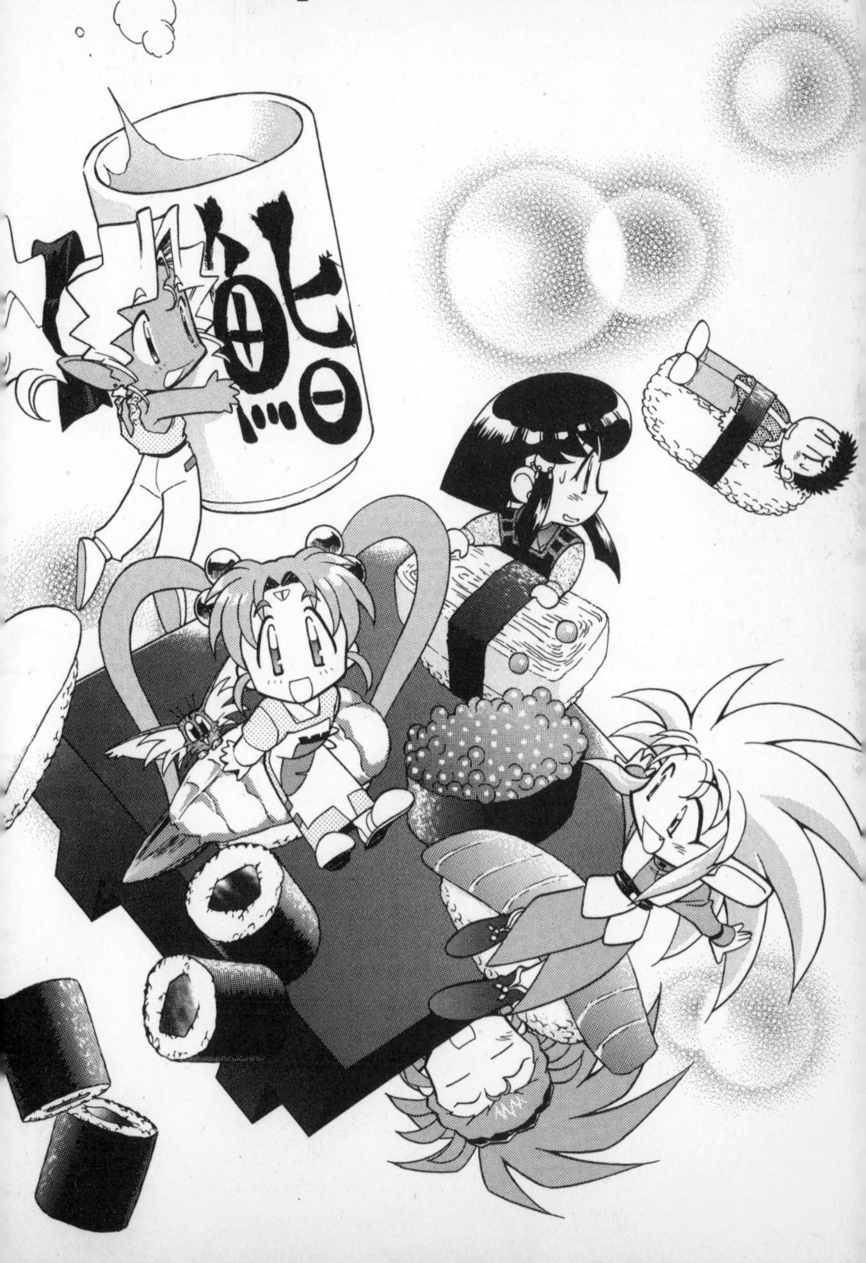

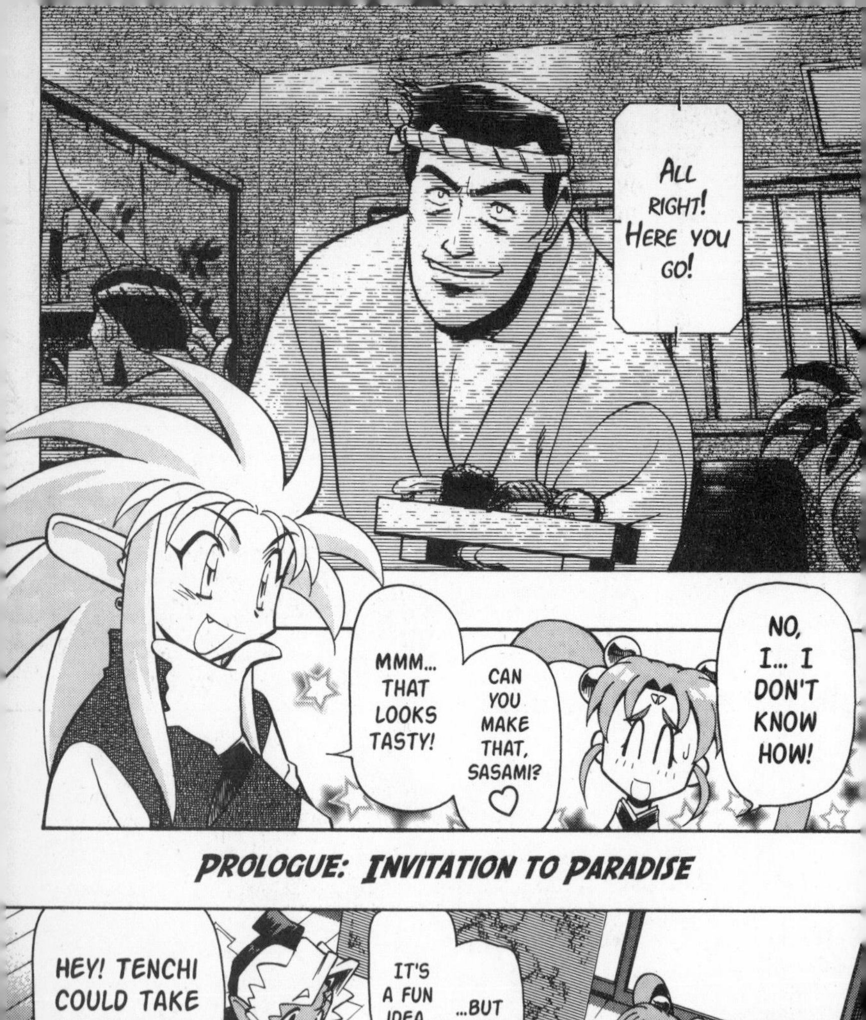
ALL RIGHT! HERE YOU GO!
MMM... THAT LOOKS TASTY!
CAN YOU MAKE THAT, SASAMI? ♡
NO, I... I DON'T KNOW HOW!

PROLOGUE: INVITATION TO PARADISE

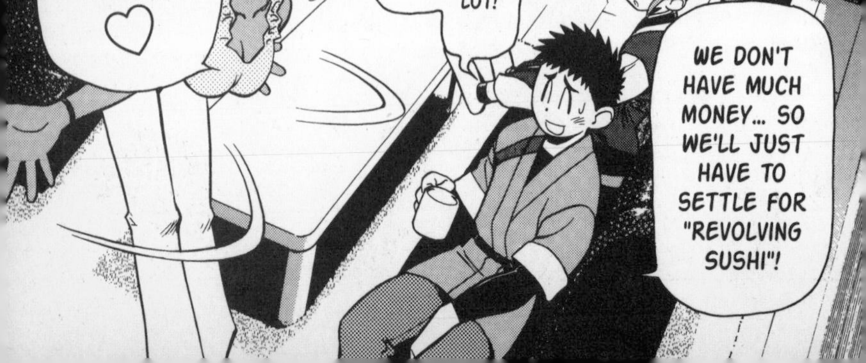
HEY! TENCHI COULD TAKE US OUT FOR SUSHI! ♡
IT'S A FUN IDEA...
...BUT IT CAN COST A LOT!
WE DON'T HAVE MUCH MONEY... SO WE'LL JUST HAVE TO SETTLE FOR "REVOLVING SUSHI"!

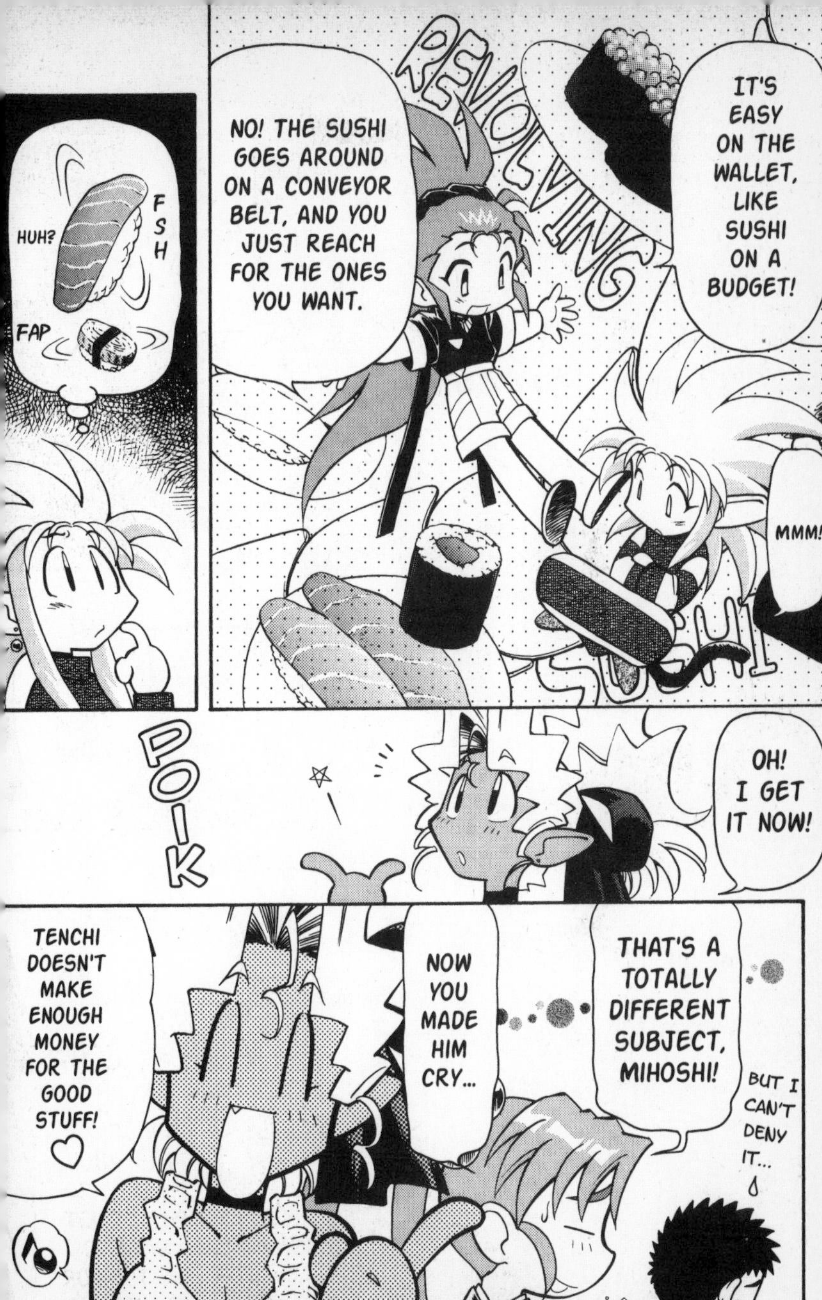
HUH?
FSH
FAP
NO! THE SUSHI GOES AROUND ON A CONVEYOR BELT, AND YOU JUST REACH FOR THE ONES YOU WANT.
REVOLVING
IT'S EASY ON THE WALLET, LIKE SUSHI ON A BUDGET!
MMM!
SUSHI
POIK
OH! I GET IT NOW!
TENCHI DOESN'T MAKE ENOUGH MONEY FOR THE GOOD STUFF! ♡
NOW YOU MADE HIM CRY...
THAT'S A TOTALLY DIFFERENT SUBJECT, MIHOSHI!
BUT I CAN'T DENY IT...

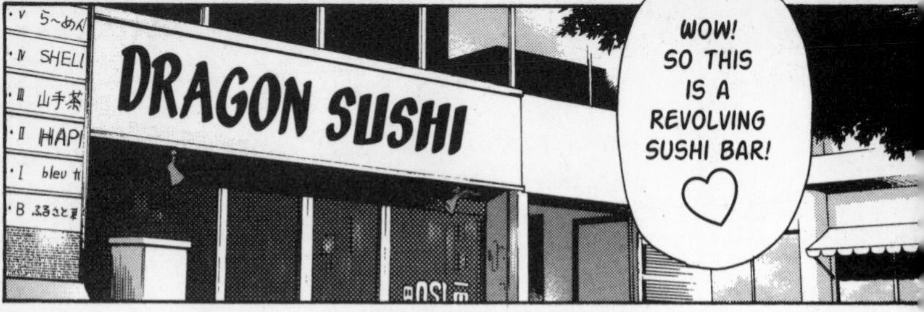

DRAGON SUSHI
WOW! SO THIS IS A REVOLVING SUSHI BAR! ♡

ACT 1: THE GATEWAY TO HELL?

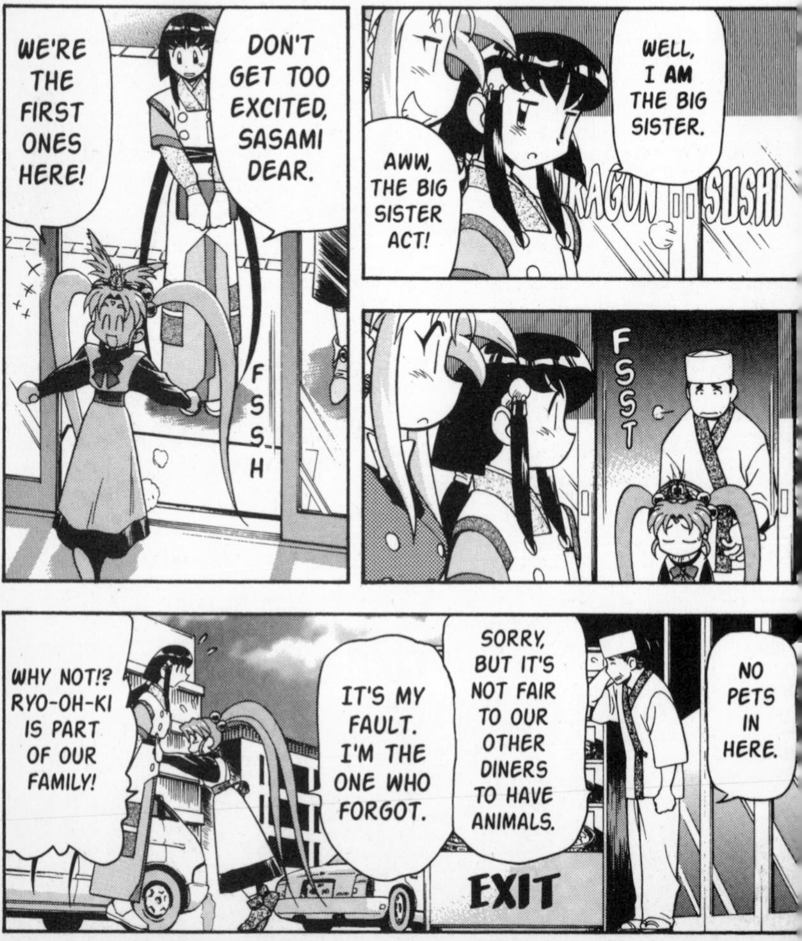

WE'RE THE FIRST ONES HERE!
DON'T GET TOO EXCITED, SASAMI DEAR.
FSSH
AWW, THE BIG SISTER ACT!
WELL, I AM THE BIG SISTER.
DRAGON SUSHI
FSST
WHY NOT!? RYO-OH-KI IS PART OF OUR FAMILY!
IT'S MY FAULT. I'M THE ONE WHO FORGOT.
SORRY, BUT IT'S NOT FAIR TO OUR OTHER DINERS TO HAVE ANIMALS.
NO PETS IN HERE.
EXIT

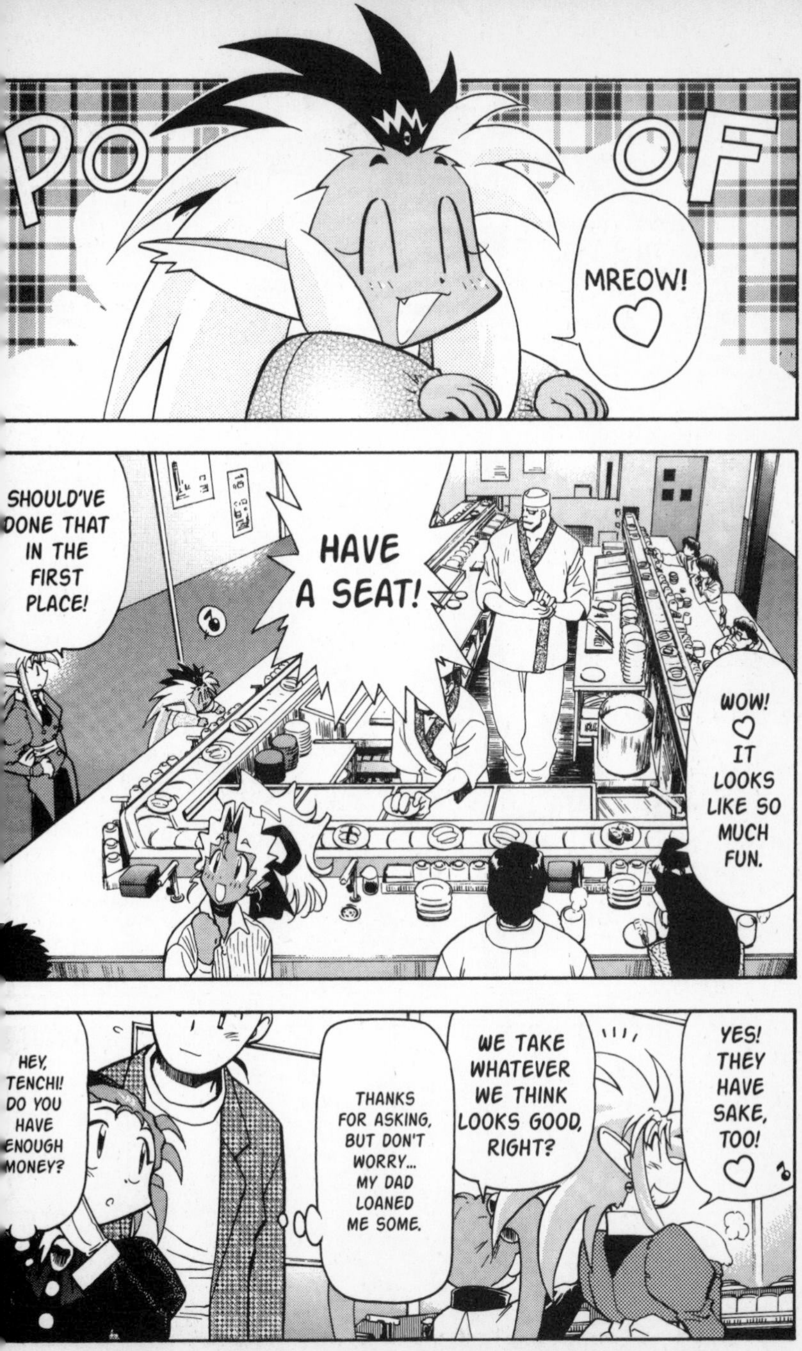
POOF
MREOW! ♡
SHOULD'VE DONE THAT IN THE FIRST PLACE!
HAVE A SEAT!
WOW! ♡ IT LOOKS LIKE SO MUCH FUN.
HEY, TENCHI! DO YOU HAVE ENOUGH MONEY?
THANKS FOR ASKING, BUT DON'T WORRY... MY DAD LOANED ME SOME.
WE TAKE WHATEVER WE THINK LOOKS GOOD, RIGHT?
YES! THEY HAVE SAKE, TOO! ♡

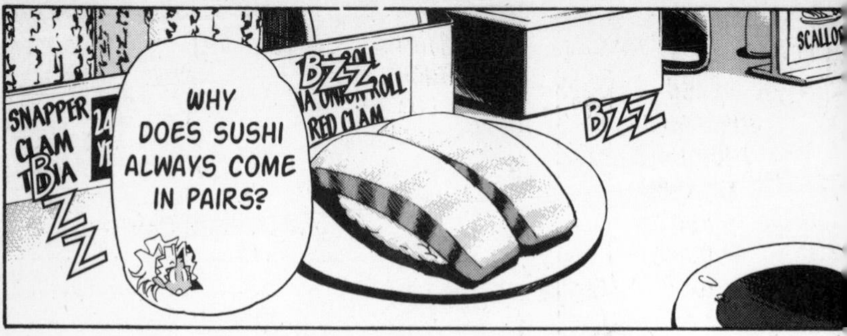
SNAPPER
CLAM
BZZ
WHY DOES SUSHI ALWAYS COME IN PAIRS?
BZZ
RED CLAM
BZZ

ACT 2: THE KING OF KNOWLEDGE

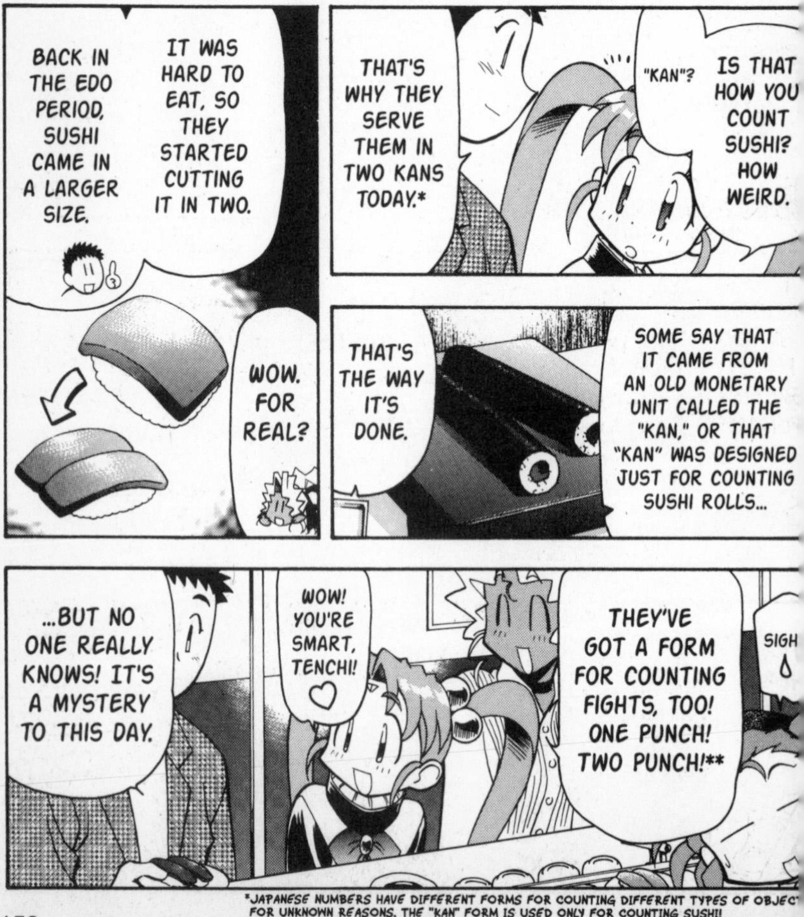
BACK IN THE EDO PERIOD, SUSHI CAME IN A LARGER SIZE.
IT WAS HARD TO EAT, SO THEY STARTED CUTTING IT IN TWO.
WOW. FOR REAL?
THAT'S WHY THEY SERVE THEM IN TWO KANS TODAY.*
"KAN"?
IS THAT HOW YOU COUNT SUSHI? HOW WEIRD.
THAT'S THE WAY IT'S DONE.
SOME SAY THAT IT CAME FROM AN OLD MONETARY UNIT CALLED THE "KAN," OR THAT "KAN" WAS DESIGNED JUST FOR COUNTING SUSHI ROLLS...
...BUT NO ONE REALLY KNOWS! IT'S A MYSTERY TO THIS DAY.
WOW! YOU'RE SMART, TENCHI!
THEY'VE GOT A FORM FOR COUNTING FIGHTS, TOO! ONE PUNCH! TWO PUNCH!**
SIGH

*JAPANESE NUMBERS HAVE DIFFERENT FORMS FOR COUNTING DIFFERENT TYPES OF OBJEC
FOR UNKNOWN REASONS, THE "KAN" FORM IS USED ONLY FOR COUNTING SUSHI!
**MIHOSHI IS THINKING OF A TV COMMERCIAL FOR THE ENERGY DRINK LIPOVITAMIN A, IN WHI
A MAN YELLS, "FIGHT! ONE PUNCH!"

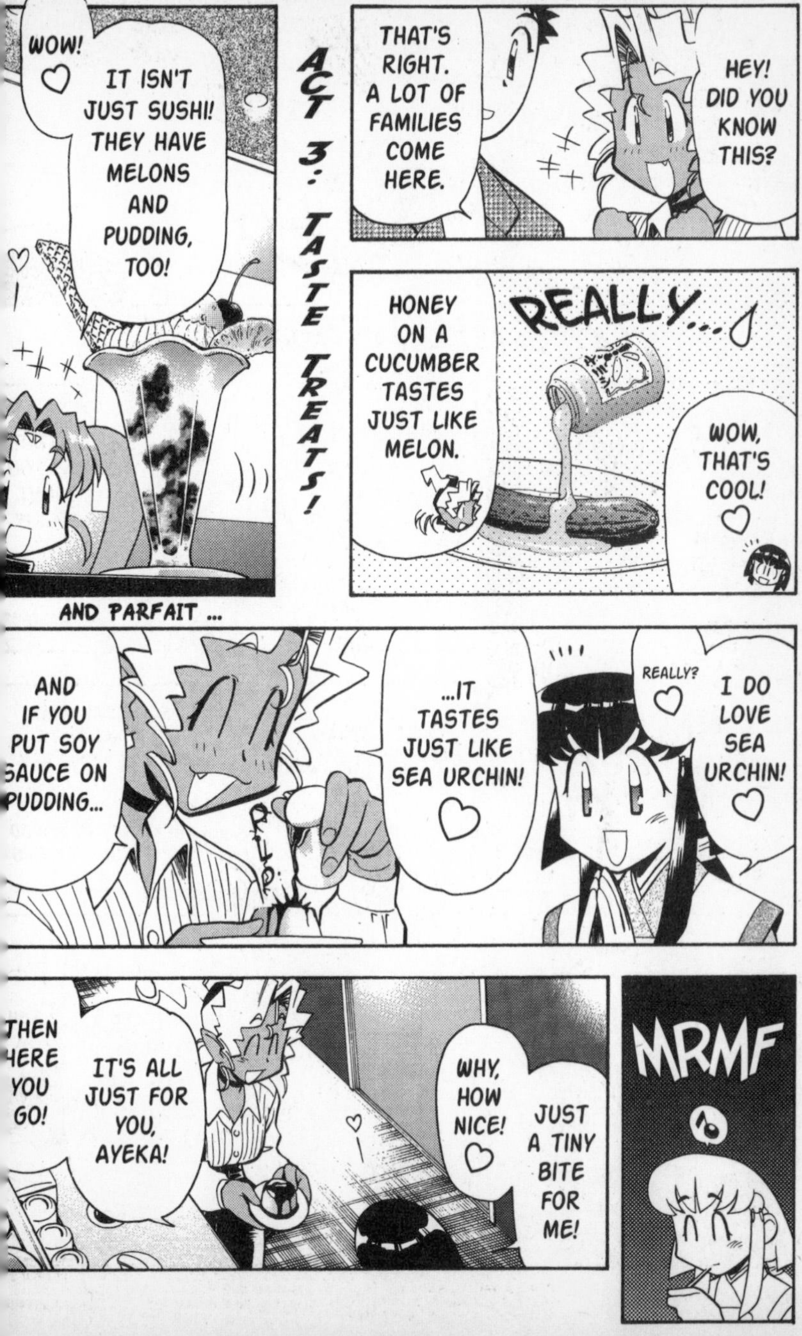
WOW! ♡
IT ISN'T JUST SUSHI! THEY HAVE MELONS AND PUDDING, TOO!
AND PARFAIT ...
ACT 3: TASTE TREATS!
THAT'S RIGHT. A LOT OF FAMILIES COME HERE.
HEY! DID YOU KNOW THIS?
HONEY ON A CUCUMBER TASTES JUST LIKE MELON.
REALLY...
WOW, THAT'S COOL! ♡
AND IF YOU PUT SOY SAUCE ON PUDDING...
...IT TASTES JUST LIKE SEA URCHIN! ♡
REALLY? ♡
I DO LOVE SEA URCHIN! ♡
THEN HERE YOU GO!
IT'S ALL JUST FOR YOU, AYEKA!
WHY, HOW NICE! ♡
JUST A TINY BITE FOR ME!
MRMF

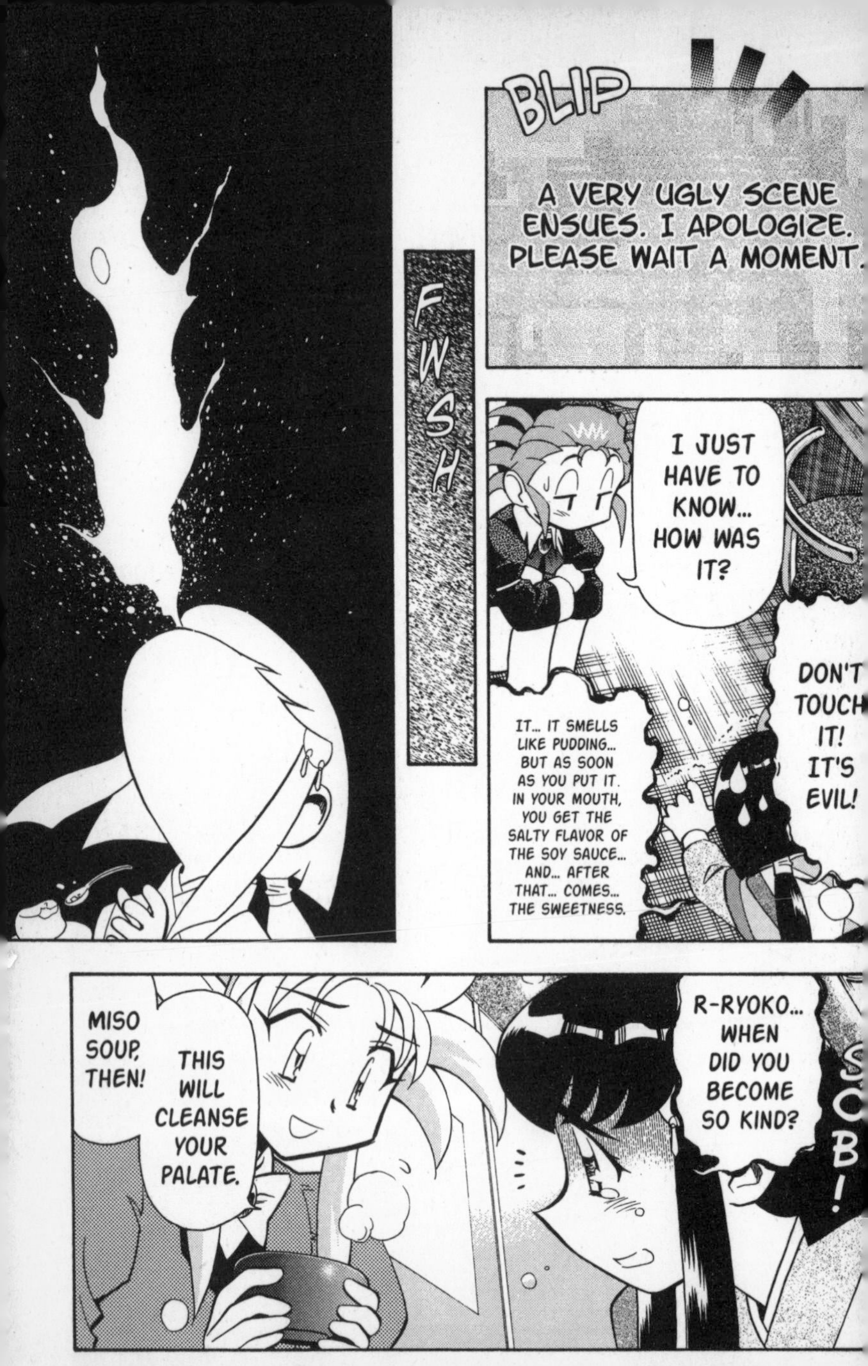
FWSH
BLIP
A VERY UGLY SCENE ENSUES. I APOLOGIZE. PLEASE WAIT A MOMENT.
I JUST HAVE TO KNOW... HOW WAS IT?
DON'T TOUCH IT! IT'S EVIL!
IT... IT SMELLS LIKE PUDDING... BUT AS SOON AS YOU PUT IT IN YOUR MOUTH, YOU GET THE SALTY FLAVOR OF THE SOY SAUCE... AND... AFTER THAT... COMES... THE SWEETNESS.
MISO SOUP, THEN!
THIS WILL CLEANSE YOUR PALATE.
R-RYOKO... WHEN DID YOU BECOME SO KIND?
SOB!

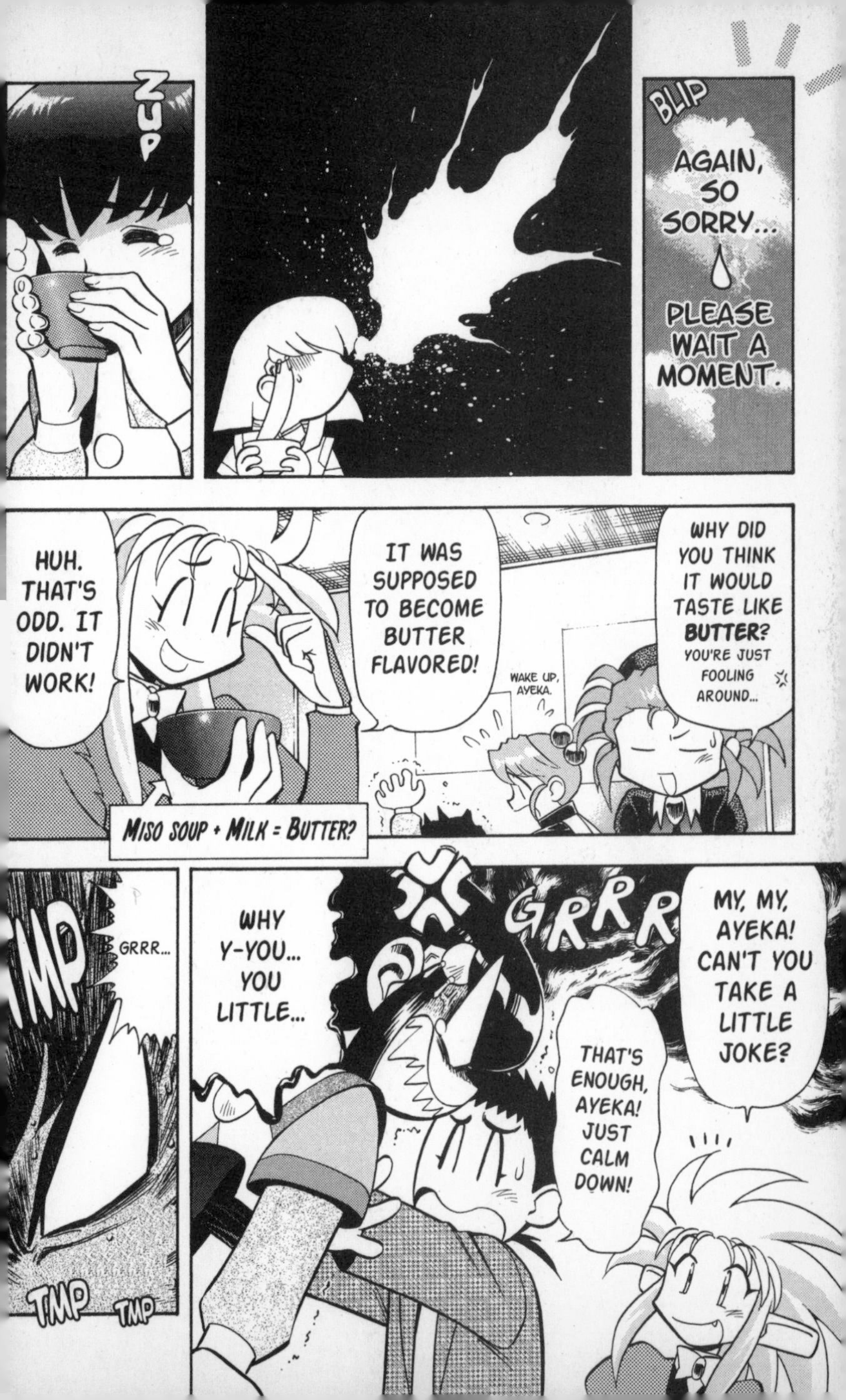
ZUP
BLIP
AGAIN, SO SORRY... PLEASE WAIT A MOMENT.
HUH. THAT'S ODD. IT DIDN'T WORK!
IT WAS SUPPOSED TO BECOME BUTTER FLAVORED!
WAKE UP, AYEKA.
WHY DID YOU THINK IT WOULD TASTE LIKE BUTTER? YOU'RE JUST FOOLING AROUND...
MISO SOUP + MILK = BUTTER?
GRRR...
TMP TMP
WHY Y-YOU... YOU LITTLE...
GRRR
MY, MY, AYEKA! CAN'T YOU TAKE A LITTLE JOKE?
THAT'S ENOUGH, AYEKA! JUST CALM DOWN!

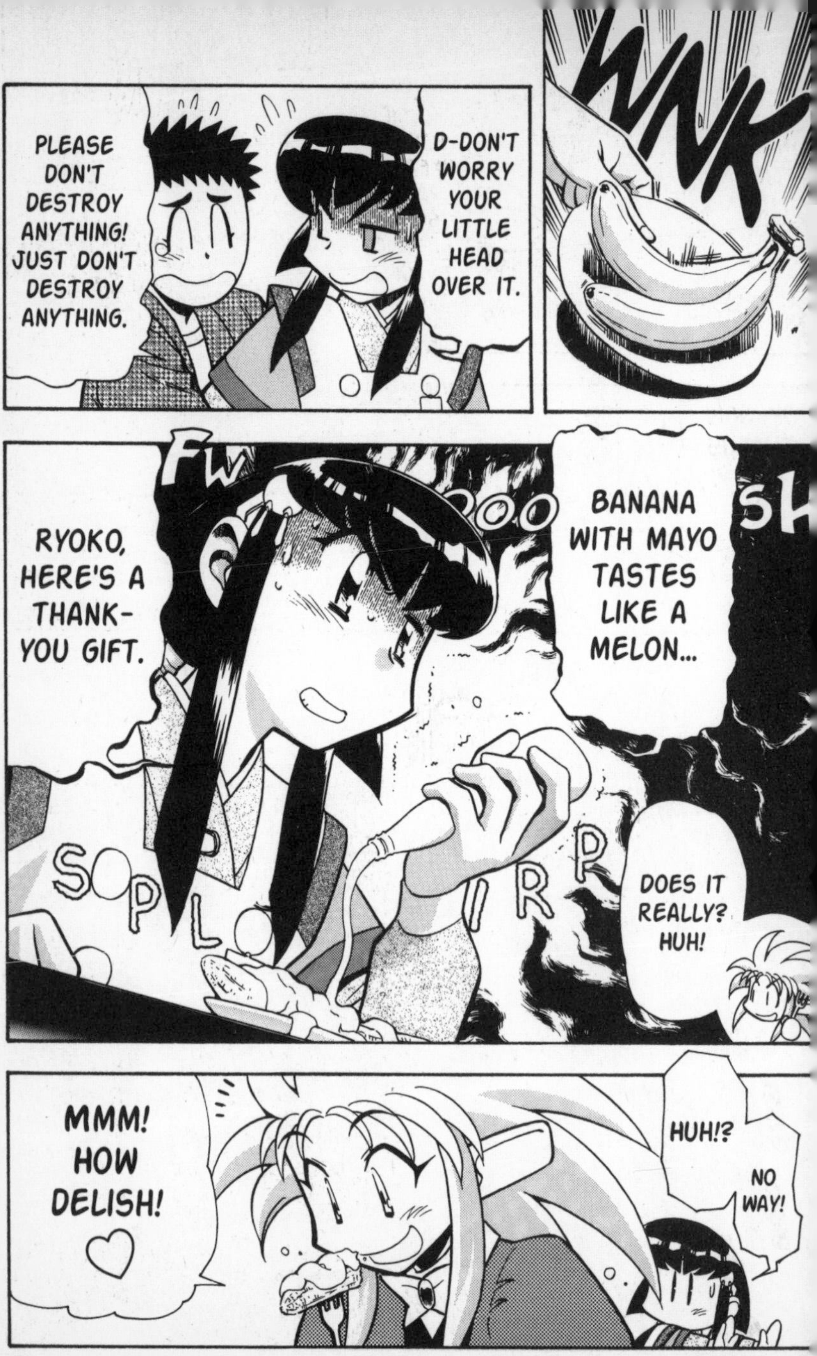

PLEASE DON'T DESTROY ANYTHING! JUST DON'T DESTROY ANYTHING.
D-DON'T WORRY YOUR LITTLE HEAD OVER IT.
WNK
RYOKO, HERE'S A THANK-YOU GIFT.
BANANA WITH MAYO TASTES LIKE A MELON...
DOES IT REALLY? HUH!
MMM! HOW DELISH! ♡
HUH!?
NO WAY!

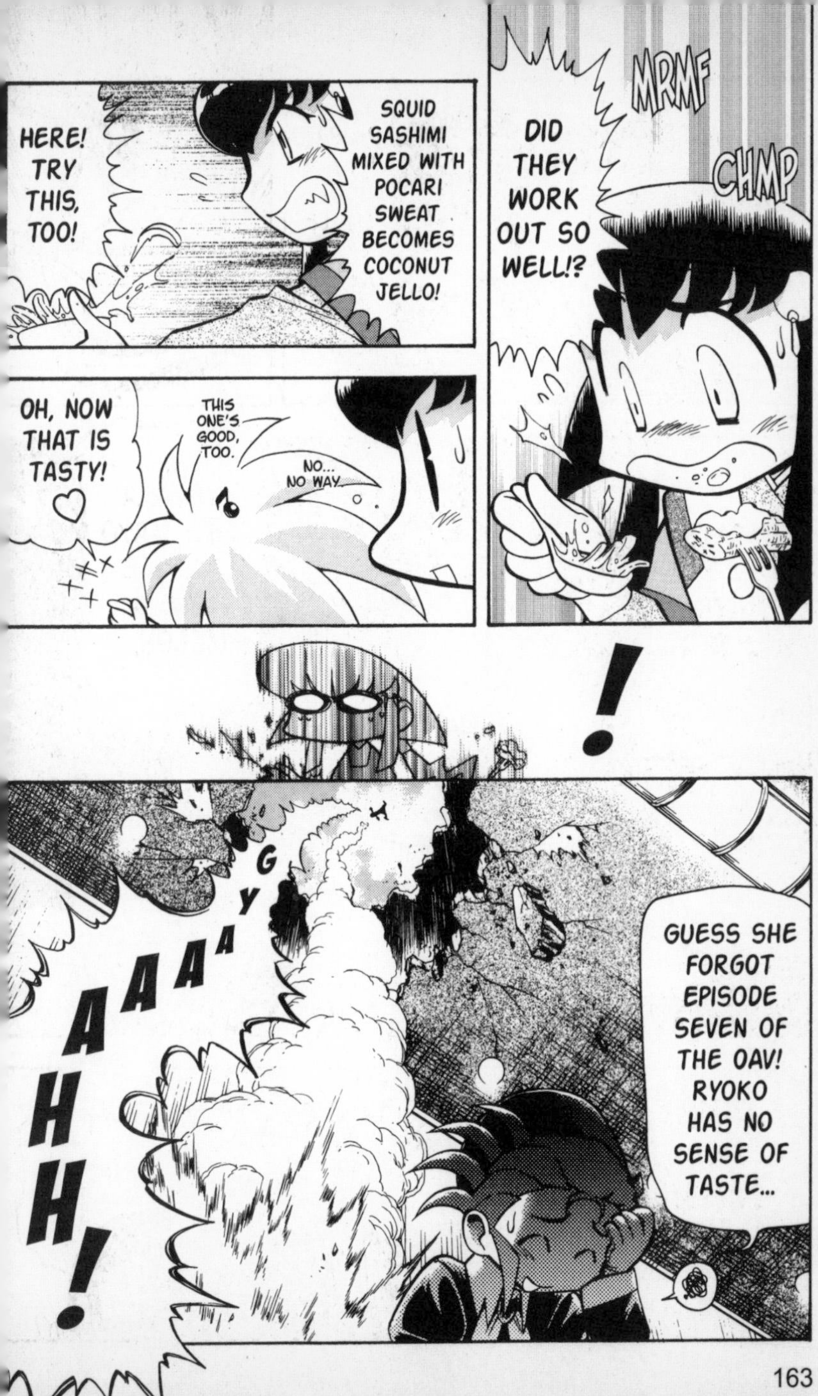
HERE! TRY THIS, TOO!
SQUID SASHIMI MIXED WITH POCARI SWEAT BECOMES COCONUT JELLO!
OH, NOW THAT IS TASTY! ♡
THIS ONE'S GOOD, TOO.
NO... NO WAY.
MRMF
CHMP
DID THEY WORK OUT SO WELL!?
!
GYAAAAAAHHHH!
GUESS SHE FORGOT EPISODE SEVEN OF THE OAV! RYOKO HAS NO SENSE OF TASTE...

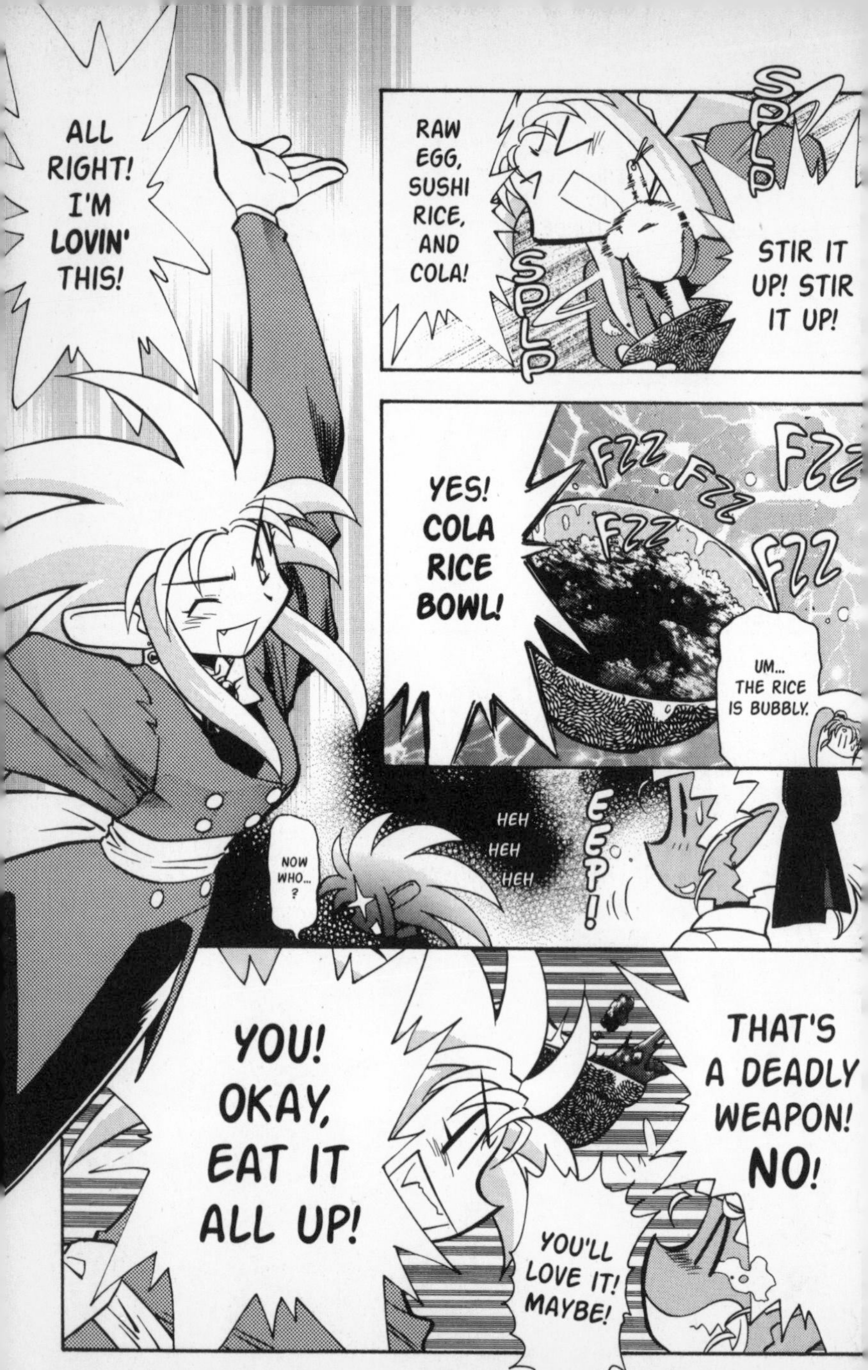
ALL RIGHT! I'M LOVIN' THIS!
RAW EGG, SUSHI RICE, AND COLA!
SPLP
SPLP
STIR IT UP! STIR IT UP!
YES! COLA RICE BOWL!
FZZ
FZZ
FZZ
FZZ
FZZ
UM... THE RICE IS BUBBLY.
NOW WHO... ?
HEH HEH HEH
EEP!
YOU! OKAY, EAT IT ALL UP!
YOU'LL LOVE IT! MAYBE!
THAT'S A DEADLY WEAPON! NO!

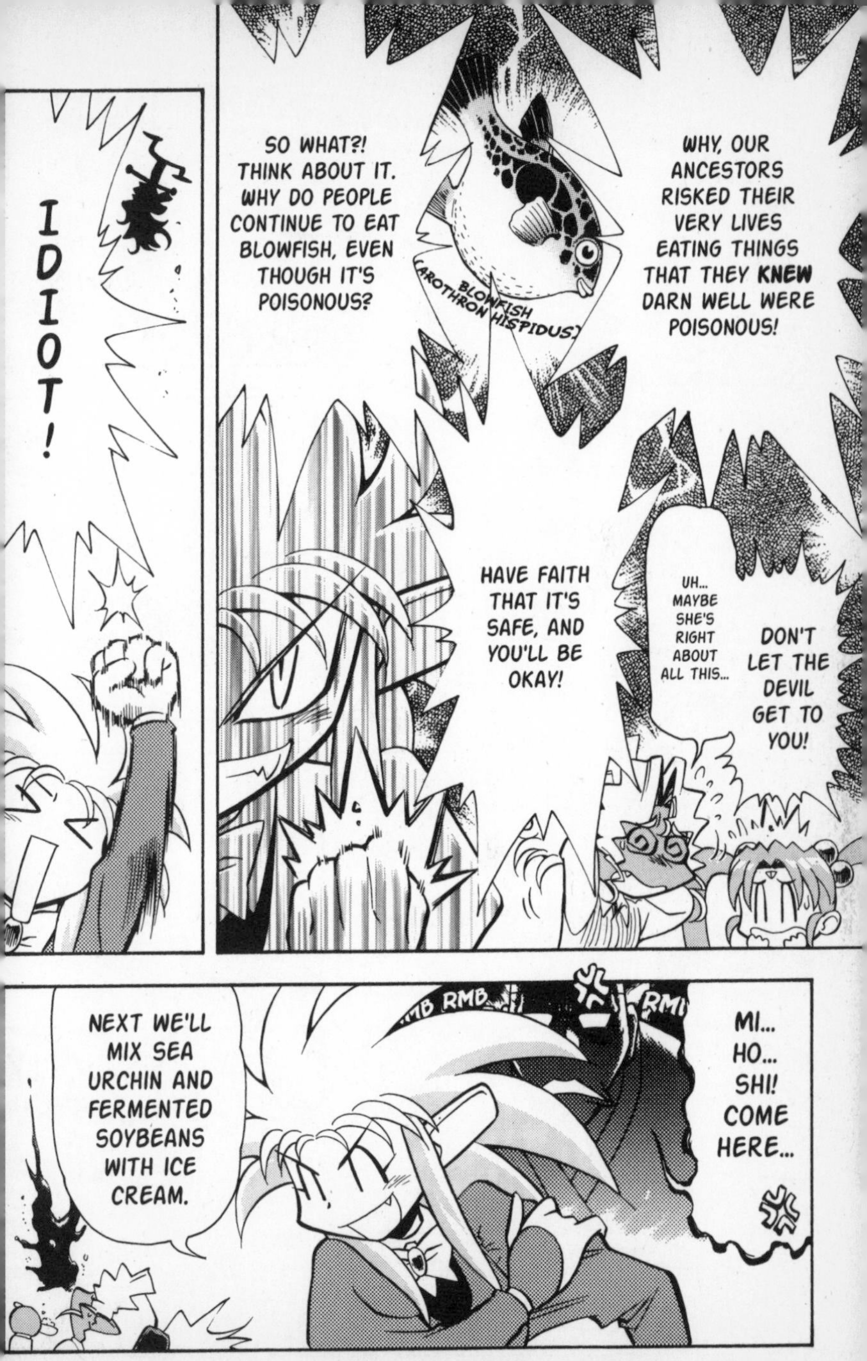
IDIOT!
SO WHAT?! THINK ABOUT IT. WHY DO PEOPLE CONTINUE TO EAT BLOWFISH, EVEN THOUGH IT'S POISONOUS?
BLOWFISH (AROTHRON HISPIDUS)
WHY, OUR ANCESTORS RISKED THEIR VERY LIVES EATING THINGS THAT THEY **KNEW** DARN WELL WERE POISONOUS!
HAVE FAITH THAT IT'S SAFE, AND YOU'LL BE OKAY!
UH... MAYBE SHE'S RIGHT ABOUT ALL THIS...
DON'T LET THE DEVIL GET TO YOU!
NEXT WE'LL MIX SEA URCHIN AND FERMENTED SOYBEANS WITH ICE CREAM.
RMB RMB
MI... HO... SHI! COME HERE...

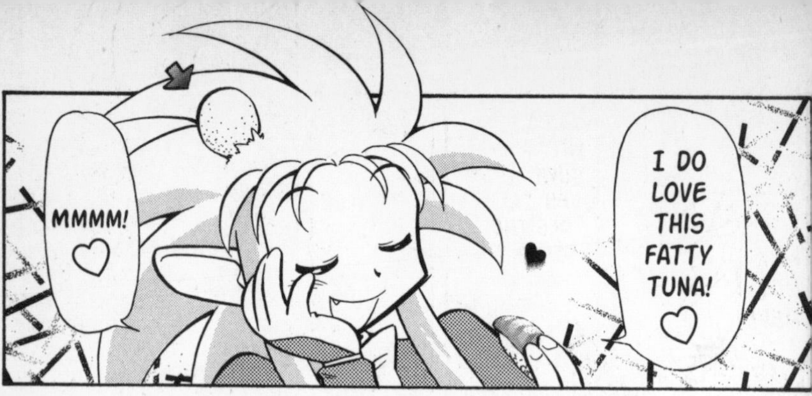
MMMM! ♡
I DO LOVE THIS FATTY TUNA! ♡

ACT 4: THE KING APPEARS

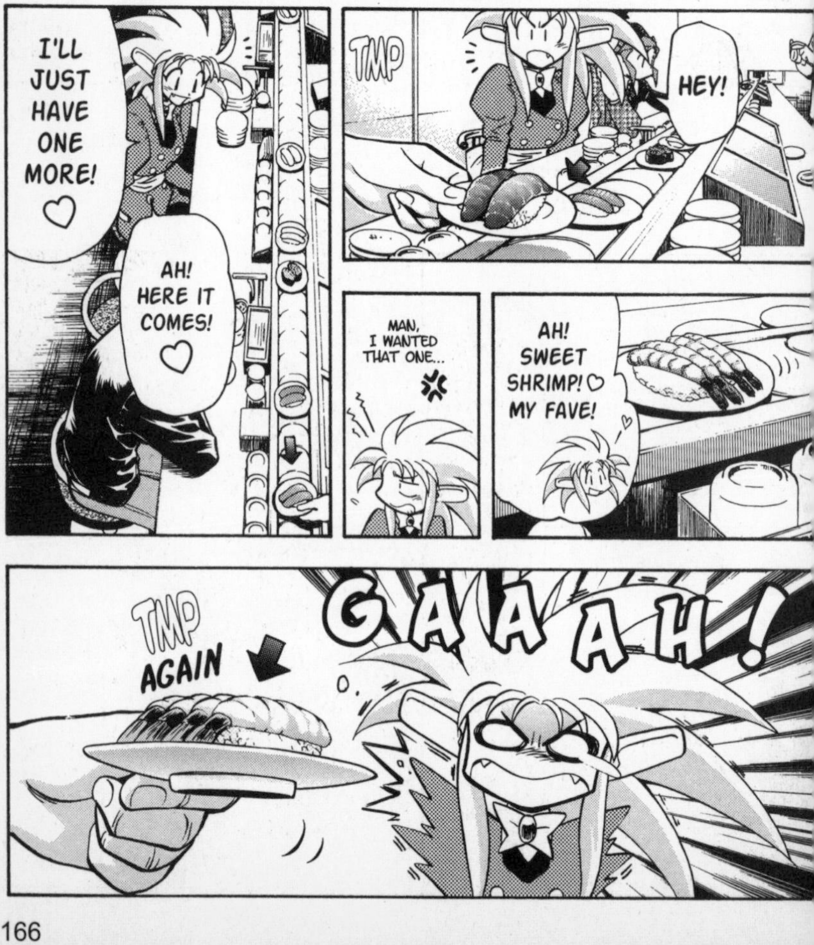
I'LL JUST HAVE ONE MORE! ♡
AH! HERE IT COMES! ♡
TMP
HEY!
MAN, I WANTED THAT ONE...
AH! SWEET SHRIMP! ♡ MY FAVE!
TMP AGAIN
GAAAH!

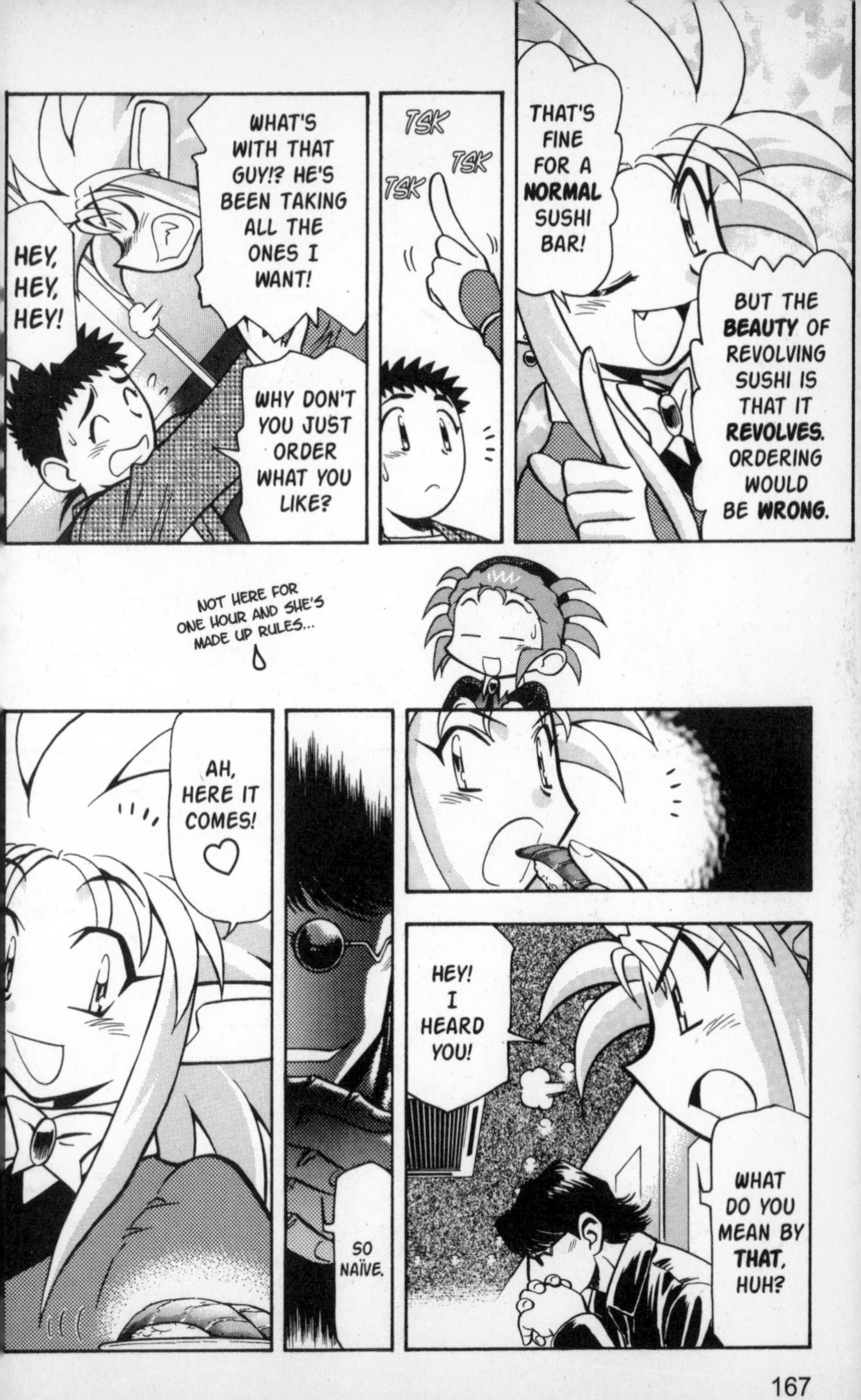
HEY, HEY, HEY!
WHAT'S WITH THAT GUY!? HE'S BEEN TAKING ALL THE ONES I WANT!
WHY DON'T YOU JUST ORDER WHAT YOU LIKE?
TSK
TSK
TSK
THAT'S FINE FOR A NORMAL SUSHI BAR!
BUT THE BEAUTY OF REVOLVING SUSHI IS THAT IT REVOLVES. ORDERING WOULD BE WRONG.
NOT HERE FOR ONE HOUR AND SHE'S MADE UP RULES...
AH, HERE IT COMES!
SO NAÏVE.
HEY! I HEARD YOU!
WHAT DO YOU MEAN BY THAT, HUH?

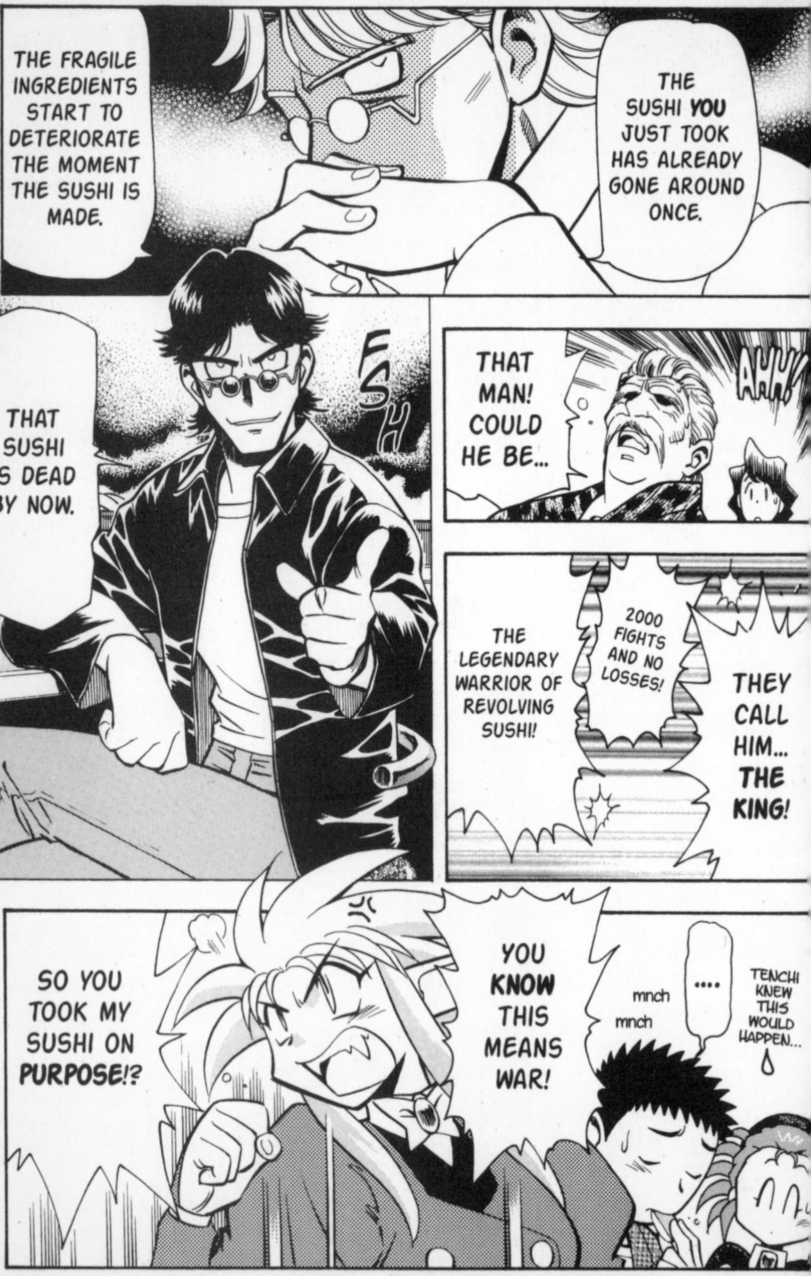
THE FRAGILE INGREDIENTS START TO DETERIORATE THE MOMENT THE SUSHI IS MADE.
THE SUSHI **YOU** JUST TOOK HAS ALREADY GONE AROUND ONCE.
THAT SUSHI IS DEAD BY NOW.
FSH
THAT MAN! COULD HE BE...
AHH!
THE LEGENDARY WARRIOR OF REVOLVING SUSHI!
2000 FIGHTS AND NO LOSSES!
THEY CALL HIM... **THE KING!**
SO YOU TOOK MY SUSHI ON **PURPOSE!?**
YOU **KNOW** THIS MEANS WAR!
mnch
mnch
....
TENCHI KNEW THIS WOULD HAPPEN...

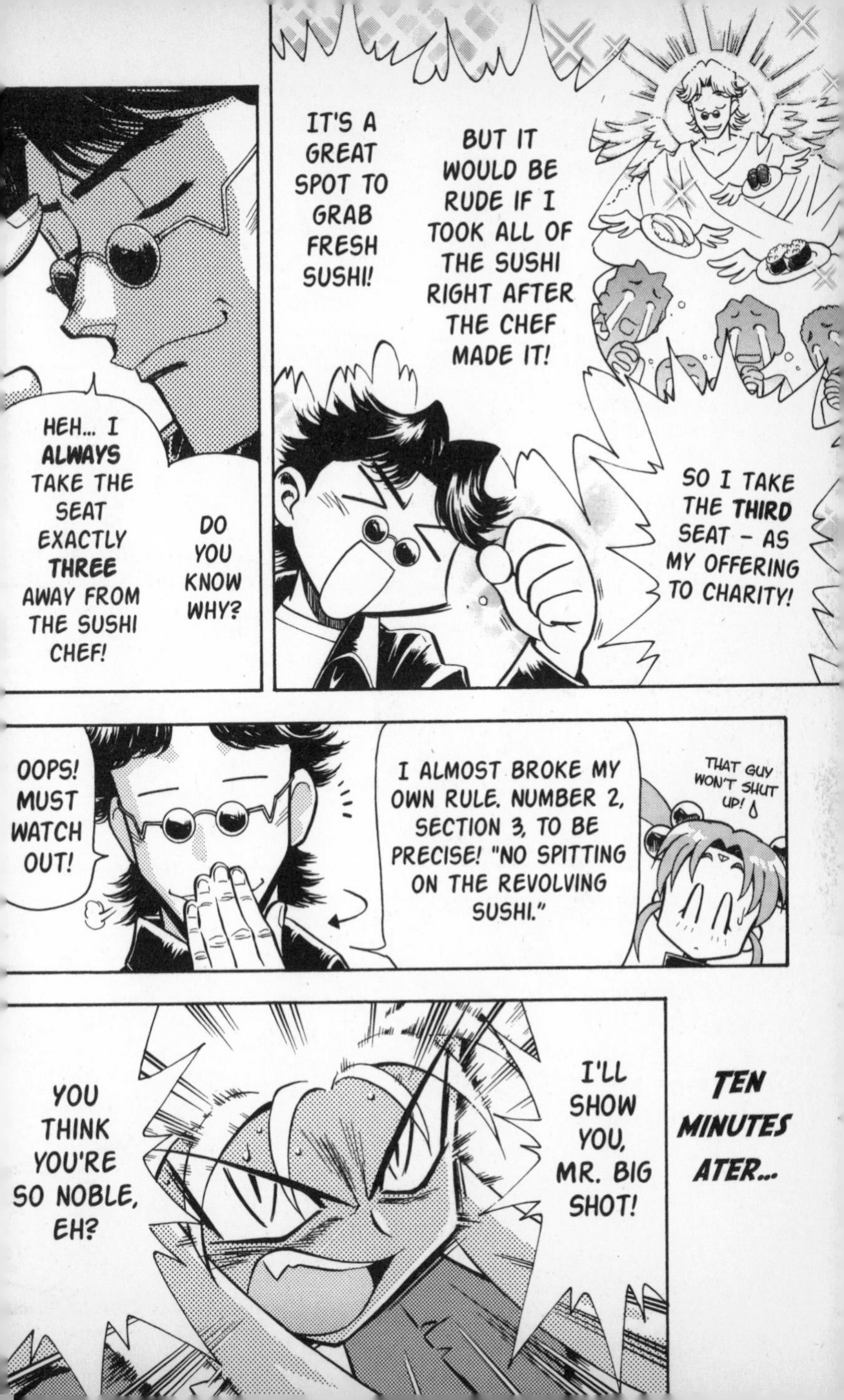
HEH... I ALWAYS TAKE THE SEAT EXACTLY THREE AWAY FROM THE SUSHI CHEF!
DO YOU KNOW WHY?
IT'S A GREAT SPOT TO GRAB FRESH SUSHI!
BUT IT WOULD BE RUDE IF I TOOK ALL OF THE SUSHI RIGHT AFTER THE CHEF MADE IT!
SO I TAKE THE THIRD SEAT – AS MY OFFERING TO CHARITY!
OOPS! MUST WATCH OUT!
I ALMOST BROKE MY OWN RULE. NUMBER 2, SECTION 3, TO BE PRECISE! "NO SPITTING ON THE REVOLVING SUSHI."
THAT GUY WON'T SHUT UP!
YOU THINK YOU'RE SO NOBLE, EH?
I'LL SHOW YOU, MR. BIG SHOT!
TEN MINUTES ATER...

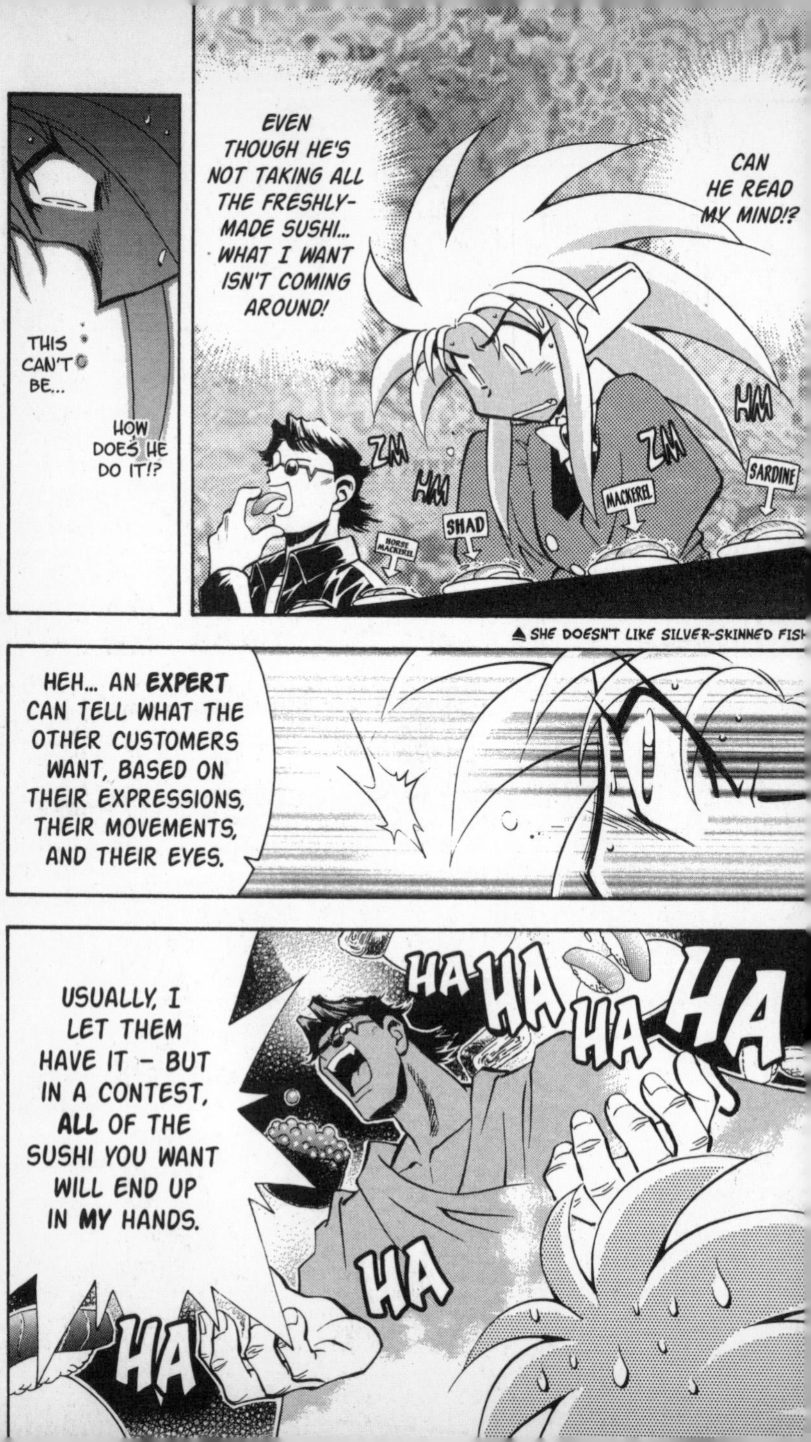

THIS CAN'T BE...
HOW DOES HE DO IT!?
EVEN THOUGH HE'S NOT TAKING ALL THE FRESHLY-MADE SUSHI... WHAT I WANT ISN'T COMING AROUND!
CAN HE READ MY MIND!?
ZM
HM
ZM
HM
HORSE MACKEREL
SHAD
MACKEREL
SARDINE
SHE DOESN'T LIKE SILVER-SKINNED FISH
HEH... AN **EXPERT** CAN TELL WHAT THE OTHER CUSTOMERS WANT, BASED ON THEIR EXPRESSIONS, THEIR MOVEMENTS, AND THEIR EYES.
USUALLY, I LET THEM HAVE IT - BUT IN A CONTEST, **ALL** OF THE SUSHI YOU WANT WILL END UP IN **MY** HANDS.
HA HA HA HA
HA
HA

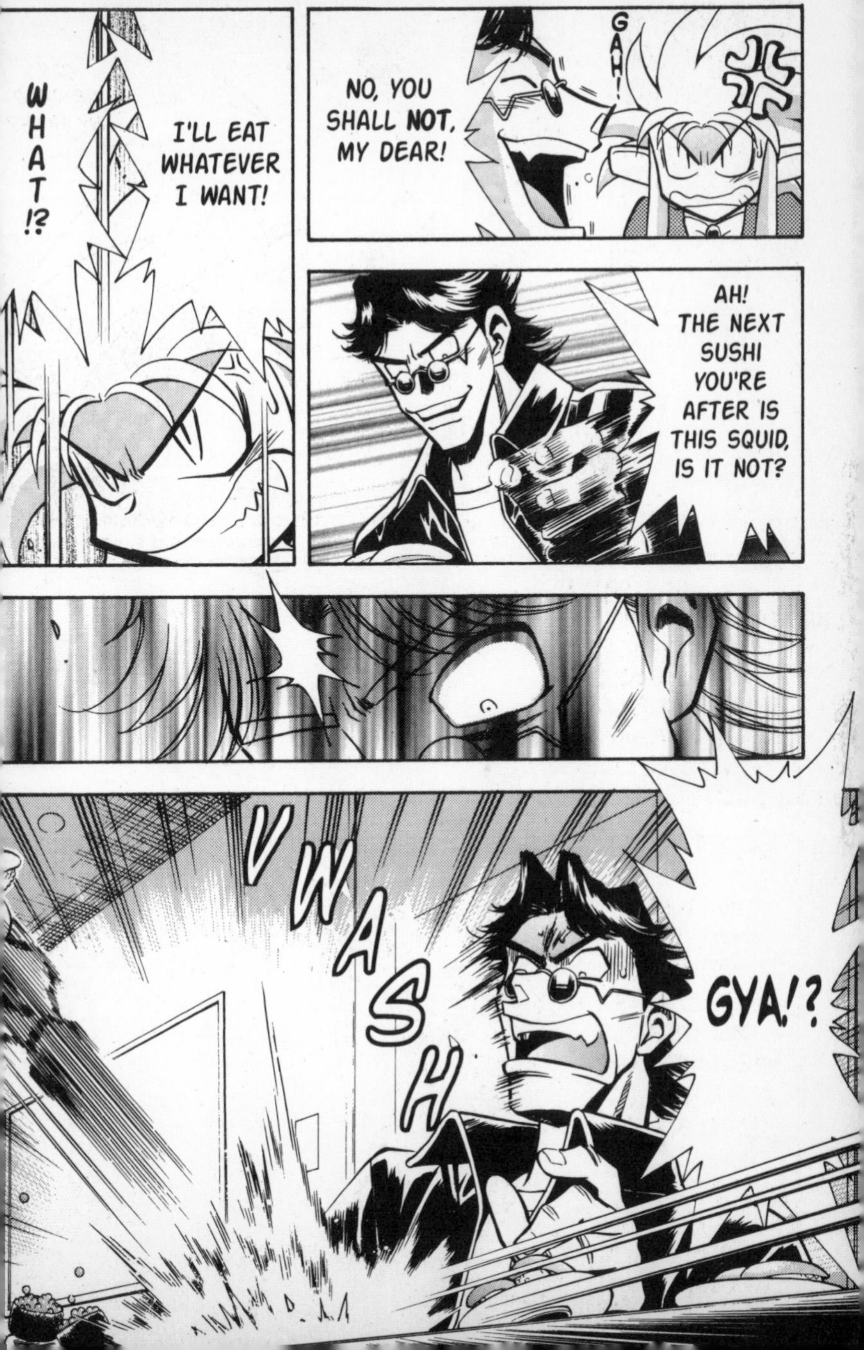
WHAT!?
I'LL EAT WHATEVER I WANT!
NO, YOU SHALL NOT, MY DEAR!
GAH!
AH! THE NEXT SUSHI YOU'RE AFTER IS THIS SQUID, IS IT NOT?
VWASH
GYA!?

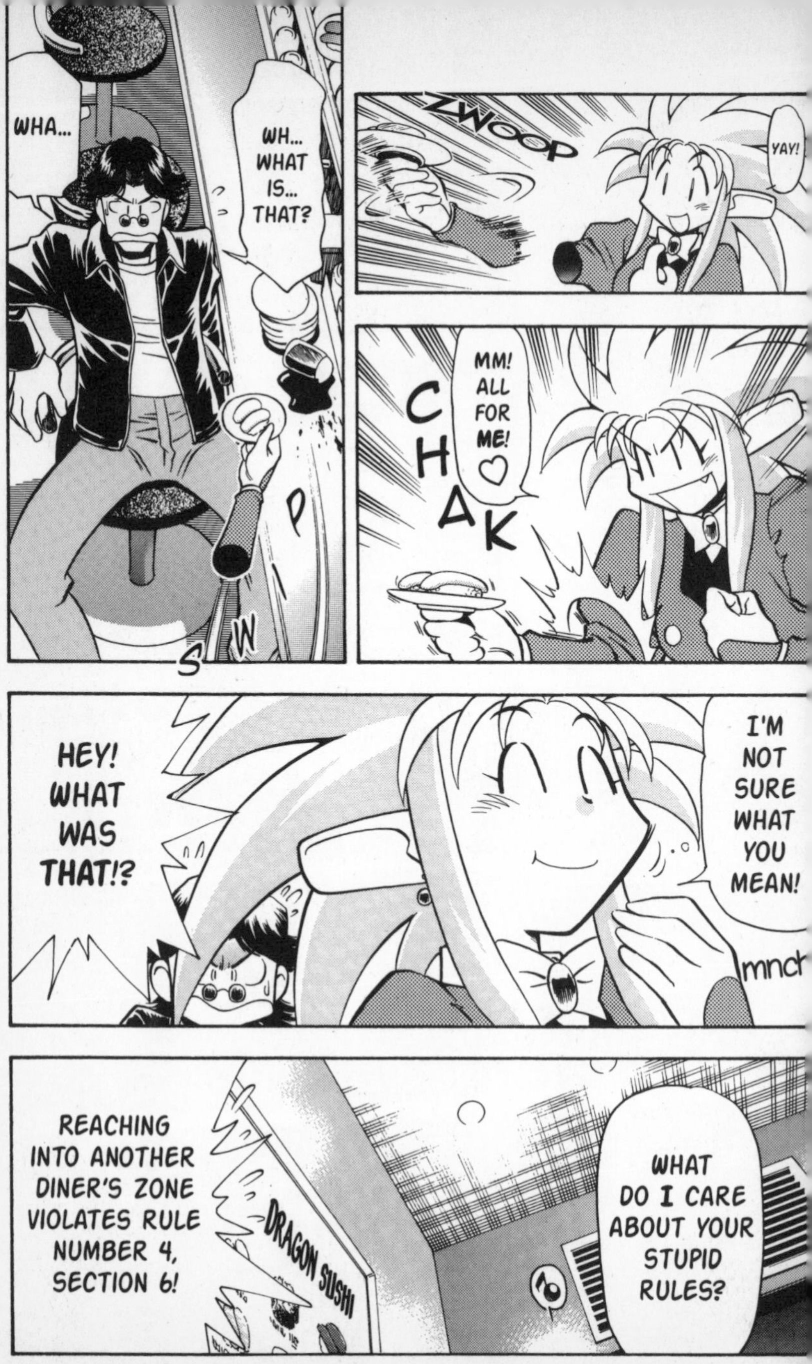

WHA...
WH... WHAT IS... THAT?
S W I P
ZWOOP
YAY!
MM! ALL FOR ME! ♡
CHAK
HEY! WHAT WAS THAT!?
I'M NOT SURE WHAT YOU MEAN!
mnch
REACHING INTO ANOTHER DINER'S ZONE VIOLATES RULE NUMBER 4, SECTION 6!
DRAGON SUSHI
WHAT DO I CARE ABOUT YOUR STUPID RULES?

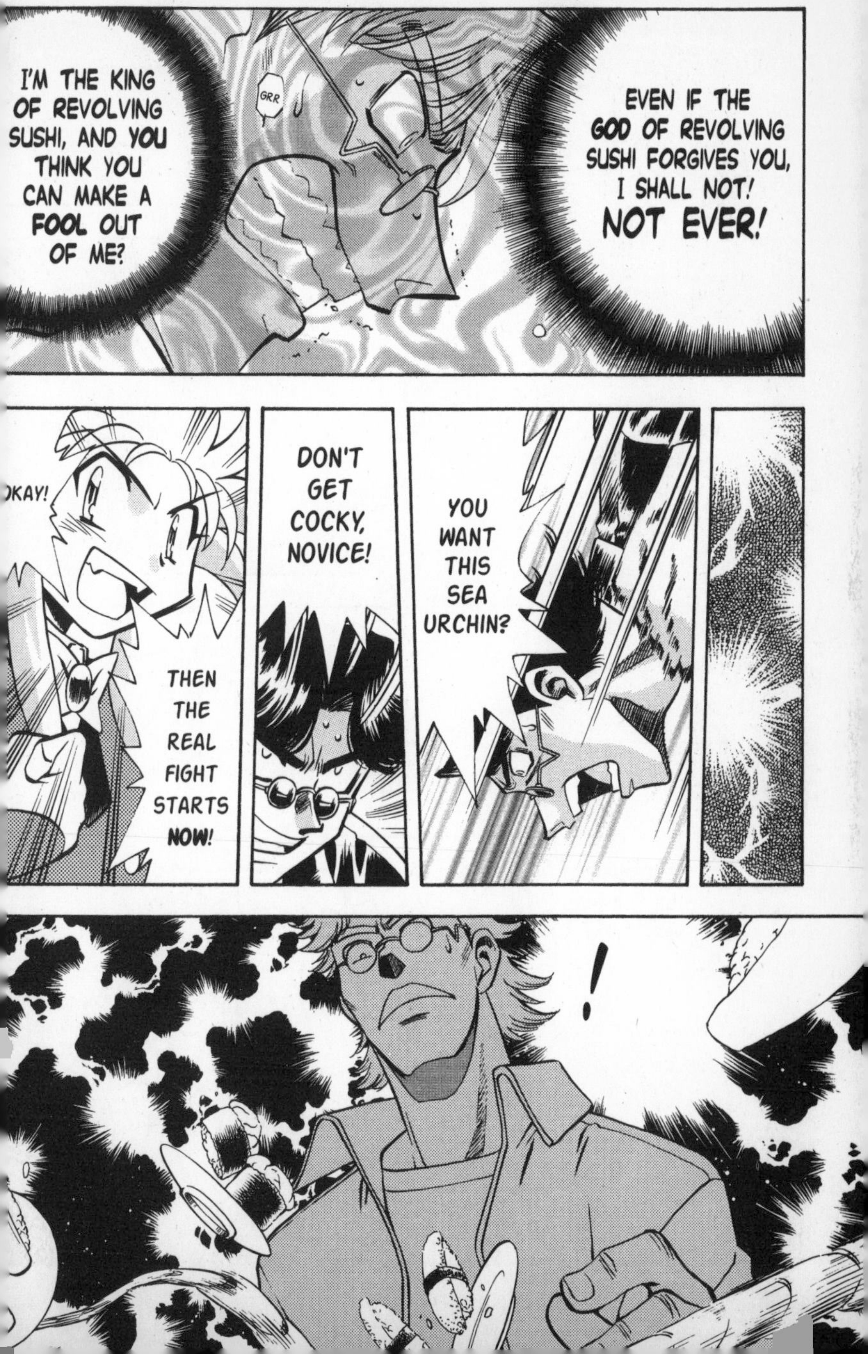
I'M THE KING OF REVOLVING SUSHI, AND YOU THINK YOU CAN MAKE A FOOL OUT OF ME?
GRR
EVEN IF THE GOD OF REVOLVING SUSHI FORGIVES YOU, I SHALL NOT! NOT EVER!
OKAY!
THEN THE REAL FIGHT STARTS NOW!
DON'T GET COCKY, NOVICE!
YOU WANT THIS SEA URCHIN?
!

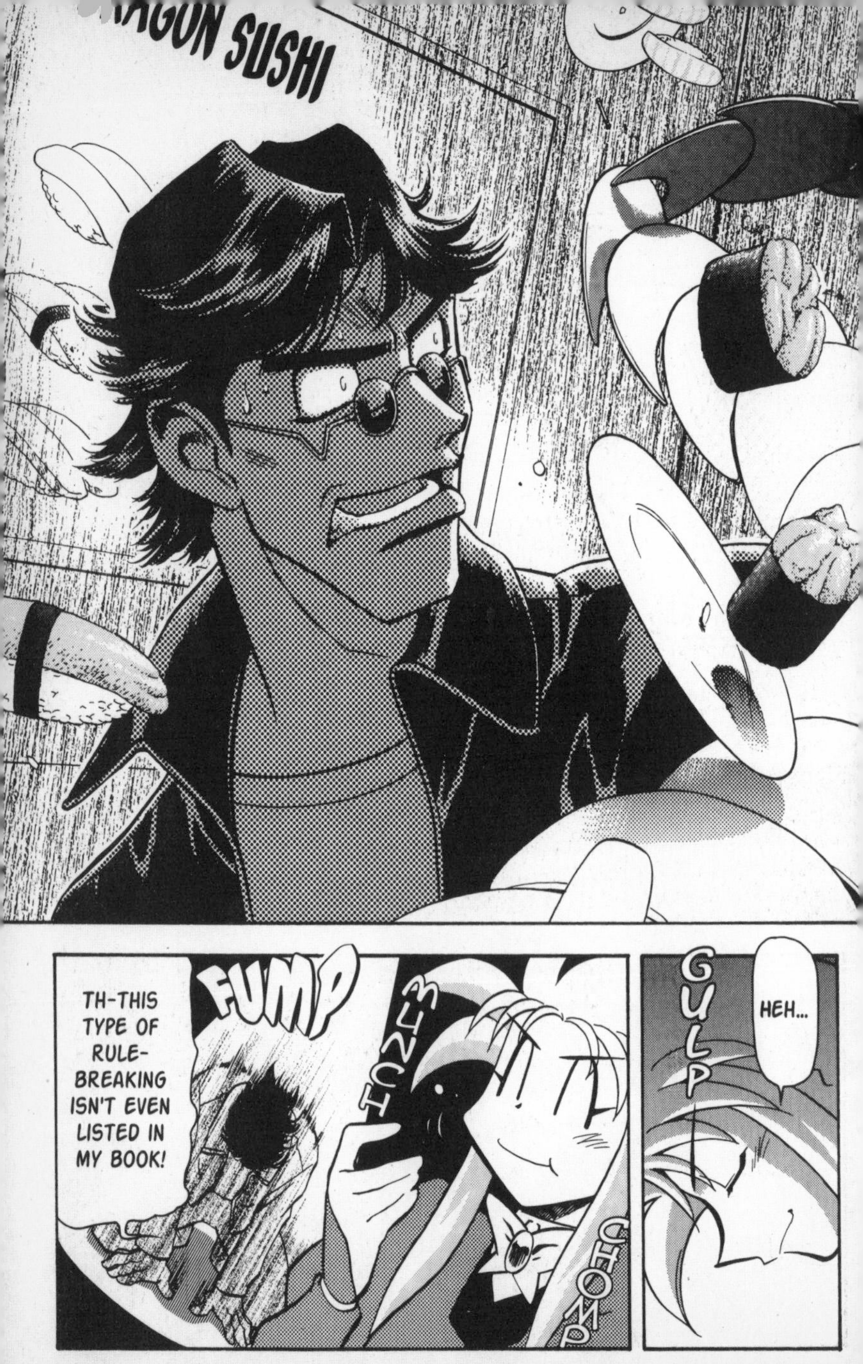
RAGON SUSHI
FUMP
TH-THIS TYPE OF RULE-BREAKING ISN'T EVEN LISTED IN MY BOOK!
MUNCH
CHOMP
GULP
HEH...

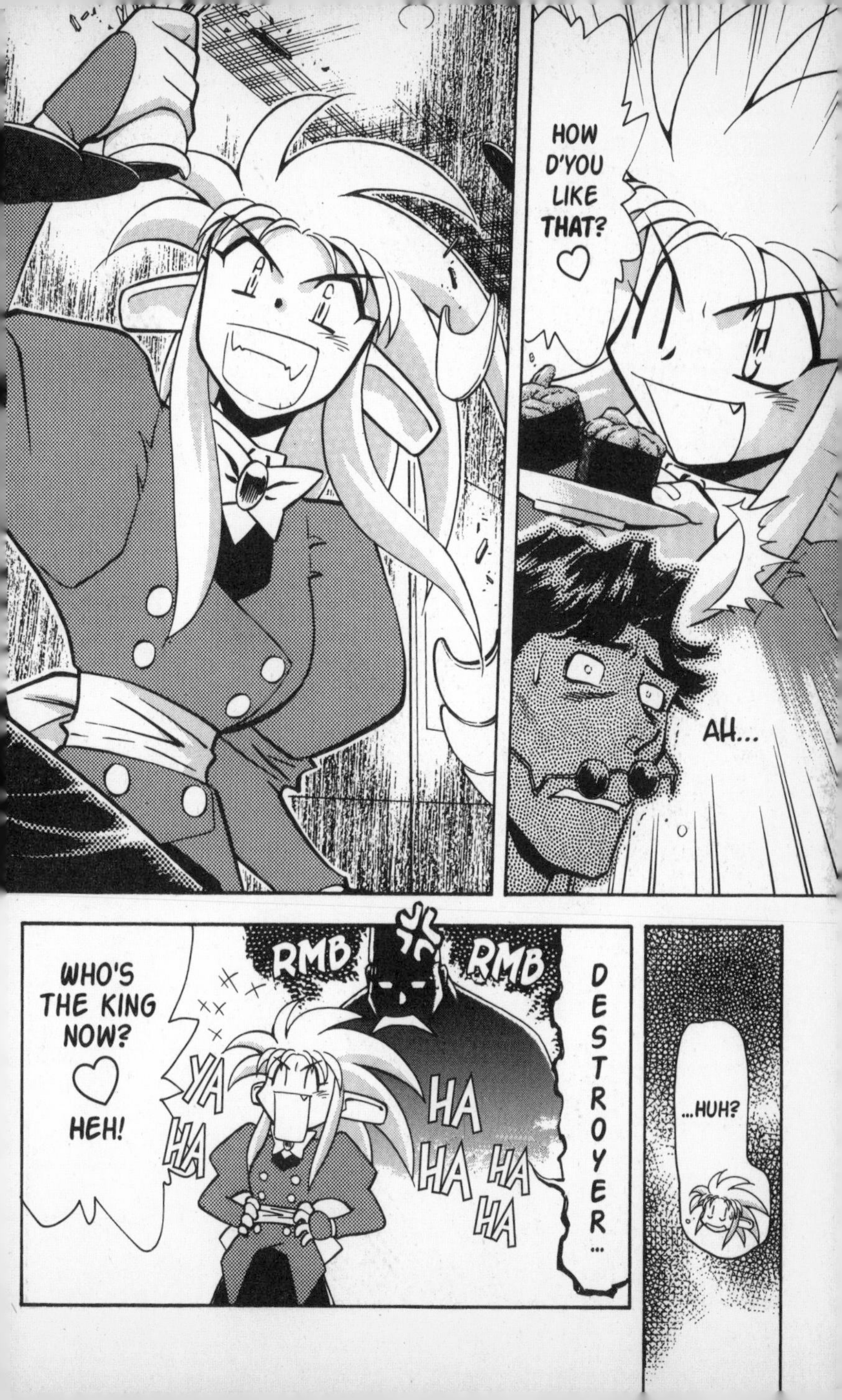
HOW D'YOU LIKE THAT? ♡
AH...
WHO'S THE KING NOW? ♡
HEH!
RMB RMB
YA HA
HA HA HA HA HA
DESTROYER...
...HUH?

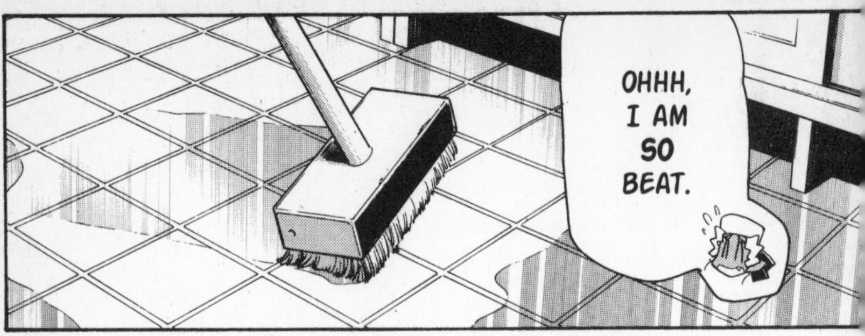
OHHH, I AM SO BEAT.

ACT 5: REPARATION FOR DAMAGES

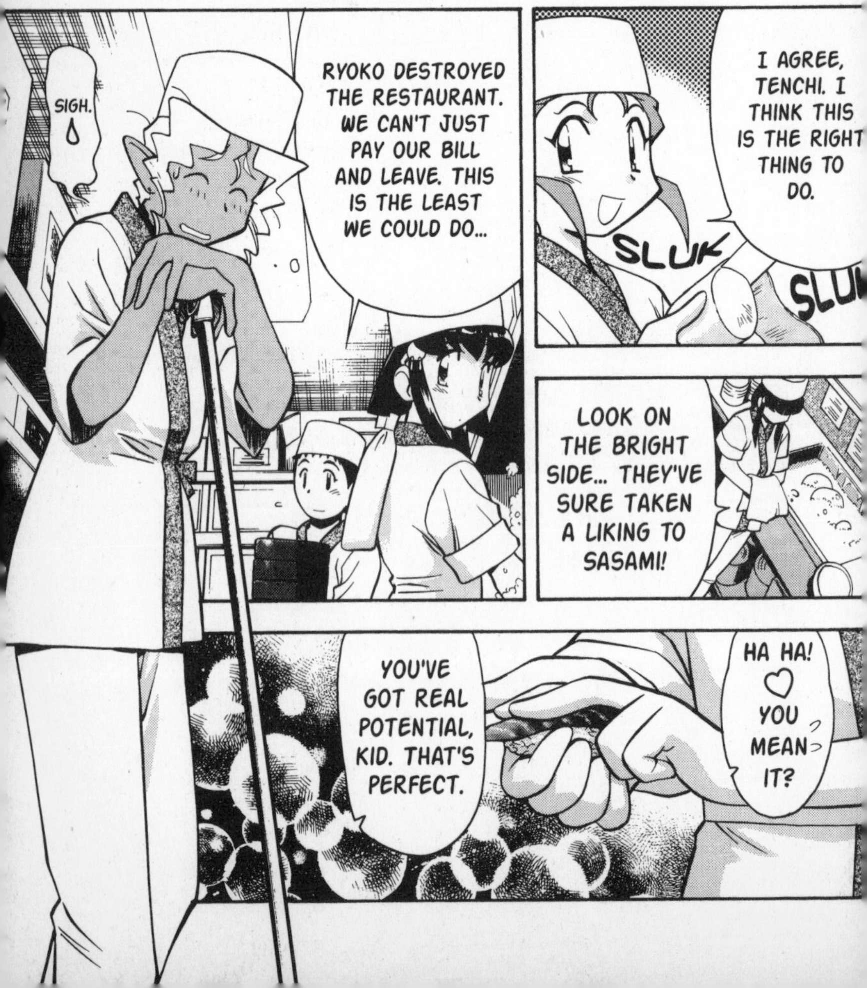
SIGH.
RYOKO DESTROYED THE RESTAURANT. WE CAN'T JUST PAY OUR BILL AND LEAVE. THIS IS THE LEAST WE COULD DO...
I AGREE, TENCHI. I THINK THIS IS THE RIGHT THING TO DO.
SLUK
LOOK ON THE BRIGHT SIDE... THEY'VE SURE TAKEN A LIKING TO SASAMI!
YOU'VE GOT REAL POTENTIAL, KID. THAT'S PERFECT.
HA HA! ♥ YOU MEAN IT?

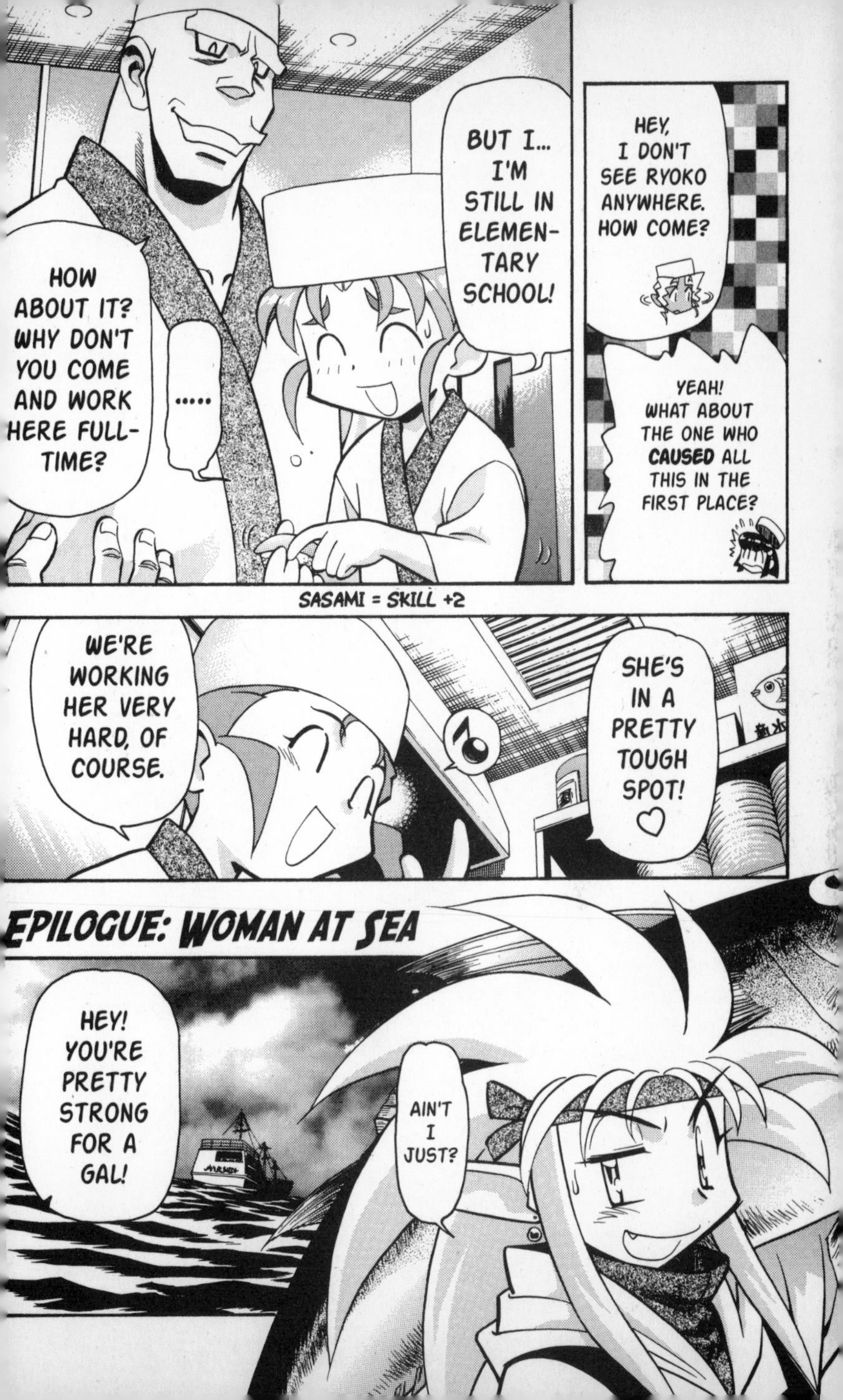
HOW ABOUT IT? WHY DON'T YOU COME AND WORK HERE FULL-TIME?
.....
BUT I... I'M STILL IN ELEMENTARY SCHOOL!
HEY, I DON'T SEE RYOKO ANYWHERE. HOW COME?
YEAH! WHAT ABOUT THE ONE WHO CAUSED ALL THIS IN THE FIRST PLACE?
SASAMI = SKILL +2
WE'RE WORKING HER VERY HARD, OF COURSE.
SHE'S IN A PRETTY TOUGH SPOT! ♡
EPILOGUE: WOMAN AT SEA
HEY! YOU'RE PRETTY STRONG FOR A GAL!
AIN'T I JUST?

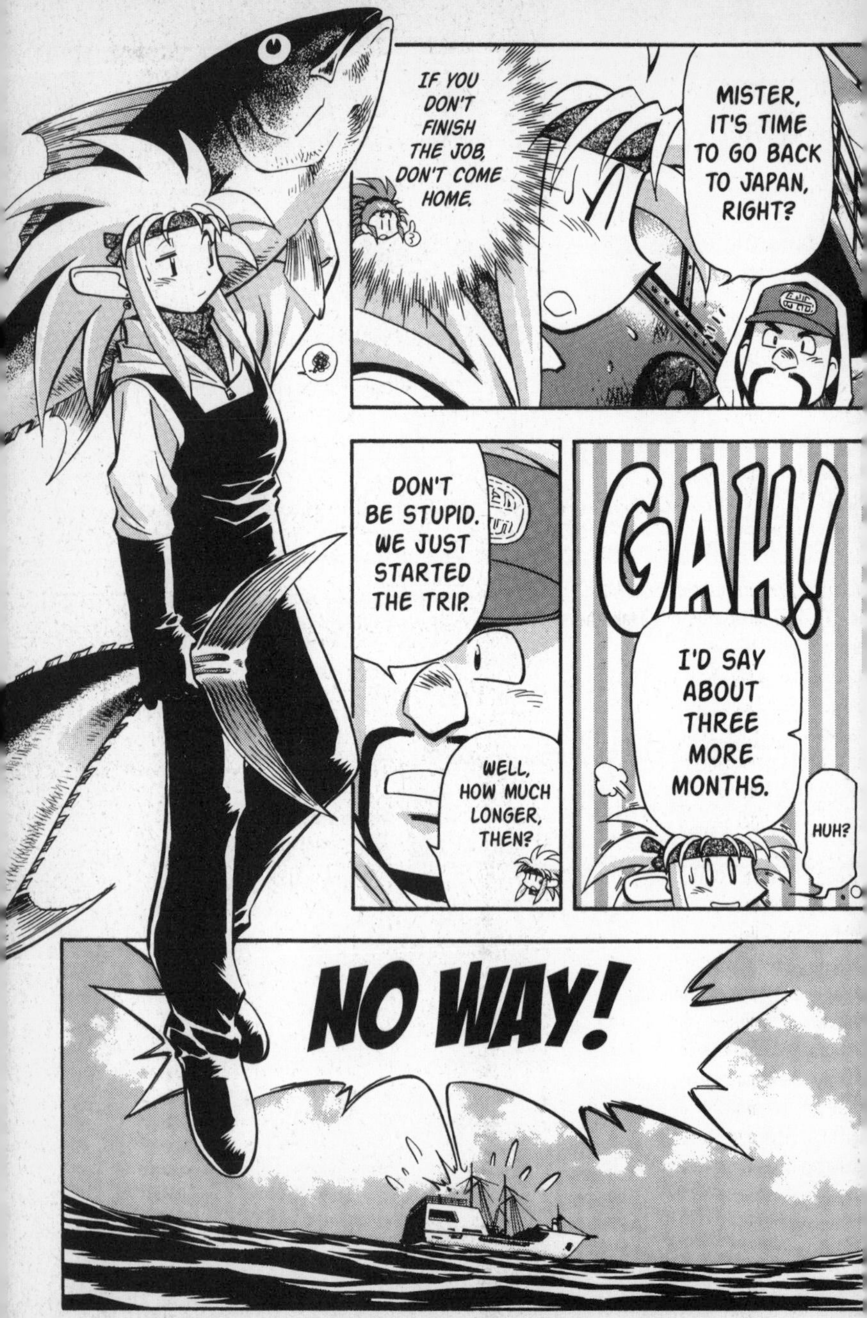
IF YOU DON'T FINISH THE JOB, DON'T COME HOME.
MISTER, IT'S TIME TO GO BACK TO JAPAN, RIGHT?
DON'T BE STUPID. WE JUST STARTED THE TRIP.
WELL, HOW MUCH LONGER, THEN?
GAH!
I'D SAY ABOUT THREE MORE MONTHS.
HUH?
NO WAY!

TO BE CONTINUED IN VOLUME 6!

Tenchi. I can't believe I'm editing Tenchi.

Like many otaku of my generation, I was introduced to anime via **Tenchi Muyô!** You youngsters in the audience may not believe it, but there was a time when very little anime or manga was available in the United States. As a college student, I spent my nights huddled on a beer-stained sofa with the other members of the campus science-fiction club, entranced by flickering images of Ranma Saotome, Lina Inverse, the Patlabor force, those ninja in **Ninja Scroll**, and, of course, Tenchi and his hyperactive harem.

When Eric Searleman, the previous **All-New Tenchi!** editor, asked me to take the reins of power, I felt that my life as an otaku had come full circle. Anime and manga had exploded onto the American market, we were flooded with more from Japan than any one fangirl could read or watch… and here I was, immersed in Tenchi all over again.

But getting back to my roots reminded me of how much I owe to those long-ago nights on the college sofas. Many of the elements I love to incorporate into my own comics – mad scientists, outlandish sci-fi concepts, and, best of all, butt-kicking women – come straight from the Tenchi mythos. And then there's the hair. Tenchi hair is a masterpiece of engineering. I'm still trying to figure out why mine just hangs there. Wood glue might help.

I'm back to Tenchi. And it feels good.

Shaenon K. Garrity
Editor of **The All-New Tenchi Muyô!**

Like Tenchi? Love Tenchi?

If so, here are some other books the editor thinks you'll enjoy:

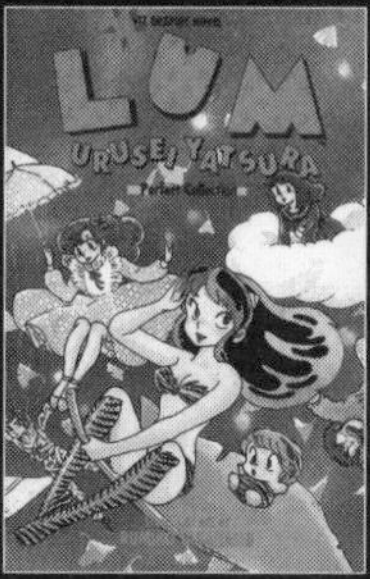
LUM
URUSEI YATSURA

© 1983 Rumiko Takahashi/ Shogakukan

Lum* Urusei Yatsura

Learn your history, kids: the harem love comedy wouldn't exist as a genre without Rumiko Takahashi's shamelessly funny sci-fi classic. A bikini-clad alien demon princess (in matching tiger-striped spaceship) rockets into a teenage boy's backyard, setting off a chain reaction of violence, chaos, and sexy extraterrestrial visitations. It's so much fun, you don't even need to recognize that, like **Tenchi**, the whole thing's an elaborate send-up of Japanese mythology. Simply the best.

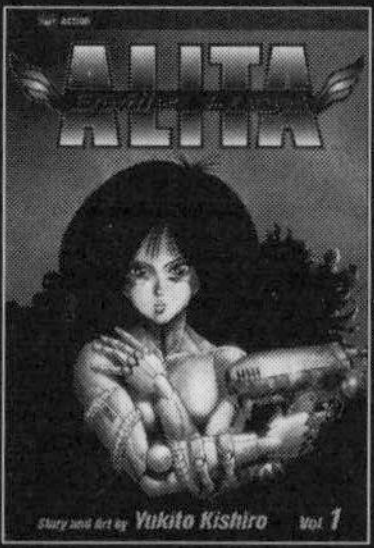
ALITA
Yukito Kishiro
Vol. 1

GUNNM © 1991 by YUKITO KISHIRO/SHUEISHA Inc.

Battle Angel Alita

If you read only one manga about cyborgs fighting for survival in a postapocalyptic future, **Battle Angel Alita** is the one to read. And if the tough-as-nails women are the reason you keep reading **Tenchi**, you don't want to miss out on this intense action saga. Rescued from the trash by an eccentric inventor, sweet but deadly Alita keeps the peace in a futuristic junkyard while searching for the secret of her lost identity. Yukito Kishiro's gorgeous, kinetic artwork makes the story sing.

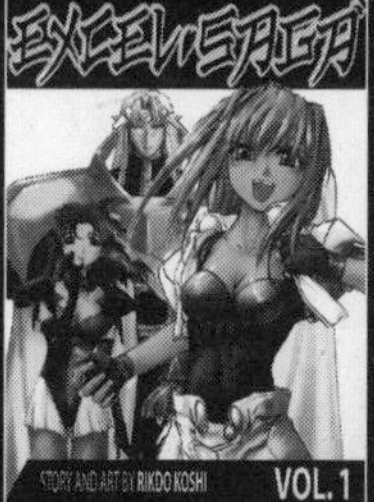
EXCEL SAGA
STORY AND ART BY RIKDO KOSHI
VOL.1

© 1997 Rikdo Koshi/ SHONENGAHOSHA

Excel Saga

What's wrong with trying to take over the world? Experience the battle for the planet from the bad guys' point of view as over-enthusiastic Excel, her sickly sidekick Hyatt, and a very unfortunate dog pool their limited resources to follow the muddled dictates of would-be overlord Il Palazzo. After you've seen what these low-budget supervillains go through just to attack their local civic center and still make it home with enough cash for a ramen dinner, you'll be rooting for the heroes to take a fall once in a while.

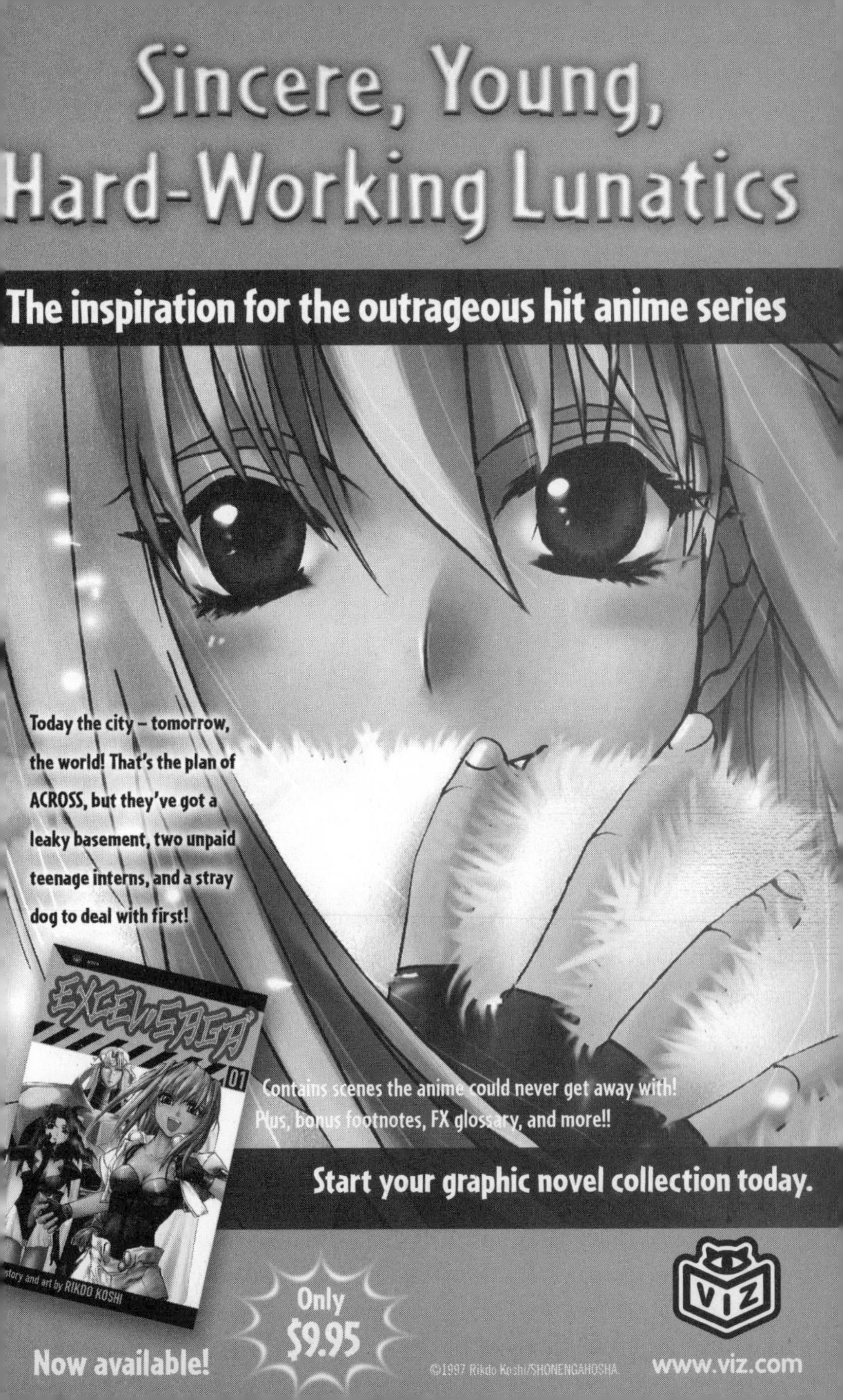
Sincere, Young,
Hard-Working Lunatics
The inspiration for the outrageous hit anime series
Today the city – tomorrow, the world! That's the plan of ACROSS, but they've got a leaky basement, two unpaid teenage interns, and a stray dog to deal with first!
EXCEL SAGA
01
story and art by RIKDO KOSHI
Contains scenes the anime could never get away with!
Plus, bonus footnotes, FX glossary, and more!!
Start your graphic novel collection today.
VIZ
Only $9.95
Now available!
©1997 Rikdo Koshi/SHONENGAHOSHA
www.viz.com

COMPLETE OUR SURVEY AND LET US KNOW WHAT YOU THINK!

☐ Please do NOT send me information about VIZ products, news and events, special offers, or other information.

☐ Please do NOT send me information from VIZ's trusted business partners.

Name: _____

Address: _____

City: _____ **State:** _____ **Zip:** _____

E-mail: _____

☐ Male ☐ Female **Date of Birth** (mm/dd/yyyy): ___ / ___ / _____ (Under 13? Parental consent required)

What race/ethnicity do you consider yourself? (please check one)

☐ Asian/Pacific Islander ☐ Black/African American ☐ Hispanic/Latino

☐ Native American/Alaskan Native ☐ White/Caucasian ☐ Other: _____

What VIZ product did you purchase? (check all that apply and indicate title purchased)

☐ DVD/VHS _____

☐ Graphic Novel _____

☐ Magazines _____

☐ Merchandise _____

Reason for purchase: (check all that apply)

☐ Special offer ☐ Favorite title ☐ Gift

☐ Recommendation ☐ Other _____

Where did you make your purchase? (please check one)

☐ Comic store ☐ Bookstore ☐ Mass/Grocery Store

☐ Newsstand ☐ Video/Video Game Store ☐ Other: _____

☐ Online (site: _____)

What other VIZ properties have you purchased/own? _____

_____

How many anime and/or manga titles have you purchased in the last year? How many were VIZ titles? (please check one from each column)

ANIME	MANGA	VIZ
☐ None	☐ None	☐ None
☐ 1-4	☐ 1-4	☐ 1-4
☐ 5-10	☐ 5-10	☐ 5-10
☐ 11+	☐ 11+	☐ 11+

I find the pricing of VIZ products to be: (please check one)

☐ Cheap   ☐ Reasonable   ☐ Expensive

What genre of manga and anime would you like to see from VIZ? (please check two)

☐ Adventure   ☐ Comic Strip   ☐ Science Fiction   ☐ Fighting

☐ Horror   ☐ Romance   ☐ Fantasy   ☐ Sports

What do you think of VIZ's new look?

☐ Love It   ☐ It's OK   ☐ Hate It   ☐ Didn't Notice   ☐ No Opinion

Which do you prefer? (please check one)

☐ Reading right-to-left

☐ Reading left-to-right

Which do you prefer? (please check one)

☐ Sound effects in English

☐ Sound effects in Japanese with English captions

☐ Sound effects in Japanese only with a glossary at the back

THANK YOU! Please send the completed form to:

NJW Research
42 Catharine St.
Poughkeepsie, NY 12601

All information provided will be used for internal purposes only. We promise not to sell or otherwise divulge your information.